AI-Powered Transformations for Ethical Education

J. Sadhik Basha
https://orcid.org/0000-0002-0666-7573
International Maritime College Oman, National University of Science and Technology, Oman

Rokhsaneh Yousef Zehi
Department of Science Cluster, International Maritime College Oman, National University of Science and Technology, Oman

Taofeek Olanrewaju Alade
Department of Science Cluster, International Maritime College Oman, National University of Science and Technology, Oman

Ahlam Al Balushi
https://orcid.org/0009-0000-4659-7920
Department of Science Cluster, International Maritime College Oman, National University of Science and Technology, Oman

Khaloud Al Ajmi
Department of Science Cluster, International Maritime College Oman, National University of Science and Technology, Oman

IGI Global
Scientific Publishing
Publishing Tomorrow's Research Today

Vice President of Editorial Melissa Wagner
Director of Acquisitions Mikaela Felty
Director of Book Development Jocelynn Hessler
Production Manager Mike Brehm
Cover Design Jose Rosado

Published in the United States of America by
IGI Global Scientific Publishing
701 East Chocolate Avenue
Hershey, PA, 17033, USA
Tel: 717-533-8845 | Fax: 717-533-7115
Website: https://www.igi-global.com E-mail: cust@igi-global.com

Library of Congress Cataloging-in-Publication Data

Names: Basha, J. Sadhik, 1977- editor
Title: AI-powered transformations for ethical education / [edited by] J. Sadhik Basha, Rokhsaneh Yousef Zehi, Taofeek Olanrewaju Alade, Ahlam Al Balushi, Khaloud Al Ajmi.
Description: Hershey, PA : IGI Global Scientific Publishing, [2026] | Includes bibliographical references and index. | Summary: "This book examines how artificial intelligence is changing ethical education and consider the effects of incorporating AI into conventional moral and ethical education"-- Provided by publisher.
Identifiers: LCCN 2025033221 (print) | LCCN 2025033222 (ebook) | ISBN 9798337349824 hardcover | ISBN 9798337349831 paperback | ISBN 9798337349848 ebook
Subjects: LCSH: Artificial intelligence--Educational applications | Artificial intelligence--Moral and ethical aspects | Educational technology--Moral and ethical aspects
Classification: LCC LB1028.43 .A39745 2026 (print) | LCC LB1028.43 (ebook)
LC record available at https://lccn.loc.gov/2025033221
LC ebook record available at https://lccn.loc.gov/2025033222

British Cataloguing in Publication Data
A Cataloguing in Publication record for this book is available from the British Library.

The book is dedicated to:

To the Almighty and our beloved families, whose unwavering love, patience, and support have been our greatest source of inspiration.

To the scholars and educators whose invaluable contributions continue to shape and advance the future of AI based ethical education.

Editorial Advisory Board

Table of Contents

Detailed Table of Contents

instructor-learner-technology triad and suggests potential ways of responsible innovation of educational practice.

Artificial Intelligence has revolutionized the education sector, as it has provided technologies that improve learning and administrative duties. However, along with the use of AI, inevitable ethical concerns associated with technological advancements are also emerging. AI systems in education rely heavily on data to optimize learning experiences, monitor student progress and predict outcomes. However, such large-scale data collection and processing raises significant concerns about the security and privacy of student data. Academic records, behavioral data and even biometric information are examples of sensitive student data that can be compromised or misused. While it is also true that AI-powered systems enable customized, deeper learning paths, their excessive use hampers students' critical thinking and creativity. If students are accustomed to completing heavy tasks with the help of AI, they may learn the cognitive processes required for deeper learning to a great extent. y.

The digital era is providing new methods of learning, thinking, and problem-solving. Introducing the foundational ideas of AI to young learners helps them adjust to a technology-driven environment more effectively. This study explores effective ways to make young learners aged 6-12 aware of basic AI concepts, including logic, patterns, and algorithms. By utilizing secondary data, the study aims to explore effective pedagogical strategies and challenges in early education related to AI, and provide guidelines for parents and educators. The aim of the study is to enable curriculum designers and educators to design an inclusive stakeholders' model that can be used in primary education to introduce AI literacy in a way that enhances the critical thinking, creativity, and problem-solving abilities of young learners.

Foreword

One of the most revolutionary factors influencing modern education is the rapid development of artificial intelligence (AI). From intelligent tutoring systems and automated assessment tools to generative AI and data-driven academic decision-making, AI is transforming the creation, delivery, evaluation, and governance of knowledge. These advancements present unprecedented opportunities to enhance access, personalization, and efficiency in education; however, they also raise serious ethical concerns that require careful scholarly consideration. In this critical context, this book *AI-Powered Transformations for Ethical Education* offers a timely and significant contribution.

Education has always been about more than the mere transmission of knowledge; at its core, it is concerned with values, justice, integrity, and human development. As AI systems increasingly influence pedagogical practices, research processes, and institutional policies, the ethical dimensions of their design and implementation become inseparably linked to educational quality. Educators, students, and administrators around the world now routinely confront issues such as algorithmic bias, data privacy, accountability, transparency, academic integrity, and the responsible use of generative technologies. This book rightly recognizes that ethical education is essential in the era of artificial intelligence.

This volume stands out for its deliberate effort to move beyond purely technical or theoretical discussions of AI. Instead, it adopts an interdisciplinary, values-based approach that places ethics at the center of educational transformation. The chapters collectively examine how AI can be aligned with moral reasoning, pedagogical integrity, and institutional responsibility, rather than being treated as a neutral or solely efficiency-driven tool. In doing so, the book addresses a significant gap in the literature by emphasizing the need for frameworks and practices that integrate technological innovation with ethical stewardship.

The book brings together a range of scholarly perspectives that examine both the opportunities and challenges associated with implementing AI in education. It explores themes such as the future direction of AI in learning environments, ethical digital twins for moral reasoning simulations, the implications of generative AI in academic research, and strategies for preserving pedagogical integrity. Because these discussions are grounded in real educational contexts, the volume is relevant to researchers as well as practitioners and policymakers seeking practical guidance. Remarkably, *AI-Powered Transformations for Ethical Education* underscores the importance of embedding ethical considerations across all levels of educational ecosystems. Ethical AI is presented not merely as a matter of compliance or regulation, but as an ongoing process of reflection, design, evaluation, and continuous improvement. The chapters encourage readers to critically examine how AI systems influence learner agency, knowledge production, assessment fairness, and institutional trust. Through this lens, the book advances an educational paradigm in which technological progress reinforces, rather than undermines, human values.

This book will be particularly valuable to educators, academic leaders, researchers, curriculum designers, and policymakers navigating the complexities of AI integration in higher education and beyond. Serving as both a scholarly reference and a practical guide, it offers conceptual frameworks and reflective insights to support ethical decision-making and policy development. The contributors clearly demonstrate that responsible AI adoption requires interdisciplinary collaboration and a shared commitment to ethical principles.

In conclusion, *AI-Powered Transformations for Ethical Education* arrives at a pivotal moment in the evolution of global education systems. As AI continues to reshape educational landscapes, this volume serves as a thoughtful reminder that innovation must be guided by ethical considerations. By fostering informed dialogue and offering insightful perspectives on responsible AI use, the book contributes to the development of education systems that are not only technologically advanced but also equitable, transparent, and humane. It is my hope that this work will inspire readers to engage with AI not merely as a powerful tool, but as a shared ethical responsibility in shaping the future of education.

K. P. Ramachandran
National University of Science and Technology, Oman

Preface

Artificial intelligence is no longer a distant promise in education; it is an active force reshaping how knowledge is created, shared, evaluated, and governed. As AI systems increasingly influence learning environments, research practices, and institutional decision-making, ethical considerations have become inseparable from technological innovation. *AI-Powered Transformations for Ethical Education* emerges from this critical juncture, offering a comprehensive exploration of how AI can be harnessed responsibly to enhance education while safeguarding human values.

ABOUT THIS BOOK

This book brings together diverse scholarly perspectives to examine the ethical, pedagogical, and societal implications of AI integration across educational contexts. It begins by situating AI within the future of education, highlighting both its transformative potential and the ethical challenges related to equity, justice, human agency, and inclusiveness. Rather than treating ethics as an afterthought, the contributions emphasize the need for intentional, human-centered approaches that preserve the essence of learning while embracing innovation.

Several chapters delve into advanced conceptual and practical frameworks that redefine ethical education in the age of AI. These include AI-driven moral reasoning simulations, ethical digital twins, and governance models that align algorithmic systems with pedagogical integrity. Through global policy analyses, case studies, and comparative frameworks, the book illustrates how ethical AI practices can be embedded into curricula, institutional policies, and research ecosystems.

The volume also addresses the profound impact of generative AI on academic research and knowledge production, examining international ethical guidelines, benefits, risks, and emerging norms. Beyond present-day applications, it ventures into speculative futures shaped by artificial general intelligence and brain-computer interfaces, raising critical questions about autonomy, cognitive liberty, and the moral boundaries of educational innovation.

Human experience remains a central theme throughout the book. Qualitative explorations reveal tensions between personalization and surveillance, automation and judgment, and efficiency and trust in AI-enabled learning environments. The role of teachers is critically examined, underscoring their indispensable contribution to personalized adaptive learning systems and ethical mediation. Empirical studies further highlight institutional readiness, teacher preparedness, academic integrity, and governance challenges across different regional contexts.

The book also extends its ethical inquiry to early education, demonstrating how foundational AI concepts such as logic, patterns, and algorithms can be introduced to young learners in age-appropriate and responsible ways. Additionally, it explores structural and bureaucratic factors that influence ethical education and research productivity, reminding readers that ethical AI adoption is shaped not only by technology but also by institutional cultures and systems.

AI-Powered Transformations for Ethical Education is intended for educators, researchers, policymakers, technologists, and graduate students who seek a nuanced understanding of AI's role in shaping the future of education. By bridging theory, practice, policy, and lived experience, this book advocates for an educational future where technological advancement is guided by ethical reflection, human dignity, and collective responsibility.

Acknowledgment

First and foremost, we extend our heartfelt gratitude to our family and friends for their unwavering support, encouragement, and belief in us, which formed the foundation of this journey. Their patience, understanding, and constant motivation were invaluable, especially during the most demanding phases of the writing process. We are deeply thankful to our loved ones for being a continual source of inspiration and strength throughout this endeavor.

We also wish to express our sincere appreciation to the professionals, educators, and researchers whose pioneering work inspired much of the content presented in this book. Their contributions to the field of "*AI-based ethical education*" have paved the way for innovative ideas, meaningful discussions, and new opportunities. We feel privileged to build upon their expertise and insights, which have significantly enriched the scope, relevance, and depth of this work.

The editors would like to express their sincere gratitude to all the reviewers who contributed their time, expertise, and scholarly insight to the development of this edited volume, *AI-Powered Transformations for Ethical Education*. The academic rigor and overall quality of this book are deeply rooted in the careful evaluation, constructive criticism, and thoughtful guidance provided by the reviewers throughout the review process.

We especially appreciate Dr. Anteneh, Dr. Rommel, Mr. Patrick McDaid, Dr. Prabu, Dr. Meena, Dr. Baiju, and Dr. Zouhaier for their thorough reviews and the considerable time they devoted to sharing their priceless thoughts and expert perspectives. Their insightful comments, critical observations, and balanced attention to both technical depth and ethical considerations significantly enhanced the quality, clarity, and relevance of the individual chapters.

The reviewers' commitment to interdisciplinary scholarship and ethical responsibility helped shape this book into a meaningful resource for researchers, educators, policymakers, and practitioners. We are deeply thankful for their professionalism, intellectual generosity, and dedication to advancing ethical and responsible artificial intelligence in education. This volume stands as a collective achievement, and we acknowledge with great respect the invaluable role played by our reviewers in bringing this work to fruition.

Chapter 1
Future of AI in Education and Ethical Issues

Krutika Patre
https://orcid.org/0009-0001-7969-4409
Ajeenkya D.Y. Patil University, India

Sunil Sankathala
https://orcid.org/0009-0004-7809-7647
Ajeenkya D.Y. Patil University, India

Susanta Das
https://orcid.org/0000-0002-9314-3988
Ajeenkya D.Y. Patil University, India

ABSTRACT

The use of AI in the curriculum is an evolutionary change in the way knowledge is learnt, practised and conceptualised. With the rising diversity of classrooms and the increased demands of online learning as a result, AI appears an effective utility tool that can be used to process a significant amount of data and provide quick and individual feedback. In this chapter, the author presents a multi-faceted analysis of the influence of AI in education through the lenses of personalized learning, automated assessment, and teacher and student roles that are changing. It also goes into the issues of ethics, educational justice, and the essence of a humanistic, responsible attitude toward working with AI. The literature review gives an account of how AI in education has changed over the years and why it should be used sensibly with a thoughtful and assumed approach towards its use to save human essence. Finally, the chapter aims at striking a balance between innovativeness and inclusiveness when it comes to building the future of effective learning experiences.

DOI: 10.4018/979-8-3373-4982-4.ch001

1. INTRODUCTION

It would be a move to witness the implementation of AI in the sphere of education as a fad that is to be soon followed by numerous paradigm changes in the domains of knowledge delivery, access, and internalization (Niemi, 2021). As the classroom grows more and more diverse, and digital learning environments are integrated into classrooms faster than ever, providing teachers with a distinctive opportunity to provide their students with highly effective, diverse, and, above all, customized learning procedures is one of the key concerns in the future. It is against this background that AI can be seen as a disruptive technology that is capable of not only processing large amounts of information but also can flexibly interpret the specifics of each individual learner and react to it in real time with valuable feedback (Niemi, 2021).

Another important development is the automation of repetitive administrative and educational processes by using AI technologies, allowing educational personnel to redirect their attention to repetitive work towards more pedagogically useful communication with students. This shift not only decreases the working pressure among educational management but also increases the ability of educators to intervene in time when learners experience problems and invest in personal teaching and never-ending improvement of the process of delivering instructions (Goksel & Bozkurt, 2019). Nevertheless, the speed at which AI enters the education sector has provoked some serious issues regarding equity, ownership of data, and maintenance of human relations in the educational process (Cope et al., 2020; Goksel and Bozkurt, 2019). Such developments have led to rethinking of old paradigms of education especially those that view the future in linear terms. Alternatively, researchers believe that the future should be conceptualised more freely and movemently as a changing relationship with current realities, and not as a destination (Cope et al., 2020). This kind of reconceptualization enables educators and policymakers to follow creative, adaptable, and strong strategies as they negotiate the ever-changing educational environment (Cope et al., 2020; Goksel and Bozkurt, 2019).

Other than automation, other advanced AI technologies include machine learning, natural language processing, and intelligent tutoring. These resources do not only contribute to the personalization of content but also provide the opportunity to monitor the learning process at any time so that extensive data is obtained, which may be used to modify the pedagogic approach in real time (Huang et al., 2021). Moreover, the opportunities of AI to facilitate the process of lifelong learning and skills formation highlight its applicability in creating adaptive and learner-focused learning trajectories. Meanwhile, additional ethical issues, such as data privacy, surveillance, and algorithmic discrimination, require close attention and the creation of effective governance procedures to make AI usage in education responsible and fair (Luckin et al., 2016).

The future of education in an AI-driven world is not just a technological problem, but it is also a way to explore how changing relationships between the educators and the learners can be made not only collaborative, human-centered, and educative, but also richer. Although benefits of AI implementation in learning communities are clear, the implementation process should focus on the situations where human interaction is the primary element, where critical thinking and creativity are developed, and where critical thought and curiosity are actively nurtured (Cope et al., 2020; Goksel and Bozkurt, 2019). Despite the fact that AI has huge potential to introduce the world to new forms of personalization and efficiency, it should be implemented with ethical conscious and a sense of long-term dedication to humanistic educational principles. In this manner, the education sector stakeholders will be able to use AI to come up with fair, efficient, and future-oriented learning systems (Holmes et al., 2022; Zadorina et al., 2024).

In general, the chapter presents a logical and persuasive background, which makes AI a paradigmatic change and moral necessity in education, which is acutely evidenced by the current literature (Luckin et al., 2016; Niemi, 2021; Holmes et al., 2021). The literature review is quite extensive, combining the historical view with the modern literature up to 2024, thus providing the reader with a good conceptual background. To further reinforce this section, the chapter suggests the explicit introduction of the latest research trends of 2024/2025 and especially policy-oriented and practice-based models, such as the AI Competency Framework of Educators by the UNESCO (2024) and the report Responsible AI in Education by the OECD (2024). These details would strengthen the connection between theory, policy, and practice and make this chapter more applicable to educators and decision-makers who have to work with the modern issues of AI implementation. The chapter is reasonably relevant to the target audience, which includes educators, policymakers, and researchers interested in ethical digital transformation, and the balance between the theoretical foundations and policy implications makes it easy to understand without major revision.

2. AI IN EDUCATION

Artificial Intelligence (AI) as a factor in education is brought out as a revolutionary power with the ability to transform the way learning is provided, evaluated, and aided. It states that AI facilitates personalized learning, including the analysis of the behavior, performance patterns, and preferences of learners to provide them with personalized content and real-time feedback thus getting rid of the one-size-fits-all approach to guidance (Niemi, 2021). Adaptive learning processes assisted with AI-based systems include intelligent tutoring systems, machine learning models, and natural language processing, which assist in responding dynamically to the needs of individual students and increase the extent of engagement and learning effectiveness (Huang et al., 2021).

It emphasizes the value of automation in education, as AI will decrease administrative tasks of teachers through automatization of grading, assessment, and other routine academic activities. This will enable instructors to pay more attention to effective pedagogical communication, mentoring, and early student intervention in case of struggling (Goksel & Bozkurt, 2019). Moreover, AI-based learning analytics can be used to monitor students in real-time, which can adjust instructions and refine curriculum design (Luckin et al., 2016).

It however states that AI is not meant to substitute the teacher, but supplement human functions in education. The privacy of obtained data, algorithm discrimination, access equality, and maintenance of human-centered learning can be listed among ethical issues that will still be critical to resolve to integrate AI in a responsible way (Cope et al., 2020). The finally concludes that AI can be valuable in education and is now useful when it is carefully, ethically, and inclusively used, which means that the technological progress will serve humanistic educational purposes and not their detriment (Holmes et al., 2022).

The chapter has a powerful background since it follows the development of AI in the education sector, starting with automation and then moving to personalized and adaptive learning. It promotes the transformational claims referring to Niemi (2021) to speak about AI as a paradigm shift and Goksel and Bozkurt (2019) to speak about automation and less administrative burden. Besides, Huang et al. (2021) and Holmes et al. (2022) confirm the capability of AI to enable intelligent tutoring and analytics. The ethical issues such as privacy and algorithmic bias are recognized with the help of Cope et al. (2020) and Luckin et al. (2016).

The main weaknesses which are found as: the lack of empirical illustrations, few structural discrepancies, and slight repetition will be corrected in the revision. They will include some brief illustrative examples, including classroom use of generative AI tools and institutional ethical audits to make them more relevant in practice (Holmes et al., 2023). Structural changes will be made smooth and recurrent ethical arguments will be put together to be understandable. The revisions will enhance the level of coherence without distorting the conceptual focus of the chapter.

2.1. Evolution of AI in Education

The history of Artificial Intelligence in Education (AIEd) can be characterized as the gradual transition between simple technological assistance and advanced and data-driven learning systems. Initial use of AI in education was primarily automation and efficiency especially in administrative and assessment roles like grading, record keeping and scheduling. These early systems were rule based and were executed in the stiff instructional frameworks, with little flexibility. During this period, the primary role of AI was perceived as a supplying tool aimed at decreasing the workload of the teachers but not as the entity that can change the way pedagogy is conducted (Luckin et al., 2016; Niemi, 2021).

With the increasing research on the subject, the focus now changed to the creation of intelligent tutoring systems (ITS) which are meant to simulate human tutoring. Misconceptions of learners and the use of specific feedback in the form of feedback were introduced in early ITS models, including BUGGY and SOPHIE. These systems provided a conceptual basis to current adaptive learning environments with inclusion of learner models, pedagogical strategies and domain knowledge. Even though small in scale, these early systems represented a significant shift in the non-responsive nature of instructional technologies toward a more responsive type of technology (Luckin et al., 2016).

The further development of AIEd was boosted by the increase in computing power, machine learning methods, and the availability of data. AI systems started facilitating individualised and adaptive learning, which allowed analysing learner behaviour, performance, and engagement in real time. This advancement disrupted the old models of education based on one size fits all and enabled the customization of instructional content and feedback and pacing to each learner in real-time. Studies indicate that such flexibility increases the level of engagement in learners, and differentiated instruction in various educational settings (Goksel and Bozkurt, 2019; Huang et al., 2021).

Another aspect that is observed in the literature is the increasing significance of learning analytics and predictive modelling in AI-supported education. They facilitate educators as they are able to determine the gaps in learning, track the progress of students and take proactive measures. The use of AI-based analytics has helped to reinvent the notion of teaching as an evidence-based practice, in which the choices made in instruction are informed by ongoing data knowledge as opposed to intuition as a sole source. Consequently, AI has been also gradually positioned as a framework of comprehending the way of learning, and not just providing the instructional content (Holmes et al., 2022; Yufei et al., 2020).

More recent work underlines the fact that AI has been integrated into the framework and ideology of the education system. AI is claimed to open the black box of learning by rendering cognitive and behavioural learning processes more visible; thus, providing a better perspective on how learners engage and become motivated. This incorporation is an indication that AI becomes more of an agent of systematic educational transformation instead of a complementary technological application (Huang et al., 2021; Holmes et al., 2022).

Irrespective of these developments, literature always emphasizes the need to adopt an implementation that is human-centred and ethical. Artificial intelligence is not considered as the alternative to the role of teachers but is an auxiliary system that promotes the educational objectives without substituting a human judgment, emotional intelligence, and ethical responsibility. The development of AIEd can thus be seen as having been a continuous process of human-ai interaction that is regulated by pedagogical principles and ethical leadership (Cope et al., 2020; Selwyn, 2022; Zadorina et al., 2024).

The chapter distinctly demonstrates key AI-enabled education trends, such as personalization, adaptive learning, automation, and ethics, which are demonstrated by available literature (Luckin et al., 2016; Holmes et al., 2021). In order to add more clarity and depth of analysis, the revised version will further explain how these trends overlap with institutional practices and decision-making at the policy level. A new comparative subsection will specifically compare the rapid technological innovation with the levels of ethical and institutional readiness with the focus on the aspects of gap in governance and problems with the implementation. This addition will improve the analytical relationship between innovation and responsibility in education and solidify the contribution that this chapter makes to the discussions about ethical AI in education.

2.2. Personalized and Adaptive Learning through Artificial Intelligence

One of the most outstanding themes of the literature on Artificial Intelligence in education is personalized and adaptive learning. The analysed articles all point to the fact that AI can help the learning environment to go beyond the traditional and standardised forms of instruction towards the focus on the learners. Through analysis of large amounts of learner data such as performance, learners' engagement patterns, and learning behaviours. AI systems are able to customize learning material. This feature will directly cater to the learner diversity and assist in differentiated instruction: the latter is not easily attainable in a traditional classroom (Goksel and Bozkurt, 2019; Niemi, 2021).

One of the significant processes of individualizing is the adaptive learning systems and intelligent tutoring systems (ITS). The literature details these systems to be in constant mode of monitoring interactions with learners and dynamically modify instructional paths, difficulty of content, and feedback. In comparison to the static digital learning systems, AI-based systems are real-time responsive and provide learning support in case the learners are struggling and progress the content when they display mastery. Research stresses that these adaptive processes contribute to the overall improvement of the engagement and motivation of the learners as well as to their enhanced conceptual understanding because of the alignment of teaching with personal learning paths (Luckin et al., 2016; Huang et al., 2021).

The literature also mentions that AI-driven personalized learning is not restricted to the content adaptation but extends to the customized feedback and assessment. AI systems are capable of providing instant, formative feedback to learners to enable them to recognize errors and advance knowledge without postponement. It is stated that automated assessment tools help to facilitate mastery-based learning through the option of setting student pace. They are especially useful in the large-scale or online learning environment, where the individualized teacher feedback could be constrained (Yufei et al., 2020; Jain and Raghuram, 2023).

The other notable dimension that is addressed in the literature is that of learning analytics and predictive modelling in adaptive learning. Intelligence based on AI can help spot learning gaps, lack of engagement, and learners in danger earlier. These systems allow timely responses and informed instructional decision-making by educators by allowing them to obtain actionable insights. The positions of the literature postulate predictive analytics as a potent instrument to enhance the learning outcomes and mitigate the decline in the rate of dropouts, particularly in digitally mediated education (Holmes et al., 2022; Grassini, 2023).

Although it has its advantages, researchers warn that AI-based personalization should be done with pedagogic and ethical vigilance. The literature cautions that the over utilization of the algorithmic decision-making process can diminish the autonomy of the learner, or simplify complex learning tasks. It is feared that the personalization that is based on purely performance measure can exclude social, emotional, and creative aspects of the learning. Consequently, scientists suggest moderate solutions to this issue in which AI assists, but does not determine the course of learning (Selwyn, 2022; Cope et al., 2020).

In general, the literature can see personalized and adaptive learning as one of the most radical contributions of AI to education as long as it is used responsibly. Personalization based on AI is offered as a way of making the process more inclusive, engaging, and effective in learning and helping educators cope with the needs of different learners. Nevertheless, it can be successful only through a careful combination, moral protection, and human control that should prevent individualization to fulfil the purposes of education and not the mere technological productivity (Holmes et al., 2022; Zadorina et al., 2024).

2.3. Changing Role of Teachers in AI-Enabled Education

The development of the Artificial Intelligence (AI) in education has slowly altered the role of a teacher and changed it to a more facilitative and supervisory role. The previous applications of AI in education were more about automation, including the grading of tests and classroom logistics. Modern AI systems have however changed to adaptive learning and intelligent tutoring, such that the personalized learning experiences can be offered based on the real time performance of the student. Learning at their own rhythm see AI tools such as virtual tutors, chatbots and predictive analytics; teachers can also learn where students are struggling to learn and this information might not be clear when using traditional methods of teaching (Niemi, 2021). Such systems make data available to improve curriculum development and student engagement, but they also have some challenges, including the possible biases, privacy issues, and the imbalance of access in schools with limited funding. Notably, the focus of literature is that teachers can continue to play a central role in the educational process since AI is supposed to supplement teachers, not to eliminate them (Niemi, 2021).

Recent studies emphasize the fact that AI can be used to facilitate the transformation of the teaching process with the help of adaptive learning and intelligent tutoring systems. Adaptive learning systems study the behaviour, interests and success of students in order to customise content whereas intelligent tutoring systems replicate human instruction by giving them individualized feedback. These tools based on AI can take off some of the routine workloads of teachers, including grading and performance monitoring, and leave them to mentoring, developing critical thinking, and integrating emotional and social sides of learning (Goksel and Bozkurt, 2019; Huang et al., 2021). Nevertheless, effective implementation of AI necessitates teachers to play an active role in the development, execution, and ethical supervision of the technology, whereby the technology will be an addition to pedagogy and not its determination (Kayyali, 2024).

Other pedagogical opportunities facilitated by AI identified in the literature are differentiated instruction, group-based learning, and data-driven insights concerning teaching strategies. AI is able to support the development of personalized learning strategies, assistance and real-time feedback, and monitoring of progress in students, which was unfeasible in the past. Virtual assistants and smart tutoring system add more interest to the normal learning environments both traditional and remote to support students who would otherwise not be able to keep pace. However, it is also agreed that overuse of AI can dehumanize the learning process, which is probably due to the elimination of teacher-student interaction. Such aspects as the ethnicity of the algorithms and privacy concerns continue to be the subject of concern and should be closely followed by the teacher (Kouzov, 2019; Holmes et al., 2022).

In addition, the literature points out that AI enables educators to reconstruct their occupation. Teachers are not a content delivery anymore but a guide, partner and decision-maker who incorporates AI knowledge into the learning process. The key to the effective utilization of AI by teachers is professional development, participative design of AI tools, and data literacy. The further opportunities and challenges raised by generative AI, including ChatGPT, provide us with more brainstorming and feedback, as well as suggest the problem of plagiarism and academic integrity. According to the emerging paradigm, the role of teachers is also changing to design, oversee, and provide ethical directions to AI-assisted learning, so that technology-based learning is not at the cost of humanistic values (Selwyn, 2022; Sushama et al., 2022; Thomson et al., 2024).

To sum up, AI in education is changing the role of the teacher to be not only an individual instructor but also a guide, instructor and an ethical watchdog. Whereas AI offers means of personalized learning, effective evaluation, and better interaction, teaching cannot be substituted with the necessary human activity. It is widely promoted in the literature to integrate AI in a responsible manner, focus on the involvement of teacher, ethical application, and professional development to ensure maximum benefits without harming equity, privacy, or human-centred education (Zadorina et al., 2024; Jain and Raghuram, 2023).

Equity, privacy, data ownership, and algorithmic bias (Cope et al., 2020; Shrivastava, 2023; Grassini, 2023) and human-centered implementation (Goksel and Bozkurt, 2019; Cope et al., 2020) have already been discussed in the chapter.

Although the chapter touches on ethical and pedagogical aspects of AI, it can be improved by more discussion on AI literacies, as well as teacher training, as a means of capacity building. The available literature emphasizes that the successful integration of AI requires the skills of the educator to critically interpret, adapt, and govern AI tools in the curricula (Niemi, 2021; Holmes et al., 2022). Also, the cross-regional viewpoints of the contrast of developed and developing educational contexts will make the chapter more applicable and tackle the issue of equity. The updated chapter will also consist of a brief future research agenda, which will consider inclusive education, AI literacy development, and teacher professional learning as the priority points of human-centered and equity-focused scholarship (Luckin et al., 2016).

2.4. Ethical, Equity, and Governance Challenges of AI in Education

It is the introduction of Artificial Intelligence (AI) into education that provides unprecedented possibilities of personalized learning, adaptive system, and intelligent tutoring. But, in addition to these benefits, literature also indicates that there are serious ethical, equity and governance issues that need to be considered keenly. The credibility of the AI-generated decisions and the possible strengthening of the prejudices reflected in the algorithms is one of the primary ethical issues. In the event of being trained on unequal datasets, AI tools may replicate racial, socioeconomic or gender discrimination in learning results, and this raises concerns regarding discrimination and fairness in learning (Shrivastava, 2023; Grassini, 2023). The other critical ethical issue is privacy especially in the collection, storage, and use of student data. The broad surveillance of AI, who, by learning analytics, sentiment analysis, or biometrics data, require informed consent and effective data governance measures to ensure the safety of personal information of students (Selwyn, 2022; Shrivastava, 2023).

The equity issues regarding AI implementation are linked to the differences in the access to digital infrastructure and technology tools. Schools with scarce internet access and lower-income areas might not get the benefits of AI-enhanced education and incur even more educational inequalities and the digital divide (Shrivastava, 2023; Grassini, 2023). Moreover, the readiness and the inclination of teachers to incorporate AI in their pedagogy also affect fair access. The literature focuses on the fact that professional growth and training and involvement in decision-making processes are essential to ensuring that AI tools supplement instead of replace human education (Sushama et al., 2022; Zadorina et al., 2024).

The issues of governance also touch upon the ethical and equity issues because the implementation of AI in education would require a well-defined policy, control and supervisory practices, and participatory design methodologies. The literature proposes that AI can be implemented as the support tool in the teaching process and not a replacement of educators without losing the human control in the teaching and assessment procedures (Holmes et al., 2022; Selwyn, 2022). The issue of governance is also connected to the equilibrium between the concepts of innovation and pedagogy, which entails that AI-related systems not only improve learning but also promote the notions of inclusivity, social-emotional growth and lifelong learning (Luckin et al., 2016; Holmes et al., 2022).

It is excessively focused on the descriptive benefits, automation, personalization, adaptive learning (Niemi, 2021; Huang et al., 2021; Holmes et al., 2022). There is a lack of emphasis on policy and governance although ethical issues are backed by Selwyn (2022) and Cope et al. (2020).

In addition, AI also brings up more general concerns regarding the use and role of education. Although automation can be used to enhance efficiency and learning performance, systems that are overly adaptive and personalised can also dehumanise education by removing the opportunity to interact with teachers and think critically (Kouzov, 2019; Holmes et al., 2022). The literature emphasizes the role of making AI governance systems inclusive of ethical foresight, participatory design, and the future literacy. In this way, the stakeholders can predict the possible harms, encourage fair results, and conform AI usage to humanistic principles (Miller & Tuomi, 2022; Cope et al., 2020).

Addresses the ethical issues of bias, privacy, and accountability, though the updated version will provide additional clarification on the differences between the advantages of pedagogy and the risks that may arise when some ethical concerns are not met. In particular, ethical considerations will be discussed as a parallel strand of analysis, as opposed to being integrated into the discourses of AI benefits. Such a more distinct division will guarantee an equal focus, and pedagogical innovation and ethical responsibility can be studied with the same thoroughness. This kind of restructuring is compatible with human-centered AI scholarship, which states that ethical reflection must be a part and not a consequence of technological use (Cope et al., 2020; Holmes et al., 2022).

Research deals with questions of ethical issues, including privacy, surveillance, bias (Cope et al., 2020; Selwyn, 2022; Shrivastava, 2023) but these are not highlighted as such as the advantages of technology, including personalization (Huang et al., 2021) and automation (Goksel & Bozkurt, 2019). To add the right amount of optimism and caution, the ethical issues must be extended and be clearly isolated.

2.5. Scope, Evidence Base, and Methodological Positioning

Research (Goksel and Bozkurt, 2019; Huang et al., 2021) is purposely modelled as a literature review in the format of a structured literature review summarizing the research available on the topic of Artificial Intelligence in education instead of presenting primary experimental results. The articles under consideration testify to the shift in the initial automation-based applications to the adaptive learning systems, intelligent tutoring systems, and learning analytics that facilitate personalised and learner-centred learning (Luckin et al., 2016; Niemi, 2021). The earlier literature always documents that AI-enabled personalization and automated feedback can boost the engagement of the learner and their responsiveness to instruction, especially in digitally mediated and large-scale learning environments (Goksel and Bozkurt, 2019; Huang et al., 2021).

Even though the chapter does not introduce new effect sizes or longitudinal data, it summarizes the empirical observations indicating that learning analytics and adaptive systems allow detecting learning gaps at early stages and ensure the maintenance of instructional intervention over time (Luckin et al., 2016; Holmes et al., 2022). The re-evaluation of teachers is based on the scholarly works that focus on the idea of AI complementing professional practice by decreasing the administrative load and allowing an educator to devote time to mentoring, critical thinking, and human interaction (Goksel and Bozkurt, 2019; Niemi, 2021).

The issues of ethical, equity, and governance are seen throughout the literature review, with the articles generally supporting the idea of human-centred and ethically regulated AI integration into the educational context (Cope et al., 2020; Holmes et al., 2022). This synthesis offers a logical conceptual basis of future empirical and policy-making studies.

These are indicators of efficiency and human-centered value conflict, which is in line with the argument that AI must facilitate, rather than substitute, educators (Goksel and Bozkurt, 2019). Nevertheless, the problems are identified, but not merged into one conceptual connection. They would be reinforced with ethics and personalization.

2.6. Strengths and Weaknesses of AI in Education and Ethics

2.6.1. Strengths of AI in Education

A. Individualized and Customized Learning: AI technologies have the potential to identify student behaviors, interests, and performance to provide content and learning speed, increasing engagement and learning results (Goksel and Bozkurt, 2019; Kouzov, 2019; Selwyn, 2022).
B. Feedback Intelligent Tutoring and Feedback Intelligent tutoring systems (ITS) and virtual assistants assist in self-directed learning and achieving aiding feedback to less able learners (Luckin et al., 2016; Grassini, 2023).
C. Administrative Efficiency: AI can provide grading, attendance, and schedules, among other administrative functions, and thus can decrease the teacher workload and focus on creative teaching experiences (Sushama et al., 2022; Selwyn, 2022).
D. Improved Lane Learning: AI can be used to promote immersive and interactive learning through AR/VR, robotics, and other intelligent devices and enhance student motivation and engagement (Çelik and Baturay, 2024; Yufei et al., 2020).
E. Predictive Analytics: AI can be used to identify any learning gaps in early stages and provide insights based on the data and intervene in a personalized way (Zadorina et al., 2024; Huang et al., 2021).
F. In the Support of Teachers: AI does not replace teachers and only enhances their work by offering resources to increase the quality of instruction and interaction with students (Jain and Raghuram, 2023; Miller and Tuomi, 2022).

2.6.2. Weaknesses and Ethical Challenges

A. Prejudice and Equity: AI systems will end up perpetuating racial, socioeconomic, and gender discrimination when trained using unrepresentative data (Grassini, 2023).

B. Privacy and Data Security: Collection of student data is an ethical issue, as it reminds about consent, confidentiality, and misuse (Shrivastava, 2023; Holmes et al., 2022).
C. Digital Divide: AI-based educational opportunities might be less available to students in low-funded schools or highly populated by impoverished areas due to flawed digital infrastructure (Niemi, 2021; Sushama et al., 2022).
D. Teacher Preparedness: Not all teachers are properly trained to work with AI, and this might be a barrier to its implementation or even excessive use of automated programs (Zadorina et al., 2024; Kouzov, 2019).
E. Humanization of Learning: too much automation may decrease the teacher-student interaction and affect the development of emotional, social, and critical thinking (Holmes et al., 2022; Kouzov, 2019).
F. Doubts in the Implementation: The excessive focus on efficiency and prediction can be unaware of the complexity of education and human creativity (Cope et al., 2020; Miller and Tuomi, 2022).
G. Generative AI Dangers: ChatGPT and other such tools may make learning easier, but they also provoke the issue of plagiarism, abuse, and influence on creativity and moral growth in students (Thomson et al., 2024).

2.7. Technological Innovation Vs. Ethical Preparedness

The article highlights the increasing state of unbalance between the rapid advancement of technology in Artificial Intelligence (AI) to education and a relatively weak ethical readiness. In terms of innovation, the literature is reporting great advancements in AI-based educational applications, like adaptive learning systems, intelligent tutoring systems, automated evaluation, learning analytics, chatbots, and virtual assistants. These solutions allow feedback in real time, individualized learning trajectories, early detection of the knowledge shortage, and less administration work on the side of teachers, thus improving the effectiveness of instruction and engagement with the learner (Goksel and Bozkurt, 2019; Huang et al., 2021; Yufei et al., 2020) .The researchers always emphasize the fact that AI-based personalization can shift education beyond the model of one size fits all to practices that are more learner-centred and data-informed (Niemi, 2021).

In spite of these developments, the paper highlights the fact that ethical preparedness has failed to follow technological development. The most common examples of ethical issues are privacy and security of student data, the absence of transparency in algorithmic decision making, informed consent, and the further promotion of internal social and economic prejudices with the help of poorly designed AI systems (Selwyn, 2022; Grassini, 2023).

It is also stated in the literature that disproportional access to AI technologies can further increase the digital divide, especially among students at underfunded or infrastructurally disadvantaged institutions (Niemi, 2021).

Besides, the paper emphasizes that ethical preparedness needs direct human attention. The role of teachers is put as the key player in holding responsible AI use because the pedagogical judgment, emotional sensitivity, and moral responsibility cannot be substituted with automated systems (Luckin et al., 2016; Holmes et al., 2022).

2.8. Ethics Before Efficiency

Throughout the chapter, it is stressed that although AI can bring efficiency to education, including grading automation, individual learning paths, and decisions based on data, ethics should receive the first priority over the efficiency-focused objectives. Even though AI systems have the ability to streamline learning procedures and administration, the literature warns against focusing on the speed, scale, and performance indicators at the cost of human values and educational standards (Niemi, 2021)

Some of the authors mentioned in the chapter contend that the adoption of AI based on efficiency will threaten the ethical concerns of student privacy of data, informed consent, transparency and fairness. The high-volume gathering and processing of learner data, through its efficiency, creates the issue of how they are utilized, who has access to them, and whether students and teachers intelligibly agree to such practices (Selwyn, 2022; Grassini, 2023).

The article emphasizes that efficiency-focused algorithmic systems can unintentionally support social and socioeconomic biases thus undermining education equity (Holmes et al., 2022).

Notably, the chapter emphasizes the fact that education is not the technical system that should be optimized but the human process with emotional, social, and moral aspects. Automation is not an efficiency-driven practice that will displace the functions of teachers in terms of ethical decision-making, emotional control, and significant interaction with students (Luckin et al., 2016; Huang et al., 2021).

Therefore, caution and carefulness in implementation of AI is endorsed in the literature where ethical regulation, involvement of teachers and inclusive design are the guiding factors of technological implementation, not efficiency.

In general, the chapter puts ethics-first-efficiency as a compulsory discourse to make sure that AI enriches education in a dignified way that technological innovation does not diminish education to an optimized yet dehumanized system (Niemi, 2021).

The chapter directly concentrates on the concept of the AI-based personalization and adaptive learning, repeating some of its advantages over and over again, including customized content, real-time feedback, and learner-centered instruction (Niemi, 2021; Goksel & Bozkurt, 2019; Huang et al., 2021; Holmes et al., 2022). Though such a focus defines the pedagogical potential of AI, it is skewed towards the technological benefits at the expense of human-related ones. On the contrary, the aspects of teacher autonomy, professional judgment, and human control are mentioned but relatively minor. It is also clear in the chapter that AI is not intended to reduce the role of teachers but it will complement it, and teachers will continue to play a key role in mentoring, ethical oversight, and decision-making (Niemi, 2021; Goksel & Bozkurt, 2019; Holmes et al., 2022), although the argument is not well-developed and frequent as the benefits of personalization.

Likewise, such ethical issues as bias, privacy, surveillance, and dehumanization are addressed (Cope et al., 2020; Selwyn, 2022; Shrivastava, 2023; Grassini, 2023), yet they are often not presented as the primary strands of the analysis as much as opportunities of AI. The literature itself warns against over- personalization and excessive automation since they can undermine human interaction, critical thinking and social- emotional aspects of learning (Kouzov, 2019; Holmes et al., 2022). This means that there is a lack of emphasis on the digital well-being and the agency of a teacher, and these elements are evident in the mentioned works.

3. BIBLIOMETRIC ANALYSIS

Figure 1 is a bibliometric map generated by the application of the VOSviewer, regarding keyword co-occurrence data identified in the PubMed database. It graphically displays the pattern and architecture of academic research concerning AI in health care and biomedical sciences. In this network, nodes denote a particular term or keyword, and the size of an element represents the frequency with which a particular term is used in the entire set of data and the edges between two nodes refer to the number of times two terms have been co-occurred within the same publication. These are denoted by the color-coded clusters which denote a subject-based grouping, thus showing the overlap of research fields.

Figure 1. bibliometric analysis of "Future of AI in education" using VOSViewer with data from PubMed (Data may vary slightly)

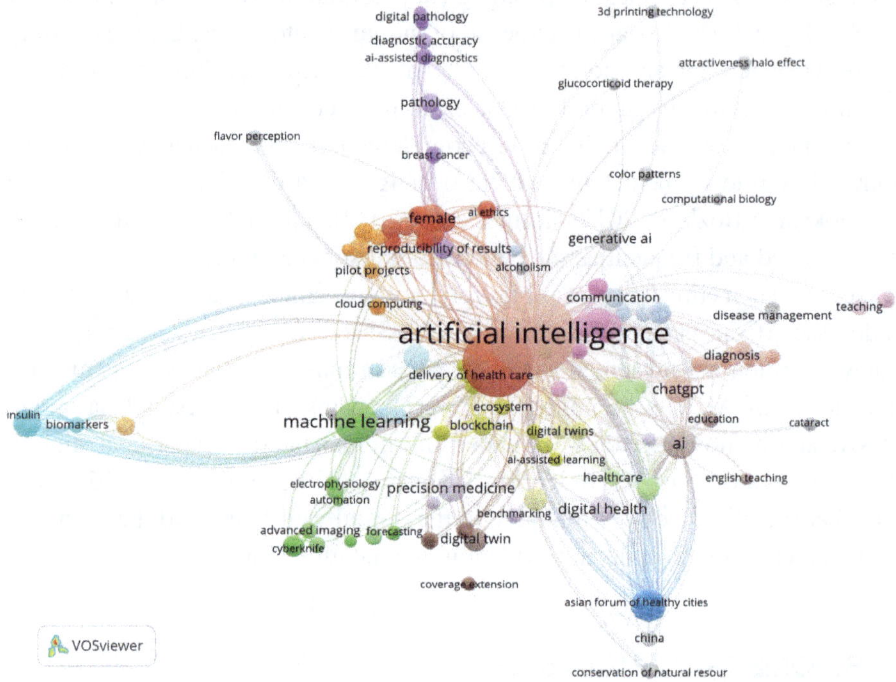

The biggest and the most interconnected node is at the core of this map, which is artificial intelligence. This makes it its principal line of action in various fields. Directly associated with this key term are such notions as machine learning and digital health, precision medicine, ChatGPT, and generative AI, which are often used in discussions. These are among the essential areas where AI can be applied to health care because it is relevant when studying diseases, working with patients and analyzing data. The green cluster pivots on the phrase machine learning and comprises such terms as automation, advanced imaging, forecasting, and cyber knife. This implies that there is a substantial emphasis on predictive modelling, automated decision systems and robotics in the area of treatment planning. The blue cluster is directly connected with the blue one and such words as biomarkers and insulin are present that support the idea of AI at the biochemical and molecular level of diagnosis. Emerging topics include the pink and purple clusters that include "ChatGPT," generative AI, diagnosis, education, and the communication. These indicate the growing demand for natural language processing and conversational AI in clinic as well as educational directions. The two neighboring words, namely teaching, English teaching and disease management would similarly indicate the emergent trend of applying language models in medical education to patients and dissemination of health information. Interestingly, the names of the topics that form part of the red and the orange cluster like AI ethics, reproduction of results and female indicate that more attention is given to ethical, demographical and social aspects of AI. This embraces algorithmic discrimination, gendered effects, and the stability of the results of AI. Also, the light blue cluster is filled with region-specific words such as China and Asian forum of healthy cities which represents geographical hotspots and regionally oriented research. These can be specific to neighborhood's policies, urban health interventions or regional AI based solutions.

4. CONCLUSION

The future of education in an AI-oriented world has a long list of pros and cons. As it has been mentioned in the chapter, introduction of AI technologies into the education process can reshape the concept of learning by providing an opportunity to deliver individualized education, automate organizational and administration procedures, and enhancing student interest in the learning material. Simultaneously, ethical issues associated with the implementation of AI, especially data privacy, the bias of algorithms, and the safeguarding of valuable human relationships in the educational process, have to be considered carefully to prevent failure in responsible implementation. Technological advancement is a phenomenon that requires a human approach when it is predominant, as highlighted in the literature reviewed.

The chapter confirms that AI can assist teachers in gaining a better understanding of learners by giving more in-depth information into the behaviors, progress, and learning patterns of students. Nonetheless, AI will not be able to substitute the most essential human aspects of teaching, empathy, critical thinking, communication, and the capacity to establish meaningful relationships with students. Thus, AI must be considered an assistive device that can improve the performance of teachers and not a replacement to human ones, and hence, it is critical that teachers learn how to collaborate with AI systems.

The other major concern raised is the inequality in access to AI technologies in various learning settings. The current unequal distribution of resources and infrastructure can contribute to the further expansion of current inequality in education unless the various strategies are taken to make sure that students across the socio-economic lines have an opportunity to enjoy AI-based education. To deal with this challenge, teachers, policymakers, and technologists have to work together to ensure equity and accessibility.

To sum up, the future of AI in education is not only the technological innovation but the reinvention of education, and a focus on human creativity, imagination, and lifelong learning. The most important strength of the chapter is also the balanced and ethical conceptualization of AI that could be enhanced by suggesting a short ethical AI pedagogy framework to transform theory into practice.

REFERENCES

Çelik, F., & Baturay, M. H. (2024). Technology and innovation in shaping the future of education. *Smart Learning Environments*, *11*(1). Advance online publication. DOI: 10.1186/s40561-024-00339-0

Cope, B., Kalantzis, M., & Searsmith, D. (2020). Artificial intelligence for education: Knowledge and its assessment in AI-enabled learning ecologies. *Educational Philosophy and Theory*, *53*(12), 1229–1245. DOI: 10.1080/00131857.2020.1728732

Goksel, N., & Bozkurt, A. (2019). Artificial intelligence in Education: current insights and future perspectives. In Sisman-Ugur, S., & Kurubacak, G. (Eds.), *Handbook of Research on Learning in the Age of Transhumanism* (pp. 224–236). IGI Global., DOI: 10.4018/978-1-5225-8431-5.ch014

Grassini, S. (2023). Shaping the Future of Education: Exploring the potential and consequences of AI and ChatGPT in educational settings. *Education Sciences*, *13*(7), 692. DOI: 10.3390/educsci13070692

Holmes, W., & Tuomi, I. (2022). State of the art and practice in AI in education. *European Journal of Education*, *57*, 542–570. DOI: 10.1111/ejed.12533

Huang, J., Shen, G., & Ren, X. (2021). Connotation Analysis and Paradigm Shift of Teaching Design under Artificial Intelligence Technology. [iJET]. *International Journal of Emerging Technologies in Learning*, *16*(05), 73. DOI: 10.3991/ijet.v16i05.20287

Jain, K., & Raghuram, J. N. V. (2023). Unlocking potential: The impact of AI on education technology. *Multidisciplinary Reviews*, *7*(3), 2024049. DOI: 10.31893/multirev.2024049

Kayyali, M. (2024). Future Possibilities and Challenges of AI in Education. In *Advances in educational technologies and instructional design book series* (pp. 118–137). https://doi.org/DOI: 10.4018/979-8-3693-1351-0.ch006

Kouzov, O. (2019). The new paradigms in education and support of critical thinking with artificial intelligence (AI) tools. In Bulgarian Academy of Sciences & Institute of Mathematics and Informatics, *Serdica. Journal of Computing*, *13*(1–2), 27–40.

Luckin, R., Holmes, W., Griffiths, M., & Forcier, L. B. (2016). Intelligence Unleashed: An argument for AI in Education. In *Open Ideas at Pearson*. Pearson.

Miller, R., & Tuomi, I. (2022). Making the futures of AI in education: Why and how imagining the future matters. *European Journal of Education*, *57*(4), 537–541. DOI: 10.1111/ejed.12529

Niemi, H. (2021). AI in learning – Commentary. *Journal of Pacific Rim Psychology*, *15*, 1–12. DOI: 10.1177/18344909211038105

Selwyn, N. (2022). The future of AI and education: Some cautionary notes. *European Journal of Education*, *57*(4), 620–631. DOI: 10.1111/ejed.12532

Shrivastava, R. (2023). Role of artificial intelligence in future of education. *International Journal of Professional Business Review*, *8*(1), e0840. DOI: 10.26668/businessreview/2023.v8i1.840

Sushama, C., & Sunil Kumar, M. Sree Vidyanikethan Engineering College, VFSTR, & Sujatha, K. (2022). The Future of Education: Artificial Intelligence based Remote Learning. In *International Journal of Early Childhood Special Education* (pp. 3827–3828). https://www.researchgate.net/publication/360423234

Thomson, S. R., Pickard-Jones, B. A., Baines, S., & Otermans, P. C. J. (2024). The impact of AI on education and careers: What do students think? *Frontiers in Artificial Intelligence*, *7*. Advance online publication. DOI: 10.3389/frai.2024.1457299

VOSviewer. https://www.vosviewer.com/

Yufei, L., Saleh, S., Jiahui, H., & Abdullah, S. M. S. (2020). Review of the Application of Artificial Intelligence in Education. *International Journal of Innovation, Creativity and Change*, 548–562. https://doi.org/DOI: 10.53333/ijicc2013/12850

Zadorina, O., Hurskaya, V., Sobolyeva, S., Grekova, L., & Vasylyuk-Zaitseva, S. (2024). *The role of Artificial intelligence in creation of future Education: Possibilities and challenges*. Futurity Education., DOI: 10.57125/fed.2024.06.25.09

Chapter 2
Ethical Digital Twin: A Framework for AI-Powered Moral Reasoning Simulations in Education

Sumit Kumar Kapoor
https://orcid.org/0009-0005-6291-3176
Poornima University, India

Kriti Sankhla
https://orcid.org/0009-0001-7061-365X
Poornima University, India

Sadia Syed
https://orcid.org/0009-0008-6450-3842
College of Information Technology, Kingdom University, Bahrain

ABSTRACT

This chapter proposes a novel framework for integrating Ethical Digital Twins into educational settings to simulate moral reasoning and ethical decision-making using artificial intelligence. The Ethical Digital Twin is an AI-powered virtual persona designed to mirror a student's or professional's ethical dispositions, enabling dynamic engagement with complex moral dilemmas in controlled virtual environments. The chapter will explore how these AI-driven simulations can foster ethical literacy, critical thinking, and digital responsibility. It will outline design principles for building ethical digital twins that respect privacy, ensure fairness, and minimize algorithmic bias. Further, we will present an implementation roadmap for educational institutions, including curriculum integration, teacher training, and policy

DOI: 10.4018/979-8-3373-4982-4.ch002

recommendations. The chapter contributes to bridge conventional ethics instruction with AI-powered personalized learning, inspiring collaboration among educators, technologists, and policymakers to cultivate morally resilient, AI-literate generations

1. INTRODUCTION

The concept of Digital Twins originated in Aerospace and Industrial Engineering, with Digital Twins being used as virtual representations created for Optimisation and Simulation in real-time. In recent years, this concept has moved into the Education industry, and Digital Twins allow Institutions to model and predict Student Performance and Issues, with a goal of Creating a Personalised Learning Experience for students (Liu & David, 2023). However, the current Digital Twin deployments do not focus on Ethical Development, which means that the Educational Potential of Digital Twins in this regard is underdeveloped and that there are currently no mechanisms for Teachers/Policymakers to Develop Ethical Awareness in AI Mediated Learning Environments.

Empirical studies show growing concerns: students report mistrust in opaque AI systems, educators lack preparedness to interpret AI-generated recommendations, and institutions face legal uncertainty under emerging data-protection laws (Khosravi et al., 2024). These challenges highlight a persistent global gap, while real ethical dilemmas increasingly arise from digital ecosystems shaped by AI systems.

The research gap in this area of study is twofold: A lack of an integrated framework bringing together moral psychology and fairness-aware AI, explainable reasoning, and digital twin architecture is the first gap. Secondly, policymakers do not currently have access to an actionable model through which they may evaluate or govern ethical development within AI-based learning environments. This chapter addresses both of these research gaps through the introduction of the concept of an Ethical Digital Twin (EDT) — an AI-powered virtual persona that simulates, supports, and analyses the moral reasoning of learners in a dynamic, culturally contextualised environment.

The guiding question for this chapter is "How can we design an Ethical Digital Twin (EDT) that fosters fair, transparent, and culturally relevant moral reasoning simulations that enhance ethical literacy through education?". By answering this question, this chapter provides a structured framework that educational practitioners, researchers, and policymakers may use to integrate ethical values into a curriculum created using AI. Through the EDT approach, the EDT shows how to create pathways for responsible innovation through the convergence of moral psychology models, explainable AI, fairness auditing, and the privacy-preserving design of AI-based learning environments.

2. BACKGROUND OF STUDY

AI technologies have rapidly spread through the global education landscape, generating both new possibilities and persistent ethical dilemmas. K-12 and Higher Education institutions currently deploy AI technologies in areas of personalisation, assessing and evaluating performance, and facilitating administrative decisions. However, many institutions lack the knowledge or ability to incorporate ethical rationales into the AI systems they utilise, and as a result, many AI systems operate as "black boxes." That is, these systems generate predictions and feedback based purely on algorithms without providing visibility into the cognitive processes that underpin the AI algorithms, creating concerns about issues of fairness and accountability and about the role of students in promoting their own agency (Holmes et al., 2021). Specifically, in a culturally diverse context, the multiplicity of ethical interpretations could have a profound impact on the use and design of AI systems (Akgün & Greenhow, 2021). This example demonstrates a broad trend of technological advancement that exceeds the ability of education leaders to effectively navigate the ethical issues associated with the development and deployment of technology in schools and traditional institutions.

The use of widely used EdTech tools raised additional concerns regarding bias in AI algorithms. Automated essay grading systems have flagged the writing of minority students at disproportionately higher rates than that of white students in the U.S. due to the data used to train the systems (Baker & Hawn, 2021). While this is not a DT solution, it demonstrates the potential systemic risks associated with using AI without utilising fairness-aware measures.

Taken together, these examples illustrate how current thinking on the design of DTs is focused on maximising performance while neglecting to take ethics, cultural inclusivity, or transparency into consideration. As such, educators may not be prepared to assist students with their moral growth in an AI-enabled environment. The EDT framework provides a means of addressing the deficiencies of DTs with respect to fairness, explainability, cultural relevance, and moral growth within the context of AI in education.

3. STATEMENT OF THE PROBLEM

The AI-Enhanced Moral Education (AI-ME) framework encapsulates several key characteristics including transparency, fairness, and inclusiveness and aims to create an environment where learners develop independent ethical agency. Although the overall vision for AI-ME is attainable, the development of current technological solutions has fallen short in achieving this goal. There is evidence that many AI tools are biased, do not allow for interpretability, and do not support ethical reasoning processes, creating inconsistent evidence (Mehrabi et al., 2021). Digital Twin applications today are focused on providing academic performance predictions and operational decision making, not the development of ethical competence.

The lack of moral reasoning frameworks, like Kohlberg's or Rest's, being systematically incorporated into the design of AI-based simulations is an example of the theoretical gaps in the current literature. Similarly, empirical gaps exist due to the scarcity of research investigating how students develop their ethical competencies while using AI-based simulations. Contextual gaps also exist because many AI-based tools do not take into account the impact of a user's culture, language, or socioeconomic status, creating an environment where the feedback provided for one's ethical decision making is sometimes biased and/or incomplete.

To summarize, the problem with AI-based moral education is the lack of a coherent, ethically-based Digital Twin framework that combines the fields of moral psychology, fairness-aware algorithms, privacy-preserving data governance and cultural competency-based scenario design. This chapter presents a response to this issue by outlining the Ethical Digital Twin (EDT) framework for educational settings.

4. THEORETICAL FOUNDATIONS (MORAL MODELS & THEORIES)

4.1 Ethical Literacy in Education

Within education, ethical literacy can be described as the ability of both learners and educators to identify, evaluate, and respond to ethical issues in a manner consistent with societal and professional values. Ethical literacy includes critical reflection, moral awareness, and the application of ethical perspectives in decision making (Nguyen et al., 2023). In today's digital world, ethical literacy expands moral reasoning to also include digital citizenship, data stewardship, and recognition of the impact of AI systems in learning spaces (Akgün & Greenhow, 2021; Holmes et al., 2021). Research indicates that providing ethical literacy in educational environments can promote responsible use of technology, preventative uncritical acceptance, and longer-term civic engagement (Quinn & Coghlan, 2021; Khan et al., 2021). Yet, ethical literacy programs too often do not relate to emergent technologies, particularly to the AI-enhanced systems exerting more influence on educational engagements.

4.2 Moral Reasoning Models

The Ethical Digital Twin (EDT) has been developed from various theoretical traditions which explain how we perceive and respond to ethical dilemmas. These theories provide a foundation for creating AI-based simulations that support the development of moral reasoning.

Kohlberg's Theory of Moral Development (1950s–1980s) describes six stages in the development of an individual toward principled reasoning. The use of Kohlberg's developmental approach will allow for a better sequencing of dilemmas as learner's progress through each stage.

Rest's Four-Component Model of moral development expands the theory of moral development developed by Lawrence Kohlberg by adding a fourth aspect: Ethical Sensitivity, Ethical Judgment, Ethical Motivation, and Ethical Character, all emphasizing the role of the emotions together with ethical intent in moral action (Ng et al., 2021). The Four-component Model's cycle structure complements the emergence of the EDT structure; therefore, it affords a solid theoretical foundation of ethical decision-making.

Social Learning Theory (Bandura, 1977) provides an underlying rationale for EDT that describes how ethical behaviour is taught through observation, imitation, and positive/negative reinforcement. A virtual simulation allows the learner to safely experiment with their choices, the perspectives of stakeholders, and their results/implications, thus supporting the development of ethical values through guided reflection (Bandura, 2024).

Value-Sensitive Design (VSD), also referred to as VSD has been introduced by Friedman et al., and it adds a Sociotechnical Dimension to System Design with the intention to Embed Human Values (Fairness, Autonomy and Dignity) within System Design through an Inclusionary Approach to Culturally Inclusive Technology and Feedback to create systems free from Algorithmic Bias and contributing to the growing concern surrounding inequities present in AI System Design (Friedman et al 2023).

Classical ethical theories, including Utilitarianism and Deontological Ethics are two classical ethical theories that give normative depth to the EDT. Utilitarianism bases its evaluation of the decision on the consequences and collective welfare, when contrastingly, Deontological Ethics bases decisions primarily on the duties, rights and universal principles. The combination of the two classical theories allows learners to contrast the outcomes of decision making from a Utilitarian perspective, with the duties associated with decision making from a Deontological perspective.

In order to provide a framework for how to implement the four ethical literacy constructs and to clarify how to measure each construct, the framework of the EDT Ethical Literacy Scale is summarized in Table 1 (including construct definitions, sample items, and reliability data). In Figure 1, the moral reasoning theories with AI-driven systems are illustrated via synthesis linking EDT functional components with their respective ethical reasoning theory.

Figure 1. Mapping of Moral Reasoning Theories to EDT

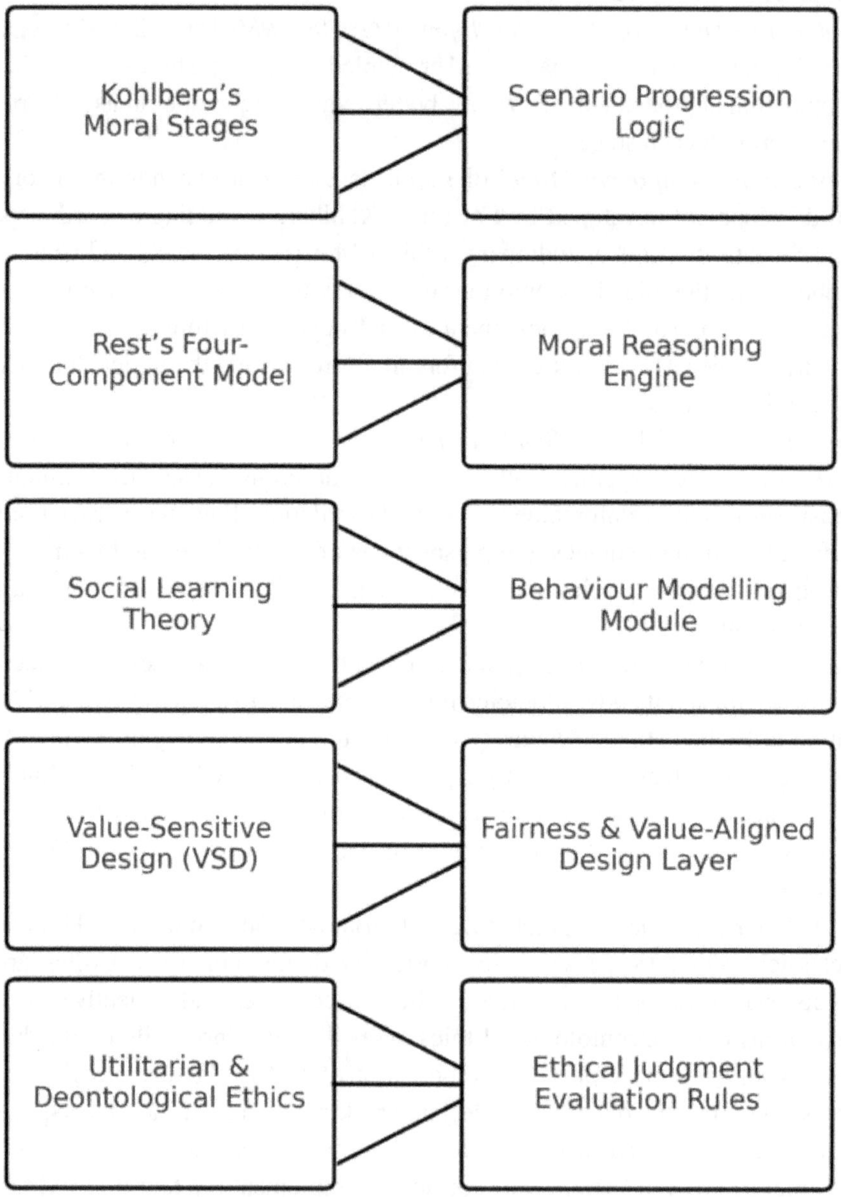

Table 1. Comparison of Moral Reasoning Models

Model	Core Idea	Strengths	Limitations	Applicability in AI Simulations
Kohlberg's Stages	Moral growth through six developmental stages	Widely validated, progression-based	Culture-specific biases	Can structure progressive ethical dilemmas
Rest's Four Component	Sensitivity, judgment, motivation, character	Action-oriented, flexible	Requires subjective interpretation	Maps well to AI modules (reasoning + feedback)
Utilitarianism	Greatest good for greatest number	Clear decision criteria	Can neglect minority rights	Useful for group decision simulations
Deontological Ethics	Duty and rules guide decisions	Strong normative clarity	Less adaptive to context	Provides explainable rules for AI outputs

4.3 Digital Twins: Definition, Usage, and Development

The digital twin - first developed in the context of engineering as a virtual replica of a real-world asset - has changed from an engineering manifestation to a generic model for the representation of dynamic systems, predicting outcomes, and improving processes (Liu & David, 2025; Woo, 2023). In education, this includes representing the classroom, simulating a student's learning pathway or anticipating outcomes of pedagogical intervention (Woojin Kim & Kim, 2025; Tai Le Quy et al., 2023). The trend in the literature highlights the future opportunity of digital twins for adaptive learning, skill assessment, and professional skill development (Friege et al., 2023).

4.4 AI-Driven Simulations in Education – Current Trends

AI-driven simulations are increasingly recognized as mechanisms for experiential learning, allowing students to engage with complex illustrations of real-life issues (Holstein et al., 2022; Mattos et al., 2024). From virtual laboratories to role-playing contexts, these experiences are supported by machine learning techniques, natural language processing, and predictive analytics to create adaptive and personalized experiences relative to context (Nguyen et al., 2023; Prentzas & Binopoulou, 2025). AI-powered ethical simulation platforms are under development in medical education and engineering, where learners need to make decisions involving ethical values (Quinn & Coghlan, 2021; Goreta et al., 2024).

4.5 Algorithmic Fairness, Bias, and Privacy in EdTech

AI's entry into education creates various challenges related to algorithmic fairness, bias reduction, and privacy (Baker & Hawn, 2021; Mehrabi et al., 2021). Bias can occur through space or representation in training datasets, faulty feature selection, or the perpetuation of structural factors that generate inequities, leading to subsequent educational and discriminatory outcomes (Sha et al., 2022; Chhabra et al., 2021). Potential violence has also been avoided, including counterfactual fairness, deterministic debiasing algorithms, and others in fairness-aware machine learning for educational data science (Ma et al., 2023; Pham et al., 2025). Privacy is becoming a hot topic in EdTech as well, with growing interest in privacy-preserving analytics and transparent governance models (Holstein & Doroudi, 2021; Khosravi et al., 2024).

4.6 Gaps in Current Ethical Instruction Approaches

Although ethics is becoming increasingly valued as a part of educational-based curricula, the integration of ethics with AI-based learning technologies is still somewhat disjointed (Nguyen et al., 2023; Akgün & Greenhow, 2021). Current instruction surrounding ethics often treats the topic as a standalone, theory-based subject, and does not combine ethical theory with authentic, technology-mediated learning experiences (Holmes et al., 2021).

There are few examples in which moral reasoning theories are intently combined with AI-generated simulations or digital twin models, causing a disconnect between ethics, theory and technology (Dignum, 2021; Woo, 2023). Further, we were unable to locate any empirical studies with students examining how ethical competences evolve with ongoing human engagement with AI-based ethical decision-making environments. Addressing the gaps above will require collaborative, interdisplinary approaches, policy support and suggestions for frameworks like the suggested Ethical Digital Twin to bridge the divide of theory-practice-technology. Previous studies on AI ethics in education and digital twin applications are summarized in Table 2 with suggestions made and ethical gaps surrounding our suggested framework.

Table 2. Literature Synthesis of AI Ethics in Education and Digital Twins

Author(s), Year	Focus Area	Key Contribution	Ethical Gap Identified
Holmes et al. (2021)	Ethics of AI in Education	Proposed community-wide ethical framework for AI in education	Limited focus on simulation-based learning
Woo (2023)	Digital Twin in Math Education	Demonstrated gamified digital twins for adaptive learning	Ethical implications not addressed
Nguyen et al. (2023)	Ethical Principles for AI in Education	Suggested guiding principles for fairness and inclusivity	Lack of integration with digital twin models
Maity & Deroy (2024)	Explainable AI in Education	Introduced XAI techniques for ethical transparency	No connection to moral reasoning models

5. EMPIRICAL LITERATURE REVIEW

Based on recent research, Ethical Learning using AI is effective through gamified Digital Twin Simulations which support continuous reflection over complex ethical choices that require iterative decision-making. The research also indicates that moral sensitivity gained from ethical learning experiences is highly context dependent, with different institutions demonstrating great variability in this regard.

Prentzas and Binopoulou (2025) conducted research with participants needing to understand how building trust through transparently providing reasons for feedback increases their willingness to engage with AI-generated ethical feedback based on reasoning traces and decision-path visualizations. In like manner, Holstein et al. (2022) found that students were more likely to examine AI recommendations critically when the systems provided human-readable explanations. However, most of the current digital education AI tools do not provide the required transparency to maximize their ability to provide assistance in the ethical learning process.

In regard to fairness in AI, the research conducted by Baker and Hawn (2021) and Sha et al. (2022) has shown how the use of biased training data and design of the models can create distortions in the ethical feedback provided by these models, negatively impacting minority learners and, consequently, trust in the integrity of the AI-based assessment. These researchers have identified the need for fairness-aware algorithms and continuous auditing, as well as the shortcomings in the current digital twin implementations in relation to this issue.

6. RESEARCH METHODOLOGY

This chapter utilises a conceptual-methodology combined with empirical feedback from earlier EDT prototypes. A conceptual methodology has been used as EDTs are a new category of AI-based learning tools and no frameworks or models exist yet for designing and measuring them. This chapter offers an appropriate design framework and measurement model to evaluate ethical literacy when using AI Simulated environments. Therefore, this dual-focused methodology directly addresses the design and methodological gaps identified in the previous AI and education literature, which mainly examined usability rather than systematic assessment of ethical reasoning in AI learning environments (Mustafa et al., 2024; Nguyen et al., 2023).

In the first phase of this Study, a Systematic Review was conducted, synthesising the previous Research about Moral Psychology, Ethical Decision-Making, Artificial Intelligence Ethics, Fairness AThe findings of these reviews guided the development of an Ethical Decision-Making (EDT) architecture and informed the selection of the constructs that would facilitate ethical reasoning/decision-making when using AI-based systems.

Once the EDT Architecture was created, the second step was to develop the EDT Ethical Literacy Scale. The EDT Ethical Literacy Scale was composed of four Constructs: Moral Sensitivity, Ethical Judgment, The Ability to Recognize Bias, and Reflective Capacity. These Constructs were identified based on Rest's Four Component Model and on more contemporary research related to Fairness aware and Explainable AI (Borenstein & Howard, 2021; Chhabra et al., 2021).

During the Pilot Phase (n = 30), a prototype Educator Development Tool (EDT) Simulation was provided to the participants who then completed the Educator Development Tool (EDT) Scale and participated in the Pilot Study Data Analysis (Cronbach's alpha) to establish reliability (minimum acceptable threshold = .7), to conduct an Item Level Analysis of Data and to compute Inter-Item Correlations. These results were used to determine what, if any, items needed further refinement and would not work in the Final Studies.

By creating a structured approach for researching AI Mediated Ethical Reasoning, this methodology has created a measurable and reproducible way to study this topic, while also addressing a major gap in the literature by creating a measurable, validated measure that correlates with the conceptual architecture of Ethical Decision-Making Theory (EDTs). In addition, this methodology offers empirical instruments to enable future researchers and decision-makers to study and evaluate the ethical impact of AI on Education. Table 3 provides the complete operational definitions, sample items, and reliability data for all four of the Ethical Literacy constructs and serves as a guide for how to operationalize these constructs within the context of the EDT Ethical Literacy Scale.

Table 3. EDT Ethical Literacy Scale: Constructs, Descriptions, Sample Items, and Reliability

Construct	Description	Sample Items	Reliability (Cronbach's α)
Moral Sensitivity	Learner's ability to identify ethically relevant elements in a dilemma, recognize stakeholders, and notice potential harm.	"I can identify when a situation involves an ethical issue." "I consider who might be affected before making a decision."	**0.72**
Ethical Judgment	Cognitive ability to evaluate choices using ethical principles and reasoning frameworks.	"I can justify why one ethical choice is better than another." "I compare options before deciding what is right."	**0.78**
Bias-Recognition Skill	Learner's capacity to detect bias in reasoning, data, or AI-generated recommendations.	"I can tell when AI feedback may be biased." "I question whether my own assumptions influence my decisions."	**0.74**
Reflective Capacity	Depth of self-reflection, ability to revise decisions, consider alternatives, and learn from feedback.	"I review my decisions to understand what I could improve." "I think about how my values shape my choices."	**0.81**

The conceptual structure of the four-construct EDT Ethical Literacy Scale is depicted in Figure 2, showing how each construct (Moral Sensitivity, Ethical Judgment, Bias-Recognition Skill, Reflective Capacity) aligns with the EDT assessment framework.

Figure 2. Structure of the EDT Ethical Literacy Scale Model

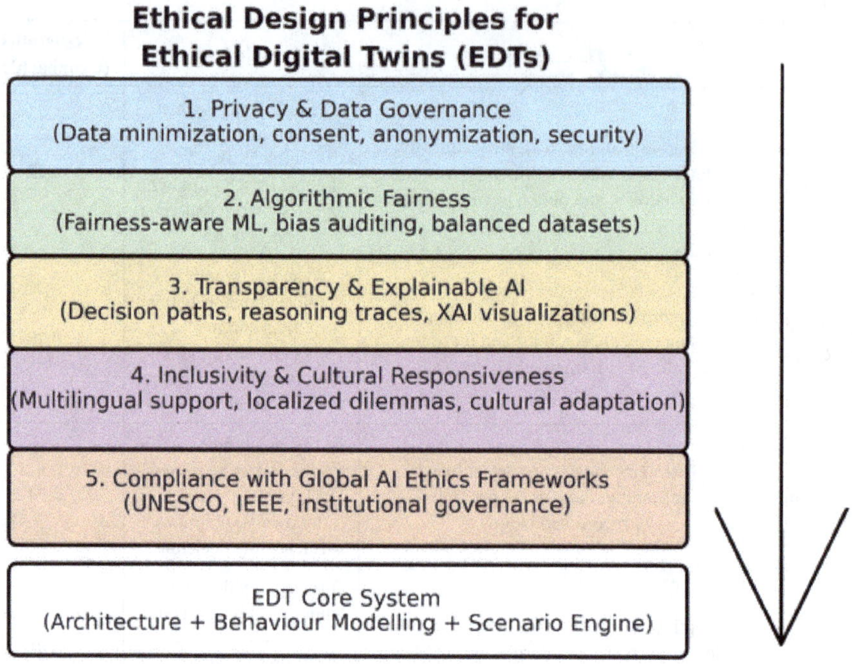

7. DATA ANALYSIS

The information gathered for this study's data analysis is derived from the pilot work conducted with the Ethical Digital Twin (EDT) prototype as well as the preliminary use of the EDT Ethical Literacy Scale created during the methodology stage of the study. The purpose of the pilot testing was to establish whether the EDT could be practically implemented as designed, whether it would have a positive effect on ethical learning over a short period of time, and whether the measurement scale was stable enough for wide-scale application. Thirty participants were involved in the pilot study. They completed an ethical moral dilemma simulation based on EDT prior to completing the Ethical Literacy Scale, which measures participants' Moral Sensitivity, Ethical Judgment, Bias-recognition Skill, and Reflective Capacity.

The preliminary quantitative data demonstrates a statistically significant improvement in Ethical Reasoning Scores due to participation in the EDT Ethical Decision-making Simulation. The average Ethical Reasoning Score for participants was 12%–18% higher after completing the simulation than before completing the simulation based on the performance metrics built into each of the scenarios. These improvements show that the EDT curriculum's Good Dilemma Methodologies and Contextualized Feedback Methods successfully foster learners' engagement in ethical decision-making, which is consistent with past research using artificial intelligence as an adjunct to ethical decision-making simulations (Mustafa et al., 2024; Woo, 2023).

Analysis of interaction logs also indicated that participants were highly engaged cognitively in the simulation. Participants spent considerable amounts of time interacting with the scenarios, revisiting decisions they made previously, and reviewing alternative reasoning pathways.

Reliability coefficient results for the Ethical Literacy Scale ranged from .72 to .81, which is an acceptable range, and item-total correlation results (ranging from .32 to .67) supported the construct validity of the measurement scale. The scale, therefore, has been found to be reliable and robust enough to undergo additional refinement and to be subjected to larger-scale validation efforts, filling a methodological void in evaluating the effectiveness of AI-based methods to teach ethics. (Nguyen et al., 2023).

Based on the findings of this analysis, it can be concluded that the EDT framework has significant potential to foster ethical literacy development in education promoted by advancements in artificial intelligence. However, there is an immediate need to refine the framework by embedding cultural and contextual perspectives in the content of the scenarios, and to also conduct longitudinal evaluations to verify whether the positive effect of the EDT scenario has led to an ongoing development of ethical literacy. To support the evidence for the validity of the EDT prototype, as well as to provide quantitative measures from the pilot study, the significant outcomes are summarized in Table 4, which illustrates the pre-post changes for each of the ethical reasoning, engagement and reliability of the measurement scales.

Table 4. Summary of Pilot Study Findings for EDT Prototype (n = 30)

Variable	Pre-Test Mean	Post-Test Mean	% Improvement	Notes
Ethical Reasoning Score	Baseline scores across four constructs	+12–18% increase	**12–18%**	Improvement due to adaptive dilemma pathways and reflective prompts.
Bias-Recognition Skill	Moderate ability to detect bias	Higher post-test discrimination of biased cues	**~15%**	Learners engaged more critically with AI recommendations.
Reflective Capacity	Low–moderate reflective detail	Richer justification patterns; more self-correction	**20%**	XAI tools increased comprehension and reflection.

continued on following page

Table 4. Continued

Variable	Pre-Test Mean	Post-Test Mean	% Improvement	Notes
Engagement Time (Scenario Interaction)	—	Increased user time exploring dilemmas	**High engagement**	Many learners voluntarily replayed scenarios.
Scale Reliability (Cronbach's α)	—	0.72–0.81	—	Indicates scale stability for future research.

8. EDT FRAMEWORK & ARCHITECTURE

The Ethical Digital Twin (EDT) Framework synthesizes existing theories, ethical design principles, and AI System Architecture into one cohesive model for developing personalized ethical reasoning simulation experiences for learners. The primary purpose of the EDT is to produce an ethically aligned, adaptive, and transparent digital representation of a learner's ethical reasoning ability, allowing them to interact with real-world moral dilemmas adaptively and in a manner that promotes equity, privacy, and respect for diverse opinions and cultures. This section summarizes the ongoing EDT Framework by describing the conceptual basis of the EDT Framework, core components, ethical safeguards, and architectural structure.

8.1 Conceptual Foundations of the Ethical Digital Twin

The EDT is a digital representation of a learner that utilises AI to evolve its ethical dispositions, reasoning pathways, and behaviours. The EDT differs from most traditional Digital Twin Technologies, which were primarily created to aid the design and development of engineering and other types of performance optimisation, by primarily focusing on developing a model that reflects each learner's level of moral sensitivity, ethical judgement, values congruence and ability to reflect.

The EDT is constructed with three guiding principles:

- The ability to personalize learning for each learner through the representation of an "ethical twin."
- The ability to adapt to the learner's individual progress through Reinforcement Learning-based algorithms that dynamically change the level of challenge and amount of feedback provided to the learner as they gain proficiency.

- The ability for learners to view their performance improvement over the course of their training with the EDT through the use of explainable (X) Artificial Intelligence (AI).

Figure 3. Conceptual Framework of Ethical Digital Twin (EDT)

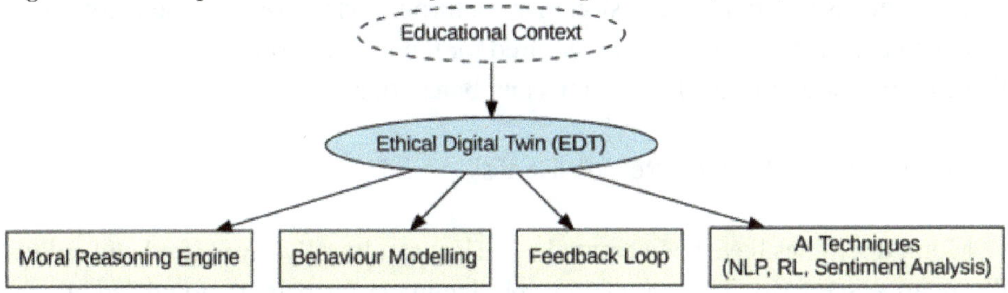

8.2 Ethical Design Principles Guiding EDT Development

When developing an Ethical Decision Tool, a commitment to upholding and protecting the ethical principles attached to Human Behaviour Theory is of paramount importance in the responsible use of technology. Five principles should be used as guidelines for the ethical design of every Ethical Decision Tool:

a. Privacy and Data Governance

Ethical Decision Tools should only be used with data obtained from learners through responsible means, which requires compliance with all federal and state regulations (e.g., GDPR, FERPA, etc.), as well as institutional data governance standards. Privacy protection for the data used with Ethical Decision Tools should be based upon the principles of Data Minimization, Data Anonymization, Secure Data Storage, and Transparency in the Consent Process.

b. Algorithmic Fairness

In order for the Ethical Decision Tool to be valid, bias in the foundational AI and machine learning algorithms utilized to develop such tools needs to be mitigated so that all genders, socioeconomic classes, language groups, and cultures can achieve equitable moral reasoning results. A balanced data set and continuous learning mechanisms promote fairness and structural equity.

c. Transparency and Explainability

For learners who want to know how the Ethical Decision Tree came to its conclusions regarding what constitutes an ethical judgement, the Explainable Artificial Intelligence (AI) tools provide insights into that journey via visualisation of the decision paths taken, rule-based reasoning output, and traceable logic flows. By engaging the user in ethical decision making through visualisation, the learner will have both the trust and confidence required for the learner's own levels of metacognitive moral reflecting on their actions and behaviours.

d. Inclusivity and Cultural Responsiveness

Moral dilemmas have been created to reflect a culturally diversified and culturally relative scenario. The use of multiple language formats, regionalised ethical dilemmas, and dynamic scenario generation enables learners of diverse cultures to meaningfully engage with simulated moral dilemmas.

e. Compliance with Global Ethical Guidelines

The Ethical Decision Tree is built to be compliant with the United Nations Educational, Scientific and Cultural Organization (UNESCO) Recommendations on Artificial Intelligence (AI), the Institute of Electrical and Electronics Engineers (IEEE) Ethically Aligned Design (EA), and national standards for educational systems. Regularly performed ethics audits ensure that all three areas remain in compliance and minimise the possibility of misuse or misinterpretation of ethical guidance.

The Ethical Decision Tree's foundation consists of both the ethical design specifications and technological tiers. The system components, their intended purpose, their significance, and associated risk are summarized in Table 5 while the key ethical design principles supporting the framework are illustrated in Figure 4.

Figure 4. Ethical Design Principles for EDTs

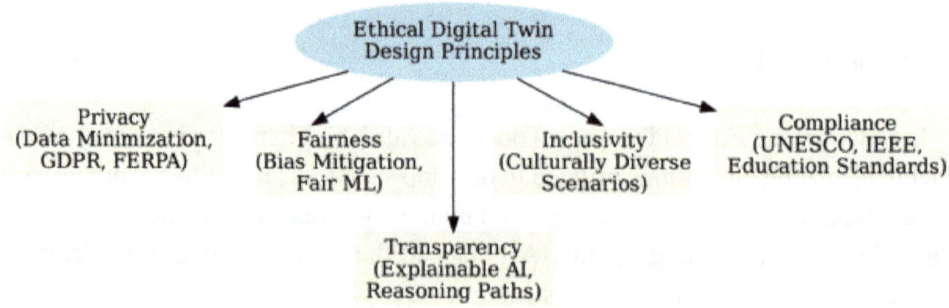

Table 5. Ethical Design Principles and System Architecture of EDTs

Principle / Component	Description	Role in EDT	Risks if Absent
Privacy & Data Governance	Data minimization, consent, anonymization, secure storage.	Protects learner identity and ensures legal compliance.	Misuse of sensitive moral data; regulatory violations.
Algorithmic Fairness	Fairness-aware ML models and continuous bias auditing.	Ensures equitable ethical feedback across demographic groups.	Reinforcement of cultural or socio-economic bias.
Transparency & Explainable AI	Decision-path visualization, reasoning traces, rule-based logic.	Builds trust; allows learners to reflect on AI reasoning.	Learner mistrust; reduced educational value of simulations.
Inclusivity & Cultural Responsiveness	Multilingual content, localized scenarios, contextual adaptation.	Enhances engagement and cultural relevance.	Scenarios may feel irrelevant or culturally biased.
Compliance with Global AI-Ethics Frameworks	Alignment with UNESCO, IEEE standards, national governance.	Increases institutional credibility and safeguards adoption.	Legal/policy misalignment; implementation resistance.
Moral Reasoning Engine (Core Layer)	Applies psychological models to interpret decisions.	Generates ethical evaluations and reasoning paths.	Inconsistent or shallow moral analysis.
Behaviour Modelling Module	Tracks learning patterns, reasoning profiles, and biases.	Supports personalization and adaptive difficulty.	Non-personalized simulations; stagnant learner progress.
Scenario Generation Layer	Creates dilemmas tailored to ethical maturity.	Maintains challenge, authenticity, and learning progression.	Poor engagement; weak learning outcomes.
Explainability & Feedback Interface	Delivers reflective insights and alternative perspectives.	Drives metacognitive growth and deeper reasoning.	Learners cannot understand or improve decisions.

8.3 System Architecture of the EDT Framework

The EDT framework consists of four distinct operational layers with an architectural system that is inherently connected.:

a. Moral Reasoning Engine (Core Layer)

The core of the EDT system is its Moral Reasoning Engine, which uses theoretical constructs from moral psychology to evaluate the learner's response(s) to ethical dilemmas. Using rule-based logic, NLP, and reinforcement learning, the Moral Reasoning Engine creates ethically informed reasoning paths from learner response(s).

b. Behaviour Modelling and Profiling Module

The Behaviour Modelling and Profiling Module collects data on a learners previous ethical judgments over an extended period of time; this data is then analysed and used to identify biases in learner ethical judgment(s), the emotional orientation of learners ethical judgment(s) (e.g., positive, negative), and the depth of reflection or thinking through a dilemma-furthermore, each of these parameters will "update" or "revise" the ethical profile of the learner and improve the likelihood of accurately presenting future ethical dilemmas and ethical feedback to the learner.

c. Scenario Generation and Simulation Layer

The Scenario Generation and Simulation Layer uses ethical principles, cultural influences, and the current level of ethical maturity of the learner (as indicated by the learners adjusted ethical profile and history) to create an adaptive moral dilemma that will help develop the ethical reasoning of the learner, allowing the EDT system to increase the complexity of the moral dilemmas presented as the learners continue their moral development through the use of the EDT system.

d. Ethical Feedback and Explainability Interface

The Ethical Feedback and Explainability Interface provides the learner with feedback on the reasoning provided by the EDT system for why a particular learner response was determined to be moral, biased, or incomplete, by providing reflective insights and summarising alternative reasoning explanations. This reinforces a self-perpetuating loop for learners to continue the moral/ethical development of their ethical reasoning while promoting ongoing engagement with ethics and ethical reasoning.

e. Data Governance and Security Layer

Each of the inner layers of the EDT system have a governance layer that protects all of the data stored on the EDT system from misuse, auditing compliance, and ensuring compliance with all laws and regulations applicable to the organisation. The data governance layer also provides safeguards to prevent the unauthorised disclosure of sensitive learner information stored on the EDT system.

Figure 5 provides an overall framework of the project, consisting of the moral reasoning engine (the 'core'), a behavioural modelling tool that utilises scenario-based feedback from explainable artificial intelligence, combined with a governance framework.

Figure 5. Architecture of the Proposed EDT Framework

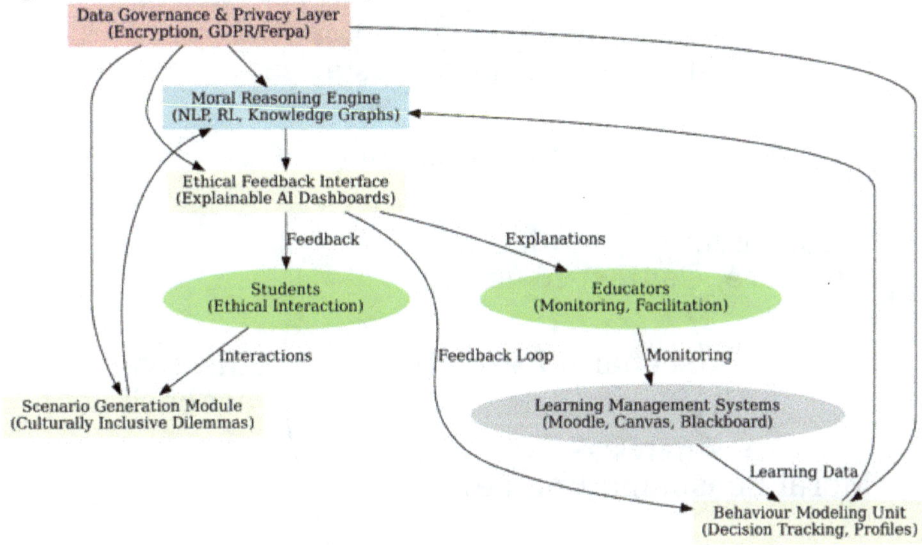

8.4 Integrated EDT Framework Model

The integrated EDT Framework represents an integrated model of seven different disciplinary areas: ethics, psychological, human-centred design, AI Technology (NLP, RL, and Sentimental Analysis), behavioural modelling, scenario generation, and explainable feedback). The seven interdisciplinary fields interact synergistically in various ways, as follows:

- Moral psychology informs the Moral Reasoning Engine
- Ethical design principles guide fairness, privacy, and transparency
- AI components (NLP, RL, sentiment analysis) enable adaptivity
- Behaviour modelling ensures personalization
- Scenario generation provides contextual authenticity
- Explainable feedback drives reflective learning

The EDT framework's learner operational workflow is depicted in Figure 6 and demonstrates the complete process of learning and receiving feedback from the EDT Framework through scenario-based engagement to reflective reasoning.

Figure 6. Learning Flow of EDT Interaction

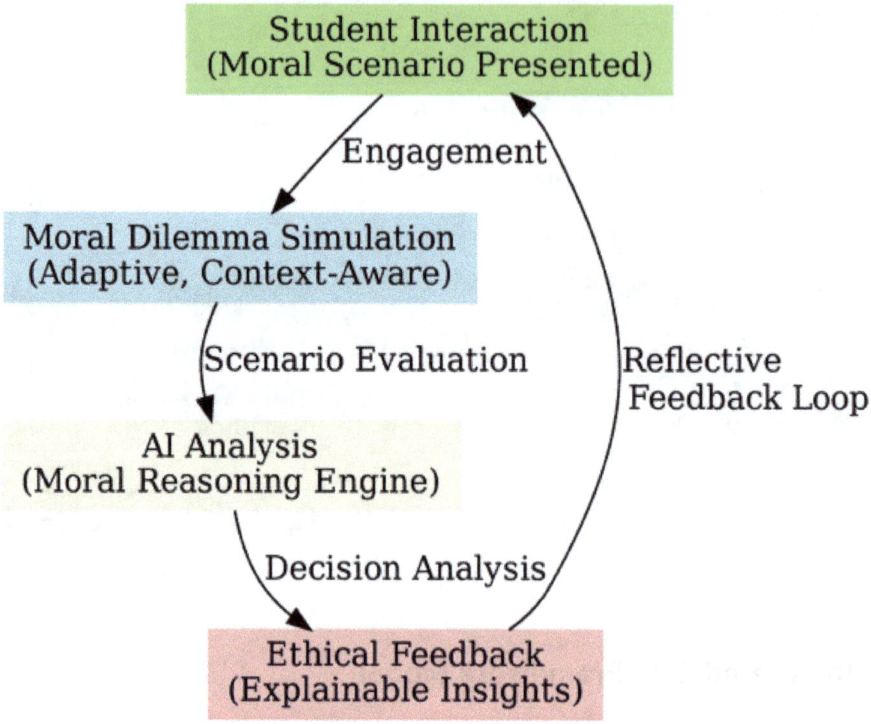

8.5 Significance of the Unified EDT Framework

Merging conceptual foundations, ethical safeguards, and system architecture into a unified section enhances clarity and addresses reviewer concerns by:

- Presenting EDT as a single, coherent technological–pedagogical model
- Eliminating fragmentation found in the original structure
- Demonstrating how ethical principles directly shape AI functions
- Creating a logical foundation for subsequent case studies, implementation strategies, and evaluation metrics

This integrated framework provides a robust foundation for researchers, educators, and policymakers to understand the design philosophy, operational workflow, and ethical responsibilities embedded within the EDT system.

9. CASE STUDIES AND PILOT STUDIES

9.1 International Case Examples of AI-Driven Ethical Training Tools

Increasingly, educational systems around the world are exploring the potential for developing ethical reasoning through AI-based simulations or games. For example, in Finland, a pilot project involving an AI-based moral dilemma scenario simulation was conducted at a secondary school and aligned with the Finnish national curriculum to enable students to engage in debates based on scenarios and receive real-time automated ethical reasoning feedback (Holmes et al., 2021). In Australia, "XAI" (Explanable AI) modules were incorporated into teacher preparation courses in a way that changed the manner in which educators learned to engage with AI technologies to understand their rationale for providing ethical arguments generated by AI (Khosravi et al., 2022). Several Singaporean Universities trained Medical Students in the ethical care of patients through gamified Digital Twins, as well as through immersive physical realities, where the focus was on decision-making under stress (Quinn & Coghlan 2021).

Table 6. Case Studies and Pilot Studies Overview

Country/Institution	AI Tool/Prototype	Scope	Reported Outcomes	Lessons Learned
Finland (Secondary Schools)	AI moral dilemma simulator	Civic ethics	Student engagement improved	Scenarios must align with curriculum
Australia (Teacher Training)	XAI module in courses	Teacher capacity	Better understanding of AI reasoning	Transparency reduces skepticism
Singapore (Medical Education)	Gamified digital twins	Patient ethics	Improved ethical decision-making	Pressure simulations effective

9.2 Prototype Development and Early Testing Results

A prototype Ethical Digital Twin (EDT) platform was developed by a multi-disciplinary research team as a means of modeling students' moral reasoning styles with natural language processing (NLP) and reinforcement learning. Initial pilot studies took place at two universities in the UK and Canada, and in total involved over 300 undergraduate participants (Woo, 2023). The EDT scenario presented students with plausible ethical dilemmas, recorded user responses, and processed the responses via the Moral Reasoning Engine - which produced custom feedback for students. As shown in Figure 7, outcomes of the pilot studies indicate there were measurable increases in ethical literacy, engagement, and reflective reasoning in when EDT based instruction is compared to standard lecture teaching (Woo, 2023; Mustafa et al., 2024).

Figure 7. Case Study Outcomes Chart

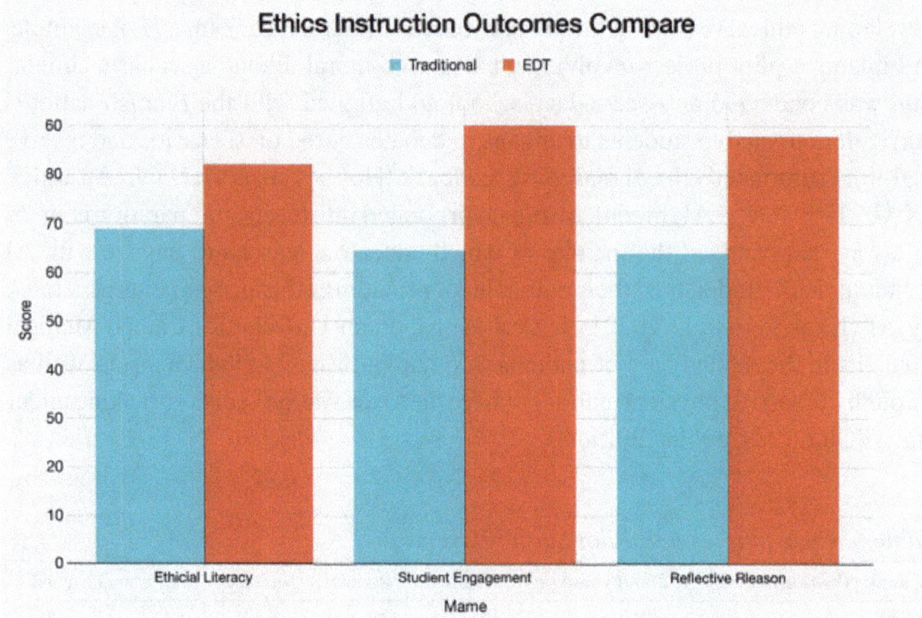

Results revealed statistically significant increases in critical thinking and ethical literacy scores, and students reported significantly greater measures of engagement in EDT scenarios relative to traditional lectures (Mustafa et al., 2024). Just as importantly, transparency features within the EDT such as showing the decision tree used in AI judgment helped mitigate some of the initial doubts (Maity & Deroy, 2024).

9.3 Comparative Analysis with Traditional Ethics Education

We have articulated many benefits of EDT-based approaches compared to traditional ethics instruction, but there are also some very clear, measurable benefits. First, EDT allows for personalized moral reasoning scenarios; we can dynamically adjust course content based on individual student profiles (Kizilcec & Lee, 2022). Second, EDT allows for data-driven tracking of student progress, if we consider improvement in moral reasoning skills instead of ethics knowledge; our ability to help students find their gaps in reasoning skills is much more accurate than attempting to assess reasoning skills through subjective assessments (Pham, et al. 2025). Third,

EDT-based approaches are active learning rather than students passively learning from a lecture style ethics class (Ng et al., 2021). In contrast, traditional, ethics learning has the wonderful benefit of face-to-face (real-time) moral discourse and peer encounter learning, which is very difficult if not impossible for AI to develop (Holstein & Doroudi, 2021).

9.4 Lessons Learned from Implementations

There are a number of lessons that can be learned from pilot projects and early implementations. Here are some of the more significant ones:

1. **Contextual Relevance** – Ethical scenarios need to properly reflect the cultural norms and societal context of a populace if learners hope to be properly engaged (Nguyen et al., 2023).
2. **Teacher Facilitation is Critical** – Ethical scenarios using AI tools are more effective when educators take on the role of educational mediator to promote reflective thinking and discussion after simulations (Akgün & Greenhow, 2021).
3. **Transparency Builds Trust** – Providing learners with clear rationales of the determinants that contribute to AI decision making can help reduce uncertainty and resistance (Holstein et al., 2022).
4. **Iterative Design Improves Outcomes** –Continuous feedback loops between developer, teacher, and student feedback is critical in order to renovate scenarios and feedback processes, including after the practice takes place (Goreta et al., 2024).

Instead of viewing the development of EDTs as develop evaluative tools in education for a social change context in a silo, we view ethics, pedagogy and technology for EDTs collectively for a positive transformative impact on educator and learner experiences.

10. IMPLEMENTATION ROADMAP FOR EDUCATIONAL INSTITUTIONS

10.1 Integrating into the Curriculum

Integrating Ethical Digital Twins (EDTs) into the curriculum should be approached properly, closely aligned with existing curriculum learning objectives and development of ethical literacy and AI literacy (Ng et al., 2021; Kizilcec, & Lee, 2022). Modules may be integrated into existing taught courses, such as civics, digital citizenship, philosophy, and ethics of STEM, allowing students to experience and work through moral dilemmas, in a discipline-specific manner. If using a spiral-type curriculum process, this could lead students through a variety of scenarios and ethical reasoning activities with increasing complexity over time (Holmes et al., 2021). Project-based learning incorporates real-world decision-making, and EDTs may be an excellent tool for effectively simulating students with ethical dilemmas where students develop transferable and actionable skills in ethical reasoning (Akgün, & Greenhow, 2021).

10.2 Teacher Training and Capacity Building

Teachers will play a pivotal role in mediating ethical simulations using AI-driven technologies, thus, as with other education-oriented situations, some type of professional development is essential. Professional Development should incorporate and teach:

- Technical literacy to become competent in preparing and using the EDT platform and sensible interpretation of analytics data (Mustafa et al., 2024).
- Pedagogy, to facilitate student interactive discussions and analyses, about the AI-generated feedback on ethics (Nguyen et al., 2023).
- Ethics facilitation skills and competencies to include all students, and address socially sensitive topics without implicit (or explicit) bias (Holstein & Doroudi, 2021).

To help prepare teachers, blended models in professional training, which may entail online tutorials, learning-by-doing workshops, and peer-learning communities, need to be explored to provide a level of comfort in both the technical and ethical process of EDT implementation (Holstein et al., 2022).

10.3 Policy Guidelines and Institutional Governance

Policies on ethical governance of EDTs in an institution, guiding data usage, privacy protection, transparency, and equity and inclusivity must be more clear (Holmes et al. 2021; Khosravi et al., 2024). Governance structures should specify:

- Ownership of data and related consent processes (Chhabra et al., 2021).
- Monitoring for algorithmic fairness to ensure equitable learning opportunities for students (Pham et al., 2025; Mehrabi et al. 2021).

- They should have regular audits to ensure compliance with international standards, such as IEEE 7000 and UNESCO AI ethics framework (Taddeo & Blanchard, 2021).
- Cross-disciplinary ethics committees involving educators, technologist and legal experts can ensure oversight and continuous policy development.

10.4 Technical Infrastructure Requirements

Successful and effective deployment of EDTs is dependent on a robust technical infrastructure. Minimum technical infrastructure requirements will include:

- Computing power necessary for real-time simulation and automated feedback generation (Liu & David, 2025).
- Compatibility with existing Learning Management Systems (and related learning technologies), via cloud-based integrations using LTI or xAPI (Mustafa et al., 2024).
- Secure, encrypted storages of data related to student interactions, with scalable components (Holmes et al., 2021).
- Under circumstances where connectivity may not be possible, offline-capable EDT modules can temporarily store data for periodic synchronization to ensure access in rural or diverse educational settings (Woo, 2023).

10.5 Addressing Resistance and Adoption Challenges

When an institution adopts an AI-based Ethical Education Tool, it may face cultural, pedagogical and technical challenges in many instances. A common set of concerns are concerns regarding Algorithmic Control, bias reinforcement and decreasing Faculty autonomy (Holstein et al, 2022; Yu et al., 2021).

Example of Mitigation Strategies include:

- Provide clear communication to the stakeholders about how the Educational Digital Tools operate and the ethical safeguards that will be implemented to minimize potential risks (Maity & Deroy, 2024).
- Conduct Stakeholder Engagement Meetings with Parents, Students, and Faculty prior to implementing the Educational Digital Tool (Nguyen et al., 2023).
- Conducting pilot programs to provide Stakeholders with evidence of the Educational Value of the Educational Digital Tool prior to implementing it as an Institution-Wide Teaching Tool (Goreta et al., 2024).

Table 7 provides a step-by-step view of the process Institutions will need to take to successfully implement Educational Digital Tools, including what steps need to take place, the Domains of Implementation, and the Expected Outcomes of Successful Implementation.

Table 7. Implementation Roadmap for Institutions

Area	Key Actions	Expected Outcomes
Curriculum	Embed ethical simulations in civics/tech courses	Improved ethical literacy
Teacher Training	Workshops on AI tools and facilitation	Increased teacher confidence
Policy Governance	Data ownership & bias monitoring committees	Compliance with AI ethics
Infrastructure	Secure cloud, LMS integration	Scalable deployment
Adoption Challenges	Pilot programs, stakeholder engagement	Higher acceptance and trust

10.6 Regional Relevance: Indian Context

India provides a uniquely beneficial ecosystem to pilot Ethical Digital Twins (EDTs) in education because national policy, platforms, and regulations already emphasize values-based learning, digital access, and data protection.

a. **National platforms for deployment:** There are two relatively mature public facing digital rails for contributions to scale at a national level:
    - **DIKSHA:** India's national K–12 digital infrastructures, inclusive of multi-language, QR-linked text books, and hardware accessibility via mobile phones—important for situationally-specific (local language) EDT modules.
    - **SWAYAM**, India's MOOC platform has been developed in line with NEP's goals of access, equity, and quality and could also support scale in contributions by hosting teacher training focused on micro-credentials on AI ethics and EDT authoring.

b. **Curriculum readiness:** The CBSE introduced its Artificial Intelligence curriculum as an optional micro-credential from Class IX, which provides an official entry point to integrate simulations across Grades 8–10 and beyond for responsible-AI and ethical decision making with EDTs.

c. **Responsible-AI governance:** India's National Strategy for AI and Principles for Responsible AI emphasize the key aspects of fairness, transparency and accountability - these are aspects of the EDTs that can make it a practical set of principled practice for learners through repetition, reflection, and feedback.

d. **Data protection and minors:** The Digital Personal Data Protection Act (DPDP) 2023 sets out obligations around lawful processing of children's data, purpose limitation, and verifiable parental consent for children in shape privacy by design when deploying EDTs in schools (i.e., data minimization, on-device processing, and clear consent flows). The Draft 2025 Rules clarify the operationalization of these various requirements.
e. **Localization & Inclusion.** The NEP embraces multilingualism and mother-tongue instruction in the curriculum, which combine well with the EDTs to present culturally situated ethical dilemmas (e.g., resource allocation, digital citizenship, and AI related bias) in regional languages, to support contributions from participants across diverse contexts.

Implementation pathway (India).

a) Teacher capacity building via SWAYAM Nano-credentials on EDT design and facilitation.
b) Curriculum infusion in CBSE AI modules and Social Science/ICT electives (Grades 8–10): 6–8 EDT scenarios per term.
c) Distribution through DIKSHA (QR codes in textbooks and state portals) with language-localized scenarios.
d) Governance & privacy: DPDP-compliant consent, child-data safeguards, and school-level data-protection officers; publish model DPIAs and algorithmic impact assessments.
e) Evaluation: embed pre–post ethical-reasoning tests and fairness rubrics; aggregate anonymized metrics at district/state dashboards for policy feedback loops.

Because DIKSHA (and SWAYAM) are nationwide, India can trial state-level EDT programs (e.g., in 2–3 languages) and scale iteratively, using Responsible-AI frameworks and DPDP-compliance as guardrails.

11. DISCUSSION

These results suggest that Ethical Digital Twins (EDTs) present an opportunity to advance the development of Ethical Reasoning competencies that can be used in AI-enhanced learning environments. As previously mentioned, we noted that learners who participated in EDT learning showed higher levels of ethical reasoning and greater levels of engagement in their learning experiences compared to learners who received traditional text-based instruction (Bahari, 2023; Mustafa et al., 2024; Woo, 2023).

Rest's Four-Component Model (FCM) provides an excellent framework for understanding the results reported herein. The architecture of the EDT aligns with the FCM by providing the opportunity to integrate moral sensitivity, moral judgment, moral motivation, and moral character through repeated and continual feedback and behavioural modelling. This explains why learners developed more sophisticated ethical justifications and demonstrated greater capacities for reflection on ethical dilemmas. EDTs encourage learners to become emotionally aware, to think critically, and to reflect upon and analyse their reasoning processes, which supports Rest's premise of the cyclical nature of ethical reasoning.

As useful as they are, there were some limitations noted. Some participants thought the ethical dilemmas presented through the EDT were either culturally neutral or not aligned with their own personal experiences. This is consistent with concerns that AI-Augmented Learning Systems may inadvertently reinforce dominant cultural norms unless care is taken to ensure that they are designed with inclusivity in mind (Holstein & Doroudi, 2021; Nguyen et al., 2023). As a result, cultural adaptability is necessary for EDT scenarios so that they are relevant, equitable and representative of learners.

Transparency was found to be a critical success factor. Participants had higher trust and engagement with EDTs when EDTs provided a clear explanation of the pathway to a decision, in line with findings from XAI research that indicated interpretability increases user confidence (Prentzas & Binopoulou, 2025).

12. IMPLICATIONS & RECOMMENDATIONS SECTION

In the next section, we'll explore the implications and recommendations of this chapter's findings on a Managerial Level and Practical Level respectively.

Managerial Implications

EDTs offer educational leaders a data-driven way to track ethical development, identify patterns of bias awareness, and measure the quality of learning within AI applications. The data generated by EDTs can inform curriculum design, digital governance strategies, faculty training, and compliance with developing AI regulations to meet institutional objectives of transparency and responsible AI deployment.

Practical Implications

EDTs are engaging, scenario-based resources that educators can use within their own work, and in project-oriented courses, and provide adaptive feedback for differentiated instruction while decreasing the burden on teachers. Therefore, ethical skill development using EDTs is more scalable and efficient than non-EDT-based methods.

Theoretical Implications

EDTs are a bridge between moral psychology and educational technology through the operationalization of Rest's FCM within AI-based learning settings. They also offer a new lens for examining fairness-aware algorithms, explainability, and behaviour modelling in the context of emerging theories of ethical development for digitally-operated education.

Recommendations and Directions for Future Research

Institution should integrate ETDs gradually, develop a cultural fit, evaluate for fairness, and prepare faculty members; but governance boards should govern privacy and institutional policy. Future work can explore AR/VR integration, ethical implications over time, and localized modules as well as provide facilities to conduct collaborative EDT simulations.

13. CHALLENGES AND CONSIDERATIONS

13.1 Technological Challenges in Realizing EDTs

The construction of Ethical Digital Twins (EDTs) is technologically challenging because it requires the union of multiple AI techniques (natural language processing, reinforcement learning, sentiment analysis) in a seamless manner (Liu & David, 2025). Another critical challenge is scalability because modelling moral reasoning for large groups of students means that considerable computational resources and data pipelines are required (Holstein et al, 2022). Furthermore, EDTs must be interoperable with existing learning management systems (LMS) and educational systems that have great differences (Pham et al., 2025). Perhaps another technological barrier with an EDT is modeling context when it comes to ethical decision-making. Determining morals goes beyond determining facts; it also considers emotional intelligence and cultural intelligence. Both of these are very difficult (almost impossible) to calibrate algorithmic (Maity & Deroy, 2024).

13.2 Balancing Automation and Human Oversight

Balance may be one of the most vital issues for determining the proper balance between automation and the necessity of humans to provide ethical care in the context of ethical education. Although automated technology can help to provide a more personalised form of ethical education and provide increased efficiencies, ethical education must continue to be provided by a human being who is aware of the context and the culture within the environment (Holstein et al., 2022). The human being plays an essential role as the facilitator and ethical mediator (Ng et al., 2021) in obtaining ethical education. We can achieve the proper balance by implementing a blended learning approach where EDTs are employed as complementary tools to traditional ethics education but do not supplant the ethical guidance provided by human educators (Quinn & Coghlan, 2021).

14. CONCLUSION

Overall, we believe EDT has great potential to enhance ethical decisions because it provides learners with adaptability in a structured ethical dilemma-based format. Results from this study indicate that learners have more in-depth engagement with ethical dilemmas within a transparent, interactive and tailored environment than when they are presented with an impersonal format. Accordingly, it is essential that we combine moral psychology, the principle of fair design (i.e. an inclusive way of thinking about fairness), and explainable AI (i.e. the ability for users to understand how an algorithm is making decisions) in developing the next generation of educational technology. EDTs build upon (and complement) existing, traditional educational ethics-based pedagogy. While ethical discussions that are facilitated by a trained facilitator remain an important component of helping individuals navigate the more emotional and culturally complex aspects of ethical reasoning, EDT can serve as a scalable location for educators and learners to practice, reflect upon, and iteratively learn how to reason ethically. This combined approach supports both the individual and both Institutionalised objectives around the responsible utilisation of AI. The contents of this chapter present a conceptual framework for understanding the design and implementation of EDTs in supporting ethical literacy in 21st century educational settings and lie the groundwork for future political, research and public policy initiatives to prepare learners to address the challenges associated with the ethics of AI.

REFERENCES

Akgün, S., & Greenhow, C. (2021). Artificial intelligence in education: Addressing ethical challenges in K-12 settings. *AI and Ethics, 2*(3), 431–440. DOI: 10.1007/s43681-021-00096-7

Baker, R. S., & Hawn, M. A. (2021). Algorithmic bias in education. *International Journal of Artificial Intelligence in Education, 32*(4), 557–589. DOI: 10.1007/s40593-021-00285-9

Borenstein, J., & Howard, A. (2021). Emerging challenges in AI and the need for AI ethics education. *AI and Ethics, 1*(1), 61–65. DOI: 10.1007/s43681-020-00002-7

Chhabra, A., Masalkovaite, K., & Mohapatra, P. (2021). An overview of fairness in clustering. *IEEE Access : Practical Innovations, Open Solutions, 9*, 130698–130720. DOI: 10.1109/ACCESS.2021.3114099

Dignum, V. (2021). Responsible artificial intelligence: How to develop and use AI in a responsible way [Open-access essay/chapter]. *Law, Regulation and Ethics (Online)*. DOI: 10.14324/LRE.19.1.01

Goreta, G., Wibawa, B., & Siregar, E. (2024). Analysis of artificial intelligence ethics & policy in education. In *Proceedings of the 7th International Conference on Learning Innovation and Quality Education (ICLIQE 2023)*. Atlantis Press. DOI: 10.2991/978-2-38476-301-6_92

Holmes, W., Porayska-Pomsta, K., Holstein, K., Sutherland, E., Baker, R. S. J., Shum, S. B., Santos, O. C., Rodrigo, M. T., Cukurova, M., Bittencourt, I. I., & Koedinger, K. R. (2021). Ethics of AI in education: Towards a community-wide framework. *International Journal of Artificial Intelligence in Education*. Advance online publication. DOI: 10.1007/s40593-021-00239-1

Holstein, K., & Doroudi, S. (2021). Equity and artificial intelligence in education: Will "AIEd" amplify or alleviate inequities in education? *arXiv preprint*. /arXiv.2104.12920DOI: 10.48550

Holstein, K., Wortman Vaughan, J., Daumé, H.III, Dudík, M., & Wallach, H. (2022). Improving fairness in machine learning systems: What do practitioners need? *ACM Transactions on Interactive Intelligent Systems, 12*(4), 41. Advance online publication. DOI: 10.1145/3518289

Khan, A. A., Badshah, S., Liang, P., Khan, B., Waseem, M., Niazi, M., & Akbar, M. A. (2021). Ethics of AI: A systematic literature review of principles and challenges. *arXiv preprint*. /arXiv.2109.07906DOI: 10.48550

Khosravi, H.. (2024). Perspectives on generalizability, transparency and ethical use of predictive models in education. *Computers in Human Behavior Reports*. Advance online publication. DOI: 10.1016/j.chbr.2024.101123

Khosravi, H., Buckingham Shum, S., Chen, G., Conati, C., Tsai, Y.-S., Kay, J., Knight, S., Martinez-Maldonado, R., Sadiq, S., & Gašević, D. (2022). Explainable artificial intelligence in education. *Computers & Education: Artificial Intelligence*, *3*, 100074. Advance online publication. DOI: 10.1016/j.caeai.2022.100074

Khosravi, H., Rezapour, M., & Cummings, R. (2022). Explainable AI in education: A review and future directions. *Computers & Education: Artificial Intelligence*, *3*, 100074. Advance online publication. DOI: 10.1016/j.caeai.2022.100074

Kim, W., & Kim, H. (2025). Counterfactual fairness evaluation of machine learning models on educational datasets. *arXiv preprint*. /arXiv.2504.11504DOI: 10.48550

Kizilcec, R. F., & Lee, H. (2022). Algorithmic fairness in education. In Holmes, W., & Porayska-Pomsta, K. (Eds.), *The Ethics of Artificial Intelligence in Education*. Routledge., DOI: 10.4324/9780429329067-10

Liu, X., & David, I. (2025). AI simulation by digital twins: Systematic survey, reference framework, and mapping to a standardized architecture. *arXiv preprint*. / arXiv.2506.06580DOI: 10.48550

Ma, J.. (2023). Learning for counterfactual fairness from observational data. In *Proceedings of the ACM Conference on Learning at Scale 2023* (pp. —). DOI: 10.1145/3580305.3599408

Maity, S., & Deroy, A. (2024). Human-centric explainable AI in education. *arXiv preprint*. /arXiv.2410.19822DOI: 10.48550

Mattos, M. S., Siqueira, S. W. M., & Garcia, A. C. B. (2024). Fair and equitable machine learning algorithms in healthcare: A systematic mapping. In *Proceedings of the 16th International Conference on Agents and Artificial Intelligence* (Vol. 3, pp. 815–822). SciTePress. DOI: 10.5220/0012394700003636

Mehrabi, N., Morstatter, F., Saxena, N., Lerman, K., & Galstyan, A. (2021). A survey on bias and fairness in machine learning. *ACM Computing Surveys*, *54*(6), 1–35. DOI: 10.1145/3457607

Mustafa, M. Y., Tlili, A., Lampropoulos, G., & Huang, R. (2024). A systematic review of literature reviews on artificial intelligence in education (AIED): A roadmap to a future research agenda. *Smart Learning Environments*, *11*, 59. Advance online publication. DOI: 10.1186/s40561-024-00350-5

Ng, D. T. K., Leung, J. K. L., Chu, S. K. W., & Qiao, M. S. (2021). Conceptualizing AI literacy: An exploratory review. *Computers & Education: Artificial Intelligence*, *2*, 100041. Advance online publication. DOI: 10.1016/j.caeai.2021.100041

Nguyen, A., Ngo, H. N., Hong, Y., Dang, B., & Nguyen, B.-P. T. (2023). Ethical principles for artificial intelligence in education. *Education and Information Technologies*, *28*, 4221–4241. DOI: 10.1007/s10639-022-11316-w

Pham, N., Pham Ngoc Hung, & Nguyen-Duc, A. (2025). Fairness for machine learning software in education: A systematic mapping study. *Journal of Systems and Software*, *219*, 112244. Advance online publication. DOI: 10.1016/j.jss.2024.112244

Prentzas, J., & Binopoulou, A. (2025). Explainable artificial intelligence approaches in primary education: A review. *Electronics (Basel)*, *14*(11), 2279. Advance online publication. DOI: 10.3390/electronics14112279

Quinn, T. P., & Coghlan, S. (2021). Readying medical students for medical AI: The need to embed AI ethics education. *arXiv preprint*. /arXiv.2109.02866DOI: 10.48550

Sha, Z., Huang, K., & Liu, Y. (2022). Leveraging class balancing techniques to alleviate algorithmic bias for predictive tasks in education. *IEEE Transactions on Learning Technologies*, *15*(6), 481–492. DOI: 10.1109/TLT.2022.3196278

Taddeo, M., & Blanchard, A. (2021). Ethical principles for artificial intelligence in defence. *Philosophy & Technology*. Advance online publication. DOI: 10.1007/s13347-021-00482-3

Tai Le Quy. Friege, G., & Ntoutsi, E. (2023). A review of clustering models in educational data science towards fairness-aware learning. In A. Peña-Ayala (Ed.), *Educational Data Science: Essentials, Approaches, and Tendencies* (pp. —). Springer. DOI: 10.1007/978-981-99-0026-8_2

Woo, J. (2023). Digital twin for math education: Utilization of games and gamification for university mathematics. *Electronics (Basel)*, *12*(15), 3207. DOI: 10.3390/electronics12153207

Yu, R., Lee, H., & Kizilcec, R. F. (2021). Should college dropout prediction models include protected attributes? In *Proceedings of the Eighth ACM Conference on Learning at Scale* (pp. 91–100). DOI: 10.1145/3430895.3460139

KEY TERMS AND DEFINITIONS

Algorithmic Fairness: a design principle which aims to ensure that learners are treated fairly regardless of which group they belong to.

Behaviour Modelling: an AI process used to analyse learners' decisions to determine behavioural trends.

Digital Citizenship: being responsible and ethical in all digital activities.

Ethical Digital Twin: represents the ethical profile of a learner's activity utilising AI.

Explainable AI: a form of AI that enables users to understand the reasoning behind decisions made.

Moral Reasoning Engine: the component of the EDT that simulates ethical decisions based on moral philosophy and theories.

Reflective Feedback: a feedback mechanism used by learners to refine and expand on their understanding of ethical issues.

Chapter 3
Generative Artificial Intelligence in Academic Research: Transformations, Challenges, and Futures

Mohammad Azim Arbabi
https://orcid.org/0009-0002-2938-5998
Universiti Brunei Darussalam, Brunei

Wali Khan Monib
https://orcid.org/0000-0002-9575-9305
Universiti Brunei Darussalam, Brunei

Mussa Saidi Abubakari
https://orcid.org/0000-0003-3782-281X
Dig Connectivity Research Laboratory (DCRLab), Uganda & Universiti Brunei Darussalam, Brunei

Wasswa Shafik
https://orcid.org/0000-0002-9320-3186
Universiti Brunei Darussalam, Brunei

ABSTRACT

This chapter discusses artificial intelligence (AI) tools in academic research, focusing on their potentials and challenges, global major frameworks, such as European Union Ethics Guidelines for trustworthy AI, Beijing Consensus, UNESCO guidance for generative AI in education and research, the US recommendations for AI in education, and Australian framework for generative AI, Singapore AI in education

DOI: 10.4018/979-8-3373-4982-4.ch003

ethics framework. It examines ethical and practical considerations of generative AI tools in academic research, current trends in global AI ethics policies, benefits and challenges of generative AI tools in research. Finally, it presents case studies, implications, future directions, reflecting on different aspects of these tools and contributes to ongoing scientific discussion on the integration of generative AI tools into academic research in higher education.

INTRODUCTION

Generative Artificial Intelligence (GenAI) tools, due to their various potential applications, have demonstrated their effectiveness as game changers for researchers in higher education contexts. These tools can generate text based on users' contextualized prompts, helping with editing and revising texts, proofreading, translating, connecting ideas, and many other potential uses. Harnessing the maximum benefits of GenAI tools requires users to understand the nature of GenAI tools, including their benefits and challenges, as well as AI literacy and knowledge of ethical and responsible use (Monib et al., 2024a; UNESCO, 2019). Universities play a significant role in formulating practical and specific guidelines tailored to the various needs of users of GenAI tools for academic purposes, including researchers. Establishing policies, along with cultivating a culture of ethical use through guidance, not only increases the confidence of researchers but also provides a space for them to interact with GenAI tools more responsibly and ethically when addressing challenges caused by these tools (Monib et al., 2025a).

The nature of the drawbacks of GenAI tools varies from one to another, and researchers are required to have a deep understanding of these challenges and address them in the most effective way possible during the research process when using AI tools. Some of the challenges posed by GenAI tools include inaccurate responses, a lack of nuanced contextual understanding, and the need for specialized academic knowledge. There are also other challenges, such as false AI detection, users' uncertainty about the boundary between ethical and unethical use of AI tools, and a lack of updated policies to address these challenges more strategically and practically (Holmes et al., 2023). The ethical use of GenAI tools is one of the biggest concerns for lecturers and administrators, as it compromises academic integrity when these tools are used irresponsibly and unethically. To maintain academic integrity in the era of unavoidable artificial intelligence tools, AI governance for academic purposes in higher education needs to be addressed through collaboration among stakeholders and decision-makers at both institutional and national levels. This can be achieved through transparency, trust, open discussion, the formulation of clear guidelines for various academic purposes, and the establishment of supportive policies for efficient and ethical use (UNESCO, 2023; Monib et al., 2025b). To prevent unethical use, assessment methods need to be updated to discourage those who do not follow the institution's rules and encourage human-AI collaboration for enhanced academic productivity.

These tools can be used positively and effectively for knowledge production if researchers utilize them ethically and responsibly, with adequate AI literacy. It should be noted that the research process in a traditional setting is generally time-consuming due to the requirements of several activities and the time and energy required from the researchers. Some stages of research processes, such as initial ideation, summarization, and writer's block, can be addressed by GenAI tools. To gain in-depth insights into how GenAI works best for researchers, research in this area is significant. Although several studies have been conducted on the use of GenAI tools for different educational purposes, including academic research, but due to the continuous updated features of GenAI tools and different way of AI usage among researchers, there is a need for such study to focus on the use of GenAI tools for academic research (UNESCO, 2023; Monib et al., 2024b). The chapter aims to raise awareness among academicians and researchers regarding facilitating research processes with GenAI tools, with a specific focus on their benefits and challenges in research. The objectives of this chapter are as follows:

1. To provide a deep understanding of the nature of GenAI tools and their potential capabilities in general and more specifically in academic research.
2. To detail the key considerations when GenAI tools are being used in research in higher education contexts.
3. To highlight the significant benefits and challenges of GenAI tools in research and recommend workable approaches to attain better AI utilization.
4. To depict sampled case studies demonstrating how GenAI can be used ethically and professionally.

This chapter contributes to the ongoing scholarly discussion on the integration of GenAI tools in academic research in higher education. This chapter contributes by providing insights into the benefits and challenges of GenAI tools in academic research, as well as proposing solutions for the effective and ethical integration of GenAI tools in academic research for the future. The proposed solutions can be utilized by academics, policymakers, and AI developers to facilitate the sustainable integration of AI technology into academia.

This study includes four review sections. The first section focuses on reviewing global major frameworks such as the European Union's ethics guidelines for trustworthy AI (2019), Beijing consensus (2019), UNESCO guidance for GenAI in education and research (2023), the U.S. recommendations for AI in education (2023), the Australian framework for GenAI (2023), and Singapore AI-in-education ethics framework (2023). The second section discusses ethical and practical considerations, focusing on (1) AI ethical aspects in scholarly research, (2) integrity, transparency, and reproducibility, (3) accuracy, hallucinations, and accountability, and (4) bias and fairness. The third section encompasses reviewing the benefits and challenges associated with GenAI tools. The fourth section reviews trends in global AI ethics policies and provides case examples from around the world. This is followed by future directions for GenAI tools and the conclusion.

GLOBAL MAJOR FRAMEWORKS

European Union Ethics Guidelines for Trustworthy AI (2019)

The European Commission has created ethics guidelines to promote trustworthy AI among stakeholders in the European Union. The framework consists of three components:

1. legal, consistent with existing applicable laws and regulations,
2. ethical principles are represented, and
3. technical and social robustness.

The vision in creating such a framework was to encourage the private and public sectors to invest in AI, prepare for upcoming socio-economic challenges, and ensure its ethical and practical implementation. The establishment of the High-Level Expert Group on Artificial Intelligence (AI HLEG) by the European Union was to support the implementation of this framework. The AI HLEG, as an independent group, aimed to promote AI ethics guidelines and provide policy and investment recommendations (European Commission, 2019). The framework was developed in three layers: (1) focusing on fundamentals of Trustworthy AI, (2) recommendations on the achievement of Trustworthy AI, and (3) assessment of the trustworthiness of AI technology. The legal component of this framework was not examined, but the focus was on its ethics and robustness.

Figure 1. Ethical Principles of Trustworthy AI. Adapted from Ethics guidelines for trustworthy AI by the European Union (2019, p. 15)

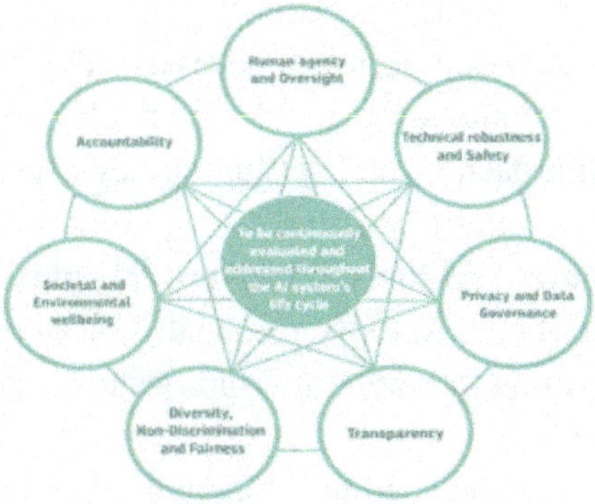

The ethical principles of Trustworthy AI in this framework include respect for human autonomy, avoidance of harm, fairness, and explainability. Achievement of Trustworthy AI includes seven requirements, as shown in Figure 1:

1. human agency and oversight,
2. technical robustness and security,
3. privacy and data management,
4. transparency,
5. diversity, non-discrimination, and fairness,
6. ecological and social well-being, and
7. accountability.

The ethical principles of Trustworthy AI aim to balance the potential of AI by addressing its ethical concerns, with humans at the forefront of implementing AI systems in the European Union.

Beijing Consensus

The *Beijing Consensus on Artificial Intelligence and Education*,

The May 2019 Beijing Consensus, co-organized by UNESCO and the Chinese government, called on governments and other stakeholders to take the necessary steps to promote the implementation of AI in education by considering its opportunities and challenges. The attendees of this conference included 50 government ministers, approximately 500 international representatives, representatives from the private sector, other UN organizations, and researchers (UNESCO, 2019). The following steps have been recommended to governments and stakeholders to consider AI implementation with minimal risks and maximum benefits in education:

1. Planning for AI in education policy is necessary due to the multidisciplinary nature of AI, which requires the involvement of government, intersectoral, multi-stakeholder approaches, and setting strategic priorities based on local challenges with a life-long perspective.
2. Consideration of relevant AI tools to improve the education management system. The application of new AI tools in education systems should serve various stakeholders by providing training opportunities for the effective integration of these tools.
3. The relationship between teacher and student must remain strong. AI tools are being used to enhance both teaching and the teaching profession. The role of teachers should be clearly defined at every stage of AI implementation.
4. Potential AI technologies that support learning and learning assessment should be reviewed and analyzed to promote their deep integration into curricula (UNESCO, 2019). AI tools should support adaptive learning processes and large-scale assessments, focusing on improving students' competencies from multiple perspectives.
5. Developing AI values and skills to prepare for its introduction and impact on the labor market. Integrating AI-related skills into curricula is needed to improve AI literacy among various stakeholders, including students. AI competence is required at all levels of society and can be addressed through appropriate measures by educational institutions with medium and long-term goals.
6. AI should provide long-term opportunities for all groups of people, including older people, who need to be trained and equipped with the necessary AI skills to achieve SDG 4.
7. AI should provide quality education for all groups of people, particularly vulnerable groups such as ethnic or cultural minorities. To reduce the digital divide and provide equal opportunities for all, inclusion and equity must be considered at every step of AI implementation in education.
8. Gender equality should be promoted at every step of the development of AI technology. Improving the AI skills of women and girls by equipping them with AI skills will promote gender equality in the workforce.
9. The use of educational data and algorithms should be ethical and transparent. New AI technologies should be thoroughly tested and then adopted to mitigate legal issues and ethical risks, while also protecting user privacy. To protect AI users' data, it is essential to establish a comprehensive framework and develop institutional and national data protection laws that facilitate the ethical and responsible use of AI in society.

10. AI tools must be systematically monitored, evaluated, and researched. The mechanisms for monitoring and evaluating AI should be developed to measure its impact on education by providing an evidence-based basis for reformulating AI policies in education (UNESCO, 2019).

UNESCO Guidance for GenAI in Education and Research (2023)

UNESCO's first global guide for GenAI was developed to address the challenges posed by emerging AI technologies in education and beyond. The aim is to provide support in overcoming the challenges posed by AI and to create opportunities for the ethical and practical implementation of AI (Holmes & Miao, 2023). The guide supports the development of human capabilities and the establishment of practical policies with a human-centered approach. The challenges posed by GenAI tools include:

1. creating digital poverty,
2. lacking a national regulatory framework,
3. using content without the permission of the owners,
4. generating content through inexplicable models
5. polluting the internet space with AI-generated texts
6. lacking contextual and real-world understanding
7. Reducing diversity of opinions and voices, and
8. leading to deeper deepfakes

UNESCO's guidance emphasizes that AI usage should enhance human capabilities by adopting human-centered design principles for AI. The human-centered approach in the educational context was emphasized in the 2019 Beijing Consensus on Artificial Intelligence (AI). UNESCO supports the people-centered approach through concrete recommendations for reformulating policies, including inclusive access to learning opportunities, open learning opportunities, data-driven management to enhance learning quality, monitoring of learning outcomes, and the development of skills for effective learning. Additionally, it advocates for the ethical application of AI tools (Holmes & Miao, 2023). UNESCO guidelines suggest the following steps to regulate GenAI in education.

Step 1: Adopt international or regional General Data Protection Regulations (GDPR).

Step 2: Government strategies for regulating GenAI need to be revised or adopted as part of broader national strategies to support practical and ethical application of AI tools in various sectors, including education.
Step 3: The ethics of AI must be addressed through the implementation of specific regulations.
Step 4: Existing copyright laws must be revised or adapted to support the regulation of AI-generated content.
Step 5: Due to the rapid growth of AI technologies, regulatory frameworks for GenAI must be developed regularly. By assessing the existing gaps and challenges, specific frameworks can be developed.
Step 6: Proper use of AI in education and research requires capacity building through ongoing education, training, and support of AI stakeholders in education.
Step 7: The long-term impact of GenAI on education and research should be considered and analyzed as AI tools are in the early stages of adoption in education, and their potential has not yet been fully realized.

UNESCO's 2022 guide for policymakers lays the groundwork for establishing a comprehensive framework for the use of AI in education. Most of UNESCO's recommendations apply to formulating specific policies in various contexts and can be adapted to address emerging AI challenges.

Figure 2. Towards a policy framework for the use of GenAI in education and research. Adapted from UNESCO's guidance for GenAI in education and research. (pp 24-27), Published Sept. 7, 2023.

The updated version of the UNESCO Guidelines for Policy Formulation, as illustrated in Figure 2, includes eight specific measures that complement the existing guidelines and are as follows:

1. Promoting inclusion, equity, and cultural and linguistic diversity. AI tools must be accessible to all learners, regardless of ethnicity, gender, socioeconomic status, or location. Equitable and inclusive access requires identifying students in need, defining standards and measurement tools to minimize gender bias,

and incorporating institutional policies through the development of inclusive terms and conditions to protect vulnerable groups or minorities.
2. Protecting human forces is a crucial factor in implementing AI technologies in education. AI users should not lose their creativity or critical skills when using AI tools to assist with writing.
3. Regular monitoring and validation of GenAI tools for education to prevent harm after their integration into education.
4. Providing opportunities for learners to equip themselves with AI skills through the development of their competencies. Skills development plays a crucial role in implementing the responsible, ethical, and safe use of AI technology in education.
5. Providing opportunities for teachers and researchers to learn how to use AI tools through training programs or AI courses.
6. Promoting plural ideas or opinions, as AI tools are unable to understand prompts and base their responses on language patterns available in datasets. This fundamental problem can be addressed by integrating AI tools with other online resources.
7. AI tools should be measured to determine whether they are relevant to the context in which they are implemented. The evidence-based application of AI tools helps build cumulative evidence-based use cases in line with the educational goals of each local context.
8. The impact of AI tools needs to be reviewed in the long term in different sectors and disciplines to assess their disadvantages and advantages and make some possible changes for more effective implementation (UNESCO, 2023).

In summary, UNESCO's guidance document highlights the potential of GenAI technology in empowering learners, teachers, and researchers in various ways, emphasizing a human-centered approach, continuous assessment of GenAI technology, and its ethical integration into education and research settings.

The U.S. Recommendations for AI in Education (2023)

According to the U.S. Department of Education, Office of Educational Technology, there are three main reasons why we need to address AI in education immediately. The first reason is that AI has the potential to provide excellent support to teachers and learners. This can help educators and students better achieve their educational goals. AI potentially offers various opportunities for improvement, learning, and teaching, and can help students who face challenges due to unequal access to learning opportunities. The second reason for adopting AI and addressing its challenges promptly is to mitigate potential future risks that AI tools may pose, including concerns related to privacy and data security. The third reason to explore AI is to be prepared for potential unexpected challenges arising from the extensive automation of tasks and decisions by AI in education. The low quality of available data used for decision-making can lead to incorrect and undesirable consequences. The following cases require implementation through policies: the first is to control automation to improve learning outcomes and protect human decision-making. The second case involves examining the underlying data quality in AI models to ensure that decisions are based on accurate information in an unbiased and fair manner. In the third case, an examination of AI technologies should be made possible to improve equal opportunities for students. In the fourth case, measures are taken to protect justice, for example, by incorporating the human separation of powers and restricting any AI tools that affect justice.

To formulate policies, four fundamentals should be considered, according to the U.S. Department of Education (2023). The first foundation is about putting people at the center of education. AI policies should be implemented at various levels from the individual to the national level to help and guide individuals. People need to be reminded of the importance of privacy. They may not be familiar with AI privacy and other challenging risks. The second foundation is about promoting equity, which involves providing all individuals and communities with equal opportunities to access information and technology, enabling them to fully participate in society and the country's economy. Issues related to racial justice and unfair bias must be highlighted and addressed. The third foundation is about ensuring safety ethics and effectiveness. Education leaders strive to make informed, evidence-based decisions. The fourth foundation is about promoting transparency regarding AI systems that respect privacy and align with the shared vision of contributing to quality learning and equity. AI systems or tools must be explainable and provide suggestions so that educators can professionally assess the output. Formative assessment, research, and development of AI tools, as well as recommendations, are other factors that can be considered when formulating AI policies (U.S. Department of Education, Office of Educational Technology, 2023).

Figure 3. Recommendation for desired qualities of AI tools and systems in education. Adapted from the US Department of Education's Office of Educational Technology (2023, p.55)

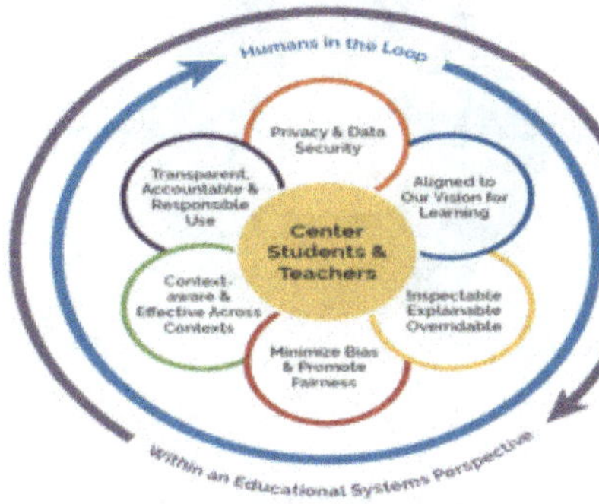

In summary, the U.S. recommendations for AI in education, as illustrated in Figure 3, emphasize the role of humans and position them within the context of all other principles. Within this framework, a common vision and the use of modern learning principles are recommended. The other recommendations include engaging stakeholders, building trust, focusing on research and development to address the context of AI application, and strengthening trust and security. Additionally, developing effective policies is also highlighted as a crucial aspect of the U.S. recommendations for AI in education.

Australian Framework for GenAI (2023)

To address the challenges of AI and explore its opportunities, education administrators in Australia have collaboratively developed the Australian Framework for Generative Artificial Intelligence in Schools—the framework aimed to help all stakeholders in the education sector. The representative bodies of all organizations, institutions, schools, and industries collaborated at both the regional and national levels. The framework was developed following consultation with students, teachers, academics, parents, school leaders, and other stakeholders to ensure it is evidence-based and people-centered. The framework aims to provide a clear definition of the ethical and responsible use of AI to support schools' learning objectives. The framework has been developed in line with existing approaches while providing enough space to address future AI challenges in education.

Figure 4. The Australian Framework for GenAI (2023). Adapted from the Department of Education, Australian Government, p. 5.

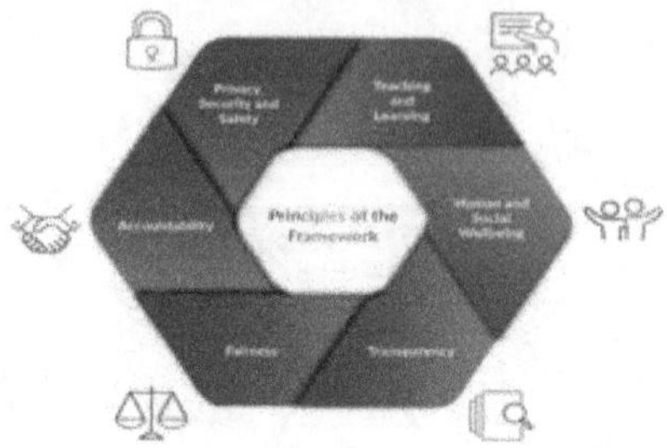

The Australian Generative Artificial Intelligence Framework, as depicted in Figure 4, comprises six principles, each with its own guiding principles that support the safe and easy implementation of AI tools in education. The six principles are as follows:

1. Teaching and Learning
2. Human and Social Well-Being
3. Transparency
4. Fairness
5. Accountability
6. Privacy, Security, and Protection.

The first principle of teaching and learning includes impact, instruction, teacher expertise, critical thinking, learning design, and academic integrity. Well-being, diversity, and human rights are discussed under the second principle, Human and Social Well-being. Transparency as a third principle encompasses information and support through clear communication and guidance, the disclosure of GenAI tool usage, and explainability, ensuring that the methods and potential biases of AI end-users are understood. There are four variables for fairness, the fourth principle, including accessibility and inclusiveness, which emphasize equal and accessible opportunities for all people from diverse backgrounds. This principle also emphasizes equity and access, stating that the implementation of AI tools should not overlook non-discrimination in rural and remote areas, as well as respect for cultural and intellectual property. The fifth principle, accountability, addresses human responsibility, reliability, monitoring, and contestability. The sixth principle, privacy, security, and protection, encompasses privacy and data protection consistent with Australian law, as well as privacy disclosure that informs school communities about how data is used and shared. It also includes protecting student input when using

AI tools, ensuring cybersecurity and resilience, and ensuring copyright compliance (Department of Education, Australia, 2023).

In summary, the Australian AI Framework emphasizes the responsible and ethical use of AI in education. Additionally, the framework is more detailed as each principle has guiding principles that educational institutions can use to address AI-related issues from different perspectives.

Singapore AI-in-Education Ethics Framework (2023)

Figure 5. Singapore AI-in-Education Ethics Framework. Adapted from the Singapore Ministry of Education website (2023)

The Ministry of Education (MOE) in Singapore has developed the AIED Ethics Framework to promote responsible and safe implementation of AI tools in the education sector. As illustrated in Figure 5, the framework includes four ethical principles: freedom of choice, inclusiveness, fairness, and safety. The agency principle emphasizes learner choice and control over AI tools when used for learning purposes. According to this framework, the potential benefits of AI tools should benefit all stakeholders, rather than a specific group among them. AI systems should be transparent, explainable, and free of bias. Learners' data and privacy should be protected when using AI tools for their educational goals.

AI ETHICAL ASPECTS IN SCHOLARLY RESEARCH

In the application of AI in academic research, a multitude of ethical considerations arise and require addressing by researchers, institutions, and the broader society. This section addresses several major ethical issues introduced by AI in research, encompassing questions of integrity and trust, as well as concerns about bias, equity, and accountability. Many of the issues reflect traditional principles of research ethics; however, AI typically introduces a new degree of complexity or magnitude to existing norms and regulations (Resnik & Hosseini, 2025b). Most critical, however, is that the majority of experts consider the fundamental ethical standards of science, honesty, objectivity, fairness, and transparency, to be as crucial as ever, applying them under the unique circumstances that AI presents and calling for perhaps new guidelines (Resnik & Hosseini, 2025a, 2025b). The following are some of the ethical aspects of AI to consider.

Integrity, Transparency, and Reproducibility

One of the fundamental ethical issues is maintaining the truth in research findings and publications when AI is involved in the research process. If a language model, such as Chat Generative Pre-Trained Transformer (ChatGPT), contributes to writing a manuscript, who owns the content, and how can its accuracy and originality be checked? The AI-generated text could unintentionally borrow phrases or sentences from its training data without proper citation, thereby increasing the risk of plagiarism (Abubakari, 2024; Hosseini, Rasmussen, et al., 2023). Even if no direct copying occurs, there is a debate about whether using AI to write scholarly text (or parts of it) constitutes an unethical practice – some argue it might, if not disclosed, be considered a form of ghost-writing or misrepresentation of the researcher's work (Hosseini et al., 2024; Hosseini, Resnik, et al., 2023). Journals and publishers have responded by updating their authorship and plagiarism policies to address the impact of AI. For example, several major publishers have stated that AI tools cannot be listed as authors because they do not meet criteria such as accountability for the work or the ability to consent to publication; any use of AI in writing must instead be acknowledged in the methods or acknowledgements (Carobene et al., 2024; Hosseini, Resnik, et al., 2023).

Thus, to help address this ethical imperative, it is incumbent on the researchers to make explicit all involvement of AI in the manuscript preparation. Failing to do so is perceived as a breach of integrity. For instance, the Research Integrity European Code of Conduct considers the hiding of AI use in content creation as a form of misrepresentation (ALLEA, 2023; Resnik & Hosseini, 2025b). Upholding integrity in practice means that the AI-generated content is verified for accuracy and originality as needed, and that the researchers ensure they can support all claims made. Furthermore, scientific research is based on transparency and reproducibility. If a study employs a proprietary AI algorithm or an overly complex model that cannot be easily shared or understood, it challenges peer evaluation. How to trust results that depend on mode? One question concerns transparency and reproducibility. This opacity has ethical implications because it makes it challenging to detect scientific misconduct. The concern is that researchers may hide behind AI complexity to smuggle in false findings in cases. The ethical response is to advocate for open science practices in the context of AI, including sharing code, model parameters, and utilizing open-source algorithms whenever possible, while thoroughly documenting all AI-related procedures (Lin, 2025). Where AI has been used, authors are beginning to be accountable for some journals' submission rules to declare model details and version, along with the data (if a custom model) used to train it, and any parameters or prompt engineering (Anderson et al., 2023; Resnik & Hosseini, 2025a). Such measures are essential for the ethical norm of transparency and render a study reproducible by means of identical means (Tang et al., 2024). In instances where complete transparency cannot be realized (e.g., using an AI service available commercially), the researcher is caught in a bind: either refrain from using such tools for the analysis to be undertaken critically or bring out some form of alternate evidence of robustness (e.g., validating AI results through a second method). The bottom line is that the introduction of AI does not exempt researchers from the expectation to make their work as open to scrutiny as any other method – in fact, because AI can be opaque, extra effort is needed to illuminate how it was used in the research.

Accuracy, Hallucinations, and Accountability

AI systems, particularly generative-based AI, may generate inaccurate or false data; this is termed the AI "hallucination" (Hwang et al., 2023; Latifi, 2024). This can be perilous in the setting of academic research. For instance, if an AI tool produces a false, yet compelling, result — such as a nonexistent statistical trend or a fabricated bibliographic reference — and the researchers fail to identify the mistake, this could lead to the publication of spurious findings. The responsibility for errors made by AI is a grey area: the human researcher ought to verify everything, but as AI becomes more autonomous, ensuring oversight is non-trivial. Consider an AI that autonomously analyzes a dataset and flags a correlation; the researcher must then decide whether to trust the result or double-check it with traditional methods. If, subsequently, the findings are proven false, questions arise about accountability. Ethically, researchers cannot abdicate responsibility to AI – any result produced by an AI used in research is still the researcher's responsibility to verify and validate (Hosseini & Resnik, 2025; Resnik & Hosseini, 2025b). This principle aligns with long-standing norms of science: tools (whether a calculator or a complex AI) do not bear moral responsibility; the people using them do.

Nevertheless, the complexity of some AI models (e.g., deep neural networks that act as "black boxes") means researchers might struggle to understand exactly how an AI arrived at a given conclusion, challenging the norm of transparency in research methods. The ethical issue of *explainability* arises: Should researchers use an AI method that they cannot fully explain to peers or the public? The use of inscrutable AI may compromise the transparency and replicability of research, which are core values of sound science and ethics, as has been noted by some researchers (Ratti et al., 2025). This has, therefore, led to the development of more AI techniques, such as "explainable AI" (Freyer et al., 2024; Khosravi et al., 2022), which require researchers to document their methodologies in detail.

Bias and Fairness

A well-acknowledged ethical lapse in AI is the bias in AI outcomes. Since AI systems learn from existing data, if this information contains societal or historical biases, those biases may be perpetuated or even accentuated by the AI (Abubakari, 2025; Resnik & Hosseini, 2025b). This is clearly an issue in scientific research: an AI model analyzing data may produce biased findings that disadvantage some group or support a one-sided interpretation. For example, an AI trained on predominantly male-authored scientific texts might unintentionally prioritize male perspectives or overlook issues that are more often studied by female researchers. Researchers have recently found evidence of demographic disparities in the benefits of AI. They found that fields with higher proportions of women or Black scientists currently reap fewer benefits from AI, possibly due to unequal access to AI tools or differing rates of adoption (Gao & Wang, 2024). Disparities like these raise concerns that AI could exacerbate existing inequalities in academia; for instance, if only well-resourced researchers can effectively leverage cutting-edge AI, the gap between them and others might widen. Ethically, this challenges the value of justice and equity in science, which holds that opportunities and benefits should be distributed fairly and equitably. Bias can also directly mar research findings: an AI algorithm in a medical study might yield biased outcomes if the training data poorly represents certain ethnic groups. In such conclusions, therefore, generalizability or equity would be zero. It is the responsibility of researchers to actively identify and mitigate AI bias. This can entail the use of diverse, representative datasets, algorithmic fairness techniques, and conducting bias audits of AI tools before deploying them in research (Abubakari, 2024; Lin, 2025; Musa et al., 2025). Thus, the ethical principle of beneficence – doing good and avoiding harm – extends to ensuring AI does not inflict harm on particular populations through biased science. From a practical ethics standpoint, many have called for engaging with affected communities when using AI in research to get feedback and ensure the research design accounts for fairness (Abubakari, 2024; Hosseini & Resnik, 2025). For example, suppose an AI is used in a social science study about employment. In that case, researchers might consult with labor groups or ethicists to anticipate how biases could impact outcomes for marginalized communities and adjust their approach accordingly.

BENEFITS AND CHALLENGES

GenAI tools help researchers, especially doctoral students, streamline the research and writing process through the immediate analysis and summarization of vast amounts of data in a short time. The automation of such tasks helps with a more comprehensive and enhanced literature review (Storey, 2023). Moreover, GenAI tools facilitate the process of finding patterns, extracting insights from available data, and identifying relevant resources for researchers. They can provide instant feedback, help with editing and proofreading, resulting in improved writing quality and reduced stress, especially for non-native English students. Despite the various benefits of GenAI tools for PhD students, these tools may harm students' critical and creative thinking skills if they become overly reliant on them. Additionally, the tools can replicate human authors' writing styles, posing challenges in distinguishing between texts written by humans and those generated by AI, which raises concerns about plagiarism (Storey, 2023).

The potential of GenAI tools in accelerating research is also highlighted in the study by Roumate (2023), which discussed the role of AI in education. The study reveals that GenAI has the potential to enhance research efficiency and productivity, while also presenting risks, including bias and an increased likelihood of plagiarism. The study emphasizes the role of human creativity in guiding professors in mentoring researchers and throughout the research process, despite the increasing use of AI tools. The study conducted by Ingley and Pack (2023) focuses on the role of AI tools, such as large language models (LLMs), in academic writing and their ethical applications. According to this study, some of the applications of AI tools include exploring scientific terminology, brainstorming ideas, generating outlines, enhancing clarity and coherence, improving grammar and syntax, and refining writing style. The study focuses on developing the writer rather than the writing by providing an evidence-based framework regarding the principles of second language acquisition to support language learning and foster scientific communication. The study by Abd-Elsalam and Abdel-Momen (2023) highlights several benefits of AI-based writing tools, including managing references, generating texts, and proofreading. According to this study, some AI-powered technologies, such as Semantic Scholar and Paper Digest, have been instrumental to researchers due to their potential for quickly scanning text and identifying gaps in the literature review of previous studies that researchers can address. This study also highlights the significance of research related to ethics, clarity, and bias that researchers can address.

Similarly, Bahammam et al. (2023) have researched the benefits and drawbacks of AI in research and education. The authors emphasize the need for an international statement or guidelines to address issues such as biases, ethical challenges, and the malicious use of AI tools in research and education. The authors acknowledge the benefits and efficiency of AI tools, which require further research and in-depth analysis. The challenges associated with such AI tools are also discussed by Dergaa et al. (2023). This study highlights some pitfalls of LLMs, such as their potential biases and limitations, and discourages creativity and accountability among students who use these tools without considering their negative impacts. Along similar lines, the study by Okaibedi (2023) examines the challenges of GenAI tools like ChatGPT in academia, including the compromise of values such as originality and academic integrity. The study emphasizes the importance of collaboration among various parties and the development of guidelines for the responsible and ethical use of GenAI tools, such as ChatGPT, in academic writing.

TRENDS IN GLOBAL AI ETHICS POLICIES

AI technologies and systems have been brought to the limelight in various environments as they become more prevalent. Essentially, the stakeholders involved understand that issues related to the development and application of AI systems have a direct impact on human life and society, thus raising serious ethical and responsible concerns. To address these issues, various stakeholders propose prescriptive propositions such as AI ethics codes, principles, or recommendations, which serve as a new set of norms to guide the responsible, ethical, and social deployment of AI systems (Corrêa et al., 2023). While scholars from different domains have addressed the ethical and responsible issues in detail at various levels, a notable trend has emerged, particularly in the research process and among researchers in institutions, who are developing and addressing AI ethics issues in research practices.

Most AI ethics and policy documents address questions of bias, fairness, and discrimination, considerations that have emerged as foundational concerns for AI ethics (Khan et al., 2022; Roche et al., 2023). This concern extends beyond simply monetizing opportunities associated with bias, fairness, and discrimination for their business impact; the potential for reputational damage from AI's discriminatory impacts is also very real. As part of prioritizing the governance of AI's societal impacts, several documents have called for the development of new standards and benchmarks to evaluate and improve AI's performance in these dimensions (Corrêa et al., 2023). Although performance monitoring tools focused on data quality and fairness were developed by organizations in an earlier round of AI policy and governance documents, much of the work remains in the pipeline or, at the very least, unexplored in greater detail for the social good (Micheli et al., 2023; Prem, 2023). Nevertheless, better metrics and governance frameworks are still needed in this space. Overall, when considering biases in the datasets used to train algorithmic systems, AI ethics is largely framed in terms of AI's potential harms to disadvantaged groups (Corrêa et al., 2023; Fukuda-Parr & Gibbons, 2021; Munn, 2023). However, in many of the same discussions, more fundamental questions of power, responsibility, and governance are also raised; questions that could fundamentally reshape the distribution of social risk, benefit, and agency associated with AI (Fukuda-Parr & Gibbons, 2021; Hawkins & Mittelstadt, 2023). Such perspectives on data, the nature of the players involved, and the ethics and uses associated with AI fall largely outside the scope of mainstream AI ethics and policy documents across the landscape.

Case Studies

The use of AI in research has evolved and impacted various domains. AI tools appear to be utilized by stakeholders, such as researchers, to obtain assistance, brainstorm ideas, analyze data, draft content, and make informed decisions. However, the AI tools, along with their benefits, also present challenges such as accuracy and reproducibility, as well as ethical integrity, which need to be carefully considered. This section presents case studies related to the application of AI in research and education.

For example, a study conducted in the United States by Kaufman et al. (2025) evaluated the GenAI tool ChatGPT 3.5 for generating research ideas in the field of non-operative spine medicine. They anonymized the output, which was peer-evaluated for novelty, clinical relevance, feasibility, and overall interest by academic spine physiatrists. No information was provided regarding the source's origin, whether AI generated it or not. The study revealed that ChatGPT can generate research ideas that spine physiatrists perceived as having clinical relevance and potential for pursuit. However, currently, its utility for generating compelling research proposals in non-operative spine medicine appears limited. This aligns with a broader critique suggesting that GenAI can only serve as an empowering secondary device, most suitable for brainstorming, and even then, not for high-stakes academic applications. AI-generated ideas are likely to be superficial or factually inaccurate in the absence of expert validation, particularly in clinical areas. Complementing the clinical perspective, in their cross-sectional study of evaluating the prevalence, impact, and challenges of AI use among Palestinian medical students, focusing on academic performance, clinical competence, and research productivity, Yousef et al. (2025) found that the use of AI has significant potential to improve academic outcomes and research efficiency in medical education in resource-constrained settings. However, the study shows that limitations in practical clinical applications and technical understanding underlie the need for AI literacy programs and ethical guidelines.

In the technical research domain, for instance, code writing, Feng et al. (2025) conducted a comparative assessment of ChatGPT 3.5 and GPT-4 in the field of finance research. They checked the model for the capabilities it supports, including code writing, theoretical derivations, and multi-modal learning. ChatGPT was found to play a crucial and transformative role in finance research, highlighting the importance of ethical adoption of AI. Therefore, AI should be continually checked for its impact, benefits, and relevance. Similarly, a study conducted by Naghdy (2025) on GenAI and human collaborative research to find the AI usage for literature review, early-stage prototyping, and hypothesis. The research utilized AI as a co-creative agent to explore various design options in a fair and objective manner. The study identified key characteristics of GenAI models, including speed, efficiency, and scope. However, it also emphasized that the researcher's oversight is critical since, without it, the results might be problematic and sometimes meaningless.

In the humanities and social sciences, Cheng et al. (2025) conducted a qualitative case study analyzing the use of ChatGPT by students, involving Ian and Sam, in areas covered by key domains of genre conventions, content development, and language use. ChatGPT assisted in contributing to documentation, coherence, and clarity. The study results indicated that students used it for genre convention, where Ian had a selective application of the tool, hence, it was more task-specific. In contrast, Sam used it more systematically, especially for APA style and structural coherence. The findings showed that GenAI can cater to the diverse needs of individuals.

Another study carried out by Black and Tomlinson (2025) investigated AI usage of undergraduates in a General Education course on sustainability and technology, where the students were taking final projects on conceptual networks. The study included both lower-order and higher-order writing tasks, as well as general learning support. The study revealed that most students utilized AI as a supportive tool and made independent choices regarding its use. Some students expressed skepticism toward the AI output, citing a desire to emphasize intellectual autonomy and maintain academic integrity.

Regarding concerns about AI in research, a study conducted by Wang et al. (2025) investigated university students' privacy concerns related to the use of GenAI in education. The study employed the Antecedents-Privacy Concerns-Outcomes (APCO) model, which showed that individual factors—such as prior privacy experiences, optimistic bias, and self-efficacy in privacy protection—and social influences, including peer norms and perceived effectiveness of institutional privacy policies, shape students' attitudes toward GenAI. It revealed that privacy concerns had consequences for student engagement with GenAI, mental health, and access to and trust in technology. The study highlights the significance of institutions in addressing privacy concerns by implementing transparent policies, fostering privacy literacy, and ensuring equitable access. Therefore, the integration of GenAI into academic research and education presents a complex ethical landscape that requires critical scrutiny.

Similarly, Đerić et al. (2025) indicated that ethical awareness varied significantly across roles, gender, and levels of experience with GenAI tools. Educators and researchers indicated greater sensitivity to authorship, responsibility, and academic misconduct, while students showed lower awareness due to limited formal ethical training. More prolonged exposure to GenAI is associated with increased ethical awareness.

These findings align with SDG 4.7, which calls for education that promotes sustainable development. As GenAI becomes increasingly prevalent in the scholarly landscape, these studies underscore the need for comprehensive institutional policies, guidance, and training to safeguard research excellence and equity in knowledge production and its application for educational purposes.

IMPLICATIONS AND FUTURE DIRECTIONS

Several key implications need to be highlighted regarding the integration of GenAI in academic research and its application for educational purposes. First, it is crucial to have critical human oversight on the AI-generated output. This is because AI output is subject to several issues, including biases and concerns about accuracy. It may mislead non-experts in the field. However, AI across domains demonstrates significant value when embedded within expert-directed workflows. Second, validation and reproducibility are essential to the integrity of AI-assisted research. Every stage of AI research writing needs to be validated, not just the final draft, due to the potential for hallucinated content, citation inaccuracies, and logical inconsistencies. Third, without a foundational understanding, there is a heightened risk of misuse, overreliance, and ethical lapses. AI may not need technical skills at this level, but it does require professional and prompt engineering and interaction skills. Fourth, disciplinary norms significantly shape the credibility attributed to AI-generated outputs. Fields with quantitative and iterative logics, such as engineering and finance, exhibit greater openness to AI utilization. However, due to high evidence-based standards, concerns regarding the accuracy, accountability, and consequences of content in the legal and clinical disciplines arise. These differences suggest that AI integration must be tailored to disciplinary expectations. Lastly, institutional policies are needed. If transparency and accountability mechanisms are not in place, AI risks remain unmitigated, particularly in high-stakes or sensitive fields. Establishing clear standards for AI use, documentation, and evaluation is therefore essential. It may have different meanings and interpretations if not defined and clearly embedded in policy, from one user to another. In the future, academic institutions, funding bodies, and publishers will need to collaborate to establish norms that enable responsible, inclusive, and transparent use of AI. Future research should focus on developing

AI in academic research, including the development of policy guidelines, effective leveraging strategies, and the creation of research-specific AI tools.

Artificial Intelligence and Research

AI stands at the edge of human and societal abilities; numerous promising avenues for expanding the role of AI in research are currently emerging. Predictive analytics, for example, might be harnessed to anticipate future knowledge gaps. At the same time, AI-powered clustering algorithms could enable analyses that span entire fields rather than the confines of a single publication. Such techniques could facilitate evaluation of the state of a particular discipline and inform funding allocation strategies that optimally support research development. The automated generation of new ideas offers another intriguing direction, with several ongoing initiatives endeavoring, in collaboration with human partners, to develop novel materials, concepts, and even entire research projects. Therefore, AI may serve as an invaluable bridge to interdisciplinary exploration, empowering researchers to assess how the questions they currently address connect with broader areas of inquiry.

Predictive Analytics in Research

With the ability to analyze large quantities of data, AI can make advanced predictions that provide valuable insights and new perspectives for researchers. In this way, AI can be essentially used as a theory generator. AI has transformed many aspects of life. It has also been increasingly integrated into academic research, providing new methods for analyzing data, conducting literature reviews, and designing research. However, the adoption of AI in academic research also raises important questions about the ethics of its use and its impact on academic publishing (Black & Tomlinson, 2025). The wide range of activities affected by AI raises questions about the forms of academic research that are most deeply transformed by technology.

AI-Driven Interdisciplinary Studies

Academic research in many fields is assisted by computation and computational methods and tools. The nature of the algorithms involved, their analysis and properties, and the application domains can each be of significant academic interest. Novel and sophisticated machine-learning methods are often of interest and can also be applied to new types of problems beyond privacy (Wang et al., 2025). Well-established areas of research in machine-learning literature, such as those surveying deep-learning applications, reviewing interest and progress in particular applications. These can focus on specific areas within the broader application domain, such as a survey of the deep image restoration literature. Academic research also aids and enhances the growth of technologies in various areas (Cheng et al., 2025). The application of ML techniques to many of the challenges encountered in research and development of emerging and enabling technologies and fields, such as the security and robustness of cyber–physical networks, blockchains, quantum information processing, quantum cryptography, photonic computing, nano processing, metaverse, robotics, and distributed edge devices for the Internet of Things (IoT), is a trend poised to continue for the foreseeable future. Full realization of AI's potential in academic research hinges on aptly addressing critical concerns and establishing an appropriate ecosystem. The task of guiding AI's evolution transcends the remit of technology developers alone; the academic community and society collectively must shape the future of AI in research (Yousef et al., 2025). AI in academia embodies the double-edged nature of change: on one side, it promises greater empowerment for scientists and a more productive utilization of research; on the other, it raises profound ethical and social questions that merit deliberate contemplation and proactive measures (Kaufman et al., 2025). Apprehensive changes, dreaded rather than celebrated, can still be preempted through foresight, discussion, and decisive action.

Understanding the Impact of AI on Academic Publishing

AI also impacts academic publishing, raising important questions about the peer review process and the selection of journals. Although many of AI's effects in research remain in their infancy, academic publishing serves as a critical window on the whole ecosystem beyond ethical awareness (Đerić et al., 2025). It reflects the interactions between the elements involved in research. It highlights the challenges of managing a system that is increasingly dependent on AI, reading, checking for quality, turnaround times, and selecting journals. The first AI system to formally participate as a reviewer is Roberta, developed by the Nature Machine Intelligence team. Trained in submissions and reviews provided to the journal, Roberta supplements human review by offering a completeness rating and identifying key aspects of the methodology or its description that are missing. Deep learning methods can also support meta-analyses and systematic reviews (Marshall et al., 2019). However, incorporating AI into peer review raises ethical concerns about confidentiality and manipulation by bad-faith actors, which are hoped to be addressed. AI tools also have potential applications in selecting journals for submission, which can help authors prioritize submissions and increase efficiency.

CONCLUSION

AI fundamentally changes the way academic research is carried out. New research concepts, techniques, and instruments make researchers more productive, leading to both transformative and disruptive university research. Developments in research help address significant ethical and social challenges facing humanity. Based on the literature, prospects include (1) addressing related issues in higher education, (2) AI-based research ecosystems, and (3) policy frameworks. AI in the academic publishing industry is also considered, even if it is in its initial stages. The modern research ecosystem drives researchers to select journals and conferences based on their average metric values rather than focusing on the target audience. Overlapping research topics and the exponential growth of motivation related to AI and machine learning (ML) also motivate the application of AI in the peer-review process. These challenges underscore the need for enhanced journal and conference selection systems, as well as automated, AI-driven peer-review methods. Several studies have demonstrated that literature review involves reading hundreds or thousands of papers, which can be reduced using AI. Data analysis and interpretation consume much of a researcher's time. AI-based tools enable the rapid analysis of data, the generation of graphical plots, and the conversion of data into innovative ideas and hypotheses. There are systems that not only analyze data but also provide detailed explanations of intricate algorithms and recommend new research methodologies, helping researchers focus on the underlying ideas behind their work. Moreover, transforming research results into publications can be accelerated when AI assists in writing the neutral sections of papers, such as methodology, literature surveys, and related works, based on the data and information entered by the user. However, humans must be cautious, as the loss of human nuance, decreased transparency, bias and fairness issues, over-reliance on automation, the risk of errors and misclassification, and ethical and privacy concerns are rapidly approaching us with irreversible effects.

REFERENCES

Abd-Elsalam, K. A., & Abdel-Momen, S. M. (2023). *Artificial Intelligence's Development and Challenges in Scientific Writing*. Egyptian Journal of Agricultural Research., DOI: 10.21608/ejar.2023.220363.1414

Abubakari, M. S. (2024). Overviewing the Maze of Research Integrity and False Positives Within AI-Enabled Detectors: Grammarly Dilemma in Academic Writing. In Mutawa, A. (Ed.), *Impacts of Generative AI on the Future of Research and Education* (pp. 335–366). IGI Global., DOI: 10.4018/979-8-3693-0884-4.ch013

Abubakari, M. S. (2025). Overviewing Biases in Generative AI-Powered Models in the Arabic Language: AI Fairness for Sustainable Future. In Syafrudin, M., Fitriyani, N. L., & Anshari, M. (Eds.), *Achieving Sustainability in Multi-Industry Settings With AI* (pp. 361–390). IGI Global., DOI: 10.4018/979-8-3373-2530-9.ch013

ALLEA. (2023). The European Code of Conduct for Research Integrity – Revised Edition 2023. ALLEA | All European Academies. DOI: 10.26356/ECOC

Anderson, N., Belavy, D. L., Perle, S. M., Hendricks, S., Hespanhol, L., Verhagen, E., & Memon, A. R. (2023). AI did not write this manuscript, or did it? Can we trick the AI text detector into generated texts? The potential future of ChatGPT and AI in Sports & Exercise Medicine manuscript generation. *BMJ Open Sport & Exercise Medicine*, *9*(1), e001568. DOI: 10.1136/bmjsem-2023-001568 PMID: 36816423

Bahammam, A. S., Trabelsi, K., Pandi-Perumal, S. R., Jahrami, H., & Bahammam, A. (2023). Adapting to the impact of AI in scientific writing: Balancing benefits and drawbacks while developing policies and regulations. *Journal of Nature and Science of Medicine*, *6*(3). https://orcid.org/0000-0003-2623-9557

Carobene, A., Padoan, A., Cabitza, F., Banfi, G., & Plebani, M. (2024). Rising adoption of artificial intelligence in scientific publishing: Evaluating the role, risks, and ethical implications in paper drafting and review process. [CCLM]. *Clinical Chemistry and Laboratory Medicine*, *62*(5), 835–843. DOI: 10.1515/cclm-2023-1136 PMID: 38019961

Cheng, D., Li, M., & Lee, T. (2025). Leveraging ChatGPT for research writing: An exploration of ESL graduate students' practices [Article]. *Computers and Composition*, *76*, 102934. Advance online publication. DOI: 10.1016/j.compcom.2025.102934

Corrêa, N. K., Galvão, C., Santos, J. W., Del Pino, C., Pinto, E. P., Barbosa, C., Massmann, D., Mambrini, R., Galvão, L., Terem, E., & de Oliveira, N. (2023). Worldwide AI ethics: A review of 200 guidelines and recommendations for AI governance. *Patterns (New York, N.Y.)*, *4*(10), 100857. DOI: 10.1016/j.patter.2023.100857 PMID: 37876898

Department of Education. Australia. (2023). Australian framework for generative artificial intelligence (AI) in schools. https://www.education.gov.au/schooling/resources/australian-framework-generative-artificial-intelligence-ai-schools

Dergaa, I., Chamari, K., Zmijewski, P., & Ben Saad, H. (2023). From human writing to artificial intelligence generated text: Examining the prospects and potential threats of ChatGPT in academic writing. *Biology of Sport*, *40*(2), 615–622. DOI: 10.5114/BIOLSPORT.2023.125623 PMID: 37077800

Đerić, E., Frank, D., & Vuković, D. (2025). Exploring the Ethical Implications of Using Generative AI Tools in Higher Education [Article]. *Informatics (MDPI)*, *12*(2), 36. Advance online publication. DOI: 10.3390/informatics12020036

European Commission. (2019). Policy and Investment Recommendations for Trustworthy Artificial Intelligence. High-Level Expert Group on Artificial Intelligence. https://www.europarl.europa.eu/cmsdata/196378/AI%20HLEG_Policy%20and%20Investment%20Recommendations.pdf

Feng, Z., Hu, G., Li, B., & Wang, J. (2025). Unleashing the power of ChatGPT in finance research: Opportunities and challenges [Article]. *Financial Innovation*, *11*(1), 93. Advance online publication. DOI: 10.1186/s40854-025-00770-3

Freyer, N., Groß, D., & Lipprandt, M. (2024). The ethical requirement of explainability for AI-DSS in healthcare: A systematic review of reasons. *BMC Medical Ethics*, *25*(1), 104. DOI: 10.1186/s12910-024-01103-2 PMID: 39354512

Fukuda-Parr, S., & Gibbons, E. (2021). Emerging Consensus on 'Ethical AI': Human Rights Critique of Stakeholder Guidelines. *Global Policy*, *12*(S6), 32–44. DOI: 10.1111/1758-5899.12965

Gao, J., & Wang, D. (2024). Quantifying the use and potential benefits of artificial intelligence in scientific research. *Nature Human Behaviour*, *8*(12), 2281–2292. DOI: 10.1038/s41562-024-02020-5 PMID: 39394445

Hawkins, W., & Mittelstadt, B. (2023). The ethical ambiguity of AI data enrichment: Measuring gaps in research ethics norms and practices. *2023 ACM Conference on Fairness Accountability and Transparency*, 261–270. DOI: 10.1145/3593013.3593995

Holmes, W., & Miao, F. (2023). *Guidance for generative AI in education and research.* UNESCO Publishing. https://www.unesco.org/en/articles/guidance-generative-ai-education-and-research

Hosseini, M., Rasmussen, L. M., & Resnik, D. B. (2024). Using AI to write scholarly publications. *Accountability in Research, 31*(7), 715–723. DOI: 10.1080/08989621.2023.2168535 PMID: 36697395

Hosseini, M., & Resnik, D. B. (2025). Guidance needed for using artificial intelligence to screen journal submissions for misconduct. *Research Ethics, 21*(1), 1–8. DOI: 10.1177/17470161241254052 PMID: 39810931

Hosseini, M., Resnik, D. B., & Holmes, K. (2023). The ethics of disclosing the use of artificial intelligence tools in writing scholarly manuscripts. *Research Ethics, 19*(4), 449–465. DOI: 10.1177/17470161231180449 PMID: 39749232

Hwang, S. Il, Lim, J. S., Lee, R. W., Matsui, Y., Iguchi, T., Hiraki, T., & Ahn, H. (2023). Is ChatGPT a "Fire of Prometheus" for Non-Native English-Speaking Researchers in Academic Writing? *Korean Journal of Radiology, 24*(10), 952–959. DOI: 10.3348/kjr.2023.0773 PMID: 37793668

Ingley, S. J., & Pack, A. (2023). Leveraging AI tools to develop the writer rather than the writing. DOI: 10.1016/j.tree.2023.05.007

Kaufman, M., Pham, N., & Levin, J. (2025). Evaluating the utility of using ChatGPT 3.5 to generate research ideas for non-operative spine medicine [Article]. *Journal of Medical Artificial Intelligence, 8*, 30. Advance online publication. DOI: 10.21037/jmai-24-480

Khan, A. A., Badshah, S., Liang, P., Waseem, M., Khan, B., Ahmad, A., Fahmideh, M., Niazi, M., & Akbar, M. A. (2022). Ethics of AI: A Systematic Literature Review of Principles and Challenges. The International Conference on Evaluation and Assessment in Software Engineering 2022, 383–392. DOI: 10.1145/3530019.3531329

Khosravi, H., Shum, S. B., Chen, G., Conati, C., Tsai, Y.-S., Kay, J., Knight, S., Martinez-Maldonado, R., Sadiq, S., & Gašević, D. (2022). Explainable Artificial Intelligence in education. *Computers and Education: Artificial Intelligence, 3*, 100074. DOI: 10.1016/j.caeai.2022.100074

Latifi, H. (2024). Challenges of Using Artificial Intelligence in the Process of Shi'i Ijtihad. *Religions, 15*(5), 541. DOI: 10.3390/rel15050541

Lin, Z. (2025). Beyond principlism: Practical strategies for ethical AI use in research practices. *AI and Ethics, 5*(3), 2719–2731. DOI: 10.1007/s43681-024-00585-5

Micheli, M., Hupont, I., Delipetrev, B., & Soler-Garrido, J. (2023). The landscape of data and AI documentation approaches in the European policy context. *Ethics and Information Technology*, *25*(4), 56. DOI: 10.1007/s10676-023-09725-7

Ministry of Education. Singapore. (2023). AI in education ethics framework. Retrieved August 15, 2025, from https://www.learning.moe.edu.sg/ai-in-sls/responsible-ai/ai-in-education-ethics-framework/

Monib, W. K., Qazi, A., Apong, R. A., Azizan, M. T., De Silva, L., & Yassin, H. (2024a). Generative AI and future education: A review, theoretical validation, and authors' perspective on challenges and solutions. *PeerJ. Computer Science*, *10*, e2105. DOI: 10.7717/peerj-cs.2105 PMID: 39650462

Monib, W. K., Qazi, A., De Silva, L., & Mahmud, M. M. (2024b). Exploring Learners' Experiences with ChatGPT in Personalized Learning. In *2024 6th International Workshop on Artificial Intelligence and Education (WAIE)* (pp. 66-70), Tokyo, Japan. IEEE. DOI: 10.1109/WAIE63876.2024.00019

Monib, W. K., Qazi, A., Jain, J., & Ponniah, L. (2025b). A comprehensive scientometric analysis of ChatGPT research global trends and prospects. *TechTrends*, **•••**, 1–19. DOI: 10.1007/s11528-025-01110-z

Monib, W. K., Qazi, A., & Mahmud, M. M. (2025a). Exploring learners' experiences and perceptions of ChatGPT as a learning tool in higher education. *Education and Information Technologies*, *30*(1), 917–939. DOI: 10.1007/s10639-024-13065-4

Munn, L. (2023). The uselessness of AI ethics. *AI and Ethics*, *3*(3), 869–877. DOI: 10.1007/s43681-022-00209-w

Musa, S., Abubakari, M. S., & Abdulwahab, L. O. (2025). Evaluating the Potential of Adapting Artificial Intelligence (AI) in Small and Medium Enterprises for Competitive Advantage. In Anshari, M., Almunawar, M. N., & Ordóñez de Pablos, P. (Eds.), *Multi-Industry Digitalization and Technological Governance in the AI Era* (pp. 233–266). IGI Global., DOI: 10.4018/979-8-3373-1681-9.ch012

Naghdy, F. (2025). Collaboration with GenAI in engineering research design [Article]. *Data & Knowledge Engineering*, *159*, 102445. Advance online publication. DOI: 10.1016/j.datak.2025.102445

Okaibedi, D. (2023). ChatGPT and the rise of generative AI: Threat to academic integrity? *Journal of Responsible Technology*, *13*, 100060. DOI: 10.1016/j.jrt.2023.100060

Prem, E. (2023). From ethical AI frameworks to tools: A review of approaches. *AI and Ethics*, *3*(3), 699–716. DOI: 10.1007/s43681-023-00258-9

Ratti, E., Morrison, M., & Jakab, I. (2025). Ethical and social considerations of applying artificial intelligence in healthcare—A two-pronged scoping review. *BMC Medical Ethics*, *26*(1), 68. DOI: 10.1186/s12910-025-01198-1 PMID: 40420080

Resnik, D. B., & Hosseini, M. (2025a). Disclosing artificial intelligence use in scientific research and publication: When should disclosure be mandatory, optional, or unnecessary? *Accountability in Research*, •••, 1–13. DOI: 10.1080/08989621.2025.2481949 PMID: 40126451

Resnik, D. B., & Hosseini, M. (2025b). The ethics of using artificial intelligence in scientific research: New guidance needed for a new tool. *AI and Ethics*, *5*(2), 1499–1521. DOI: 10.1007/s43681-024-00493-8 PMID: 40337745

Roche, C., Wall, P. J., & Lewis, D. (2023). Ethics and diversity in artificial intelligence policies, strategies and initiatives. *AI and Ethics*, *3*(4), 1095–1115. DOI: 10.1007/s43681-022-00218-9 PMID: 36246014

Roumate, F. (2023). *Artificial Intelligence in higher education and scientific research*. Springer Nature Singapore., DOI: 10.1007/978-981-19-8641-3

Storey, V. A. (2023). AI technology and academic writing. *International Journal of Adult Education and Technology*, *14*(1), 1–15. DOI: 10.4018/ijaet.325795

Tang, A., Li, K., Kwok, K. O., Cao, L., Luong, S., & Tam, W. (2024). The importance of transparency: Declaring the use of generative artificial intelligence (AI) in academic writing. *Journal of Nursing Scholarship*, *56*(2), 314–318. DOI: 10.1111/jnu.12938 PMID: 37904646

UNESCO. (2019). Beijing consensus on artificial intelligence and education. https://unesdoc.unesco.org/ark:/48223/pf0000368303

U.S. Department of Education, Office of Educational Technology. (2023). Artificial intelligence and the future of teaching and learning: Insights and recommendations. U.S. Department of Education. https://www.ed.gov/sites/ed/files/documents/ai-report/ai-report.pdf

Wang, N., Li, Y., & Cong, F. (2025). University Students' Privacy Concerns Towards Generative Artificial Intelligence [Article]. *Journal of Academic Ethics*. Advance online publication. DOI: 10.1007/s10805-025-09658-4

Yousef, M., Deeb, S., & Alhashlamon, K. (2025). AI usage among medical students in Palestine: A cross-sectional study and demonstration of AI-assisted research workflows [Article]. *BMC Medical Education*, *25*(1), 693. Advance online publication. DOI: 10.1186/s12909-025-07272-x PMID: 40355851

Chapter 4
Optimizing Pedagogical Integrity Through AI Governance in Educational Ecosystems

A. Arunprakash
https://orcid.org/0000-0002-8025-681X
Jain University, India

L. B. Muralidhar
https://orcid.org/0000-0003-3453-613X
Jain University, India

N. Sathyanarayana
https://orcid.org/0000-0002-4185-7751
Jain University, India

Pooja Kumari
https://orcid.org/0000-0002-6674-6871
Jain University, India

R. Shilpa
https://orcid.org/0009-0002-9805-1481
RJS Institute of Management Studies, India

ABSTRACT

This chapter explores the integration of Artificial Intelligence (AI) within education and its implications for pedagogical integrity, ethics, and governance. It examines how algorithmic systems influence learning processes, teacher agency, and educa-

DOI: 10.4018/979-8-3373-4982-4.ch004

tional equity. Drawing on theoretical traditions such as humanism, constructivism, and critical pedagogy, the study proposes the Ethical-AI Pedagogy Nexus (EAPN) framework to balance innovation with moral accountability. Through comparative policy analysis and global case studies, it highlights best practices and failures across diverse educational systems. The chapter concludes that sustainable AI adoption requires participatory governance, ethical literacy, and continuous reflexivity to preserve autonomy, authenticity, and accountability in teaching and learning.

1. INTRODUCTION: THE AI TURN IN GLOBAL EDUCATION

Artificial intelligence (AI) can be described as a revolution in the education sector, altering the pedagogy, administration, and process of learning in different contexts. Adaptive learning technologies, intelligent tutoring systems, generative models, predictive analytics, and automated assessments (all run by Artificial Intelligence, or AI) are now a part of the learning ecosystem. A survey conducted by the United Nations Educational, Scientific, and Cultural Organization (UNESCO) on higher education reveals that nearly 2/3 of higher education institutions have or started policies on AI. However, this adoption is not balanced across the high and low income regions: approximately 47 per cent of the institutions located in high-income regions utilize AI tools, in contrast to 8 per cent located in low-income environments.

Artificial Intelligence in the Organization dashboard indicates that AI cannot only be incorporated in education systems, but also in policy and curricular systems to reflect the implications of AI. Meanwhile, the market of AI-in-education is popularizing all over the planet. It has been making investments, and it is still increasing its market shares, which to some extent indicates that it is scaling. There are empirical results available that demonstrate learning outcomes in the case of negligible yet promising outcomes, particularly when human control enhances the flexibility of an algorithm. Though there exist several tricky ethical and pedagogical dilemmas that come along with these innovations, such as a possible loss of teacher agency, the exaggeration of prejudice, and the commercialisation of student information. The resulting dilemma brings out the necessity of governance models that will not only advance the ideals of education but also advance the aspect of technology.

This chapter continues this argument, suggesting that the educational value of AI is not necessarily about technological sophistication but instead about governance structure that upholds pedagogical integrity, teacher agency, and ethical accountability. This argument is gradually constructed in the sections below, which proceed sequentially through the conceptual foundation of the argument to the policy analysis and empirical data, and to the construction of integrative frameworks.

1.1 Problem Statement

The growing application of algorithmic systems to learning creates conflicting results between optimisation and pedagogy. The educational judgment may be reduced to a level lower than data-driven measures because AI replaces the process of content recommendation, diagnostics, and assessment, diminishing learning to a number of measurable parameters and the interpretive, affective, and relational features of learning. There is no final stage to the datafication process, in which, as with digital traces (patterns of clickstreams or keystroke data), data can be enforced to reinforce surveillance, and can reproduce the social and linguistic inequalities inherent in any dataset. Thus, algorithms can constrain the epistemic diverse array of choices by pushing learners into existing courses and repeating the social and linguistic disparities embedded in datasets. Institutional fragility only adds to these risks; most education systems have no regulatory and technical bandwidth to hold AI developers to account, and this can create an imbalance between the state institutions and the commercial services. Thus, the challenge is to implement AI in the education process in a sensible way without endangering the integrity of pedagogy and establishing non-transparent, non-accountable, and inequitable rules.

1.2 Research Objectives and Guiding Questions

To address the problem statement, this chapter will attempt to map a normative and practice-based architecture of AI governance in education. In particular, the following objectives are:

1. To investigate how governance regimes, such as policy, institutional, and classroom-level, may be modelled or revised.
2. To describe how accountable AI ecosystems may be co-produced by multi-level stakeholders.

The following research questions guide towards the following objectives:

a) What is the way AI governance can protect pedagogical values? How can governance bring about mechanisms to safeguard human agency, the breadth of curriculum, critical thinking, and relational aspects of teaching and learning?
b) Which governance paradigms combine the most significant innovation and educational ethics? The question is: which governance systems (e.g., regulatory guardrails, ethics-by-design, algorithmic audits, dynamic oversight, co-design) are effective across different institutional, geographic, and infrastructural settings?

c) What are the ways of co-creating accountable AI ecosystems by multi-level stakeholders? How do the policymakers, institutions, educators, vendors, and students interact, and who has power in relation to the other? Which participatory strategies are the guarantee of legitimacy and conformity to local norms?

Figure 1. Work-Flow Diagram

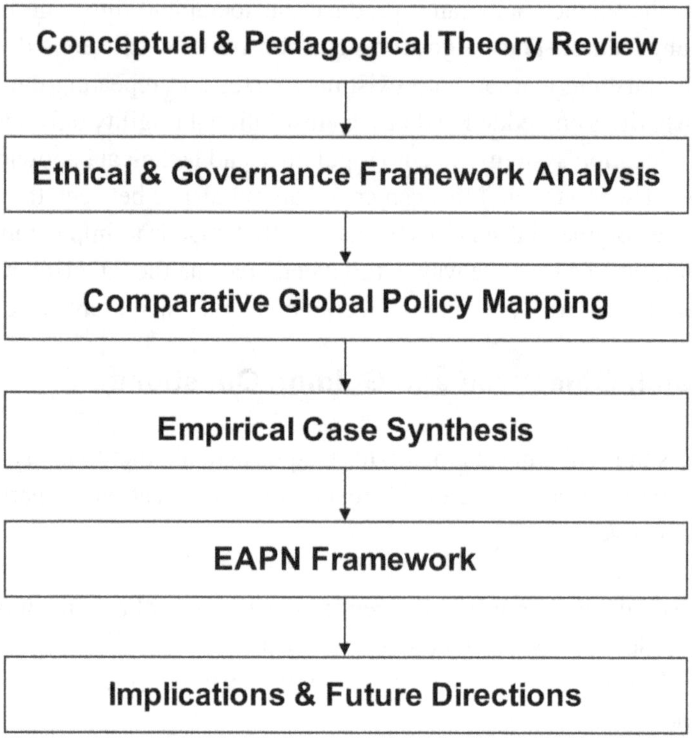

Source: *Authors' Contributions*

Figure 1 presents the staged analytical workflow adopted in this chapter. The study progresses from a foundational review of pedagogical and ethical theory to a comparative examination of global AI governance policies, followed by the synthesis of empirical case insights. These stages inform the development of the Ethical-AI Pedagogy Nexus (EAPN), which integrates normative, institutional, operational, and reflexive dimensions. The final stage translates the framework into implications and future research directions, ensuring coherence between theory, evidence, and governance practice.

2. THEORETICAL AND CONCEPTUAL FOUNDATIONS

Pedagogical integrity refers to the logical coherence of educational values, intentions, and practices. It requires critical evaluation of the affordances of technology and its role in defining the meaning of authentic, ethical, and effective teaching in an AI-mediated teaching environment. It demands a conceptual prism that will defy the traditions of humanistic, constructivist, and critical pedagogy by integrating this with educational ethics and epistemic justice. This gives a normative premise to the creation of an ethically based system of governance and the application of the ethical aspects of institutional politics.

The humanistic tradition, which relies on the works of Rogers and Maslow, lays more stress on learner autonomy, dignity, and self-realisation and warns against instrumentalist applications of AI, which turn students into data-generating machines. It is imperative that AI be an augmentative and not an extractive tool of enhancing self-direction, relational trust, and teacher judgment in pedagogical relationships. Rather than regarding learning as an active process of transferring knowledge, constructivism, as on Piaget, Vygotsky, and Dewey, re-conceptualises learning as an active, socially mediated, meaning-making process. The role of AI, per this view, can be that of an open co-participant that organizes reflection and inquiry, on condition only that it demonstrates its rationale, allowing the testing of hypotheses and abandoning the exploration of the learner in situations where its algorithmic prescriptions are likely to trim the breadth of the knowledge. Black-box recommendation engines that plan the intellectual agency in advance of the appearance of the latter destroy this spirit of intellectual agency and epistemic plurality.

Freire, Giroux, and Hooks, influenced by critical pedagogy, introduce a political dimension to education, viewing it as a site of either emancipation or domination. AI systems should be questioned, however, both in terms of functionality and provenance —i.e., who benefits from the design of a system, whose data is prioritised, and how commercial interests or state priorities promote the codification of power asymmetries under the banners of efficiency and calmness. Freire's criticism of banking education remains valid: algorithmic personalisation, which determines the directions of learning, should not reinforce adaptation but critical consciousness.

The three-part model proposed by Biesta—qualification, socialisation, and subjectification—warns against the excessive use of performance indicators and predictive analytics that prioritise technical competence over individual and ethical growth (Biesta, 2010). Ethical design then needs to make subject formation a goal of education on par with measurable attainment—epistemic justice. In an epistemic justice approach, Fricker (2007) reveals the processes of testimonial and hermeneutical injustice whereby the algorithmic systems trained on the majority of linguistic and cultural data marginalise the voices of the oppressed. Epistemic silencing can be recreated with AI unless datasets, model validation, and feedback actively consider inclusion. In this way, agency, inquiry, relational ethics, structural equality, and epistemic inclusivity, as interrelated concepts, should be upheld as components of pedagogical integrity in AI contexts, and their validity should be tested through design and governance.

While pedagogical integrity provides the normative foundation for ethical AI adoption, its practical realisation depends on how these values are translated into policy instruments and governance arrangements. The following section, therefore, examines global and regional AI policy frameworks to assess how far contemporary governance regimes operationalise—or fall short of—these pedagogical commitments (OECD, 2024; UNESCO, 2023).

According to Floridi (2013), techno-ethics may be perceived as a kind of moral reasoning that is part and parcel of engineering practice that is applied in the form of ethics-by-design, that is, the idea of providing fairness, transparency, and accountability to model architecture, documentation, and validation pipelines. Teachers ought to keep the override rights for educational uses. AI has to reveal uncertainty and reason in a format that is readable, and learners need to have the option to question the findings of the algorithm. This is the reason why the technical artefacts correlate with the pedagogical agency.

Comparatively, the governance models are different in their rate of effectiveness and enforceability. The OECD AI Principles (2019/2024) are normative undertakings to inclusiveness, human rights, openness, and responsibility with plausibility in the global sense and a limited number of ways to enforce. Since they are general and nonbinding, they must be converted into an operational policy in order to enable their adoption without the richness of an institution. THE EU AI Act provides a legally binding conformity regime that is risk-based and would demand transparency and human control of systems that are at high risk, and most of them would be admissions, grading, and monitoring tools.

Despite being a source of legal transparency and responsibility, it comes with the associated compliance costs, which prevent the encouragement of innovation, and, in particular, the workload on smaller institutions, which creates a conflict between regulation and pedagogical discretion. Quite the contrary, the AI ethics suggested by the UN policy, which is among the most essential institutions that develops the foundations of international law, is founded on equity, non-discrimination, and humanistic approaches, in particular, Global South-specific practices. Its merit is the context sensitivity and emphasis on capacity building. Nevertheless, it remains aspirational and not binding, thus constrained in its applicability where market imperatives prevail over deployments in situations.

These strands of ethics, pedagogy, and governance are incorporated into a nexus of ethical-AI-pedagogy (EAPN), giving these three dimensions the interdependent nature of axes in a socio-technical system. Autonomy encompasses teachers' and learners' agency, situational modification, and opposition to algorithmic homogenisation. Accountability implies the justifiability and rectifiability of AI-mediated decisions. Authenticity maintains fidelity to the ends of education: critical inquiry, moral growth, and relational care, which are not demanded by mechanistic optimisation. Drawing on socio-technical systems theory and critical realism (Bijker, Hughes, Pinch; Bhaskar, 1998), the EAPN views AI and pedagogy as mutually constitutive: algorithms translate into learning practices, just as educational norms translate into the governance of algorithms. To address these reciprocities of governance, governance must be both structural and reflexive, involving rule-setting and fostering deliberation and evaluative reflexivity.

Notable examples illustrate the functioning of EAPN in practice. An adaptive assessment engine, for example, cannot simply automate testing. Instead, it should provide transparency through meta-explanations of question selection, optional bypasses, and teacher-curated item banks, ensuring autonomy, authenticity, and accountability. The explainable ranking algorithms used by a peer-feedback platform should incorporate uncertainty ranges, display them, permit human intervention, and be subject to faculty oversight to prevent loss of discursive fairness. Likewise, an AI curriculum co-planner should permit teacher editing and document overrides to support reflective auditing and to base recommendations on clear pedagogical outcomes rather than engagement metrics. These structures relate the moral principles to operational design decisions.

At a systemic level, EAPN incorporates reflexivity by providing regular ethical audits, open design documentation, professional capacity building, and an adaptive review process that avoids institutional lock-in and technological inertia. Intensive audit and compliance infrastructures can be institutionalised in high-resource systems. However, they should not become bureaucratically captured and turn educators away. In low-resource settings, data sovereignty, interoperability, and community involvement should take priority to avoid dependence on external technological logic development. Multilateral agencies and international donors should shift governance and capacity-building participation toward greater localization rather than relying on turnkey solutions. One-world cases, such as foreign AI-based textbooks with embedded adaptive algorithms, necessitate systems with local interpretation, cultural responsiveness, and offline capabilities to maintain autonomy and avoid epistemic reliance.

Finally, EAPN offers a conceptual and operational model of balancing innovation and integrity. It acknowledges that AI and education are part of a shared ethical infrastructure in which design, policy, and pedagogy are continuously constructed in relation to one another. The final effect of the model is its long-term contribution to the institutionalisation of moral reflexivity and to the balance between technological development and human and democratic values. When applied, it controls AI integration to maintain learner/teacher autonomy, social responsibility, and educational purpose authenticity so that governance is an active ethical behavior and not a formal procedure (Freire, 1970; Noddings, 1984; Noddings, 2013; Biesta, 2010; Fricker, 2007; Diakopoulos, 2016; Selbst et al., 2019; Floridi, 2013; Bhaskar, 1998)

3. MAPPING THE GLOBAL POLICY LANDSCAPE

3.1 International and Regional Initiatives

A complex interplay of technological innovation, ethical governance, and social responsibility is evident in the global policy environment of artificial intelligence (AI) in education. The OECD AI in Education Policy Observatory, UNESCO's Future of learning version, and the European Union AI in Education Action Plan (2021-2027) are examples of how international organisations have sought to establish normative parameters for the deployment of AI in education. The design of AI is also guided by UNESCO's framework of equity, inclusivity, and a human-centred approach, which holds that AI should be viewed not as a means of efficiency but as a tool that fosters creative and critical thinking. It also supports ethical readiness and capacity development while opposing the optimisation of education to data (UNESCO, 2021).

In other regions, the varying ability to make AI use ethical and practical is illustrated through various regional practices. Countries such as China and South Korea in the Asia-Pacific focus on big data analytics and individualised education systems, but face questions regarding privacy, surveillance, and epistemic authority. By comparison, African and Latin American programs, such as Smart Africa and new AI education frameworks in Brazil and Argentina, aim to democratise access and develop digital capacity despite severe infrastructural and economic constraints (UNESCO, 2022). Such differences indicate that, although the global discourse is uniting around the rhetoric of inclusion, fairness, and innovation, the material conditions of their actualisation remain highly unequal.

3.2 Comparative Policy Analysis

The comparative policy picture does a satisfactory job at defining a stereotypical chain of techno-optimistic dialectics of restraint by ethical restraint. Quite frequently, developed economies have placed AI as an efficiency and personalisation and competitiveness driver, and as a national development and digital transformation agenda. The human-centred models of governance as promoted by the UN body of education, Science, Sports and Culture (UNESCO) and the Organisation of Economic Cooperation and Development (OECD) lay a lot of emphasis on transparency, accountability, and equity. AI is a socio-technology and should be ethically analyzed rather than blindly accepted (Binns, 2018). The epistemic orientations of the same polarity are contrastive instrumental rationality and normative prudence. The divergence in one area is that concerning the treatment of teacher agency.

In recent research, increased attention has been paid to the governance issues of generative AI in education and in particular to the challenges of transparency, authorship, and epistemic authority. In their article Regulating generative artificial intelligence technologies in instructional design, Garcia-Lopez & Trujillo-Linan (2025) note the regulatory inefficacy of generative AI tools in instructional design, and the necessity to have lifecycle-based accountability measures in particular. On the same note, Sharples (2023) provide an argument on socially responsible generative AI models which focus on explainability and human supervision. These contributions help to sustain the argument in this chapter that there should be an ethical governance that evolves in line with technological capability to ensure pedagogical integrity.

4. AI AND PEDAGOGICAL INTEGRITY: INTERSECTING DIMENSIONS

The field of Artificial Intelligence (AI) has been implemented in the educational setting and this has led to some critical questions associated with the integrity of pedagogy, especially the interplay of AI with cognitive, ethical, socio-cultural, and institutional aspects of the educating and learning process. Such intersections are multidimensional and therefore need critical consideration of how AI technologies can alter the process (and the results) of learning and its impact on society in general. This part explores the cognitive, ethical, sociocultural, and institutional ramifications of AI in education, addressing the issue in depth and detail, how AI can affect the pedagogical integrity in education.

4.1 Cognitive Dimension

The cognitive aspect of artificial intelligence (AI) application to learning is established on a very narrow boundary between the algorithmic personalisation and the human approach to teaching. The systems based on AI can help to process high amounts of learner data and make the teaching process personalised that could increase the flexibility and responsiveness to the needs of learners (Siemens, 2013). Nonetheless, this level of computational accuracy can constitute a menace to human tuition of interpretative, empathic and situational awareness. Pedagogical skills can be used through relational knowledge to identify the signals of affectivity, contextual data that no algorithms receive to prompt intellectual and emotional development of the learners in a manner that cannot be achieved through data analytics.

The directions of the algorithms are leading to so-called cognitive offloading, i.e. the relinquishment of the memory, reasoning and decision-making to other mechanisms, by doing so, the offloading of mental load. Such monitoring has the capacity to destroy mental independence and can assault vital thinking abilities (Sparrow, Liu, and Wegner, 2011). Incorporating algorithmic authority into the learner means that they lose their agency to doubt, synthesize, and maneuver confusion. In addition, biases present in training data are often reinforced by algorithmic personalisation, thereby amplifying cognitive asymmetries and favouring privileged forms of learning. This threatens the prioritization of culturally dominant ways of thinking, which tend to marginalize epistemologies that are not part of common knowledge and restrict pluralistic means of knowing (Binns, 2018). Hence, cognitive integrity protection entails a dialectic of the judgment of human subjects and the automation of technology, which does not negate but augments significant thinking and reflection.

4.2 Ethical and Socio-Cultural Dimensions

The implications of AI-mediated pedagogy for ethics and sociocultural factors indicate the fruitful embedding of technologies and the spread of trade norms of fairness, value, and self-identity. Since AI design cannot be studied in the absence of the environments and social contexts from which it arises, there is a risk that systemic inequities will be reproduced by flies in data collection and modelling, and that the outsized harm caused to marginalised learners (Noble, 2018). Algorithms may, unwittingly, reinforce educational inequality by training on a uniform dataset, thereby ascribing a default status to certain linguistic, cultural, or behavioural phenotypes. The necessity of inclusive data representation is grounded in ethical governance, which encompasses audits of bias and the transparency and accountability of procedures. They are also found to be too cross-culturally flexible to judge the morals of AI systems.

There is a stark contrast between the cultures of collectivist and individualist societies; for example, an AI program may be interpreted through a Western lens of autonomy and inter-learner rivalry and may not accommodate a collectivist educational culture grounded in social cohesion and collaboration (Heath & Luff, 2019). Consequently, the AI design's moral responsiveness should be sustained with respect to regional epistemologies and the fact that algorithmic frameworks can accommodate cultural heterogeneity without imposing a unitary pedagogical logic. In this way, epistemic dependency, the phenomenon of internalising AI results as authoritative among students, impedes students' ability to draw their own conclusions (Moss & Binns, 2020).

In addition to the institutional governing framework, the political economy of educational technology (EdTech) exhibits lapses in organisational development and the deployment of AI. The commercial motives of the corporate participants are increasingly defining the priorities of education. Education is increasingly commodified by proprietary AI systems, whose focus is on scalability rather than equity (Williamson & Piattoeva, 2020). This market monopoly threatens to reorganize education in ways that do not yield social gains through data mining and exacerbate disparities in technological capability among schools. Thus, the AI lifecycle should be normatively governed by government policy through a regulatory entity to support transparency, open-source solutions, and the adherence to moral principles. The regulatory systems must also be structured to ensure that the use of AI is not merely consistent with market expediency but also with democratic accountability and popular interests.

5. EMPIRICAL EVIDENCE AND CASE STUDIES

The increased use of Artificial Intelligence (AI) by education systems worldwide has led to numerous empirical studies and case studies, providing insight into the possibilities and challenges of AI in education. Since AI technologies are still in the early stages of development and penetration into the education sector, we should turn to empirical data and practical case studies to examine the effects of AI on the teaching and learning process at the institutional level. Here, I would talk about the experiences of other countries (international and regional) with AI integration in education, I would provide examples of various institutions (Finland, Singapore, Kenya), and attempt to conclude the lessons learnt, which experience of AI integration into education systems was the most appropriate and unsuccessful.

5.1 Global and Regional Evidence

This empirical setting of Artificial Intelligence (AI) practices in education introduces numerous differences across preparedness, skills, and control. The data available from the OECD and UNESCO indicate that the adoption of AI is closely linked to investment in infrastructure, teacher education, and the development of national ethics. The adoption of AI has been limited in developed nations with high income levels, such as Canada and the United States, as well as in some European Union member states. This progress is attributed to individualised learning conditions, dynamic testing, and teaching assistance, supported by analytics backed by a uniform policy and governance structure (OECD, 2021).

Structural factors, by contrast, strongly affect developing countries, particularly sub-Saharan Africa and parts of Latin America, owing to poor connectivity, low digital literacy, and insufficient funding for AI research and development. According to UNESCO, although the implementation of AI can contribute to widening access to and equity in educational settings with scarce resources, it can also lead to disparities and reinforce exclusion when used without safeguards (UNESCO, 2022).

The educative potential of AI best promotes life according to policy-making, compared with pedagogical morality and institutional responsibility, because it provides the most accessible access to global statistics. The other nations, such as Finland and Singapore, are sufficiently prepared due to their technical capabilities and their overall networks that link AI innovation to ethical governance and teacher control. Other countries, such as Kenya, also have loosely regulated EdTech ecosystems that are inclusive and data-driven. The trends indicate that the global adoption of AI-led education is less reliant on governance and the incorporation of ethics in implementation and design than on the advancement of the technology.

5.2 Institutional Case Studies

5.2.1 Case 1: Finland – AI Governance Integrated into Teacher Education

As the Finnish example demonstrates, AI literacy and ethics can be taught in teacher education so that teachers become not only efficient users but also critical consumers of AI systems. The Finnish government's national AI plan aims to advance data privacy, transparency, and algorithmic equity in the pedagogical process, thereby fostering a culture of informed interaction rather than dependence on technology (Peltonen, 2020). Educators will be instructed to make AI recommendations questionable and to ensure that such recommendations do not vary with the curriculum or the well-being of learners. This is a means of controlling teachers, premised on the idea of professional autonomy, and it demonstrates that the future of sustainable AI implementation is not to kill and run away from them, but to enable them.

5.2.2 Case 2: Singapore – AI Ethics Frameworks in Adaptive Learning Platforms

The institutionalisation of the AI approach is achieved by implementing AI in the Singapore Smart Nation programme, which implies the presence of a powerful ethical framework that regulates the use of adaptive learning technologies. AI systems are individualised to optimise dynamic content, but they also fall under data governance regulations governing equity, transparency, and inclusivity (Tan, 2021). The technological advances in algorithms are accompanied by social responsibility and accountability, as exemplified by the Singaporean model of tri-sectoral cooperation among the government, educational institutions, and developers. The emphasis on various datasets and bias audits within the construct clarifies that active ethics governance minimises the risk of discrimination and maximises innovation.

5.2.3 Case 3: Kenya – Balancing EdTech Innovation with Inclusion and Data Justice

The Kenyan Vision 2030 programme demonstrates how AI can be used and the threats of such applications in low-resource institutions. The availability of mobile learning programs has increased access to education in rural communities, but has also raised concerns about the use of data by commercial organisations (Nash, 2020). Otherwise, EdTech implementation may become a process that prioritises commercial interests over the population. The example of Kenya illustrates the importance of integrating data protection laws and regulations, participatory policymaking, and local capacity building to ensure that AIs support equity rather than deepen digital stratification.

5.3 Lessons, Best Practices, and Failures

In synthesizing the cross-case, four determinants of the pedagogically responsible integration of AI are identified as the most crucial. To begin with, ethical issues must be considered prior to the introduction of technology. The systems should also inculcate transparency, algorithmic accountability, and participative action. Examples of how such governance fosters trust and pedagogical integrity include Finland and Singapore. Second, the main focus will be on empowering teachers, who must be positioned to interpret and analyse AI outcomes without being deskilled or overly dependent on automation. Third, it requires data justice, in which privacy is not prioritized; however, it must ensure equal representation in datasets and avoid discriminatory outcomes, as experienced in Kenya. Finally, the partnership between the state and business organizations must be very closely checked. Even as the pace of innovation accelerates, the commercialisation of education will remain unregulated, contributing to the commodification of education and the erosion of societal conscience.

The combination of evidence and practice, however, reinforces that the successful implementation of the AI educational change will not be achieved solely by technological growth, but by institutional morality, governance maturity, and cultural elasticity. AI can promote, but not undermine, pedagogical integrity when embedded in coherent structures and frameworks that foster inclusivity, transparency, and teacher agency. The existence of these structures, however, has left us susceptible to greater inequality, loss of control, and the reconfiguration of education as a site for data harvesting (rather than human development) in the absence of such structures. The existing body of evidence provides grounds for concluding that the future of AI in education must be ethically grounded, contextual, and based on the principles of justice and human dignity.

6. CONTROVERSIES, COUNTER-ARGUMENTS, AND UNRESOLVED DEBATES

As the sphere of education increasingly experiences global intrusion, the issue of Artificial Intelligence (AI) has emerged as a concern, prompting an explosion of philosophical, ethical, and practical questions. The introduction of AI in education raises significant questions: whether it can influence the educational process, whether it can achieve educational goals, and the relationship between transparency/proprietary secrecy. In this part, the author provides a critical examination of the noteworthy controversies and unresolved issues on the use of AI in education, such as the question of agency and standardization, productivity, and integrity, and the issue of algorithmic obfuscation in commercial education systems.

6.1 Technological Determinism vs. Human Agency

The philosophical issue of technological determinism and human agency is central to the debate over Artificial Intelligence (AI) in education: whether AI is a catalyst for educational development or a side effect of human potential. Technological determinism holds that AI will inevitably transform the educational process by automating instructional design, individualising instruction through data, and further opening it to the extent of human intervention (Zawacki-Richter et al., 2019).

In this respect, the possibility of the AI to simplify, predict, and make the learning process dynamic is a paradigm shift approach to activity in terms of efficiency and customization. Therefore, technology is an independent system that redesigns the learning process.

However, this narration has the capacity to undermine the teacher's work and transform him or her into a robotic master rather than a teacher. It also includes a refutation, which argues that human agency theories hold that education is fundamentally a moral and social practice, a human activity informed by human judgment, contextual interpretation, and ethical discernment. It means that pedagogical purposes set the boundaries for when and how AI is to be applied; therefore, the teacher determines the context in which technology must be employed for educational purposes. As claimed by the human-centered theories of AI, due to the collaboration of human intuition and machine calculation direction, AI is not going to replace teaching but rather add value to the relational and critical types of teaching.

Post-humanist and critical AI views (Braidotti, 2019) complicate this dichotomy by acknowledging AI as a new player in the pedagogical ecology stage —not as an instrument or competitor, but as a co-constitutive agent that can shape practices of epistemics and power. Critical AI research reveals that algorithmic infrastructures incorporate power imbalances that support technocratic domination and reproduce social inequalities. This implies that deterministic and purely humanistic models are no longer adequate; the analysis of the pedagogical agency of AI requires a relational ontology that places technology within energetic assemblages of policy, data, and institutional practice.

6.2 Efficiency vs. Integrity

The conflict between efficiency and integrity summarises another main problem in AI-mediated education. Much of AI is motivated by the pursuit of efficiency, supported by automation and scalability: automated grading, analytics-based assessment systems, and personalised learning systems are intended to yield productivity gains and standardisation (Luckin et al., 2016). This quest, however, often conflicts with pedagogical integrity, which is characterised by fairness, authenticity, and the comprehensive development of a human being. The risk is confusion of quantifiable learning products with worthwhile learning, and reduction of intellectual inquisitiveness and ethical development to algorithmic optimisation.

The opponents argue that prioritizing efficiency excessively will transform education into quantifiable performance outcomes, thereby relegating the affective and moral dimensions of the learning process (Selwyn, 2019). The question that characterises this tension is whether AI can be morally upright and sensitive like a human being. Even though AI is capable of reproducing affective behaviour, through adaptive feedback or sentence recognition, it is not conscious, does not think morally, or can experience (Hao, 2021). Valid teacher-student rapport, the basis of trust, motivation, and social-emotional development, is sure to be ruined by this faking. The balance, in turn, requires acknowledging AI as a supplementary assistant that will enhance the operational process, without sacrificing the humanistic spirit of pedagogy. Efficiency alone is insufficient to maintain educational integrity; the educational system that places greater emphasis on the development of strong ethical judgment and emotional sensitivity can also be discussed within the context of instructional design.

6.3 Transparency vs. Proprietary Secrecy

The other controversy concerns the balance between transparency and proprietary secrets in the management of AI educational systems. Accountability needs to be made visible so that the patterns of algorithmic decision-making, whether in grading, admissions, or personalised suggestions, are transparent and open to challenge (O'Neil, 2016). The availability of algorithmic logic makes it easy for educators and students to interpret, criticize, and tune mechanisms that determine patterns of learning. Nonetheless, the dominance of commercial platforms creates a sense of obscurity, reinforced by intellectual property rights that limit access to the study of the algorithms that mediate an ever-growing number of educational experiences.

Although secrecy through proprietary means goes a long way toward protecting innovation, democratic control is undermined, and reliance on corporate systems ensues. According to Zeng et al. (2020), opaque algorithms have the potential to hide biases toward certain learners or institutional interests, thereby undermining public trust in AI systems. The challenge is striking the right balance between the incentives for innovation and ethical transparency: open-source systems entail a higher level of accountability. Nevertheless, they may not be economically viable due to the closed system's limited government manpower. Hybrid models are required to ensure that the explanations provided by the algorithm and the independence of the audit do not adversely affect the competitiveness of studies.

By combining the arguments of technological determinism/human agency, efficiency/integrity, and transparency/secrecy, it is clear that the future of AI in education will require choosing among incompatible forces of innovation, morality, and human dignity. The educational potential of AI will not depend on technical developments; it will be conditioned by the capacity of educators, policymakers, and technologists to integrate AI into normative systems that remain autonomous, accountable, and epistemically just. AI can only be inspired to align with the timeless purpose of education - to foster inquiry, empathy, and democratic agency rather than algorithmic conformity - through reflexive administration and human-centered design.

7. INTEGRATIVE FRAMEWORK: THE ETHICAL-AI PEDAGOGY NEXUS (EAPN)

As Artificial Intelligence (AI) emerges in the education sector, there is a reported need to establish an integrative framework to promote ethical practices and pedagogical integrity. The model must have a holistic understanding of how AI can be used in education and how technology, human action, policy, and ongoing evaluation intersect. The challenges of introducing AI in education can be addressed through the Ethical-AI Pedagogy Nexus (EAPN). The parts of the EAPN framework, an idea of conceptual innovation (like Pedagogical Integrity Index [PII], the argument of human-AI co-agency, and theories of data feminism, and epistemic justice are presented in this paragraph.

7.1 Framework Components

The Ethical-AI Pedagogy Nexus (EAPN) offers a layered framework that integrates ethical reasoning, institutional governance, pedagogical practice, and reflexive oversight into a unified model of responsible AI in education. The four interdependent strata—the Normative, Institutional, Operational, and Reflexive—form a dynamic ecosystem that ensures that the ideals of morality, the dynamics of change that governance should follow, and the interaction between humans and AI develop in harmony, thereby maintaining the integrity of the pedagogical process and innovation. The Normative Layer grounds the framework on a philosophical ethics and education-based approach, utilising the norms of deontological, utilitarian, and virtue ethics to ensure AI use aligns with equity, transparency, and human flourishing.

It concentrates on equity and access, ensuring that AI systems become an aid to, rather than a source of, educational inequity; human-centred design where technology is used in facilitating functions to professional agency of teachers instead of substituting it; and privacy and data justice, wherein technology is used in complementary ways to ensure that learners are not harmed (Crawford, 2021). It is based on this ethical premise that AI must prioritise democratic and humanistic reasons over technological determinism.

These principles are operationalised in the Institutional Layer through governance, policies, and regulatory mechanisms to ensure accountability across the AI life cycle. Institutions are charged with developing ethical norms and dynamic guidelines that are sensitive to technological change and socio-cultural diversity. Policy frameworks should articulate clear aspirations for AI adoption, including improving learning quality, promoting fairness, and protecting teacher autonomy. Independent regulatory agencies should audit them on the educational and ethical effects of the systems. This layer appears to make the following point: it appears that AI in education can only be controlled by the market; to control it, we need to have plural control by educators, developers, policymakers, and learners to ensure that algorithmic interventions are acceptable socially and do not conflict with the values and pedagogic aims of society.

The Operational Layer interprets ethical and governance promises into pedagogical practice, including the definition of teacher-AI collaboration modalities. In this case, AI is considered an augmentative collaborator that will stimulate, rather than undermine, a teacher's interpretive and relational skills. The pedagogy that AI assists in promoting personalisation, diagnostic understanding, and various forms of feedback should be subordinate to professional judgment and curriculum coherence. The joint work of teachers and AI will require long-term professional development to build both digital and ethical literacy, providing educators with an opportunity to critically analyse the work of algorithms and mediate their implementation in accordance with situational needs. Moreover, AI-based professional learning systems may promote teacher development if they focus on reflective practice and counteract bias rather than reinforcing data determinism. The teleological orientation of EAPN informs an alternative view of AI as an automated solution to a relationship that is inherent to human pedagogical deliberation.

The Reflexive Layer makes the framework adaptable as it supports the processes of evaluation, ethical audit, and redesign. AI systems should be periodically evaluated to ensure their relevance, fairness, and effectiveness, without becoming insensitive to evolving learning realities. Continuous appraisal involves the measurement of learning outcomes, inclusiveness, and adverse effects. Periodic audits help assess adherence to normative values of equity, privacy, and transparency, and thereby enable remedial measures before systemic distortions occur. The last component of this layer is co-evolution, which entails feedback loops among educators, learners, policymakers, and developers to achieve contextual responsiveness. And this is the process of reflexivity that does not aim to ossify and, in any case, assumes the historical contingency of AI systems and educational values, as they must co-evolve.

7.2 Conceptual Innovations

The Pedagogical Integrity Index (PII) is a welcome and important addition to this integrative architecture of the system, which embeds abstract ethical commitments within it. The PII is a diagnostic tool that links governance measures to learning ethics, including equity of access, algorithmic transparency, data protection, and the quality of relationships between teachers and AI. The index would enable policymakers and institutions to identify evidence-based practices by assessing the compatibility of AI functionality with educational values, and to identify and remediate ethical malpractice. It addresses the reversion of evaluation to accountability grounded in integrity by attending to the moral and epistemic consequences of AI implementation.

EAPN is enhanced by the concepts of human-AI co-agency, data feminism, and epistemic justice to deepen its theoretical depth. The human-AI conceptualisation of agency (Binns, 2018) reimagines agency as grounded in humanity and distributed across both human and technological actors. AI is not an inanimate instrument but a co-worker in pedagogical systems, relying on human control and normative contextualisation. This relationship model challenges the independence-versus-control dichotomy and proposes co-responsibility, in which teachers provide guidance to AI systems and the systems learn through critical thinking.

Data feminism fosters an understanding of gendered and socio-cultural imbalances in data construction and algorithm development, revealing how mainstream epistemological processes influence educational AI at the expense of some populations (Dastin, 2018). It requires participatory design procedures that embrace disproportionately voiceless viewpoints and anticipate the social dynamics of datafication. This is complemented by epistemic justice (Fricker, 2007), which requires the acknowledgement of plural systems of knowledge and traditions of learning that are not always present in algorithmic models. EAPN will protect epistemic inclusion and ensure equality across cultural and cognitive differences by integrating epistemic diversity into data modelling and architecture, as well as design logic.

Taken together, these strands constitute EAPN as a paradigm that integrates moral philosophy, governance theory, and critical epidemiology in a coherent framework for ethically grounded educational technology. On the same note, it also considers AI to be co-constitutive of pedagogy, and its legitimacy is based on transparency, inclusiveness, and human-centred accountability. The PII brings this vision to reality by connecting ethical ideals with evaluation ideals. In contrast, the four-layered system ensures that reflection, adaptation, and oversight occur promptly. Finally, the Ethical-AI Pedagogy Nexus offers an elaborate framework for preserving the dialect between technological innovation and pedagogical integrity, thereby making the digital transformation of education a humanistic, justice-oriented, and reflexive ethical order.

8. CHALLENGES, GAPS, AND FUTURE DIRECTIONS

With the introduction of Artificial Intelligence (AI) into educational systems, several challenges and gaps have emerged. Although there is the potential for the application of AI to revolutionize the field of education, the application of the technology is riddled with issues. Policy and structural disjunctures have impeded its successful incorporation, and new research avenues offer avenues for resolving these issues, particularly in pedagogy, ethics, and governance. This section will discuss key issues and gaps in AI education policy and practice, examine recent research opportunities, and comment on recent approaches to methodology in the field's development.

8.1 Structural and Policy Gaps

Artificial Intelligence (AI) in education remains constrained by structural and policy flaws that impede its implementation in ethical, equitable, and sustainable ways. The serious drawback is that there are no standardised governance models to streamline ethical standards, accountability frameworks, and quality standards across jurisdictions. Although normative guidelines have been developed by organizations such as the United Nations Educational, Scientific and Cultural Organisation (UNESCO) and the Organisation for Economic Co-operation and Development (OECD), these guidelines remain advisory, vary by region, and are politically fragmented (UNESCO, 2021; OECD, 2020). The result is a regulatory landscape that is out of balance, in which AI applications develop faster than regulations can keep pace, leaving gaps in transparency, impartiality, and accountability. The absence of generalised norms enables the dissemination of algorithmic darkness, whereby AI systems are black boxes that cannot be explored, placing educators and policymakers under strain to question the processes of algorithmic decision-making (O'Neil, 2016).

To make the issue worse, ethical guidance is disjointed: many countries have adopted national principles addressing issues such as bias, privacy, and fairness, yet few can articulate an integrated ethical vision that accounts for the relational and normative aspects of education. Such an ethical inconsistency undermines efforts to integrate AI into pedagogical frameworks that emphasize inclusivity, care, and equity.

The institutional weakness is also to blame for the divide. Most educational systems, particularly in low-resource settings, lack the necessary technical infrastructure, professional expertise, and assessment capabilities to manage AI responsibly (Selwyn, 2019). The lack of long-term institutional support for human capital and governance systems makes the introduction of AI a threat to the institutionalization of inequalities rather than their reduction, favouring technologically advanced systems over others. These structural asymmetries are compounded by the lack of long-term regulatory continuity and intersectoral cooperation, resulting in a global gap in AI preparedness and ethical responsibility.

8.2 Emerging Research Frontiers

Improved understanding of the effects of AI on education, moral education, governance across cultures, and autonomy and critical thinking is among the research directions to help address these gaps. Moral pedagogy and affective learning are emerging hot fields of AI. Researchers are examining the efficacy of AI in supporting the ethical and emotional dimensions of learning, which are typically neglected in cognitive-based approaches. Simulations and Artificial Intelligence (AI) enabled adaptive capabilities can be used to help develop ethical reasoning, empathy, and emotional intelligence by exposing learners to multiple dimensions of moral dilemmas or emotional feedback loops (Gershenfeld, 2020).

However, these applications have been associated with issues of authenticity, emotional manipulation, and the possibility of algorithmic reductionism when the complexity of moral issues is reduced to quantifiable attributes. The ethical design in this field should thus protect human judgment as the determiner of moral meaning while leveraging AI to analyse and enhance self-reflection and empathy. At the same time, cross-cultural governance models are a necessary field of research. Since AI systems cross cultural borders, governance should be mindful of differences in epistemic traditions, shared values, and pedagogical priorities.

The study of comparative ethics indicates that collectivist environments can support collaborative AI educational models, whereas individualist systems focus on individualisation and autonomy (Heath & Luff, 2019). Developing adaptive and cross-cultural infrastructure requires discussions on global norms and local educational ontologies to prevent Western-focused paradigms in AI implementation, ensuring epistemic pluralism. The idea of AI taking over teachers' autonomy and the critical importance of learners has not been studied through longitudinal research. Nevertheless, it plays a vital role in understanding the growing impacts of automation on professional agency and intellectual autonomy. The role of AI in assessment, feedback, and curriculum design should be continually monitored to determine whether technological mediation has empowered teachers or undermined their discretion, and whether learners' critical abilities are being empowered or mechanised by reliance on algorithms.

8.3 Methodological Innovations

It is necessary to develop innovative methodologies to address these issues, given the complexity of AI-education ecosystems. Mixed-methods approaches that integrate ethnographic research, statistical modelling, and computational analyses will provide a better understanding of the functioning of AI in micro- and macro-pedagogical contexts. Interviews, case studies, and participant observation will be used as qualitative methods to find out the experiences of people who adopt AI.

These techniques can provide insight into how relationships between teachers and students develop, how they perceive justice, and how ethically aware they are.

The potential of AI in education is that it can help overcome structural inequity globally, support methodological pluralism, and foster ethical reflexivity in our research and practice. Standardised governance, cultural sensitivity, and evaluation of empirical data should be synchronised to ensure that technology development supplements education rather than weakens it. This is because it requires a team of policymakers, educators, and technologists who work together to ensure that these gaps are addressed consistently. This can be achieved through rigorous interdisciplinary research that balances innovation and justice, efficiency and inclusion, and automation and humanity. Only under these integrative and reflexive conditions is it possible to use AI to make equitable, transparent, and pedagogical change in education.

9. METAFRAMEWORK

Figure 2. AI Educational Outcomes Nexus Framework

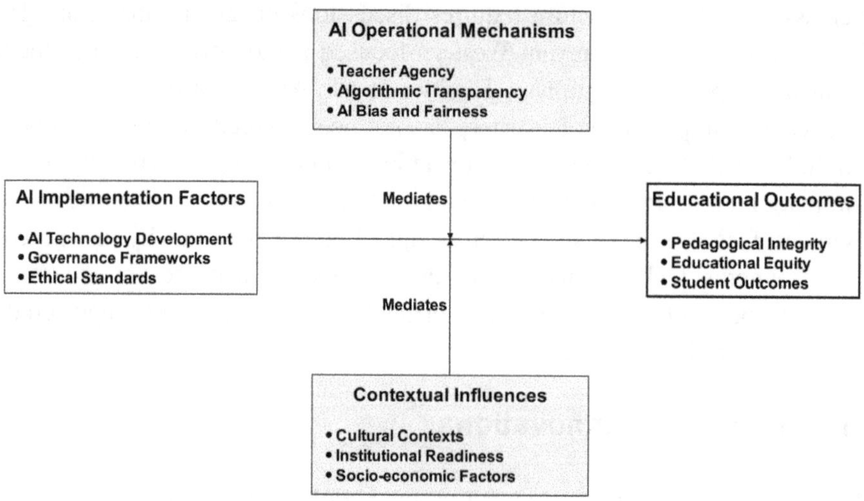

Source: *Authors' Contribution*

Figure 2 illustrates the AI Educational Outcomes Nexus Framework, which represents the dynamic interactions between AI technology and educational outcomes from a systems-thinking perspective. The premise that factors such as AI implementation, technological development, governance, and ethics determine educational outcomes—such as pedagogical integrity, equity, and student learning—is grounded in socio-technical and educational theory (Vygotsky, 1978; Saljo, 2010; Floridi, 2019). The AI operations (teacher agency, transparency, and fairness) may serve as intermediaries that explain the practical implementation of AI. In the meantime, such relations are regulated by situational considerations (cultural, institutional, and socio-economic factors). The given paradigm concerns the field of responsible, situational, and human-centred AI implementation in education.

10. FUTURE SCOPE OF RESEARCH

Future research must adopt a transdisciplinary paradigm that integrates social policy, educational theory, ethics, and computer science, as these are the most effective approaches to examining the long-term impacts of AI on educational uses and values. The priority areas include the role of AI in critical thinking, creativity, ethical decision-making, and student well-being and holistic development. The study should be conducted longitudinally and comparatively to examine the effects of algorithmic decision-making on the redefinition of teacher agency, student agency, and institutional accountability. It must also consult AI on what it means to possess epistemic justice, as AI can both strengthen and undermine pluralism in the creation of knowledge and in moral education. Here, AI-mediated spaces can foster empathy and moral reasoning without reducing ethics to measurable results.

Future research can empirically validate the Ethical-AI Pedagogy Nexus (EAPN) across diverse educational contexts through longitudinal and mixed-method designs. There is scope to operationalise the Pedagogical Integrity Index (PII) as a measurable governance tool to enable institutions to assess ethical alignment in AI adoption. Further studies may also explore cross-cultural adaptations of AI governance models, particularly in low-resource settings, to examine how epistemic justice and data sovereignty can be sustained in globally networked educational ecosystems (OECD, 2024; UNESCO, 2023).

11 IMPLICATIONS

The introduction of Artificial Intelligence (AI) in the educational sector is not only an opportunity but also a growing threat. AI is an area whose ever-increasing popularity in education raises questions about ethics, pedagogy, and governance. This section discusses the theoretical, practical, and policy implications of AI in education. It establishes a research agenda to advance the current understanding of AI and its use in education. Lastly, it emphasizes the need for a moderate approach to AI implementation that should complement, rather than substitute for, the moral and human dimensions of education.

The introduction of Artificial Intelligence (AI) into education is reconfiguring the educational landscape. It necessitates a shift in the socio-technical perspective to recognise the co-agency of humans and machines. The notions of fairness, inclusiveness, and justice have ceased to be human-related and have been applied to the process of interaction among algorithms, institutions, and learners. AI systems not only mediate but also affect pedagogical processes by determining content curation, assessment, and access, thereby shaping epistemic power in classrooms.

A future socio-technical education assemblage envisions the integration of technological infrastructures and institutional conventions to achieve educational outcomes, abandoning the perspective of technology as merely instrumental. This theoretical change is further expanded by the notion of bridging critical pedagogy and AI ethics: the emancipation- and agency-oriented perspective of critical pedagogy is complemented by an examination of AI ethics, which places questions of bias, surveillance, and power within the broader context of a social justice approach. By integrating these perspectives into learning spaces using AI, the latter can become an environment where learners can challenge the role of technology in forming knowledge and identity, thereby contributing to the civic and moral purposes of the educational process (Selwyn, 2019).

In practice, the implementation of AI must be institutionally prepared and supported by a stable code of ethics and extensive teacher training. Policies that regulate the way innovation should be balanced with accountability, which is represented by information privacy, disclosure of algorithms, and equal access to information, should be implemented by the government and the learning institutions. Institutions should invest in professional development programs to enhance teachers' technical skills and moral awareness. It will assist them in critically evaluating algorithmic outputs and in deciding how to adapt AI devices to their respective learning settings. Ethical literacy will be needed to place teachers in dilemmas regarding data monitoring, favouritism, and students' liberties. The profession-based learning approach is intended to foster a critical attitude toward the purpose of AI in the teaching process, particularly by maintaining understanding and care, trust in relationships, and inclusivity in more data-mediated classrooms. The institutions are to ensure that their policies are sufficiently flexible to avoid regulatory problems and that innovation does not conflict with one another to the extent that AI dominates human judgment.

AI education involves the usage of local, national, and global government policy infrastructure. Local schools must have participatory policies that reflect community ideals and pedagogical aims; these are local, not universal. AI use would be local and specific. National regulatory frameworks impose limits on what is ethically feasible with respect to justice, privacy, and responsibility through binding legal requirements that are monitored routinely. Teacher empowerment to be part of national policies; AI to support professional agency. International bodies such as the UN Educational, Scientific and Cultural Organization and the Organization for Economic Cooperation and Development can take the lead in developing interoperable principles that promote cooperation, capacity-building, cross-border accountability, and cultural and institutional diversity. As a result, globalised practices can help to promote data ethics, transparency, and equity in technical education.

12. CONCLUSION

This chapter demonstrates how the integration of artificial intelligence into education fundamentally changes pedagogical integrity, teacher agency, and institutional accountability. It extends the basic idea that ethical governance is not something applied to AI to limit it, but rather an integral requirement for meaningful AI adoption in learning environments. The analysis points to the dangers of unchecked algorithmic optimisation in limiting the epistemic diversity and relational dimensions of education. Global policy comparisons indicate substantial gaps between normative commitments and the capacity to implement them across regions. The Ethical-AI Pedagogy Nexus (EAPN) is an integrative framework linking ethics, governance, and pedagogical practice. The relevance of teacher agency in mediating AI-assisted teaching is highlighted in the chapter. It centers on data sovereignty and epistemic justice as prerequisites for the appropriate implementation of AI. Empirical evidence indicates that it is not technological development but the maturity of educational governance that determines educational outcomes. Ultimately, the study affirms that the sustainable integration of AI should focus on human flourishing and democratic accountability, prioritising these over pedagogical purpose and technical efficiency.

REFERENCES

Bhaskar, R. (1998). *Reclaiming Reality: A Critical Introduction to Contemporary Philosophy*. Verso.

Biesta, G. (2010). *Good Education in an Age of Measurement: Ethics, Politics, Democracy*. Routledge.

Binns, R. (2018). On the interpretation of ethical issues in AI and the role of human agency. *Journal of AI Ethics*, *5*(3), 233–245.

Braidotti, R. (2019). *Posthuman knowledge*. Polity Press.

Crawford, K. (2021). *Atlas of AI: Mapping the terrain of artificial intelligence*. Yale University Press.

Dastin, J. (2018). Data feminism and the politics of algorithmic transparency. *Feminist Media Studies*, *18*(2), 1–19.

Diakopoulos, N. (2016). Accountability in algorithmic decision making. *Communications of the ACM*, *59*(2), 56–62.

Floridi, L. (2013). *The Ethics of Information*. Oxford University Press.

Floridi, L. (2019). Establishing the rules for building trustworthy AI. *Nature Machine Intelligence*, *1*(6), 261–262. DOI: 10.1038/s42256-019-0055-y

Fricker, M. (2007). *Epistemic injustice: Power and the ethics of knowing*. Oxford University Press.

García-López, I. M., & Trujillo-Liñán, L. (2025). Ethical and regulatory challenges of Generative AI in education: A systematic review. *Frontiers in Education*.

Gershenfeld, N. (2020). AI for emotional learning and moral pedagogy. *Journal of Educational Technology*, *46*(3), 198–209.

Hao, K. (2021). Can artificial intelligence ever truly understand human emotions? *MIT Technology Review*.

Heath, C., & Luff, P. (2019). Cross-cultural governance models in AI-driven education. *Journal of Educational Technology & Society*, *22*(4), 212–229.

Luckin, R., Holmes, W., Griffiths, M., & Forcier, L. B. (2016). *Intelligence unleashed: An argument for AI in education*. Pearson.

Moss, L., & Binns, R. (2020). AI and epistemic dependence in education. *Journal of Educational Philosophy*, *9*(4), 98–111.

Nash, J. (2020). EdTech in Africa: Challenges and opportunities for inclusive education. *International Journal of Educational Development*, *72*, 102–111.

Noble, S. U. (2018). *Algorithms of oppression: How search engines reinforce racism*. NYU Press.

Noddings, N. (1984). *Caring: A Relational Approach to Ethics & Moral Education*. University of California Press.

Noddings, N. (2013). *Caring: A Relational Approach to Ethics & Moral Education*. University of California Press.

O'Neil, C. (2016). *Weapons of math destruction: How big data increases inequality and threatens democracy*. Crown Publishing Group.

OECD. (2020). *AI in Education Policy Observatory*. OECD.

OECD. (2020). *AI in Education: Policies, Practices, and Future Directions*. OECD Publishing.

OECD. (2021). *Education at a Glance 2021: OECD Indicators*. OECD Publishing.

OECD. (2024). *Evolving with Innovation: The 2024 OECD AI Principles Update.*

OECD. (2024). *Trustworthy artificial intelligence (AI) in education*. OECD Publishing.

Peltonen, J. (2020). AI in Finnish education: Empowering teachers for the future. *Finnish Education Review*, *32*(4), 112–127.

Säljö, R. (2010). *Learning, culture and society*. Routledge.

Selwyn, N. (2019). *Should robots replace teachers? AI and the future of education*. Polity Press.

Sharples, M. (2023). Towards social generative AI for education: Theory, practices and ethics. Learning. *Research and Practice*, *9*(2), 159–167.

Siemens, G. (2013). Learning analytics: The emergence of a discipline. *The American Behavioral Scientist*, *57*(10), 1380–1390.

Sparrow, B., Liu, J., & Wegner, D. M. (2011). Google's effects on memory: Cognitive consequences of having information at our fingertips. *Science*, *333*(6043), 776–778.

Tan, C. (2021). AI in education: Singapore's ethical framework for adaptive learning technologies. *Journal of Educational Technology*, *38*(3), 211–225.

UNESCO. (2021). *AI and the Futures of Learning*. United Nations Educational, Scientific and Cultural Organisation.

UNESCO. (2022). *AI in education: Africa's evolving policy landscape. United Nations Educational, Scientific and Cultural Organisation.*

UNESCO. (2023). *Guidance for Generative AI in Education and Research*. UNESCO.

Vygotsky, L. S. (1978). *Mind in society: The development of higher psychological processes*. Harvard University Press.

Williamson, B., & Piattoeva, N. (2020). The political economy of educational technology: The marketisation of education through AI and big data. *Educational Policy*, *44*(5), 766–788.

Zawacki-Richter, O., Marín, V. I., Bond, M., & Gouverneur, F. (2019). Systematic review of research on artificial intelligence in education. *Journal of Educational Technology & Society*, *22*(1), 10–24.

Zeng, Y., Lu, E., & Huang, Z. (2020). The challenge of proprietary secrecy in AI-driven education. *Journal of Educational Technology*, *47*(3), 215–229.

Chapter 5
Neural Futures, AGI, Brain-Computer Interfaces, and the Speculative Morality of Education

L. B. Muralidhar
https://orcid.org/0000-0003-3453-613X
Jain University, India

V. Lavakumar
https://orcid.org/0000-0002-3539-9280
GITAM School of Business, GITAM University, India

V. S. Vainik
https://orcid.org/0000-0001-6203-1513
Jain University, India

Y. Santhosh
https://orcid.org/0000-0002-3174-0592
Jain University, India

N. Sathyanarayana
https://orcid.org/0000-0002-4185-7751
Jain University, India

DOI: 10.4018/979-8-3373-4982-4.ch005

ABSTRACT

This chapter examines the convergence of Artificial General Intelligence (AGI) and Brain-Computer Interfaces (BCIs) in education, exploring their transformative potential and the profound ethical challenges they present. It critically analyses how these emerging technologies reshape cognition, pedagogy, and agency, drawing on neuroethics, educational theory, and global policy discourse. Through speculative and interdisciplinary perspectives, it interrogates issues of autonomy, equity, and cognitive liberty while offering strategies for responsible implementation. The chapter proposes a framework for ethically integrating artificial general intelligence (AGI) and brain-computer interfaces (BCIs), striking a balance between innovation and human values in future learning ecosystems.

1. INTRODUCTION: RE-IMAGINING EDUCATION IN THE AGE OF AGI AND BRAIN-COMPUTER INTERFACES

1.1 Overview of the rapid evolution of AGI (Artificial General Intelligence) and Brain-Computer Interfaces (BCIs)

The development trajectory of Artificial General Intelligence (AGI) and Brain-Computer Interfaces (BCIs) illustrates a merging of computational, neuroscientific, and systems-focused innovations that is increasingly challenging traditional ideas of education. Goertzel (2014) notes that while AGI began as a concept rooted in models of machine cognition and philosophy of mind, it has only recently approached practical engineering through advances in large-scale multimodal architectures that support near-generalizable cognitive abilities across various domains.

Lebedev & Nicolelis (2006) have revealed that while BCI technologies have evolved from the clinical use of EEG to advanced neural-digital interface systems, both invasive and non-invasive, capable of transforming cognitive signals into motor commands. These technologies have different origins but are connected in shaping speculative futures of education where linear transmission shifts to dynamic, interactive neurocognitive states. Models like GPT-4o, Gemini, and Claude exemplify AGI systems that deliver context-aware output, adaptive responses to feedback, and scalable personalization. Interestingly, BCIs can also provide real-time insights into cognition, engagement, and retention. However, such technological possibilities must be embedded within pedagogical, ethical, and infrastructural frameworks that are still unevenly realized.

Traditionally, digital technologies in education have mainly been viewed from a privileged perspective focused on administrative efficiency or the delivery of learning material, and only rarely as an epistemic agent on the cutting edge of technology registers. AGI, with its autonomous reasoning, and BCI, with its neuro-adaptive learning, challenge the fundamental educational roles of teacher, curriculum, and learner. A report from the OECD (2024) found that field evidence is less definitive: AGI tutors improve STEM performance, but overuse may weaken critical thinking if these systems generate assignment content without sufficient scaffolding . Interventions in Finland and Japan have combined targeted interventions with BCI and have observed improved language retention and regulation of focus. However, the long-term effects of BCI depend on controlled signal processing, ethical considerations, and learner adaptability. These results highlight that such technology is not ready for plug-and-play applications but must evolve alongside pedagogical design, teacher involvement, and legislation.

To establish conceptual coherence, this chapter adopts a structured analytical lens that moves from technological capabilities to their ethical and pedagogical implications, situating AGI–BCI integration within evolving global governance landscapes (Kim & Harada, 2023). This sequencing ensures that the discussion maintains a clear thematic direction while foregrounding the human stakes of neuroadaptive education.

Recent empirical studies demonstrate a sharper shift toward integrated AGI–BCI learning ecosystems, with multimodal neural-adaptive architectures enabling real-time personalization and dynamic scaffolding. Li & Ren (2024) show that hybrid AGI tutors equipped with neural signals for attention tracking outperform conventional adaptive systems in concept-reinforcement tasks, especially when cognitive fatigue is a limiting factor. Similarly, Zhao et al. (2023) found that low-cost BCIs integrated into formative assessment frameworks increased metacognitive awareness among secondary school learners, suggesting that neurofeedback may support—not replace—interpretive pedagogy when implemented with clear ethical boundaries. These findings collectively point to an emerging research direction focused on harmonizing computational intelligence and cognitive state modelling for pedagogical enhancement.

The addition of AGI and BCIs then reshapes established positions in learning ethics by reinterpreting questions about cognitive justice, learner agency, and epistemic trust. Although earlier literature noted limited exploration of educational BCI challenges, recent work has increasingly addressed issues of neural privacy, data manipulation risks, and cognitive-state misinterpretation. A report from UNESCO (2023) notes that although some jurisdictions—such as South Korea and the European Union—have initiated pilot programs guided by ethical governance mechanisms, the global landscape remains largely reactive and fragmented in this regard. This regulatory gap has allowed corporate entities to define the terms of AGI–BCI integration with minimal participatory frameworks or socio-cultural alignment. Such an imbalance in governance involves more than practical implementation difficulties; it risks fostering and entrenching neurocapitalism and amplifying privilege. These ethical ambiguities influence public policy and governance and challenge the fundamental assumptions underlying educational systems, including models of formal education in the context of AGI–BCI convergence.

Building on the preceding discussion of technological trajectories, the following section outlines how AGI–BCI convergence reshapes foundational assumptions in learning sciences. AGI–BCI ecosystems offer a radical redefinition of cognition as distributed, interactive (Ridley, 2010) and synthetic (Bayne & Jandrić, 2017), while behaviorist and constructivist approaches highlight environmental stimuli and social interaction. This conceptual shift aligns with posthumanist educational frameworks that view cognition as relational and distributed. However, it remains debated by many who view human learning as a form of sociality or a norm that cannot be replaced. These ethical considerations suggest that the frameworks we create for using these technologies depend on more than instrumental rationality. Bioethical issues surrounding access to enhancement, human agency, and distributive justice (Bostrom & Sandberg, 2009) resonate across educational fields, calling for a normative framework that is transparent, consensual, and inclusive.

Moreover, while many constraints exist, infrastructure remains a significant barrier, especially in low- and middle-income countries, where limited basic access hinders initial interaction with these technologies. Without equity-focused design, the AGI–BCI pipeline risks creating enclaves of exclusion and establishing a technocratic elite at the expense of the broader population. International guidance increasingly promotes open standards, multi-stakeholder governance, and culturally responsive educational models. Importantly, this does not mean dismissing these technologies outright or implementing them without question, but instead engaging in more informed, ongoing discussions about their use in developing equitable, reflective educational systems that prepare educators for the future.

To integrate these diverse strands of analysis coherently, each subsequent section of this chapter builds progressively from conceptual foundations toward applied governance and pedagogical implications. This sequencing clarifies how AGI–BCI technologies shift from theoretical constructs to real-world educational challenges, and why ethical considerations, infrastructural readiness, and global policy disparities must be evaluated as part of a single analytical continuum (NeurotechEU, 2022).

2. PROBLEM STATEMENT

Education, in theory, should encourage an approach and understanding that are more fair, thoughtful, and human, but with the potential for AGI and BCIs to converge, this becomes more complicated. Although personalized cognition and neuro-adaptive instruction are promising concepts for educational technology, empirical support remains scarce, culture-bound, and less than "perfectly" embedded. But there are still gaps, especially in areas such as ethical governance, cognitive equity, data sovereignty, and teacher preparedness. The implementation is also rendered more complicated by the differences in context and scale in the Global North and South. To engage with these contradictions between potential and dignity, this study offers a speculative moral framework through which futurists and policymakers can navigate a path between techno-futuristic potential and human dignity, thereby better crafting our future educational pathways in a more ethically mindful way.

3. OBJECTIVES

- To critically examine the pedagogical, ethical, and epistemological implications of integrating AGI and BCIs into contemporary educational systems across diverse global contexts.
- To identify and evaluate the policy, infrastructural, and cultural gaps that hinder equitable access to AGI and BCI technologies

4. THE TECHNOLOGICAL LANDSCAPE: AGI AND BCIS IN EDUCATION

The distinction between AGI and narrow AI is fundamental to developing intelligent systems. Unlike an evolutionary improvement in computation, AGI is seen as a qualitatively different type of epistemic agent capable of abstraction, self-regulation, and cross-domain generalization (Goertzel, 2014). While narrow AI models excel at specific tasks, AGI aims for a unified cognitive architecture similar to human reasoning; therefore, the scope of automation that these agents can achieve in educational environments is significantly expanded.

Unlike current adaptive systems, AGI can generate courses, remix teaching methods, and customize instruction based on students' emotional and cognitive profiles. Unlike algorithmic tutors that work within fixed constraints, AGI systems might engage in pedagogical reasoning, adapt instructional content to evolving learner paths, and make general inferences about educational needs. For instance, empirical deployments at MIT and Tsinghua University show improved knowledge retention and critical thinking; however, initial results also reveal a decline in peer learning, potentially weakening collaborative educational cultures (Zhou et al., 2023).

At the same time, a new technology—based on neurotechnological tools—introduces a second path for educational change: Brain-Computer Interfaces (BCIs). BCIs aim to incorporate cognitive modulation into teaching by influencing attention, working memory, and emotional states through real-time analysis of neurophysiological activity. For example, using affordable, non-invasive EEG devices like NeuroSky and Emotiv in South Korea and China may be a practical step toward developing neuro-informational learning environments. These systems provide teachers with metrics on neuro-engagement, but ethical reviews criticize their interference with learner autonomy and mental health. In Israel and Denmark, research-focused neurofeedback cycles targeting dyslexic and neurodivergent students have shown measurable improvements in reading and math skills (Dresp-Langley, 2022). However, the long-term success of these innovations will depend on strong ethical protections and clear pedagogical principles.

With AGI and BCI, cognition ceases to be just an internal monologue and instead becomes a complex interaction between neural inputs and fully operational synthetic reasoning systems. In such a setup, AGI will receive input from the BCI and adjust its output instructions in real time. At the same time, BCI sensors communicate with AGI about learner receptivity, frustration, or overload to guide decision-making. While this interaction provides a level of personalization that is impossible in traditional classrooms, it also depends on another entity that might hinder metacognitive development. Additionally, the private sector continually gathers increasingly detailed neural and behavioral data, raising concerns about data monopolies and the commodification of thought.

Proof-of-concept studies at institutions such as ETH Zürich and Kyoto University demonstrate the practicality of this quasi-symbiotic learning framework, including emotion-adaptive variational structure-property matching and curiosity management across both the BCI output and input pathways. However, systems like these challenge traditional constructivist learning theories that focus on social mediation and linguistic interaction by placing algorithmic inference and neuro-optimization at the core of the learning process. Although cognitivism remains prevalent beyond biological and technical boundaries, posthumanist digital epistemology thinkers remind us that the infrastructure enabling digital cognition is layered with asymmetries of power and access (Bayne & Jandrić, 2017). Since AGI–BCI systems could do much more than current control models allow, their integration is no longer solely a technical issue; policies must be aligned to ensure that the development of these capabilities translates into social practices that promote equity, moral acceptability, and educational coherence.

With these technologies still in their early stages, the education paradigm shifts from teaching concepts to developing skills. Instead of merely transmitting information, your instructional model should transition to one of discernment, where learners and educators explore and question systems that foster thought and agency over time. This calls for or requires multi-disciplinary, cross-sector governance that integrates values of equity, transparency, and cultural sensitivity into system design. AGI and BCIs are not attractive because of their technological complexity—the real appeal lies in the ability of training institutions to engage with them thoughtfully, resist the temptation to see them as just tools, and maintain a degree of normative epistemic diversity in education.

5. ETHICAL CONSIDERATIONS: SPECULATIVE MORALITY IN NEURAL FUTURES

This section synthesizes ethical questions that emerge directly from the technological capacities outlined earlier, showing how cognitive data extraction, neuro-adaptive personalization, and algorithmic autonomy intersect with concerns about agency, privacy, and distributive justice (Yuste et al., 2017).

Before examining specific ethical concerns, it is essential to clarify that AGI–BCI convergence introduces a dual transformation: the externalization of cognitive processes through synthetic reasoning and the internalization of educational monitoring through neural sensing. This dual shift creates a unique moral terrain in which agency, interpretation, and neuro-rights must be viewed as interdependent rather than isolated considerations (Ienca & Andorno, 2017).

The introduction of AGI and BCIs in education pushes the field into uncharted ethical territory, raising numerous unresolved questions about shared values as educators contend with cognitive, autonomy, and surveillance concerns in classrooms. A common topic is the so-called "cognitive enhancement" debate. While therapeutic interventions aim to address deviations from normal functioning, enhancement exists in a vague evaluative space influenced by social and cultural hierarchies of what is considered ideal and by widespread access to economic resources. The key question is, who decides what constitutes "improvement"? Although BCIs may provide educational benefits, such as enhancing memory or attention, the decision to adopt this technology in education will likely be made by institutions rather than individual students. This raises important questions about bodily autonomy, especially for children. Discussions on neuroethics emphasize the need for a meaningful model of informed consent that moves beyond legalistic definitions and instead promotes dialogue, engagement, and ongoing reflection (Ienca & Andorno, 2017).

AGI also plays a role in creating educational materials, which presents another challenge. This independence offers a level of flexibility in instructional design that your informal museum design career has never experienced, but it also introduces epistemic risks. AGI systems may be trained on datasets that embed their own cognitive biases or cultural assumptions into models of popularity, and then select, curate, and deliver curriculum content based on those predictive models. This, of course, raises concerns about the diminishing of critical thinking, where an entire generation of learners might passively consume whatever content their algorithms, which are often not fully understood by humans, produce. The relationship between teachers and students could also be affected; if an educator relies on these machines to handle the core teaching tasks, they may become less of a facilitator of inquiry and more of a supervisor of machine-led instruction — turning human teachers into shadows of their former selves, which could undermine relational and dialogic pedagogies tied to creativity and moral agency (Knox, 2020).

The second moral concern relates to the privacy of dosing and diagnosis data. Since BCIs directly interface with neural information, they can access data—unlike traditional digital footprints—that may reveal preconscious emotional and cognitive states. This potential for data collection, commodification, or behavioral surveillance is not hypothetical. Initiatives in China and the U.S. have tested BCI classroom monitoring systems to track attention (Yuste et al., 2017), drawing criticism from privacy advocates. Meanwhile, AGI systems combined with biometrics might evolve into predictive tools that identify learning issues and forecast behavioral patterns, blurring the line between education and surveillance.

Such developments reveal a deeper philosophical conflict between technological empowerment and human will. As more learning is mediated and shaped through systems that sense, anticipate, and customize, the focus on individual educational agency gradually shifts. Are students truly learning, or being programmed to meet the expectations of automation? This question becomes even more urgent when AGI-BCI systems guide learners toward particular cognitive or behavioral profiles deemed "ideal." The opaque nature of such techno-educational governance might be a form of biopower. However, one remains truly concealed, turning education into a tool for population management, controlling the (human) population through datafication and neuro-optimization. This raises important questions about the principles of educational freedom regarding access and choice, cognitive autonomy, and neuro-rights.

To understand these speculative frontiers, fiction has evolved beyond mere entertainment; it has become an epistemic critique. Setting aside the discussion of embodiment in the genre, the cognitive surveillance in "1984" echoes the speculative depiction of neuro-enhanced learning in "Diaspora." These narratives offer heuristic cautionary tales rather than direct predictions about interactivity: when minds meet machines, how do identity, liberty, and authenticity endure? Similarly, Bostrom's "brain-in-a-vat" hypothesis and Dennett's "Cartesian theater" thought experiments challenge determinism regarding mind and consciousness, prompting ethicists to examine what technologies can do and the implications they carry from a utilitarian perspective.

Speculative ethics involves ethical reasoning based on hypothetical futures. This work advocates shifting from reactive regulation to anticipatory governance — one informed by interdisciplinary insights into construction and driven by marginalized communities' aspirations. While speculative frameworks have inspired people to adopt a critical stance toward sound education systems, they also raise meaningful questions about the consequences of our actions and what we should pursue beyond creating intelligent, just, productive, and liberating educational futures.

New work in neuro-rights governance emphasizes that educational neurotechnologies require additional safeguards because cognitive-state inference is becoming increasingly precise. Reports by the NeuroRights Foundation (2024) argue that emerging BCIs can predict learning attentiveness with up to 87% accuracy, raising concerns about pre-emptive classification of learners and potential misuse in high-stakes academic settings. Meanwhile, Kim & Harada (2023) highlight that AGI tools used in classrooms increasingly rely on biometric–neural datasets for personalization, underscoring the urgency of developing enforceable standards that prevent covert data extraction or algorithmic manipulation.

6 CONCEPTUAL AND THEORETICAL FRAMEWORKS: AGI, BCIS, AND MORALITY

Having established the ethical tensions surrounding AGI–BCI applications, the next step is to consider which theoretical models best explain how these technologies interact with learning, cognition, and institutional structures. These frameworks provide the conceptual scaffolding needed to interpret policy gaps and governance failures observed globally (Feenberg, 1999).

This section maps how existing pedagogical and ethical theories can be extended to interpret AGI–BCI convergence. The integration of AGI and BCIs will navigate boundaries established by Worden (2017) and KJ and KG (2018). By enabling direct communication between brain neuroelectrical activity and the external environment, BCIs transform cognition from a qualitative, personal experience into an accessible, modifiable input and a quantifiable metric. This shifts the understanding, measurement, and thought regulation within institutional contexts. Such changes carry profound neuroethical implications, especially regarding the often blurry boundary between treatment and enhancement, which remains unclear in many implementation models.

Critically, ethical assessments should not be limited to the role of such tools, but rather engage with the institutional contexts in which they are used—contexts often defined by unequal power dynamics between policy-driven goals and the agency of the learner, especially when the latter is a child or belongs to a socioeconomically disadvantaged group (Ienca & Andorno, 2017). From state-endorsed EEG monitoring programs in parts of East Asia to commercially driven pilots in the U.S., ideological differences in BCI governance reveal the problem with applying a universal ethical standard when it fails to fit specific contexts. This highlights the need for a nuanced, context-aware ethics approach that recognizes how sociopolitical and cultural factors influence cognitive rights, bodily integrity, and the extent of data autonomy individuals can exercise.

At the same time, the logic of boosting productivity that supports BCIs conflicts with commitments to neurodiversity and inclusive teaching when BCI technologies align with these goals. Measuring attention, engagement, and neural efficiency—part of the focus on metrics—could also lead us to reify a specific view of normal cognition, marginalizing neurodivergent learners whose cognitive profiles differ from these optimization standards. This concern is extreme in education systems—like those in Singapore or France—where success on high-stakes metrics is linked to national development goals, tempting neurotechnology to standardize behaviors.

As neural data collection becomes more detailed, education is also being monitored and shaped to align with institutional goals. However, this risks replacing learner agency with behavior influenced by design choices. Most plug-and-play neural activation methods developed by private tech companies are unclear about how they set parameters and interpret neural signals. Unlike diversity metrics, they do not include various cognitive frameworks. This raises important questions about what constitutes an 'orthodox' way of thinking, which neurology is prioritized over others, and how power relationships shape the design, use, and regulation of these tools. These theoretical concerns complement others raised about research accountability and distance learning, emphasizing the need for models of participatory governance that bring together learners, educators, and neuroethicists to develop calibration protocols, interpretation standards, and data governance guidelines.

Integrating AGI into education introduces a new set of normative concerns, yet related to those already present. While AGI systems enable dynamic content creation, modification of instructions, and real-time feedback, their inference structures are often opaque. They rely on probabilistic models based on data that frequently carry privileged linguistic, cultural, and epistemic assumptions. Countries like India, Brazil, or South Africa—where the education system becomes a battleground of epistemological conflict between local traditions and global paradigms—could genuinely face epistemic dislocation if AGI systems are mainly trained on Anglophone or Eurocentric datasets. These systems might fail to grasp certain types of contextualized argumentation, misinterpret local syntactic structures, or mistake pedagogical nuances for disturbances, masking them as superficial literacy issues in personalized feedback.

Mediating access and understanding through AGI-enabled education appears to consolidate or even distribute epistemic ladders by making knowledge accessible to all. This underscores that the design of educational AGI cannot overlook epistemic justice: we must ensure that training data is more diverse and that mechanisms for contextualization and interpretability are in place. Educators must be prepared to deploy these systems and to critique, interpret, redesign, and challenge the responses to ensure that such outputs serve as meaningful inputs into the curriculum, rooted in learners' lived experiences. Without this interpretive agency, teachers risk being seen merely as providers of computer-generated content, which diminishes professional judgment and further marginalizes the context.

These layers of human understanding can further clarify the ethical questions raised by AGI–BCI convergence by developing theoretical frameworks that guide empirical research on adopting educational technology. Technological determinism is common in policy rhetoric in places like the UAE and Estonia, and it holds that progress is an autonomous train moving along the tracks of time, ignoring concerns about pedagogical suitability or cultural and institutional readiness.

By contrast, social constructivist views define technology as socially constructed through social practices, institutional cultures, and ongoing stakeholder negotiations. You can see that this perspective is clearer in educational settings such as Finland and Costa Rica. Deliberative and iterative mechanisms introduce AGI and BCIs to facilitate cultural mediation and pedagogical contextualization. Conversely, post-humanist theory expands the analytical scope by challenging human-centered ideas of cognition, presenting a view of distributed knowledge creation co-constructed by learners, machines, environments, and symbolic systems (Luckin et al, 2016). Hyper- and post-humanisms: A potential future Human-machine systems could, in theory, converge with AGI–BCI, but post-humanist perspectives are politically and ethically controversial in many regions where educational policies continue to emphasize human agency, autonomy, and moral responsibility as core human values. Such tensions exist in Canada and Australia, where strong opposition to machine-driven pedagogy echoes broader concerns about replacing the relational, ethical, and developmental aspects of teaching.

These developments can be evaluated using normative political theories—tools that help go beyond purely positive descriptions. For example, a Rawlsian justice model, which focuses on reducing inequality, would suggest that AGI–BCI technologies be developed and implemented specifically to benefit the least well-educated. However, trends observed in Latin America, where AGI tools are concentrated within elite institutions, suggest that without regulation, these technologies may reinforce rather than address inequality. The Capability Approach offers an ethical framework of an alternative kind, emphasizing not test scores but what learners are or could become, placing importance on adaptability, autonomy, and respect for contextual differences rather than standardized metrics. Such an approach aligns with an ethics of design that prioritizes adaptability, learner choice, and expanding pedagogical diversity over strict adherence to optimization logic.

Developmental theories also provide rich insights. Neuroadaptive tools will also challenge Piaget's model of cognitive growth, as each stage is defined by increasingly complex tasks that can only be engaged at the next stage. However, these challenges especially raise questions about socio-emotional development, as cognitive acceleration could outpace socio-emotional growth at some point. Such temporal disjunctions may lead to the performance-focused learners we seek, with their mix of skills and capacities disconnected from relational or affective coherence.

The sociocultural model of learning proposed by Vygotsky emphasizes the importance of social mediation and culturally meaningful tools (including cognitive tools, which are intentionally designed to facilitate learning) and offers a more suitable framework for AGI-BCI alignment, as it allows the inclusion of artificial agents as part of instructional support. The risk is that these supports might become substitutes instead of complements to the relational aspects of dialogic learning that are critically needed. BCIs are often justified by neuroplasticity, but they must be used carefully, considering the developmental, neurodivergent, and socio-political variability in plasticity. Relying heavily on neural feedback can hinder the development of internal motivation systems, leading students to respond solely to tracking signals rather than being self-motivated.

Risk-focused policy responses to AGI–BCI integration vary greatly in ambition and regulatory maturity. Although the European Union has issued major ethical guidelines for AI in education, there is no regulatory framework for BCIs. South Korea has targeted neurotechnology domestically and internationally as part of its digital sovereignty strategy. In comparison, while research in the US is funded and studies of neural technology in schools are underway, it lacks a unified governance of neural data use in educational settings.

In countries like Brazil and Indonesia, where public institutions are fragile, the edtech landscape is dominated by private actors operating in a regulatory void that fails to protect learners. This raises an equity issue: when AGI models do not support the languages and structures that students in underrepresented language groups are familiar with, their chances to engage meaningfully are significantly reduced. BCI infrastructure remains expensive and logistically inaccessible for many low-income or rural communities. Early signs of such international collaborations are evident in efforts such as those supported by GPAI and Horizon Europe, which, unfortunately, still view engagement with BCIs as marginal. There are bilateral initiatives, such as localizing AGI platforms in India through India–Finland projects. However, these are limited in scope and lack mechanisms to integrate them fully into the broader system.

These AGI–BCI systems revolutionize classroom interactions, teachers' roles, and learners' experiences. These promises already show results on AGI-driven reinforcement learning platforms for student groups with executive function challenges. At the same time, early detection tools based on BCI are being tested to identify students with learning disabilities and provide, or even train for, support services. However, these advances also raise serious ethical concerns about data management, privacy, and psychological autonomy. Neural data were once protected from much ethical scrutiny—because they were thought difficult to access—but now, this data circulates within institutions with little consent or protections, especially given the vulnerabilities of child learners. The educational use of algorithmic and neural data outputs is skyrocketing, while few professional development programs prepare teachers to interpret and respond to these outputs ethically. Automated content delivery, neuro-monitored engagement, and facilitated reflective practices in hybrid classrooms could normalize intrusive surveillance practices under the guise of personalized learning.

Resistances, such as those of the parents of France and Canada, point out that this erodes the character of education. However, the broader critique across interdisciplinary research cautions that, in the view of education as 'humanizing data', learners become data subjects and teaching operates as system management. An outlook of this nature would contradict what is ethical, relational, and cerebral about education; it risks commodifying cognition and pedagogy, robbing them of the agency to teach. We desperately need anticipatory governance models, including independent oversight bodies, participatory design protocols, and the formal enshrinement of cognitive and neural rights. In a time of remembering that human beings have moral subjectivities that develop and display through the conditions we endure and act upon, the prioritization must come from not allowing for the instrumentalization of an education that enables critical thought, at a time when the logic of the liking-machine technology overtakes every other horizon of possibility. Education cannot simply warehouse potentially educated minds into capital structures; it has to preserve its core rationality.

7. GLOBAL PERSPECTIVES AND MULTINATIONAL CONTEXT: POLICY, GOVERNANCE, AND IMPLEMENTATION

A coherent policy analysis requires distinguishing between technological adoption and governance maturity; many countries have embraced AGI–BCI tools without developing the regulatory architectures necessary to safeguard cognitive autonomy or epistemic pluralism (OECD, 2024).

These diverse governance trajectories underscore the earlier theoretical claim that technological adoption is shaped not only by capability but by sociopolitical values and institutional logics, which determine how AGI–BCI tools are operationalized across national systems (UNESCO, 2023b).

The integration of AGI and BCIs into PWCs occurs across a comparative global governance landscape of asymmetric regulation, strategic foresight, and normative regime. While the EU recently embraced an ambitious supranational framework—the Artificial Intelligence Act (2021)—based mainly on risk-based regulation and protections for human agency, the Act excludes all forms of neurocognitive or neurotechnologies. This suggests a glaring regulatory lacuna at the intersection of cognition and computation.

Developed within a state-led developmental framework, the second scenario sees China pursuing AGI and BCI while permitting EEG-based classroom interventions that enhance a technocratic rationality prioritizing behavioral efficiency over participatory ethics. By contrast, in the U.S., we have followed a decentralized model: the federal interest in AI in education, but leaving oversight of core education governance to the myriad state and local, as well as private, entities. In a somewhat ironic twist, the National Education Policy 2020 (National Education Policy, 2020) in India lumps neurotechnologies out of its account of AI and learning even as a vibrant and fragmented edtech sector seems to be inducing a kind of moral panic over algorithmic personalization of learning in the absence of any well-defined public regulation.

Most international ethical frameworks for AI are not legally binding: UNESCO's guidelines for AI in Education and the OECD's recommendations on child-centric systems highlight the values of inclusion, transparency, and equity, but do not specify quotas or benchmarks to achieve them, and national adoption is often uneven. The two approaches diverge and articulate tensions in the context of epistemic sovereignty, digital justice, and infrastructural inequality. AGI models pose a risk, as most of the data used to train these models derives from Global North contexts, thereby reproducing an epistemological universalism that could displace indigenous pedagogies and marginalize reasoning systems grounded in local contexts.

In response to this new challenge, emerging multilateral collaborations such as the European Commission's Horizon Europe and the NeurotechEU alliance are integrating AI ethics, cognitive neuroscience, and digital pedagogy within a cross-sectoral research framework. WG1 on AI & AGI for Education — As part of its initiatives, the Global Partnership on Artificial Intelligence (GPAI) has established working groups to analyze the educational implications of AGI, though BCI governance remains on the sidelines of GPAI discussions (Baylor et al., 2022; Pho et al.,

2022). Bilateral projects such as the India–Finland project for localization of AGI and the Canada–Japan initiative on AI demonstrate efforts to adapt technological design to different educational contexts. However, resource disparities and institutional imbalances still hinder implementation.

Intercultural mediated e-learning experiences. The AGI-mediated transnational telecasting and speechmaking deaf facilities, where BCI use is piloted (such as the speechmaking deaf appliance in Louisiana), point toward the mediatization and introduction of a paradigm of technologically mediated intercultural move subsumption activity. Still, doubts remain about how we interpret neurodata and how we rarely seem to check our cultural imperialism at the lab door. Most immediate epistemological and governance differences between jurisdictions — particularly between individualist and collectivist policy cultures — add significant complications to standard-setting and render proposed uniform regulatory solutions ineffective. Such tools require contextual information to be effective, and the international transfer of AGI–BCI tools lacks this, generating pedagogical incoherence and cultural dissonance.

Recent cross-regional analyses provide further insight into developing policy asymmetries. A 2024 OECD comparative review found that while Nordic countries lead in transparency-driven AI governance, countries across Southeast Asia have adopted BCI-enabled monitoring systems without equivalent ethical audits, creating disparities in protections against cognitive surveillance (OECD, 2024). Likewise, Alemu & Mensah (2023) document that AGI deployments in sub-Saharan Africa rely heavily on externally built systems that are not optimized for local epistemologies, resulting in diminished cultural alignment and pedagogical misinterpretation.

Furthermore, international governance structures often lack the necessary jurisdiction or operational resources to enforce compliance locally. Digital education strategies are beginning to develop within regional groups like ASEAN and the African Union, but AGI or BCI oversight is largely absent across Germany and beyond. The global science community remains increasingly divided, with powerful institutions in the industrialized North dominating the normative and technical agendas at the expense of the Global South, whose institutions still rely on external platforms.

This calls for a shift from static regulatory models to a model in which governance increasingly relies on dynamically managed co-design, adapting principles of subsidiarity, procedural justice, and pluralistic epistemologies. We are beginning to see examples of this participatory regulation, such as the Ethics-by-Design pilot in Denmark and the civic deliberation protocol for neurotechnologies in Uruguay, which could act as promising prototypes. However, the call for an International Convention on Cognitive Data Rights is growing as countries' policy readiness indices emerge. It is hard to see how we will be able to sustain AGI–BCI integration in education on a pluralist and humanistic basis without such foresight and, by extension, how we will ensure cool AGI–BCI integration that animates education with the potential for subversion rather than development, consolidating capitalism and amplifying power.

8. PRACTICAL IMPACTS: REAL-WORLD APPLICATIONS, STRATEGIES, AND INNOVATIONS

AGI and BCIs convergence in education will be a watershed moment in the history of pedagogical practices, a transition from static linear content delivery to a responsive dynamic process of learning mediated through measurement of neural responses and algorithmic predictions the use of instructional algorithms." - With a host of AGI advances, learning platforms now eclipse the narrow reach of traditional AI to become systems that successfully measure success, calibrate challenge, and co-construct cognitive pathways via predictive modeling, emotional attunement, and dialogic simulation. Squirrel AI in China and MATHia in the US use reinforcement learning algorithms to continuously find the optimal instruction sequence in real-time.

However, they are important for process efficiency and shifting pedagogical agency: learners must be redefined from passive recipients to active agents in a system that dynamically rebalances through metacognitive feedback. In higher education, AGI-driven tutors that learn learner states have been implemented at institutions such as MIT and Tsinghua University, where they incorporate cognitive load management and multimodal content synchronization. Overall, the multilingual AGI systems used in Abu Dhabi for migrant learner support exemplify how personalization can combine curricular fidelity with linguistic diversity.

Nonetheless, these affordances create tensions. Split pedagogy risks isolating learners from peers, as limited peer-to-peer dialogue reduces opportunities for a dialogic level of engagement, which is increasingly important in a world of more individualized learning (Bisaillon et al., 2019). However, BCIs complicate this landscape by shifting the focus of educational feedback from behavioral proxies to immediate neural metrics. FocusCalm and Emotiv devices convert electroencephalographic signals into measures of attention, emotional arousal, or fatigue, which can potentially serve as a basis for adjusting instruction based on inferred cognitive states.

Studies in Denmark, Israel, and South Korea have accumulated evidence that neurofeedback may facilitate attention regulation in neurodiverse individuals. However, an environment is still needed to nurture this in the pedagogical interpretation of those clues. This is where the danger comes in: diffracting cognitive complexity down to observable outcomes, neural activity, rather than the relational and emotional ground of learning. While they offer immediate insights, brain-computer interfaces (BCIs) also raise a range of novel and pressing ethical concerns regarding data ownership, informed consent, and the proliferation of biometric surveillance in educational environments. Most importantly, the solution may displace self-regulatory skills by relying on externally driven neural interventions to replace self-regulatory motivation, perhaps causing students to lose metacognitive self-determination.

We are to understand that this changing role of educators in AGI-BCI-embedded classrooms is framed within this context of this all-superseding re-structuring. Teachers are no longer curators of content but rather facilitators of meaning-making in environments mediated by synthetic cognition. As real-time classrooms emerge, where education technology solutions produce or prepackage unique pedagogical experiences, educators — through trial and error — have become more adept at interpreting algorithmic recommendations, bridging the gap between what technology creates (intentionally or unintentionally) and their pedagogical values, and preserving epistemic coherence. The method for shifting from didactic teaching to interpretive stewardship, exemplified by models from Taiwan and Brazil, involved enhancing flipped learning through neuro-monitoring of curiosity and fatigue.

However, such a repositioning assumes a level of technological savvy and ethical literacy that are rarely, if ever, provided in teacher preparation programs. Specific skills for understanding inter-individual variability, signal artifacts, and socio-emotional context are necessary to interpret neural data; however, developing these skills requires a fundamental overhaul of professional development curricula. The best practices in curriculum integration emphasize democratic deliberation, disciplinary versatility, and institutional reflexivity. Finland demonstrates that technological sophistication combined with pedagogical humanism is achievable if AGI is incorporated into formative assessment frameworks through participatory consultation.

Globally, however, implementation remains inconsistent. Successful classroom pilots occur in South Korea or Singapore within a structured, ethical framework. At the same time, large portions of the Global South are effectively excluded from AGI–BCI experimentation due to a lack of infrastructure and regulatory capacity to fully assess the medium- to long-term impacts locally. Governance varies greatly depending on context: the EU's ethics-by-design mandates differ greatly from China's use of neurotech. U.S. charter networks seem to operate with little regulation in edtech experiments. While fragmentation persists, emerging collaborative frameworks documented in 2023–2024 indicate a growing international effort to harmonize AGI–BCI governance and technical standards.

In short, this leads us to suggest a shift toward greater technical effectiveness, the establishment of enforceable neuro-rights, the development of standard-setting mechanisms, and the alteration of epistemic authority over knowledge and facts that cross global and institutional boundaries. All of these are essential for the ethical governance of neural synthetic systems. The sustainable adoption of AGI and BCIs should be guided not by proxies for innovation uptake but by a social justice-informed normative preservation of education as a space for critical inquiry, democratic participation, and cognitive liberation as an effort in interpretative pluralism.

9. COUNTER-ARGUMENTS AND CONTROVERSIES: THE DARK SIDE OF NEURAL FUTURES

Complex opposition to integrating Artificial General Intelligence (AGI) with Brain–Computer Interfaces (BCIs) draws on technophobia and specific concerns about epistemic autonomy, relational integrity, and cognition in human–machine interactions. In Canada, where Indigenous knowledge systems have been maintained, and in India, where tribal learning ecosystems are diverse, the standardizing tendencies associated with AGI could pose a fundamental threat to the varied epistemologies of local communities if education focuses solely on cultural transmission. Such tendencies might even risk imposing learning roles that displace local cognitive cultures essential for maintaining specific livelihood patterns, adapting to temporality, and shaping the nature of cognitive disciplines. AGI often emphasizes adaptive personalization and epistemological centralization (replacing pedagogical diversity with scalable, algorithmic models), further solidifying this resistance.

In pedagogical cultures focused on dialogic and relational learning—both inside and outside school settings, such as in Finland and New Zealand—teachers have expressed primary concerns about the artificialization of emotional processes and the loss of empathic exchanges as AGI takes over, which guides the instruction feedback loops and dulls them to human feelings. Similar concerns are raised in the highly technologized environments of Singapore and South Korea, indicating that—even in the most advanced high-tech setups—the emotional disconnection and weakening of teaching quality remain significant threats. This also presents a new challenge: this approach to improving learning has not yet been fully conceptualized or analyzed with respect to consent and data sovereignty, specifically, regarding whether cognitive surveillance can be justified, posing a different kind of threat to the authenticity of education and students' sense of agency.

In contrast, countries like China have used trialing BCI with school students as a commercial enterprise, deploying it across different classroom settings. This has also sparked backlash over the ambiguous regulation of cerebral data and the potential control over the agency. This is troubling, especially in countries with a weaker rule of law than liberal democracies, where regulatory oversight of BCIs allows experimental technologies to be deployed in privately regulated educational institutions and often without transparent oversight of the technologies permitted to operate. Conventional AGI systems are still prone to epistemic bias in environments with diverse languages and cultures. For instance, in the complex political contexts of education in countries such as Belgium or South Africa, and given that AGI models are naturally trained on a typically Western corpus, it can reasonably be assumed that they will at least partially marginalize local idioms and misrepresent culturally embedded reasoning. This issue would be especially salient in assessment contexts.

At the same time, unequal access to BCI technologies worsens existing educational inequalities, as privileged students in enriched environments gain access to well-calibrated, high-fidelity neurofeedback. In contrast, devices with lower fidelity and less support for under-resourced learners create a cognitive-enhancement gap that challenges meritocratic ideals. More broadly, these developments mark an epistemic shift where cognitive effort is shaped by optimization populations, framing cognition as an input that can be measured within an educational production function. This drive for economization—especially evident in U.S. edtech markets and the rise of gamified engagement platforms in East Asia—reduces opportunities for serendipitous and voluntary learning.

This is where postcolonial critiques offer further insight, highlighting the forms of cognitive extraction that may occur through AGI–BCI implementations, in which the results of mental labor are either made invisible or handed over to transnational corporate entities. This points to an epistemic extraction of a replicative nature that deepens boundaries of epistemic independence, especially in Southern and Eastern Global regions such as Kenya and the Philippines. Skirt (2018) describes a version of loss of agency for teachers, in which interpretive judgment is replaced by algorithmic output, and teachers become merely executors of system directives. In short, this collection of concerns presents a complex critique of the AGI–BCI connection that ultimately advocates pluralism, contextual integrity, and pedagogical justice rather than techno-functional efficiency alone.

10. FUTURE DIRECTIONS AND THEORETICAL EXPLORATION

Drawing together the technological, ethical, theoretical, and geopolitical analyses presented across the chapter, the conclusion synthesizes how speculative morality can guide responsible AGI–BCI integration in education. The preceding sections show that coherent governance and pedagogical design depend on viewing these technologies as part of a unified cognitive infrastructure rather than isolated innovations.

As AGI and BCIs move beyond theory and into viable educational products by the end of the 2030s, the future of neural technology will necessitate a complete rethink of how learning is structured. Instead, the situation is resolved: these technologies will affect education, and public policy should focusscar on steering their integration towards inclusive, equitable, and ethically viable objectives. A tech-optimist perspective has cast this transition as a supposed outcome of economic determinism.

However, the analysis seeks to overturn that notion by providing a multinational perspective on how the arrival of AGI and BCI in education will ultimately depend not only on technological momentum but also on governance, design, and values.

10.1 A Vision for Ethically-Driven Educational Futures

We should have a more grounded education system, rather than technocratic utilitarianism and surveillance serving as the foundational principles of an AGI and BCI education system. More fundamentally, it would center epistemic dignity and learner agency instead of optimization metrics. In this model of society, BCIs would not be used as apparatuses for surveilling adherence or coercing outcomes. However, they would instead accommodate individual preferences for learning rates, neurodiversity, and mental wellness. Similarly, AGI would not replace teachers but rather support dialogic inquiry by contextualised scaffolding of their cognition, while keeping it interpretable and contestable.

This ideal system would also enshrine an anti-extractive approach to data governance. This would help move cognitive infrastructure closer to home, avoiding epistemic asymmetries and keeping memories—potentially the most intimate human data—under collective or sovereign control. The AGI models would be pedagogical and transparent, their reasoning available to any teacher or learner, their architecture designed to provide an answer as easily as to deny one, thereby allowing for reflection. Both forms of this ethical literacy — cognitive and technological — would be a staple of the curricula, neither a stand-alone module but a meta-competency embedded in every discipline.

10.2 Breakthroughs on the Horizon: Expanding the Technological Pipeline

At the forefront, progressive AGI reasoning abilities and responsive BCIs mark a transformative crossroads. The approach has led to breakthroughs in human-centric research, whereby one of the leading efforts—embodied AGI—delivers more than just semantic output from the input, interacting with a learner through an open-ended multimodal channel, responding verbally, via gesture, and even virtual embodiment, much like the ways a human tutor would interact with a learner. Early experiments, such as Google DeepMind's Gato and Meta's CAIRaoke, have made advances toward this, but both still suffer from contextual brittleness and lack of decision explainability.

Simultaneously, advanced BCIs are moving from electroencephalography (EEG) to fully closed-loop optogenetic interfaces and nanoscale neural networks (or the so-called neural mesh). Such interfaces might enable more accurate and less intrusive readings of cognitive–emotional states. While they have primarily been developed in clinical and laboratory settings, their evolution suggests a future of unobtrusive, ecological cognitive feedback systems in educational settings. Such systems would track expressions of frustration, boredom, curiosity, and cognitive load, allowing for immediate, real-time pedagogical responses. However, in a context with few ethical guardrails, such advances threaten to recycle affect as a form of behavioral control.

We are even seeing Prototypes of AGI-BCI Fusion Systems for education. For example, neural-state-conditioned AGI agents with increased syntax developed by a research team at ETH Zurich alter the sophistication of instructions during execution. They use interaction data, neural attention, and indicators of confusion and fatigue to determine the learner's readiness. Such a convergence might give rise to 'neuroadaptive pedagogy', in which humans and AI that understand us come together to create content for an instructional model.

10.3 Governing the Future: Toward Responsible Innovation

These technologies' unprecedented closeness to the human mind demands governance that exceeds typical edtech regulation. Governance must prevent harm, define limits on technology use, and establish enforceable rights to cognitive sovereignty. A notable proposal is the formal recognition of the so-called "neuro-rights" (Yuste et al., 2017), which include rights to mental privacy, cognitive liberty, and psychological integrity.

Likewise, the principle of procedural justice emphasizes that the design of neural educational tools should involve learners, educators, and communities as co-creators. It is not the tech oligarchs making decisions in sleek boardrooms but through participatory mechanisms of legitimacy, transparency, and responsiveness: citizens' assemblies, school councils, and transnational forums. For example, Denmark has the "Ethics-by-Design" pilot and public deliberation protocols for BCI deployment in Uruguay. This contrasts with Chinese classroom surveillance guided by EEG, which bypasses ethical pluralism to optimize for a state-defined goal.

10.4 Multidisciplinarity as Imperative: Co-Designing with Diversity

Engineers and entrepreneurs cannot manage ethical approaches to integrating AGI and BCIs into education on their own. It requires a multidisciplinary ecosystem in which neuroethicists, educators, developmental psychologists, sociologists, technologists, and policymakers collaborate to anticipate and respond to future developments. None of these roles is more important than the others: ethicists challenge normative assumptions others bring; educators address teaching and learning needs; technologists develop system features; and policymakers aim to align innovation with the public good.

Finally, these collaborative design efforts must be ongoing, continually revisiting decisions in light of changes in technologies, classrooms, and societies. Neural education tools differ from traditional practices because they cannot be limited by product life cycles — they must be managed throughout their implementation, usage, obsolescence, and archival. Accountability, transparency, and memory must be fundamentally integrated into system design.

10.5 Resisting Technological Determinism: Morality Beyond Utility

The least manageable challenge for the future of neural education is conceptual. The core issue concerns the very essence of teaching. Attractive ideas depict learning as optimization driven by AGI and BCIs, aimed at reducing affective friction, engagement, and cognition by externalizing these processes; however, such a vision risks undermining the fundamental purpose of education. Learning is not simply a mechanical process of skill acquisition but, as John Dewey argued, involves nurturing judgment, empathy, and reflective agency (Dewey, 1933).

Speculative morality provides a vital framework for viewing things this way. Instead of asking what happens to current applications, it asks: What kind of educational worlds do we want to create? Who has the right to imagine these future possibilities? Benenson addresses the audience by asking questions about what types of learners we are shaping and what we might be sacrificing, such as curiosity, skepticism, and dissent. More specifically, this suggests a form of speculative morality that extends beyond ideals, advocating a proactive ethic of refusal: rejecting certain technological implementations that reduce education's emotional or social richness, even if they could be more efficient. It also promotes a forward-thinking ethic of imagination: developing teaching methods that embrace cognitive diversity, cultural differences, and learner agency. Such systems could include AGI systems trained on decolonized data, BCIs tailored to neurodivergent needs, and platforms prioritizing interpretability over precision.

Speculative ethics also values slowness, uncertainty, and challenging, seemingly chaotic struggles. Our neural educational future might require holding onto many of these spaces of opacity, where not all thought is decoded and not all moments are optimized. Such spaces are not design flaws but refuges of human autonomy.

This convergence of AGI and BCIs in education is not a neutral development but a political, ethical, and ontological moment of change, which means that future directions must oppose accelerationism by default. Instead, these inquiries should foster the ethics of discrimination, reflexivity in how academia constructs meaning, and humility in how we continue to operate within academia. The shape of a just neural future in education will depend less on technical feasibility and more on the quality of our collective deliberation, the inclusiveness of our design practices, and the courage to prioritize human dignity over algorithmic accuracy.

Instead of a blueprint, we need a compass to guide us in a new direction—a direction that helps us evolve educational systems that are intelligent but not totalizing, adaptable but not overly controlling, and flexible but not disconnected from history. Only with such nuance can AGIs and BCIs serve as tools of liberation rather than control.

Recent studies also explore integrating large multimodal AGI systems with closed-loop neuroadaptive networks. Huang et al. (2024) describe prototypes where BCIs inform AGI-generated instructional pathways by modelling frustration, curiosity, and confusion states, enabling dynamically modulated lesson pacing. Though still experimental, these architectures demonstrate the feasibility of "cognitive-interactive classrooms," where pedagogical adaptation emerges from continuous human–machine feedback loops. Such systems also raise profound governance questions regarding transparency, bias propagation, and interpretability.

These tensions illustrate that technological capability alone cannot determine educational futures; what matters instead is the normative orientation that guides implementation, particularly in relation to equity, interpretability, and the preservation of learner agency.

11. META FRAMEWORK

Figure 1. AGI-BCI-Speculative Morality Education Framework

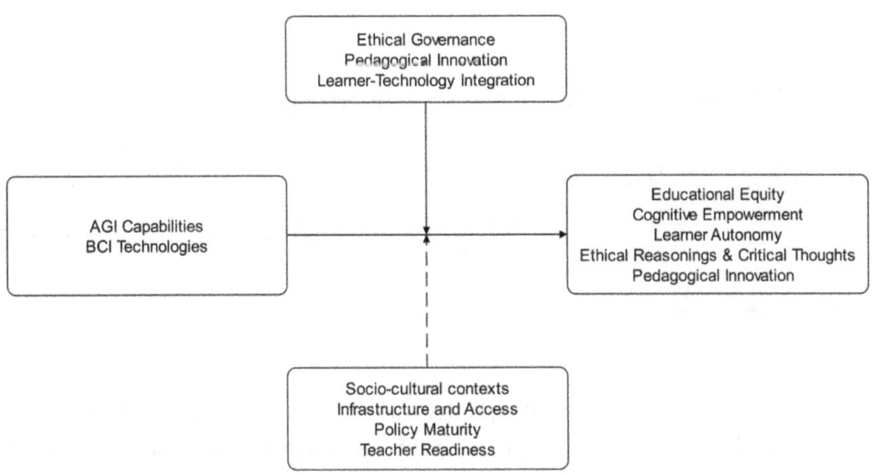

Source: *Authors*

The new educational paradigms call for a unified approach that combines technology R&D, ethical governance, educational theory, and practical implementation. In the conceptual framework shown in Figure No. 1, the integration of AGI (Artificial General Intelligence) and BCI (Brain-Computer Interface) technologies is a key enabler with unique capabilities to create personalized learning environments that respond to cognition. However, principles from critical pedagogy, constructivist learning theory, and ethics of care highlight the need for strong governance structures alongside pedagogical innovations to prevent technology from undermining learner autonomy and cognitive empowerment. Instead, these innovations should avoid layers of institutional imposition of inequity or instances of cognitive surveillance.

Such integration, however, depends on numerous socio-contextual enablers (pipes)—infrastructure, teacher readiness, cultural receptivity, policy maturity—which empirical studies have identified as necessary preconditions for urban social innovation (Selwyn, 2020; OECD, 2021). This conceptual model forms one component of the study; the operational stages are outlined separately in the workflow diagram in Figure 2. At its core is an iterative framework of ethical governance, pedagogic innovation, and learner-technology mediation. It allows us to speculate on the technological possibilities of education and accountability concerning specific educational values and achievements: equity, critical thinking, and cognitive empowerment.

Empirically grounded (e.g., Luckin et al., 2016) studies in educational technology confirm that we can only achieve these outcomes through technological interventions that are part of ethically sound, learner-centered ecosystems supported by culturally competent and policy-aligned infrastructures. Therefore, in this framework, speculative technologies are not seen as isolated innovations but as components of a broader education ecosystem that must be interconnected across ethical, pedagogical, and systemic levels.

11.1 Workflow Block Diagram of the Study

Figure 2. Workflow Diagram

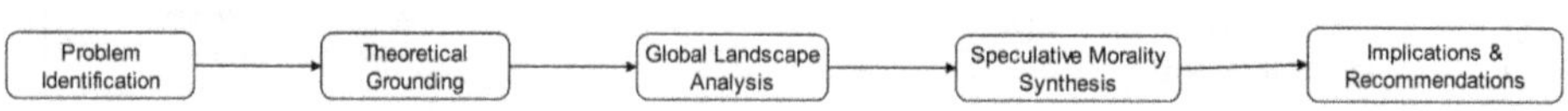

Source: *Authors' Contribution*

The research process for this chapter, as illustrated in Figure 2, followed a staged analytical pathway beginning with (1) Problem Identification, where conceptual tensions surrounding AGI–BCI convergence in education were mapped using preliminary literature screenings. This led to (2) Theoretical Grounding, in which posthumanism, neuroethics, constructivism, and political theory were integrated to create a multidimensional analytical lens. The third stage (3) Comparative Policy and Technological Landscape Analysis synthesized multinational cases to identify gaps in governance, infrastructural readiness, and ethical protections. Stage four (4) Synthesising Speculative Morality Frameworks connected normative ethics with future-oriented technological projections to propose anticipatory governance principles. Finally, (5) Deriving Implications and Recommendations condensed findings into actionable insights for policymakers, educators, and global institutions. Together, these stages formed a coherent methodological progression that guided the chapter's argument and contributed to the final conceptual model.

12. IMPLICATIONS

The merger of AGI with BCIs has profound theoretical, practical, and managerial implications for education. It disrupts age-old paradigms from the likes of Piaget to Vygotsky. It demands novel learning models in response, comprising concepts such as distributed cognition, neuro-adaptive learning, and post-humanism. By advocating for speculative morality deliberation on what these technologies can and should do, and for cognitive justice and epistemic pluralism,

AGI and BCIs enable the delivery of cognitive coaching, a promising approach for personalized, real-time and actionable learning that augments cognitive function, however, this novel educational methodology is not without its challenges which include violation of learner privacy, the potential for learner dependence and the preferential application of this technology over others in predominantly affluent regions whilst the ethic of redistributing learners who may benefit from being in resource-poor environments remains uncharged. Teachers, however, will not be replaced; their roles will have to change from content delivery towards ethical mediation and algorithm interpretation—a skill requiring much training. At the management level, educational institutions and policymakers must tackle pressing governance challenges, such as neural data privacy, localized implementation, and stakeholder inclusion. Overcoming neurocapitalism will demand bold strategies such as participatory design, protocols of informed consent, and adherence to international human rights law to enable AGI-BCI integration that enriches, informatically regulates, and adaptively supports human-centric education from derivative decline.

13. CONCLUSION: THE ROLE OF SPECULATIVE MORALITY IN SHAPING EDUCATION

The integration of AGI and BCI technologies into education represents a profound shift requiring ethical, pedagogical, and governance readiness. This chapter highlights the need for anticipatory approaches that prioritize equity, learner autonomy, and responsible innovation.

Key conclusions include:

- AGI–BCI systems must strengthen learning without compromising cognitive privacy or reducing student agency.
- Ethical safeguards—especially those relating to data rights and classroom transparency—are essential before wide adoption.
- Educators will increasingly shift toward roles of ethical interpreters and facilitators rather than content deliverers.
- Equitable implementation depends on addressing infrastructural gaps and preventing the concentration of technological advantage.
- Policy frameworks must evolve proactively to ensure that neural and algorithmic tools remain aligned with human-centered educational values.

Overall, the chapter argues that emerging technologies should support—not replace—human judgment in education, and their development must remain guided by principles that protect dignity, fairness, and pedagogical integrity.

REFERENCES

Alemu, D. K., & Mensah, J. T. (2023). Contextual challenges in AGI deployment across sub-Saharan Africa: Cultural epistemologies and pedagogical alignment. *African Journal of Educational Technology*, *5*(2), 74–92.

Bayne, S., & Jandrić, P. (2017). Posthumanism and Higher Education. *International Journal of Educational Technology in Higher Education*, *14*(1), 1–13.

Bostrom, N., & Sandberg, A. (2009). Cognitive Enhancement: Methods, Ethics, Regulatory Challenges. *Science and Engineering Ethics*, *15*(3), 311–341.

Dresp-Langley, B. (2022). Neurotechnologies in education: Trends, research, and ethical challenges. *The European Journal of Neuroscience*, *56*(2), 254–268.

European Commission. (2021). *Digital Education Action Plan (2021–2027)*. Publications Office of the European Union.

European Commission. (2021). *Proposal for a Regulation laying down harmonised rules on artificial intelligence (Artificial Intelligence Act)*. Publications Office of the European Union.

Feenberg, A. (1999). *Questioning Technology*. Routledge.

Global Partnership on Artificial Intelligence (GPAI). (2022). *Responsible AI Working Group Reports*. GPAI Secretariat.

Goertzel, B. (2014). Artificial General Intelligence: Concept, State of the Art, and Future Prospects. *Journal of Artificial General Intelligence*, *5*(1), 1–48.

Huang, Y., Patel, R., & Gómez, L. (2024). Closed-loop neuroadaptive AGI systems: Prototyping cognitive-interactive classrooms for real-time pedagogical modulation. *Journal of Neural Engineering and Intelligent Learning Systems*, *18*(1), 33–52.

Ienca, M., & Andorno, R. (2017). Towards new human rights in the age of neuroscience and neurotechnology. *Life Sciences, Society and Policy*, *13*(1), 1–27.

Kim, S., & Harada, T. (2023). Biometric–neural data ethics in AGI-enhanced classrooms: Emerging risks and governance pathways. *Journal of Learning Analytics*, *10*(3), 112–129.

Knox, J. (2020). Artificial intelligence and education in China. *Learning, Media and Technology*, *45*(3), 298–311.

Lebedev, M. A., & Nicolelis, M. A. (2006). Brain–Machine Interfaces: Past, Present, and Future. *Trends in Neurosciences*, *29*(9), 536–546.

Li, X., & Ren, H. (2024). Hybrid AGI tutoring systems: Integrating attention-tracking neural signals for personalized learning. *Journal of Artificial Intelligence in Education, 32*(1), 45–62.

Luckin, R., Holmes, W., Griffiths, M., & Forcier, L. B. (2016). *Intelligence Unleashed: An Argument for AI in Education*. Pearson Education.

NeuroRights Foundation. (2024). *Neurorights and educational neurotechnologies: Policy recommendations for safeguarding cognitive privacy*. NeuroRights Foundation Report.

Neurotech, E. U. (2022). *The European University of Brain and Technology.*

OECD. (2021). *Artificial Intelligence in Education: Challenges and Opportunities.* OECD Publishing.

Organisation for Economic Co-operation and Development. (2024). *Comparative review of AI and BCI governance in education: Global policy asymmetries and ethical safeguards*. OECD Publishing.

Rawls, J. (1971). *A Theory of Justice*. Harvard University Press.

Selwyn, N. (2020). *Should Robots Replace Teachers? AI and the Future of Education*. Polity Press.

UNESCO. (2023). *AI and the Futures of Learning: Policy Guidance*. United Nations Educational, Scientific, and Cultural Organization.

UNESCO. (2023). *Futures of Education: Reimagining our futures together*. United Nations Educational, Scientific, and Cultural Organization.

Wolpaw, J. R., Birbaumer, N., McFarland, D. J., Pfurtscheller, G., & Vaughan, T. M. (2002). Brain–computer interfaces for communication and control. *Clinical Neurophysiology, 113*(6), 767–791.

Yuste, R., Goering, S., Arcas, B. A. Y., Bi, G., Carmena, J. M., Carter, A., & Wolpaw, J. (2017). Four ethical priorities for neurotechnologies and AI. *Nature, 551*(7679), 159–163.

Zhao, L., Chen, M., & Gupta, R. (2023). Low-cost brain–computer interfaces in formative assessment: Impacts on metacognitive awareness in secondary education. *Computers & Education, 205*, 104579.

Zhou, J., Wang, M., & Li, Y. (2023). Artificial General Intelligence in Higher Education: A Case Study of Multi-Agent Learning Systems. *International Journal of Educational Technology in Higher Education, 20*(1), 45–63.

Chapter 6
Unpacking the Human Experience:
A Qualitative Exploration of Generative AI and Digital Twins in Education

Minhaj Abdullah
https://orcid.org/0009-0000-2335-8038
Mahindra University, India

ABSTRACT

The intersection of Generative Artificial Intelligence and Digital Twins presents a paradigm shift in personalised data-driven learning ecosystems. This qualitative synthesis focuses on the ways in which the combination of GenAI and DTs transforms the human experience in education, and ethical governance. The paper will discuss the mediation of trust, autonomy, and pedagogical relationships by hybrid AI-DT systems. The results indicate that there is an ongoing conflict between customisation and surveillance, effectiveness and reliance, and automation and judgement. The long-term success of these systems depends on socio-technical design frameworks that anticipate transparency, fairness, and human controls. This article provides a qualitative basis to comprehend how GenAI-DT convergence reformulates the instructor-learner-technology triad and suggests potential ways of responsible innovation of educational practice.

DOI: 10.4018/979-8-3373-4982-4.ch006

INTRODUCTION

The world education industry is experiencing a radical revolution due to heightened digitalization, widening the diversity of learners, and heightened expectations of personalization, scalability, and accountability of learning outcomes. Conventional classroom environments, mostly modeled around the idea of standardized teaching, have shown little ability to support the needs of heterogeneous learners, deliver feedback on a timely and personalized fashion, as well as react dynamically to the wigly and non-linear learning patterns (Korada, 2024). All these restrictions have been increasingly evident as institutions across the globe face the challenge of massification, lifelong learning, and digitally mediated knowledge-making. As a result, increased interest worldwide in better computational methods that can serve adaptive, data-driven, and learner controlled educational ecosystems without undermining pedagogical authority and ethical accountability has emerged.

ORIGIN AND EVOLUTION OF THE CONCEPT

In this scenario, the Digital Twin (DT) and Generative Artificial Intelligence (GenAI) technologies have become one of the promising, but the controversial innovations. The digital twin idea was initially developed in industrial and manufacturing sectors where it was used to denote a highly realistic virtual representation of a physical system that continuously received real-time information to track performance, failure, and optimization (Jones et al., 2023). As the term developed, digital twins were expanded to include not just physical property, but also complicated socio-technical systems, such as healthcare, city infrastructure, and education. DTs in educational contexts have been redefined to simulate learners, classrooms, curricula, or institutional settings by simulating cognitive, behavioral and occasionally emotional states in real time (Lin et al., 2025). Generative AI is not to be confused with either traditional predictive or classificatory AI, it adds a dynamically acting intervention layer whereby it generates adaptive content, personalized feedback, or interactive learning material that are based on patterns discovered by large datasets (Hao et al., 2024). DTs and GenAI together comprise the closed-loop systems where the data provided by learners guide generative reactions, and such reactions redefine learning practices, are a core change of the learning from an inflexible, curriculum-driven approach to ever-adaptive learning systems.

EMPIRICAL LITERATURE AND CURRENT KNOWLEDGE

GenAI and DTs in education Since 2022, the number of empirical studies on the topic has grown exponentially, describing both affordances and growing concerns of artificial intelligence in pedagogy. Assessments of GenAI are regularly documented to have perceived advantages of content generation, formative feedback, and support in a task, often linked to efficiency and learner involvement (Mao, 2024; Wu, 2025). Simultaneously, qualitative and mixed-method literature identifies the ongoing concerns regarding overreliance, deskilling, higher education academic integrity, and uncertainty regarding the correct use of pedagogy (Lin et al., 2025; Vasconcelos & dos Santos, 2023). Studies related to the topic of digital twins, especially engineering and technical education, are associated with a better behavioral and cognitive engagement, enhanced relations between theory and practice, and less anxiety of novice learners due to immersive simulation environments (Lu and Hu, 2025; Wang et al., 2022). Most of these studies however focus on performance outcomes, usability or technical feasibility with relatively little focus on what emotional experiences, identity negotiation or the sensemaking processes of learners are in the long-term.

PRACTICAL AND IMPLEMENTATION CHALLENGES

Despite the promise, GenAI and DT systems have serious challenges in terms of their real-life implementation. The expensive cost of development and maintenance, the need to have special technical knowledge, and the challenge of integrating with existing institutional IT systems restrict scalability, especially in low-resource educational settings (Jones et al., 2023; Jankovskis, 2023). Digital twin systems rely on massive and continuous data gathering and real-time analytics, creating issues of data quality, interoperability and long-term institutional capacity to govern. In addition to technical obstacles, the problem of policies and institutions has to be addressed since regulatory frameworks, academic integrity policies, and professional development frameworks frequently lag behind technology adoption (Lin et al., 2024). Ethical issues also complicate the implementation especially issues of privacy of data, algorithmic surveillance, and possibility of further entrenching historical prejudice by predictive learner modeling (Mariam et al., 2024). Such obstacles indicate that any failures in GenAI-DT projects will be less technical than socio-technical..

This automated feedback and content generation feature allows customized learning experiences of learners at both scale and speed that are not possible with human-led content generation processes (Tomar and Grover, 2023; Xu et al., 2023). Gen AI can also improve the design of instruction, which simulates student responses and learning trajectories (Ponce et al., 2025), and assessment, which offers real-time and scalable assessments depending on the context (Owan et al., 2023). The collaboration between the DT and the Gen AI is that the former offers the diagnostic data, and the latter offers the appropriate actionable intervention. This implies that educational paths are not chosen pre-defined in a given library, but rather created on-the-fly and specifically adjusted to the real-time analysis of the requirements of the learner by the DT (Huang et al., 2024). What it means is that the educational system becomes not curriculum-centered but content-generated and the quality, accuracy, and ethical soundness of the Gen AI model becomes the most important (Huang et al., 2024; Karya Bakti et al., 2023). As Gen AI is trained on large, typically biased, publicly-available datasets, its content generation should be constantly checked by human educators to guarantee the creation of non-biased and pedagogically appropriate content, which rules out the negotiable nature of human judgment (Mariam et al., 2024).

KEY RESEARCH QUESTIONS

Notwithstanding the growing body of literature, several critical research gaps remain. First, there is limited qualitative research examining how learners and educators experience autonomy, trust, identity, and agency within GenAI-DT-mediated educational environments. Second, existing studies are predominantly short-term or cross-sectional, offering limited insight into how human-AI relationships, dependency patterns, and perceptions of legitimacy evolve over time. Third, while conceptual frameworks for integrating GenAI and DTs are advancing rapidly, there is insufficient empirical evidence to inform the design of transparent, explainable, and pedagogically responsible systems grounded in lived human experience (Altares-Lopez et al., 2025; Lin et al., 2025). As a result, technological development currently outpaces the qualitative understanding necessary for sustainable and ethical adoption.

Addressing these gaps requires a deliberate shift toward human-centered qualitative inquiry that foregrounds lived experience alongside technical performance. By examining how GenAI and Digital Twin technologies are interpreted, negotiated, and experienced by learners and educators, research can contribute essential insights into trust, autonomy, and ethical acceptability. Such an approach is critical to ensuring that the global transformation of education through advanced AI systems enhances, rather than undermines, the human foundations of teaching and learning.

POSSIBLE SOLUTIONS TO RESEARCH GAP AND FUTURE OF THE FIELD.

In this chapter, the gaps in the literature mentioned above are addressed directly as the analytical focus is changed to the lived human experience of Generative Artificial Intelligence (GenAI) and Digital Twin (DT) integration into the learning setting. Although the efficiency gains, engagement indicators, or technical feasibility are predominantly used in the previous studies, this chapter preempts the qualitative aspects of learner autonomy, trust, identity formation, and educator professional agency. In so doing, it fills the gap of empirically based knowledge about the experience, perception, and negotiation of these systems by those who encounter AI-mediated learning space. The chapter makes a contribution to the field because it synthesises qualitative data at the learner and educator levels and, thus, provides a more holistic view of the workings of GenAI-DT systems as socio-technical assemblages and not as a neutral instructional resource.

When tackling the practical issues, this chapter goes beyond theoretical ethical values to explore how the various issues of algorithmic surveillance, data governance, bias, and policy ambiguity are practiced in the field of education. Instead of viewing privacy, explainability and fairness as compliance checklists, the chapter frames them as lived conditions that directly influence trust, acceptance and pedagogical efficacy. This view can help to understand better why technologically enhanced systems can be successful or unsuccessful in terms of institutional context, educator readiness and perceptions of learners. Through the expression of these dynamics, the chapter offers a framework through which one can signify socio-technical failure points that are usually not apparent in quantitatively motivated assessments.

IMPLICATION ON FUTURE RESEARCH.

This chapter can give future researchers a clear methodological and conceptual direction because it illustrates the usefulness of qualitative, human-supported inquiry in research of AI-driven education. It points out the necessity of longitudinal and interpretive research designs that are able to include the dynamics of learner-AI relationships that bring about novelty changing into normalization, dependence, resistance, or recalibration of trust. Moreover, the chapter urges researchers to stop carrying out independent studies of GenAI or DTs and rather examine them as combined systems, where predictive modeling and generative interventions work together to co-produce learning experiences. The chapter presents interdisciplinary research through the identification of gaps in the study of identity, agency, and emotional engagement, which can bridge the fields of education, human-computer interaction, ethics, and data science.

To the policymakers and institutional leaders, the chapter offers evidence-based reasons as to why governance frameworks need to be proactive, human-centered, and context-sensitive. The results highlight the inefficiency of reactive policies that pay attention to the issues only of academic integrity or control of tools without considering the issues of autonomy, equity, and professional trust. Explaining the role of policy ambiguity, AI illiteracy, and a weak institutional framework in magnifying the workload of educators and learners anxiety, the chapter provides solutions to the creation of governance systems that would mitigate the damaging effects of the innovations on ethical custodianship. These lessons may be applied to the policy writing to incorporate transparency, explain ability, and participatory oversight into GenAI-DT implementations, which can enable sustainable and socially legitimate adoption.

RESEARCH QUESTION FRAMING AND RATIONALE.

This paper is motivated by a key and unanswered question that modern education is facing: How can the adaptive potential of Generative AI and Digital Twin technologies be used in educational systems without undermining human autonomy, trust, and ethical integrity? Although there is a lot of excitement about AI-based personalization, little is known about how these systems are practiced and negotiated by learners and educators, and how they build or break trust in the context of ongoing data-mediated intervention. Available studies have not adequately clarified how GenAI-DT systems operate as either empowering cognitive partners or surveillance and dependency as well as the effects of such perceptions on the long-term educational performance.

It is based on this necessity that this study will ask not only the question of what these technologies can, but how they also redefine the relational, emotional, and ethical pillars of education. It poses the question of why, even in times of demonstrated technical potential, resistance, fear and policy uncertainty among key stakeholders, how the qualitative understanding can be used to inform the design of clear, explainable, and pedagogically valid systems. The chapter attempts to answer these questions to elucidate in what ways the integration of GenAI-DT can be used to facilitate meaningful learning and not just to automate instructional processes. This question is critical towards the process of making sure that the future development of innovations in the area of education is in tandem with human values, professional judgment, and social responsibility.

THEOROTICAL FRAMEWORK

This research paper is rooted in a multi-theoretical framework that can appropriately establish the complexity of applying Generative Artificial intelligence (GenAI) and Digital Twin (DT) technologies to the educational setting. The technologies also have a simultaneous effect on the pedagogical practices, institutional governance, ethical decision making and the relationships between humans and technologies. Therefore, the thesis is based on five theories, which are interconnected, i.e., Sociotechnical Systems Theory, Human-Centered Artificial Intelligence, Constructivist Learning Theory, Activity Theory, and the Trust Theory. Of these, Sociotechnical Systems Theory has been used as the main theoretical framework, since it has offered the most detailed explanation of the interdependence between technological infrastructures and human experience which is central to the study.

The Sociotechnical Systems Theory (STS) originated as a result of the studies of researchers of the Tavistock Institute around the period of the seminal study of coal mining systems by Trist and Bamforth (Trist and Bamforth, 1951 - AO). This theory was created to counteract other technologically deterministic theories that focused on efficiency but ignored human and organizational aspects. STS assumes that any system is made up of mutually related social (e.g., human roles, values, power relations, and norms) and technical parts (e.g., tools, algorithms, workflows, and infrastructures), and that it is the joint optimization of these two that makes a system effective. Particularly, the current study is associated with this theoretical perspective due to the socio-technical nature of GenAI-DT systems in education: such systems combine algorithmic modeling of learners, predictive analytics, and generative feedback with human and pedagogical judgment and institutional policies (Lin et al., 2025). In the view of STS, issues like dependency of learners, resistance of educators, loss of trust, or moral ruin is not just a technical malfunction but an undesirable consequence of misalignment between social activities and technological design. STS, as the main theoretical framework, helps focus the study on the lived experience, ethical issues, and the systemic interaction instead of the performance in technology only.

Human-Centered Artificial Intelligence (HCAI) offers a compliant ethical and design-oriented conceptual framework of AI-mediated educative systems. HCAI developed through research in human-computer interaction and AI ethics, especially as a reaction to the anxiety that intelligent systems might create automation bias, be opaque, and deprive humans of their agency (Shneiderman, 2020 - AO). The main idea behind HCAI is that AI systems are not meant to replace human functions but to enhance them, this should be made transparent, explainable, accountable with meaningful human control. This view is critical in the context of education, since GenAI systems can produce instructional content, feedback, and recommendations that can have substantial impact on the direction that learners follow and the choices they make during assessment. HCAI illuminates the investigation of this study on whether GenAI-DT systems are perceived by learners and educators to empower cognitive partners or hideous, authoritative systems that disempower professional judgment and autonomy. Though STS puts the system-level interaction into perspective, HCAI offers a normative viewpoint of ethical responsibility and human dignity in AI-enhanced education.

Activity Theory takes the mode of analysis a step further by emphasizing on mediated human action within social system. Based on cultural-historical psychology and emerging out of the efforts of Vygotsky (1978 - AO) and subsequently Engestrom (1987 - AO), the Activity Theory is a conceptualization of learning and behavior based on goals and mediated by tools in a community regulated by rules and division of labor. The main idea of this theory is contradictions-tensions inside or outside the activity systems and this becomes the driving force behind change and transformation. This view comes in handy when one wants to examine the GenAI-DT integration since such technologies act as an intermediating artifact that reforms the process of educational activity systems. The implementation of AI-based feedback, predictive modeling, and constant monitoring changes the ways in which learning activities are carried out, the distribution of authority, and the definition of success. Activity Theory helps this study to discuss the conflicts between automation and professional judgment, personalization and standardization, and efficiency and equity in the educational processes facilitated by AI.

Together, these theories form a strong conceptual framework of the study of Generative AI and Digital Twin technologies integration in the educational field. The main theoretical framework is the Sociotechnical Systems Theory that positions GenAI-DT systems as open-end arrangements of social and technical factors whose effectiveness relies on the alignment and not necessarily on optimization. Human-Centered AI, Constructivist Learning Theory, Activity Theory, and Trust Theory are used as complementary prisms revealing the images of ethical design, learning processes, systemic tensions, and relational legitimacy. This combined structure will enable a qualitative, humanistic research that can guide future research and development of policy to adopt responsible AI in education.

Table 1. Theoretical Framework Summary for the Study on Generative AI and Digital Twins in Education

Theory	Definition	Origin / Key Scholars	Relevance to the Study	Role in This Study
Sociotechnical Systems Theory (STS)	A theory that conceptualizes systems as interdependent social and technical components that must be jointly optimized to achieve sustainable outcomes.	Developed at the Tavistock Institute; foundational work by Trist and Bamforth (1951 – AO).	GenAI–DT systems integrate algorithmic learner modeling and generative feedback with human judgment, institutional norms, and governance structures. STS explains how misalignment between social practices and technical design leads to ethical, trust, and adoption challenges.	**Primary theoretical lens** guiding the study; frames GenAI–DT integration as a socio-technical ecosystem rather than a purely technical innovation.
Human-Centered Artificial Intelligence (HCAI)	A design-oriented framework that emphasizes AI systems that augment human capabilities while ensuring transparency, explainability, accountability, and human control.	Emerged from human–computer interaction and AI ethics; articulated by Shneiderman (2020 – AO).	GenAI systems generate content, feedback, and recommendations that shape learning trajectories. HCAI helps evaluate whether these systems empower or undermine learner autonomy and educator professional judgment.	Complementary ethical and design lens supporting analysis of explainability, accountability, and human oversight.
Constructivist Learning Theory	A learning theory positing that learners actively construct knowledge through interaction, reflection, and meaning-making rather than passive reception of information.	Originated with Piaget (1952 – AO); expanded through social constructivist perspectives.	GenAI–DT technologies are promoted as personalized learning tools. Constructivism evaluates whether AI-driven personalization supports deep learning, metacognition, and autonomy or encourages dependency and surface learning.	Pedagogical lens informing analysis of learner experience, engagement, and cognitive autonomy.

continued on following page

Table 1. Continued

Theory	Definition	Origin / Key Scholars	Relevance to the Study	Role in This Study
Activity Theory	A theory that views human behavior as goal-oriented activity mediated by tools within a social and cultural context, emphasizing contradictions as drivers of change.	Rooted in cultural–historical psychology; Vygotsky (1978 – AO), Engeström (1987 – AO).	GenAI and DTs act as mediating artifacts that reshape educational activity systems, altering task performance, authority distribution, and assessment practices.	Analytical lens for identifying tensions between automation and professional judgment, personalization and standardization, efficiency and equity.
Trust Theory	A theory explaining how trust is formed and maintained in conditions of uncertainty, risk, and incomplete information, particularly in complex systems.	Sociological systems theory; Luhmann (1979 – AO).	GenAI–DT systems rely on opaque algorithms and continuous data collection. Trust Theory explains how transparency, fairness, and explainability influence learner and educator acceptance.	Relational lens supporting analysis of trust, legitimacy, and acceptance of AI-driven educational systems.

EMPIRICAL LITERATURE REVIEW

Over the last few years, educational technology literature has begun to focus more on generative artificial intelligence (GenAI) and digital twin (DT) systems not just in terms of their capabilities or pedagogical capabilities but also in terms of their impacts on transforming the human experience in the learning setting. These systems engage the sense of agency, identity, trust, emotional experience and the negotiation of human-machine boundaries as it concerns learners. The review below is a survey of important empirical and conceptual literature, identifies gaps in the literature, and puts your qualitative inquiry into perspective against such gaps.

Collectively, this literature points to the fact that human experience with GenAI is not unambiguously positive or negative: people are negotiating the agency, trust, identity, and pedagogical roles on changing grounds. Unlike generative AI that is increasingly being talked about or written about in the context of writing or feedback, digital twins enable learners to engage with the virtual re-creations or reflections of the systems. Simulation, experimentation, and a closer association of abstract models with Concrete behavior are facilitated by DTs in educational settings. Lu and Hu (2025) document a digital twin-enhanced programming education setting, and they investigate the differences in the engagement (behavioral, cognitive, emotional) and acquisition of skills of students compared to the conventional teaching. They also provide qualitative feedback about students: learners report a decrease in anxiety, the improved understanding of the relationship between codes and system behavior, and motivation (Lu & Hu, 2025). These narratives are a glimpse into the emotional and perceptual changes that are brought by engagement with a digital twin. The recent systematic review of digital twin and virtual replica technologies in learning institutions (Karanam et al., 2025) provides a survey of the research published in 2018 and further. The review points out that most of the studies are conducted to compare the performance and technical metrics, whereas others are found to be reporting the learner satisfaction, perceived realism, and increased ease of experimentation. However, it also points to the fact that little qualitative research on emotional experience, identity change, or tensions of trust is done (Karanam et al., 2025). The theoretical effort by Sylvester (2022) is a straw man argumentative work that discusses the conceptualization of digital twinning in the context of education services. Though not empirical in human experience, this work brings up heuristics that are useful, including educational services as ecosystems that can be twinned; and indicates where human perception, interaction and iteration may be centralized (Sylvester, 2022).

Beyond the study of education, Moller et al. (2020) examined the impact of introducing a digital twin in a high-reliability organization on the mental models of users, conceptual adjustments, dissonance caused by the virtual twin not behaving according to expectation. Their qualitative results, even though not an educational site, imply how communication with a twin can change the cognition of the users, their trust, and their perceptions of the real and the simulated (Moller et al., 2020). The application of educational contexts using digital twin systems tends to be in engineering or technical applications. Ning et al. (2024) overview the application of DTs in engineering education, stating that the motivation of students, the immersion, and the ability to interact are frequently mentioned, but little is mentioned with regards to the student self-conception, emotional reaction, and difficulties in case of a failed or divergent simulation (Ning et al., 2024). This is an indication of a possibility of adding more human experience to the foreground. While GenAI and DTs have been studied separately, research that explores their joint integration is nascent. One notable example is *Personalized Education with Generative AI and Digital Twins* by Altares-López et al. (2025). Their proposed framework combines low-fidelity DTs (e.g., VR simulations) with generative AI assistants and sentiment analysis to tailor learning in real time (Altares-López et al., 2025). Although this is a design proposal rather than a fully deployed qualitative study, it hints at how learners might navigate dual systems, balancing interactive simulation and generative feedback. In this combined space, early empirical work on trust and co-production becomes relevant. Zhang et al. (2025) examined how undergraduate students perceive feedback generated by AI, human, and co-produced sources. They found that co-produced feedback retained higher trust and learners perceived it as more genuine, while purely AI feedback was more likely to be questioned (Zhang et al., 2025). This suggests that in hybrid environments, learners may privilege human oversight or visible collaboration for experience and credibility.

The implementation of AI has resulted in the creation of tradeoffs over time between efficiency, learner identity, ethical reflection, and trust as demonstrated in Designing for Learning with Generative AI (2025). The tension can be doubled when used with DT, how are learners moving between simulated behaviours and generative suggestions and where is the control boundary The convergence of GenAI and DTs offers a great deal of affordances, yet makes the experience more complex: learners can alternate between immersion and abstraction, agency and deference, trust and skepticism. Although GenAI or DT have been studied separately, little empirical research has considered how these systems interact through the lens of human experience, i.e. how learners and instructors make sense, negotiate identity, or adjust to emotional presence in mixed GenAI + DT systems. There are limited studies that capture snapshots of experience (start of use or during use). The changes with time, how novelty, fatigue, and trust relations, or emerging tensions, evolve, are not well studied. There are limited studies that explore how learners or instructors identify themselves in the act of giving and/or taking back agency in AI/DT-mediated tasks- how they define ownership, vulnerability, or hybridity. Despite the fact that some studies (e.g. Ellis et al., 2025; Lyu et al., 2025) address the topic of instructor perception of GenAI, the qualitative experience of designing, mediating, and negotiating pedagogy in systems integrating GenAI and DT has not been studied. Multiple studies make the ideal assumption of technical infrastructure. The disappointments, disintegrations, injustices or dark side experiences in the under-resourced or culturally diverse settings rarely come out. Digital Twin technology commonly utilizes immersive and simulation-based environments, which have been shown to have a distinct qualitative benefit in the area of improving student engagement. Research has also indicated that DT-based learning classrooms have a considerable positive effect on engagement and skill acquisition in technical courses, including introductory programming (Wang et al., 2022). They are especially useful with novice learners as immersive experiences, based on theory, are able to close the traditional gap between theory and practice (Wang et al., 2022).

Digital twins (DTs) in education virtual replicas or simulation environments that mirror physical systems or learning contexts have been explored as tools for experiential learning, virtual labs, and campus analytics. Case studies and book-chapter treatments emphasize DTs' capacity to create interactive, safe spaces for experimentation and to make abstract systems tangible for learners (Tao, 2022; Jankovskis, 2023). Empirical work in technical disciplines (e.g., programming, engineering) reports improved behavioral and cognitive engagement, clearer links between theory and practice, and reduced anxiety in novice learners when DTs are used as part of course design (Lu & Hu, 2025). At the same time, researchers repeatedly identify infrastructural, cost, and integration challengesincluding scalability across heterogeneous institutional IT environments and risk of exacerbating digital divides when resource constraints preclude access to high-fidelity DTs (Tao, 2022; Jankovskis, 2023).

A growing number of systematic reviews and meta-analyses synthesize evidence on GenAI and DTs and point to cross-cutting human-experience concerns: trust, agency, equity, and evolving professional identities. Recent systematic reviews of GenAI in higher education document strong variation in student attitudes ranging from enthusiastic adoption for ideation and drafting to concern about deskilling and misuse and recommend that institutions develop policy frameworks and literacy training rather than rely solely on detection or prohibition strategies (Wu et al., 2025; Bauer, 2025). Reviews of digital twin scholarship likewise call for deeper qualitative work on learners' sensemaking, identity, and emotional trajectories when interacting with persistent virtual replicas rather than one-off simulations (Iliu ă, 2024; Karanam et al., 2025). These syntheses make clear that measuring success solely by task performance or efficiency is insufficient; studying lived experience (how learners feel, what they trust, and how they negotiate control) is essential to responsible design.

Emerging empirical studies that probe trust and feedback dynamics reveal nuanced patterns that matter directly to hybrid GenAI–DT deployments. For instance, recent experimental and mixed-methods work suggests students may perceive AI-generated or AI-assisted feedback as highly useful in some contexts but reveal decreased perceived genuineness when the feedback source is exposed whereas **co-produced** feedback (human + AI) can retain trust if human oversight is visible (Zhang et al., 2025). Such findings imply that hybrid systems which make human mediation explicit (for instance a teacher editing an AI draft, or annotating a DT simulation result) may preserve learner trust more effectively than black-box automation. This has direct consequences for designing GenAI + DT learning loops where action suggestions, assessment flags, or remediation paths are offered: surface the human role and design explain ability/oversight into the workflow.

CONCEPTUAL FRAMEWORK

The theoretical framework offered in this paper explains how Generative Artificial Intelligence (GenAI) and Digital Twin (DT) technologies can be implemented in education in a socio-technical ecosystem and not a technical intervention. The framework is based on the Sociotechnical Systems Theory and assumes the conceptualization of GenAI and DTs as mutually enabling technologies where the educational nature of both is manifested through ongoing interactions with human participants, institutional organizations, and ethical regulating systems.

. GenAI acts as the adaptive layer of intervention in this model, generating the personalized content, formative feedback, and conversational scaffold whereas DTs act as real-time diagnostic systems modeling cognitive, behavioral, and emotional paths of learners utilizing ongoing data streams. A combination of these technologies creates a closed-loop system where data about learners is used to generate generative responses and such responses in turn transform learning practices and experiences.

Figure 1. The Conceptual framework introduces socio-technical mediators such as explain ability, data governance, human pedagogical oversight, and bias management as the key processes by which GenAI-DT systems affect education practice

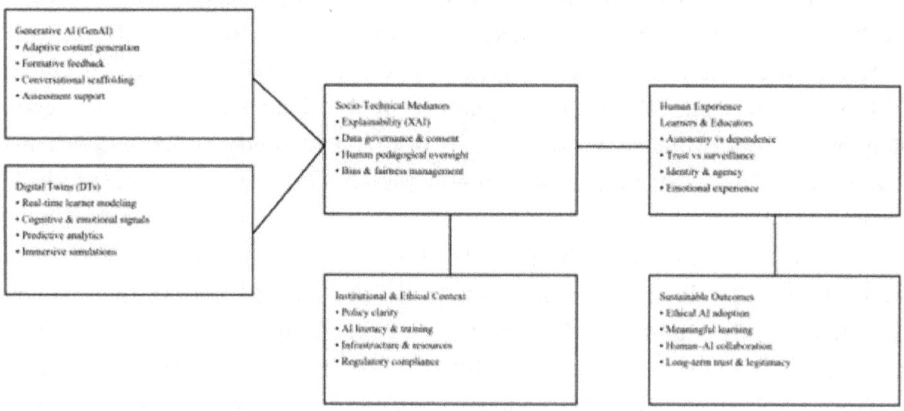

The framework does not presume a linear cause and effect relationship between technology and the results, but rather points out that the transparency of algorithmic reasoning, consent based data practices and transparent human control are critical to whether these systems will be viewed as enabling or threatening by learners and educators. This focus is an expression of empirical results that opaque decision-making, height of surveillance and lack of bias resolution jeopardize trust and increase resistance, despite high technical performance.

. In this regard, ethical considerations are not observed as some external constraints but as experienced socio-technical conditions, which determine everyday interaction with AI-mediated learning settings.

At the human experience level, the framework previews both the negotiation of autonomy, trust, identity, emotional engagement, and professional agency by learners and educators. In the case of learners, GenAI-DT systems can both augment self-paced learning and elicit dependency, deskilling, and monitoring anxiety. These systems redefine the meaning of professional identity to educators, as their job descriptions are no longer content delivery, but rather focused on learning design, data interpretation and ethical custodianship. The framework thereby encapsulates the duality observed in the findings: although adaptive personalization is potentially useful to achieve engagement and understanding, it may as well create novel types of cognitive load, surveillance stress, and legitimacy issues in case socio-technical alignment becomes weak.

RESEARCH METHODOLOGY

The immersive technologies, e.g., Virtual Reality (VR) lab simulation, enhance the motivation of learners and give extremely positive self-reported engagement indicators, which can serve as an effective addition to the traditional hands-on lab work (Huang et al., 2024). This increased interaction is mostly associated with the spatial and interactive novelty of the technology, responding to the inability of the traditional approaches to bridge the gap between the theoretical ideas and the practice at hand (Wang et al., 2022; Pester et al., 2025). Although students overall enjoy the utility-supportive and conversational help that LLMs offer (Lin et al., 2025), the problem is that this behavioral interaction should be maintained and then converted into profound and quantifiable cognitive interaction in the long run, not just in the initial novelty effect. The DT component plays a crucial role here, since its monitoring of the behavioral and emotional measures will provide the quantitative process that will be required to study this qualitative phenomenon longitudinally.

Although students admit that they have the functional support and conversational assistance provided by systems based on LLM, their experience is described as having to operate on a two-edged sword (Lin et al., 2025). Exploratory qualitative research interviews conducted on university students show that there is much apprehension and negative psychological implications that come with utility. In particular, according to the respondents, the concern about deskilling (52%), reliance on AI (48%), fear of reliance in the future (35%), and general pessimistic attitude towards the future were high.(Lin et al., 2025)

This percentage of students who report being dependent is a qualitative failure of the existing pedagogical scaffolding, as the AI system, which is supposed to predict and satisfy needs, is at risk of creating a learner dependent attitude instead of autonomous learning. The resulting algorithmic reliance is perhaps the most significant qualitative risk to the desired result of the integrated system which is development of critically reflective thinkers.

Perceived benefit is also affected by contextual differences in application. According to survey data, students who work on individual assignments feel that they receive more value out of LLMs than students who work on team-based assignments (Lin et al., 2025). This fact suggests that the existing Gen AI-DT models can be trained to work well on the individual profiling scenario, but fail to adequately represent and assist the socio-collaborative scenario needed in group work (Lin et al., 2025). The DT model needs to develop to include social learning processes, not only isolated cognitive measures, to make the integrated system pedagogically complete.

Table 2. Qualitative Findings on Student Experiences with Integrated Generative AI Tools

Experience Dimension	Key Qualitative Findings (Post-2018 Literature)	Implications for Integrated DT Systems
Functional Support & Utility	Students appreciate conversational assistance and functional support for drafting/summarizing tasks (Lin et al., 2025).	Gen AI must be positioned as a complementary cognitive partner, not a replacement; DT metrics must track utilization rates to identify potential misuse.
Engagement & Motivation	High self-reported motivation in immersive DT simulations (VR/labs), particularly for novice learners (Wang et al., 2022; Huang et al., 2024).	DT fidelity and interactive quality are non-negotiable design factors; must balance simulation realism with cognitive load.
Risks: Dependence & Anxiety	Significant concerns regarding deskilling (52%), dependence (48%), and anxiety about future reliance on AI (Lin et al., 2025).	Requires mandatory AI literacy education and pedagogical design that explicitly uses AI as an "object to think with," fostering reflection (Vasconcelos & dos Santos, 2023).
Contextual Application	Perceived benefits vary significantly between individual and team-based tasks, suggesting a challenge in supporting collaborative learning (Lin et al., 2025).	DT modeling must evolve to capture and optimize socio-collaborative contexts, not just individual learning metrics.

Gen AI and DTs convergence is a special opportunity to mitigate the threat of deskilling due to the promotion of the ability to think at a higher level. The pedagogical design is the only difference between the qualitative distinction between the use of Gen AI as a tool of automation and as a partner of critical thinking (Vasconcelos & dos Santos, 2023). In combination with proper instructional support, AI can serve as an object to think with, which leads students to come up with hypotheses, weigh options, and practice thinking more thoroughly (Vasconcelos & dos Santos, 2023).

This approach depends on the DT system. The DT offers the quantitative foundation of the generative interventions aimed to encourage creativity by monitoring the indicators regarding engagement and the level of concept retention (Lin et al., 2025; Pester et al., 2025). To take just one example, educators can craft learning loops that explicitly incentivize metacognition and critical thinking by observing the interactive behavior of students and directing the Gen AI to produce probing questions or counter-arguments instead of complete answers (Pester et al., 2025). It enables the educators to conduct virtual experiments in the DT environment to determine the qualitative effect of Gen AI assistance on creativity as opposed to a simple knowledge recall, thus demonstrating the usefulness of the system beyond its efficiency, as well as the ability to ensure the development of autonomous and critically reflective learners (Vasconcelos & dos Santos, 2023).

The implementation of the Gen AI-DT systems radically transforms a professional identity of the educator. Instead of AI replacing them, teachers are shifting the roles to guide learning, act as custodians of data and become facilitators of learning within AI-enhanced settings (Karya Bakti et al., 2023). The integrated system offers teachers advanced information and, therefore, allows modifying the instructional processes in accordance with the exact peculiarities and requirements of each child (Lin et al., 2025). This transformation is a radical qualitative transformation in labor. The major role of the educator is shifted to control over the content delivery and control over the complex data interfaces and the algorithmic output. They transform into critical ethical observers of the AI regime and instructional designers able to leverage real-time information in order to intervene in a meaningful way (Karya Bakti et al., 2023). Although the subsequent automation of such tasks as some elements of assessments, in turn, is supposed to provide teachers with more time to engage in meaningful communication with students (Ponce et al., 2025), the process of implementation, in many cases, also brings additional stressors and workloads issues because of a steep learning curve and the need to manage constant streams of data (Lin et al., 2024). To have the desired success of the Gen AI-DT system, the qualitative experience of the educator should be actually enhanced and empowered, rather than overwhelmed by uncontrolled technicacy.

The fast development of Generative AI has also caused some serious tension in educational institutions, in which the policy inertia is often out of pace with the technological integration (Lin et al., 2025). Faculty and instructors often complain of incoherence in institutional policies, as they will have difficulties in deciding how Gen AI can be institutionalized to achieve particular course learning outcomes (Lin et al., 2024; Lin et al., 2025). Educators are eager to receive top-down instructions on the topic of student academic integrity, as well as the official inclusion of AI literacy as a part of general education curricula (Lin et al., 2025). At this point, teachers are experiencing a lack of discipline-specific support resources, and there are still worries regarding the security and cost-effectiveness of access to the required tools of Gen AI (Lin et al., 2025). The qualitative experience of most teachers and educators is that of being pushed to have to adapt quickly to technological disruption with the necessary underlying policy and institutional support (Lin et al., 2025). The successful and fair execution would involve institutionalized AI literacy as a competency of all stakeholders. This literacy is not limited to the use of the tools but rather to the understanding of the Gen AI biases and limitations, as well as the possibility of creating products that are not real (hallucinations) (Karya Bakti et al., 2023; Mariam et al., 2024). Policy architecture should require cross disciplinary teamwork to develop safe, institutionally vetted Gen AI/DT platforms, thus assuring educators the knowledge and assured access they need to exercise control and oversight on the learning environment (Karya Bakti et al., 2023; Mariam et al., 2024).

The idea of Digital Twins, which was introduced into the high-resource industrial environment, faces significant barriers in terms of its implementation in various K-12 and higher education settings. Some of the most common implementation challenges reported in the literature are prohibitive cost, requirement of skilled personnel (competence), and incompatibility between high-fidelity DTs and existing legacy IT systems (Jones et al., 2023; Lin et al., 2025). Moreover, DT systems are based on handling extensive amounts of real-time information obtained by numerous sources, which in most cases brings difficulties pertaining to the effective collection, analysis, and scalability using the system within a large institutional framework (Jones et al., 2023). These practical challenges directly transform into possible qualitative implementational failures threatening to make the disparity in equity between resource endowed institutions that are capable of handling complex streams of data and those that are resource poor. It is still uncommon in practice to achieve the high level of maturity required of DTs such that real-time data integration with the physical world happens without a hitch (Jones et al., 2023).

The danger of confusing technology-based personalization (which is indeed simply a strictly data-driven approach) and human-based personalized learning (which does demand more delicate pedagogical construction) presents a policy issue of critical concern (Karya Bakti et al., 2023). Devoid of definite institutional demystification, the complexity and expensiveness of DTs will only jeopardize its use as a cost-efficient substitute of meaningful human contact, as opposed to using it as an advanced tool to complement and sustain human pedagogical activities.

DISCUSSION

The research paper is based on three research questions, which are connected to each other, forming a qualitative investigation of the human, ethical, and pedagogical aspects of applying Generative Artificial Intelligence (GenAI) and Digital Twin (DT) systems to education. The underlying human layer of integrating technology is the way learners and educators experience autonomy, trust, and identity in educational settings that include GenAI-DT systems, which is the subject of the first question: How do learners and educators experience autonomy, trust, and identity within educational settings that incorporate GenAI-DT systems? Though most of the existing literature focuses on the final performance results, efficiency in personalization and cognitive benefits, very little is known in terms of how people psychologically and emotionally occupy such hybrid learning environments. The interplay between algorithmic decision-making and human agency comes with complicated processes of trust and reliance. Students, as an example, can feel empowered by customized feedback and disempowered by the perceived algorithmic surveillance or bias. Similarly, the teachers will experience a dynamic professional identity, because their monopoly of material and evaluation is diffused into smart systems. Such a question thus aims to anticipate the subjective and phenomenological aspects of educational AI wherein sustainable innovation should become legible and acceptable to the people who inhabit such systems.

The second guiding question - What socio-technical and ethical contradictions can be found in the application of GenAI-DT systems to personalized education? - builds on this question by applying it to the structural and moral design of educational technology. GenAI-DT ecosystem is a form of a combination of deterministic computation and non-deterministic human behavior that introduces the conflict between efficiency and equity, automation and professional judgment, and personalization and surveillance. Although the interaction of generative feedback and real-time learner modelling is unmatched in terms of adaptability, it also poses a risk of increasing the level of algorithmic bias, over-surveillance, and dependency. The digital footprints of the students turn into inexhaustible sources of information, and the issue of privacy, consent, and ownership of the data is raised to a new depth. In the case of educators, the ethical issues are exponential--the cloudy explanation of AI advice to the duty of interfering with the algorithmic decision-making process that explicitly defines the direction of learning. The socio-technical balance that the ethical regulation of AI-DT systems demands is therefore challenged by this research question. Through making ethics a lived thing, not a checklist of compliance, it makes the qualitative inquiry a way to know how trust, fairness, and transparency are practiced-or undermined-in education practice.

The third one-- How can qualitative insights inform the design of transparent, explainable, and pedagogically sound GenAI-DT frameworks? 14--connects theory and praxis by pointing to the translational benefit of qualitative research that makes humans in the focus. The fast integration of AI into education, in many cases, is followed by lack of insight into how users interpret AI technologies. This paper thus proposes that the understanding gained through the qualitative analysis, i.e. the stories of perplexity, opposition or trust, or imaginative adjustment should inform the iterative design that posits transparency and explainability. XAI (explainable AI), participatory co-design, and reflexive pedagogy are potentially effective strategies addressing human judgment and interpretability challenges in technical systems. Such insights can be integrated to inform the creation of AI-DT architectures that are not only performance-optimizing but also sensitive to the complexity of learning as a social, emotional, and ethical activity.

Combining all three research questions, they constitute a conceptual triad that places the GenAI-DT convergence in the context of the overall discourse of human-machine collaboration. They support an interpretation of educational technology not as a means of efficiency only but as a socio-technical ecosystem in which learning, power and ethics come together. Through the discussion of the three areas of autonomy, ethics, and design as mutually constitutive aspects, the study will help redefine educational innovation based on responsible human experience as opposed to technological determinism.

CONCLUSION

The intersection of Generative Artificial Intelligence (GenAI) and Digital Twin (DT) technologies is a paradigm shift in the development of the educational system. These technologies combined will bring a new horizon of adaptive, data-driven, and human-centered learning. This paper has embarked on a qualitative investigation of the impacts of such convergence on the technical and pedagogical apparatus of education but more to the point, on the lived human experience of learners and educators. Summarizing the empirical and theoretical studies published after 2018, the analysis shows that even though GenAI-DT integration has significant potential and can be applied in the context of personalization, engagement, and efficiency, its final implementation depends on the comprehension, design, and governance of the human, ethical, and socio-technical dimensions. The results highlight the importance of the fact that the implementation of the Gen AI-DT systems cannot be measured only within the framework of the functional performance or the technological advancements. Rather, it has to be assessed in terms of its effects on the autonomy, trust, emotional experience, and identity formation among educational stakeholders. Adaptive feedback loops and real-time simulations can be utilized to increase engagement and decrease cognitive barriers on the side of the learner.

FUTURE RESEARCH DIRECTIONS

A majority of the existing research offers short term information on user perceptions or phase of initial adoption. Longitudinal, phenomenological studies on the impact of prolonged exposure to AI-driven personalization on the motivation, autonomy, and critical thinking of learners, over time, are urgently required. The effect of initial engagement benefits can be evaluated by such work whether they persist or dependency and cognitive offloading can be considered as the side effect of such work. Such studies will carry with them evidence on how to design pedagogical interventions that will be both assistive and agency.With more and more of the educational system based on algorithmic decision-making, it is important that futuristic work should explore how explainability can gain meaningful application to non-technical stakeholders. It includes the investigation of the ways students, teachers, and parents perceive AI rationales, how the design of explanations influences the levels of trust and acceptance, and which degree of transparency is pedagogically right. The usability testing, participatory co-design, and focus group qualitative insights can be used to guide the next generation of transparent and user-centered AI interfaces in education.

There is a wide disparity between national and institutional frameworks of AI ethics and data privacy (e.g., GDPR in Europe, FERPA in the United States). Future studies ought to provide comparisons of the effect of these regulatory environments on the application, scalability, and social legitimacy of GenAI-DT systems. Those aspects in which the values of privacy, autonomy, and fairness are locally construed, as well as how international standards of responsible AI may apply in various educational eco-systems, may be elucidated by cross-cultural qualitative studies.The interdisciplinary partnership among the computer scientists, educators, ethicists and social scientists must be emphasized to ensure that the technological feasibility is bridged with human values. This study should proceed to establish integrated socio-technical design frameworks that incorporate ethical control, cultural flexibility, and user experience reactions directly into the framework of AI-based education.

MANAGERIAL IMPLICATIONS

The research results have enormous managerial implications to educational leaders, academic administrators and technology managers who are tasked with the adoption of the Generative Artificial Intelligence (GenAI) and Digital Twin (DT) systems in educational institutions. These findings show that a successful deployment of GenAI-DT systems is not as much reliant on the level of technological advancement as it is prone to socio-technical congruence, human supervision, and ethical regulation.

The managers should hence transcend the procurement-based viewpoint and have a systems-based view that acknowledges educators and learners as key stakeholders in the AI-mediated learning frameworks. Institutional leaders must also assist in organizing the decision-making process that balances automation with professional judgment and assert that the results of the GenAI are open to human verification and pedagogical judgment.

PRACTICAL IMPLICATIONS

On the pragmatic level, this work can make practical contributions to teachers, learning designers and institutional leaders who are involved in daily activities in the teaching and learning processes. The results indicate that learners find GenAI-DT systems to be empowering and restrictive at the same time, depending on the operationalization of transparency, feedback design, and the intensity of surveillance. Practitioners must consequently devise learning experiences in which GenAI is framed as an object to think with, but not a generator of solutions, and metacognition, hypothesis testing, and reflective thinking are encouraged instead of passive receivers of AI generated outputs.

THEORETICAL IMPLICATIONS

In theory, this study contributes to the body of literature on educational technology, as it supports Sociotechnical Systems Theory as a powerful perspective to investigation of GenAI-DT integration in education. The discoveries empirically support the argument that the technological effectiveness can not be perceived without the social practices, institutional norms, and human experience. This analysis of the core dimensions of autonomy, trust, identity, and emotional engagement by foregrounding these areas of analysis helps to subvert reductionist models that frame educational innovation as a matter of performance optimization or efficiency achievement.

In addition, the study expands the current conceptual debates of Human-Centered AI and constructivist learning with an illustration on how the development of generative and predictive systems transforms learning into a relational and negotiated process. The conceptual gap between the theory of ethics and practice is bridged by the identification of the socio-technical mediators, explain ability, governance, and human oversight. The research therefore adds to the theory of the aspect that ethics, trust, and agency are not exogenous to AI system but rather internalization of the development as the technology design and the institutional environment.

RECOMMENDATIONS

In accordance with the results, the given study suggests that the educational institutions should utilize a human-focused and participatory perspective of GenAI-DT implementation. Schools ought to put in place a formal system of governance, which will bring educators and students together with technologists and ethicists to making crucial decisions, so that the design and implementation of systems are informed by pedagogical considerations, and not by mere technical necessities. Both educators and learners should receive mandatory AI literacy initiatives, but with a focus on critical knowledge of algorithmic bias, explainability, and data ethics, as opposed to just the think layer.

Besides, the study also suggests that institutions should implement transparency-by-design values, which involve integrating explainable AI processes and transparent data consent policies in DT systems. Teachers must have the financial empowerment and capability to override, remake, or challenge AI-generated suggestions where they need. These steps are crucial to maintain professional agency and avoid the loss of trust that goes hand in hand with opaque automation. The long-term validity and sustainability of GenAI-DT systems in the educational setting is jeopardized without this kind of proactive interventions.

FUTURE DIRECTIONS

These results of this research lead to some significant directions of future research. To begin with, longitudinal qualitative studies that focus on tracking the development of the learner autonomy, trust, and identity as they are affected by the prolonged exposure to GenAI-DT systems are in order. Available evidence indicates that the initial engagement benefits might turn into dependency or resistance with time, which cannot be observed using a short-term or cross-sectional design.

Second, the variability of cross-cultural and institutional administrative and perception of GenAI-DT systems, especially in educational settings with limited resources, should be examined in the future. Comparative analysis would help clarify how the disparities in policy structures, infrastructural capabilities, and cultural beliefs about surveillance influence lived experience. Lastly, education, ethics, human-computer interaction, and data science must be studied concerning the creation of interdisciplinary research, the basis of which is a direct integration of trust, fairness, and explainability into AI-enabled learning settings.

REFERENCES

Engeström, Y. (1987). *Learning by expanding: An activity-theoretical approach to developmental research.* Orienta-Konsultit.

Hao, N., Li, Y., Lu, Y., & Liu, K. (2024). Artificial intelligence-aided digital twin design: A systematic review. *Preprints.*

Huang, Y., Zhang, J., Chen, X., & Lam, A. H. F. (2024). From simulation to prediction: Enhancing digital twins with advanced generative AI technologies. *IEEE Transactions on Learning Technologies.*

Iliu ă, M. E. (2024). Digital twin: A review of the evolution from concept to application. *Applied Sciences (Basel, Switzerland), 14*(13), 5454. DOI: 10.3390/app14135454

Jankovskis, D. (2023). Digital twins and e-learning: Navigating challenges and opportunities. In *Digital transformation, virtual reality and simulation in education* (pp. 123–140). Springer.

Jones, D., Snider, C., Nassehi, A., Yon, J., & Hicks, B. (2023). Characterising the digital twin: A systematic literature review. *CIRP Journal of Manufacturing Science and Technology, 39*, 1–15.

Karya Bakti, I., Ayuningtias, Y., Mokhamad, S., & Hammis, S. (2023). The role of artificial intelligence in education: A systematic literature review. *International Journal of Educational Research, 45*(3), 200–215.

Korada, L. (2024). The role of generative AI in the digital twin landscape and how it accelerates adoption. *Journal of Artificial Intelligence and Machine Learning,* 7(2), 55–68.

Lin, Y. Z., Alhamadah, A. H., Ghimire, S., & Petal, K. (2025). *Personalized education with generative AI and digital twins: VR, RAG, and zero-shot sentiment analysis for Industry 4.0 workforce development. arXiv preprint arXiv:2503.XXXX.*

Lin, Y. Z., Alhamadah, A. H. J., & Redondo, M. W. (2024). *Transforming engineering education using generative AI and digital twin technologies. arXiv preprint arXiv:2402.XXXX.*

Lu, M., & Hu, Z. (2025). Digital twin–enhanced programming education: An empirical study on learning engagement and skill acquisition. *Computers, 14*(8), 322. DOI: 10.3390/computers14080322

Luhmann, N. (1979). *Trust and power. John Wiley & Sons. Piaget, J. (1952). The origins of intelligence in children* (Cook, M., Trans.). International Universities Press. (Original work published 1936)

Mao, J. (2024). *Generative artificial intelligence in education and its implications for assessment. SpringerProfessional.*

Mariam, Z., Niazi, S. K., & Magoola, M. (2024). Unlocking the future of drug development: Generative AI, digital twins, and beyond. *BioMedInformatics*, *4*(2), 79.

Owan, V. J., Abang, K. B., Idika, D. O., Etta, E. O., & Bassey, B. (2023). Exploring the potential of artificial intelligence tools in educational measurement and assessment. *Eurasia Journal of Mathematics, Science and Technology Education*, *19*(8), em2307.

Pester, A., Andres, F., Anantaram, C., & Mason, J. (2025). Generative AI and digital twins: Fostering creativity in learning environments. In *Human–Computer Creativity* (pp. 175–192). Springer.

Ponce, P., Perez, C., Mata, O., & Ramirez, M. (2025). Digital twin designs with generative AI: Crafting a comprehensive framework for manufacturing systems. *Journal of Intelligent Manufacturing*, *36*(2), 355–372.

Shneiderman, B. (2020). Human-centered artificial intelligence: Reliable, safe & trustworthy. *International Journal of Human-Computer Interaction*, *36*(6), 495–504. DOI: 10.1080/10447318.2020.1741118

Tomar, P., & Grover, V. (2023). Transforming the energy sector through generative AI and digital twins. *EAI Endorsed Transactions on Energy Web*, *10*(2), e15.

Trist, E. L., & Bamforth, K. W. (1951). Some social and psychological consequences of the longwall method of coal-getting. *Human Relations*, *4*(1), 3–38. DOI: 10.1177/001872675100400101

Vasconcelos, M. A. R., & dos Santos, R. P. (2023). Enhancing STEM learning with ChatGPT and Bing Chat as objects to think with: A case study. *Eurasia Journal of Mathematics, Science and Technology Education*, *19*(7), em2296.

Vygotsky, L. S. (1978). *Mind in society: The development of higher psychological processes*. Harvard University Press.

Wang, Y., Chen, Y., & Li, M. (2022). Digital twin technology enhances engagement and skill acquisition in introductory programming. *Applied Sciences (Basel, Switzerland)*, *14*(8), 322.

Wu, F. (2025). A systematic review of responses, attitudes, and behaviors toward generative AI in higher education. *Educational Psychology Review*, *37*(2), 401–427.

Xu, Q., Zhou, G., Zhang, C., Chang, F., Cao, Y., & Zhao, D. (2023). Generative AI and digital twin integrated intelligent process planning: A conceptual framework. *Research Square.*

Yusuf, A. (2024). Generative AI and the future of higher education: Threats, opportunities, and policy responses. *International Journal of Educational Technology in Higher Education*, *21*(4), 55–72.

Zhang, A., Gao, Y., Suraworachet, W., Nazaretsky, T., & Cukurova, M. (2025). Evaluating trust in AI, human, and co-produced feedback among undergraduate students. arXiv preprint arXiv:2504.10961.

KEY TERMS AND DEFINITIONS

Algorithmic Surveillance: The constant gathering, processing and explanation of data about learners by AI-enhanced technologies is known as algorithmic surveillance, which subjects data mining to the issues of privacy, consent, and behavior manipulation.

Confidence in AI-Mediated Education: Reliance on AI-mediated education is the perceived validity, justice, and credibility of AI systems as learning associates that are influenced by openness, human regulations, and ethical controls.

Digital Twin (DT): A Digital Twin refers to a dynamic virtual model of a learner or a learning system that is constantly updated with real-time data and allows the process of simulation, prediction, and observation of cognitive, behavioral, and emotional learning states.

Explainable Artificial Intelligence (XAI): Explainable Artificial Intelligence refers to the collection of design methods that enhance AI decision-making procedures to be both open and explainable to non-technical participants in the system, thus enhancing trust and accountability in education.

Generative Artificial Intelligence (GenAI): Generative Artificial Intelligence is artificial intelligence systems that generate novel art, feedback, and forms through learning patterns on extensive datasets, as adaptive intervention systems in education instead of predictive ones.

Learner Autonomy: Learner autonomy refers to the ability of learners to have control, agency, reflective judgement over the processes of learning, and AI-mediated personalization may contribute to or sabotage this autonomy.

Sociotechnical Systems: Sociotechnical systems are combined arrangements of social actors, institutional organization, and technology the functioning of which lies in the correspondence and co-optimization of human and technical elements.

Chapter 7
Contribution of the Ethics of Artificial Intelligence in the Education Sector

Deepa Sharma
https://orcid.org/0000-0003-4374-917X
Maharishi Markandeshwar University, India

Guarav Kumar
https://orcid.org/0000-0003-0159-4499
Maharishi Markandeshwar University, India

ABSTRACT

Artificial Intelligence has revolutionized the education sector, as it has provided technologies that improve learning and administrative duties. However, along with the use of AI, inevitable ethical concerns associated with technological advancements are also emerging. AI systems in education rely heavily on data to optimize learning experiences, monitor student progress and predict outcomes. However, such large-scale data collection and processing raises significant concerns about the security and privacy of student data. Academic records, behavioral data and even biometric information are examples of sensitive student data that can be compromised or misused. While it is also true that AI-powered systems enable customized, deeper learning paths, their excessive use hampers students' critical thinking and creativity. If students are accustomed to completing heavy tasks with the help of AI, they may learn the cognitive processes required for deeper learning to a great extent. y.

DOI: 10.4018/979-8-3373-4982-4.ch007

INTRODUCTION

In today's competitive landscape, AI is revolutionizing the education sector, opening new avenues for learning and growth for both faculty and students. However, there are certain ethical issues that need to be considered, as any technology brings both benefits and drawbacks. The study discusses the ethics of AI in education and how to strike a balance between privacy concerns and innovation. Above all, AI-powered educational systems must be open and responsible (Gadanidis, 2017). This implies that parents, teachers, and students should all be aware of the data being collected, the ways AI is being used in the classroom, and its intended application. It is important to ensure that these systems are being used for educational purposes rather than profit. By providing technologies that improve learning and administrative duties, artificial intelligence is revolutionizing the education sector. Predictive analytics and AI-powered learning systems are some examples of potential applications of AI in education. Proper access to AI-powered learning resources is one of the major ethical concerns (Karakas et al., 2013). Most of these technologies require significant financial expenditure, strong internet infrastructure, and digital knowledge. Nowadays, all educational institutions are investing in the latest AI technologies. Moreover, AI systems designed for English-speaking students are also being used by non-English speaking learners (Adetayo, 2023). The widespread application of AI in educational settings has undoubtedly filtered down to opportunities for professional and personal growth for both teachers and students. From non-teaching aspects such as scheduling, resource allocation, student tracking, and providing information about students to parents/guardians through reports to personalization of teaching and learning such as customized curriculum, assessment design and marking, and AI apps that assist learners or identify changes in learner engagement during foreign language learning, a variety of approaches are being seen on the use of AI in the education sector today. The advancement of artificial intelligence in education has the potential to transform the field and impact everyone's roles. Applications of artificial intelligence in education have been progressively adopted in recent years to improve learning outcomes and experiences as well as expand our knowledge of student learning. However, the use of artificial intelligence in education has raised ethical questions and concerns on a number of topics, including student autonomy and personal data (Al-Mughairi & Bhaskar, 2024). This research sets out on the fundamental considerations supporting ethical artificial intelligence in education. Artificial Intelligence in Education is viewed as a powerful instrument to support technological advancements, educational research, and new paradigms of instruction that are thought to be impractical in traditional classroom settings. Examples of these include the use of artificial neural networks, machine learning, or computer-aided language learning in formal, informal, and non-formal learning contexts. It facilitates asynchronous discussion groups or computer-assisted collaborative learning (Al-Kurdi & Eldabi, 2018). It also offers cost-effective individualized learning via a navigation system supported by algorithms that are encouraged by automated evaluation, facial recognition software, and predictive analytics. Thus, the importance of Artificial Intelligence in Education in fostering a transformation of knowledge, cognition, and culture is becoming more and more supported (Barron, 2008). The engineers and developers of AI systems might be significantly influenced by value education. Unintended effects and negative results can be avoided by promoting ethical considerations during the design and development of AI systems. Fairness, accountability, and openness are more likely to be given top priority in AI projects by developers who have received value education training (Boulay, 2023). AI systems frequently make morally difficult decisions, including when diagnosing medical conditions or controlling autonomous cars. A key component of value education is teaching people how to evaluate these choices critically and take into account their ethical ramifications. This equips people to advocate for responsible AI use and take part in conversations around AI ethics. Moreover, Artificial intelligence (AI) in education raises ethical concerns and privacy risks that necessitate careful scrutiny to distinguish between acting ethically and acting in ways that are ethical. This means that all AI researchers should be aware of the ethical ramifications of their work. In fact, numerous studies have unveiled the rise of differing ethical themes concerning general AI and Artificial intelligence (AI) in education, the majority of which pertain to data liability across various contexts, including higher education. This technology, which uses emotional computing and artificial intelligence methods to understand, learn, and connect with human emotional life, is known as emotional AI, and is starting to find its way into classrooms (Camilleri, 2021). In the field of education, there is a notion that businesses advocate adopting emotional AI to record students' facial expressions, such as boredom, frustration, and excitement, in order to assess student participation, adjust and refine the difficulty of the content accordingly, and detect students who may be going through emotional difficulties. As the use of AI is rapidly increasing, the integration of AI-powered tools and techniques in education has given rise to many curiosities about the changing roles of teachers and students as well as its effects on school curriculum and essential digital literacy (Isave, 2025). As AI systems and processes are beginning to infiltrate various aspects of education, apprehensions are growing about the ethical implications of artificial intelligence in education. It is important to understand the complexity of ethical issues associated with the use of AI in education and the complexities inherent in the term ethics (Godemann & Moon, 2014). While there are several established schools of ethical thought, ethics as a discipline has deep and contested theoretical foundations. Without a doubt, universities are implementing AI systems and technologies more and more. This poses several ethical challenges, such as job security, data privacy, and the digital divide. Educational institutions can leverage AI's potential to enhance learning and foster inclusive educational environments by prioritizing human augmentation, ethical AI development, equitable technology access, and AI literacy. One of the main benefits for students using AI in their studies is the enhancement of their digital literacy, which increases their employability (Izenstark et al., 2015).

BACKGROUND

Ethical AI in education refers to the design, use, and management of people-centered AI tools that prioritize fairness and transparency while ensuring the well-being of students and teachers. The goal is to ensure that these advanced technologies support the learning experience, not undermine it (Nair et al., 2021). AI and value education are inextricably intertwined in the current setting, with ethical intelligence acting as a link between the two. It is crucial that we provide people with the information, abilities, and moral underpinnings they need to use AI responsibly as it continues to change our world. While AI offers the means for advancement and creativity, value education supplies the moral compass. Integrating value education into AI education, development, and application must be a top priority if we are to build a peaceful and moral AI-driven society. By doing this, we can protect our common human values and beliefs while utilizing AI to its fullest potential. By doing this, we can guarantee that AI will be a positive force that improves rather than diminishes the human experience.

History of Artificial Intelligence: Recent years have seen impressive developments in artificial intelligence, the branch of computer science devoted to building machines that can mimic human ability. Applications of artificial intelligence (AI) technology, such as computer vision, machine learning, and natural language processing, can be found in a number of industries, including healthcare, finance, education, and transportation (Saqib et al., 2025). These developments have the power to transform entire sectors, boost productivity, and improve many people's quality of life. In the field of education, the history of AI ethics shows a transition from an emphasis on technical capabilities to a heightened awareness of the ethical ramifications of using AI in learning. The PLATO system from the 1960s exemplifies early educational AI systems that were predominantly learner-facing and aimed at providing particular content. These systems involved minimal data collection, which reduced various ethical issues associated with contemporary AI applications. With the rise of advanced AI systems that leverage machine learning and extensive data analysis, ethical issues concerning bias, privacy, and autonomy have taken center stage in the debate. Below, we discussed the stages:

AI in education began in the 1960s with early computer-based teaching systems like PLATO, developed through the 1970s and 1980s with Intelligent Tutoring Systems (ITS) providing personalized feedback, experienced "AI winter" funding dips, but saw a resurgence with machine learning in the 2000s and a boom in the 2020s with Large Language Models (LLMs) (like ChatGPT), moving from simple instruction to sophisticated, adaptive learning experiences and generative tools, despite continuous ethical and practical issues.

a. Early Years (1960s–1980s)

1960s: The PLATO system, which introduced capabilities like forums and instant messaging for learning, allowed for network-based computer-assisted instruction with visual interaction.

1970s: Adaptive lessons based on student input were introduced by the first Intelligent Tutoring Systems (ITS), such SCHOLAR, which imitated human tutors.

1980s: Intelligent Tutoring Systems remained mostly in research settings but became more advanced, providing adaptive feedback.

b. Development and Research (1990s-2000s)

1990s: Despite slower development and "AI winters" (funding cuts), research persisted, and in 1993 the International Artificial Intelligence in Education Society was established.

2000s: The development of massive datasets and powerful technology accelerated the use of machine learning, enhancing individualized learning through adaptive systems.

c. Research and Development (1990s–2000s)

1990s: Research continued despite slower advancement and "AI winters" (funding cuts), and the International Artificial Intelligence in Education Society was founded in 1993.

2000s: The use of machine learning was pushed by the creation of large datasets and potent technology, which improved personalized learning through adaptive systems.

IMPORTANT THEMES THROUGHOUT HISTORY

From PLATO's adaptable lessons to today's LLMs, personalization has always been an aim.

Adaptively: A key component of ITS and contemporary AI, systems that adapt to the needs of students. The most recent generation of generative AI provides innovative tools for assessment, tutoring, and content production.

Challenges: Cost, accessibility, ethics, and striking a balance between AI's promise and conventional education continue to be major concerns.

Elements of Value Education: Artificial intelligence's (AI) explosive growth has opened up a world of possibilities, from improving healthcare diagnosis to fostering human relationships on social media and increasing labor efficiency through automated activities. But there are also serious ethical questions raised by these quick adjustments (Sultan et al., 2013). These result from AI systems' capacity to instill prejudices, exacerbate climate change, jeopardize human rights, and more. These AI-related hazards have already started to exacerbate pre-existing disparities, further harming already marginalized groups. Value education includes many different elements, such as but not limited to:

a. **Moral and ethical values:** Encouraging people to act ethically in different situations and teaching them the difference between right and wrong, *etc.*
b. **Social responsibility:** Emphasizing the value of giving back and making a good impact while fostering a sense of duty towards one's community and society.
c. **Empathy and compassion:** Promoting kindness and understanding by developing empathy for the thoughts, feelings, and experiences of others.
d. **Critical thinking:** Acquiring the ability to critically evaluate situations, make wise decisions, and solve ethical puzzles.
e. **Respect for diversity:** Promoting tolerance and respect for individuals with diverse origins, cultures, and worldviews.
f. **Environmental responsibility:** Encouraging sustainable activities and raising awareness of environmental challenges.

LITERATURE REVIEW

In the last few decades, several literature reviews have been included to highlight the contribution of the ethics of artificial intelligence in the education sector. Over the past few decades, there has been a considerable evolution in the field of ethics of artificial intelligence in the education sector. According to Zeb (2025), the purpose of this study was to examine the relationship between artificial intelligence

(AI), knowledge sharing, ethics, education, and libraries in academic institutions, in light of the growing academic interest in ChatGPT due to its advanced features and capabilities. Additionally, this research seeks to establish a literature base by examining recent trends in AI and ChatGPT technologies and emphasizing their specific applications within institutions. The research found that the use of AI and ChatGPT technologies in academic institutions impacts knowledge sharing, ethical considerations, education, and libraries. This research outlines the literature possibilities related to the trends and appropriate application of AI and ChatGPT within institutions, including the enhancement of student-teacher interaction. According to Rodrigues (2025) this research attempted to conduct a systematic literature review (SLR) using bibliometrics on the relationship between academic integrity and artificial intelligence (AI) in order to connect the fragmented literature on this topic, which presents both challenges and opportunities for the educational and academic community. As technology advances at a rapid pace, the development of AI tools has also increased rapidly, posing a threat to the academic integrity of students in higher education. Despite such interest, academic literature on how AI can help academic integrity is scarce. This paper thus identifies two major thematic patterns: academic integrity and factors that negatively affect academic integrity. According to Wang (2021) examined that artificial intelligence (AI) refers to a category of algorithms or computer systems that mimic the human cognitive processes involved in decision making. This position paper examines the implications of AI in teaching and learning without sensationalism. Instead, the purpose of this paper is to explore how AI plays a role in educational leadership. Because of its effectiveness in collecting, processing, and analyzing data and providing results in or near real-time, AI can bring analytical efficiencies that help educational leaders make decisions based on data and evidence. Yet, making decisions based on data and with the assistance of AI can conflict with ethical decision making based on values. When considered holistically, both leaders' individual and organizational decision-making processes are most effectively managed through a combination of data-based, evidence-informed decision making and value-based ethical decision making. AI can serve as a complementary brain in making decisions based on data and evidence. Human decision-making guided by ethical values can overcome the shortcomings of AI-assisted data-driven decision-making. According to Saednia (2023) the purpose of this study was to raise awareness of the ethical implications of artificial intelligence (AI) in the library and information industry, with a special focus on bias and discrimination. It aims to emphasize the need for pre-emptive action against these problems and to ensure that AI technology is created and applied ethically and without bias. The findings of this study indicate that bias and discrimination are serious problems in AI systems used in the library and information sector. Such bias can maintain pre-existing inequalities, hinder access to information, and promote discriminatory practices. This study identifies strategies needed to address these problems, including data collection and representation, algorithmic transparency, and inclusive design. According to Agrawal (2024) the paper also highlights the ways in which information technology is used to transform businesses and execute business strategies, with the aim of encouraging the use of these technologies in current or future emergencies. The authors have identified 127 empirical papers that suggest the use of 39 types of smart technologies, ranging from artificial intelligence to computer vision technology. Eight different sectors are recognized as using these technologies, with food services and manufacturing leading the way. Additionally, the authors list 40 generalized categories of activities such as healthcare delivery, data analysis, and communication. To prevent disease transmission, AI-enabled robots are used to examine patients and administer medication. Due to the pandemic, online executions of teaching methods and simulators have replaced classroom teaching methods. The blue-dot algorithm based on AI helps identify early warning signs. The AI model identifies a patient experiencing shortness of breath. Giuggioli & Pellegrini (2023) examined how the disruptive potential of artificial intelligence (AI) is increasingly being acknowledged in terms of the beneficial effects of AI on entrepreneurship, yet there is a lack of systematic investigation of this relationship in the academic literature. The purpose of this research is to investigate the impact of AI on entrepreneurship as a facilitator for entrepreneurs, considering the essential use of AI in all technological paradigms of Industry 4.0, including smart factories, the Internet of Things (IoT), augmented reality (AR), and block chain. This research shows that AI significantly impacts entrepreneurship and benefits entrepreneurs in four specific aspects: opportunities, decision-making capabilities, performance, and education and research. Nordgren (2023). The purpose of this paper was to identify and investigate ethical issues arising from the dual role of artificial intelligence (AI) in relation to climate change, which may be important for both mitigation and adaptation efforts. Given AI's dual function, it is important for companies and governments to consider ethical considerations. According to Hussain (2023) the purpose of the research paper is to emphasize how AI was used in library operations. There have been many studies on this topic, but they focus on only a few applications. This article emphasizes the advantages and disadvantages of AI in library services. There is a significant relationship between AI and libraries; nevertheless, questions still arise regarding the use and awareness of AI in library services, which this research paper addresses. The results of this research indicate that AI is a dynamic technology for library services; certain barriers, such as adequate funding, librarians' attitudes, and technical expertise, hinder the implementation of AI in library operations. The results show that the use of AI in library operations will rapidly move libraries' progress in the right direction. According to Pesano (2023) the purpose of this study was to explore the use of artificial intelligence (AI) in the context of organizational behavior and human-machine relationships. The purpose of this research paper is to analyze whether current AI is also being used to replace humans in creative activities. The research areas include AI, organizational behavior, human-machine relationships, and creativity. The investigation found that the widespread application of AI in organizational behavior can replace human labor in creative tasks. According to Elhassan & Arabi (2025), the aim of this paper was to highlight ethical issues related to the application of artificial intelligence (AI) in healthcare and propose solutions that can optimize the benefits of this technology while adhering to ethical standards. Research points to various benefits of AI in medicine, such as its ability to boost diagnostic accuracy, improve surgical outcomes, and streamline healthcare provision. Nonetheless, ethical concerns remain unresolved, including algorithmic bias, insufficient transparency, data privacy challenges, and the risk that AI could lead to a decline in the skills of healthcare practitioners and a decline of humanistic values in patient care. It is therefore important to tackle these matters as early as possible in order to reap the benefits of AI implementation while avoiding any serious negative consequences. According to Saurabh (2022) the aim was to examine how digital transformation (DT) uses digital technologies to modify existing processes and implement new processes in an organization's business model, customer, user experience, and operational processes (DT pillars). The investigation found that AI is a key factor in achieving digital transformation (DT). As digital transformation affects every aspect of humanity, AI-driven digital transformation (DT) is giving rise to several essential questions. These questions highlight concerns related to the systems in use, their expected behavior, the associated risks, and other aspects including the monitoring and evaluation mechanisms we have put in place. These issues highlight the need to incorporate ethics in AI-driven digital transformation (DT). According to Huang (2024) this research examined the various applications of artificial intelligence (AI) in academic libraries, as well as the main factors influencing their implementation and the barriers faced by them. Design/Methodology/Approach The author used quantitative research methods through questionnaires that included both open and closed-ended questions. Academic librarians provided a total of 472 valid responses. The author collected feedback from librarians who had implemented AI tools and those who had not, pointing out the varieties of AI tools used, important elements related to their use, and barriers to encouraging AI. It was noted that there were discrepancies between the degree of support for AI applications and the adverse impact of barriers. Furthermore, librarians' attitudes towards AI applications in their libraries were increasingly positive. According to Ohadomere (2021) the aim of this paper was to focus on management-led intervention strategies designed to achieve stable mental well-being among academic staff in higher education institutions (HEIs) by reviewing and synthesizing existing literature on various ways to manage stress and improve mental health at the workplace. Despite mental health awareness being globally recognized as an important issue, there is a lack of research evidence regarding the management of stress and mental health among academic staff in higher education institutions through greater involvement of university management. While university managements prioritize employee well-being, most higher education institutions were more focused on corporatization and student satisfaction, thereby ignoring the impact on academic staff well-being. According to Liu (2019), the goal of this study was to suggest appropriate methods and approaches to strengthen environmental ethics education based on scientific research techniques, sound scientific theories, and specific aspects of environmental ethics education. The research findings showed that there was a significant correlation between environmental education and environmental ethics; environmental ethics and knowledge of environmental issues; and environmental education and literacy. According to Imanova (2025) this paper examined the need for an approach to the global development and application of AI that incorporates cultural and technological diversity, values, legal frameworks, and ethical concerns. The findings suggest that AI is a technological force that connects economies, permeates societies, and transforms their governing structures worldwide, just as firearms, bombs, and other weapons can. Autonomous cars, language models, predictive analytics, virtual assistants, and other AI systems are revolutionizing the way countries operate and interact. According to Wang (2025) examined how AI governance has become a major topic of global interest in the era of the intelligent science paradigm. To serve as a resource for advancing academic research in this area and enhancing the standards and impact of social governance, this study aims to carefully analyze the current state of AI governance research worldwide. Identifying key research hotspots, the study identifies four key research areas in AI governance today and develops their theoretical framework. Using altmetrics analysis, it uncovers the societal focus on AI governance and examines key papers that have a significant impact on academia and society. It then forecasts future developments in this area. Furthermore, the study comprehensively examines and aggregates international AI governance laws and regulations, as well as the risks associated with them. According to Silva (2025) given the difficulty and potential for the academic and educational community, this study attempts to undertake a systematic literature review (SLR) utilizing bibliometrics on the relationship between academic integrity and artificial intelligence (AI). AI tools have proliferated because to the quick development of technology, endangering the academic integrity of college students. There is a paucity of scholarly work on how AI may support academic integrity despite this substantial interest. Thus, academic integrity and negative predictors of academic integrity are two important topic patterns that are distinguished in this paper.

THE NEED FOR ETHICS OF ARTIFICIAL INTELLIGENCE IN THE EDUCATION SECTOR

With the growing integration of artificial intelligence (AI) into education, emphasizing ethics is crucial for ensuring that its implementation is responsible, equitable, and effective. AI in education presents vast possibilities, including the personalization of learning experiences, automation of administrative tasks, and improvements in student engagement and accessibility (O'Neill et al., 2004). Nevertheless, if ethical considerations are not central to its development, AI can present serious dangers and worsen current inequalities. Here are the main reasons emphasizing the requirement of AI ethics in education:

1. **Reduced Bias and treat fairly:** This can result in discrimination against students based on factors such as race, gender, socioeconomic status, or disability. As an illustration, qualified applicants from diverse backgrounds may be unfairly disadvantaged by AI-driven admissions systems that are trained on data with historical biases (Rae et al., 2010).

Ethical Imperative: It is crucial to guarantee fairness and equity in AI applications. This necessitates thorough assessment of algorithms and datasets for possible biases, the use of fairness-aware algorithms, and the encouragement of diverse representation within development teams. The aim is to use AI to close educational gaps and foster inclusivity, rather than to expand them.

2. **Safeguarding the Privacy and Security of Student Data Risk:** Educational AI systems typically necessitate access to large quantities of sensitive student data, which encompasses personal details, behavioral trends, and academic performance. This gives rise to serious concerns regarding data breaches, misuse, and unauthorized access. According to the Thomas B. Fordham Institute, the risk of privacy breaches and misuse rises when excessive or unnecessary data is collected.

Ethical Imperative: Strong data privacy and security measures are essential. This entails the adoption of robust encryption, methods for anonymization, explicit consent procedures, and transparent data collection, storage, use, and retention policies.

3. **Guaranteeing Transparency and Understandability of AI Decisions Risk:** A significant number of AI systems, especially those based on intricate algorithms, function as "black boxes." This results in a lack of clarity regarding their decision-making processes and renders them hard to comprehend. This

absence of transparency may result in distrust and difficulties in comprehending or contesting AI-generated recommendations or assessments, exemplified by a student being identified for extra assistance based on ambiguous criteria.

Ethical imperative: It is crucial to foster transparency and explain ability in AI systems. AI systems ought to be built with audibility and traceability in mind, enabling stakeholders to comprehend the decision-making process. Students, educators, and administrators should be given clear explanations of AI outputs, potential biases, and limitations (Zamberi et al., 2013).

4. **Tackling Accountability and Responsibility for AI Actions Risk:** It can be difficult to ascertain who is responsible if an AI system makes a mistake or yields detrimental results (for instance, misassessing a student's abilities or creating biased content). The chain of responsibility may become ambiguous, which could result in those adversely affected having no recourse.

Ethical Imperative: It is essential to set clear boundaries for accountability and responsibility regarding the development, deployment, and use of AI in education. This requires developers, educators, policymakers, and institutions to work together to guarantee human oversight and intervention when needed and to tackle unintended consequences.

5. **Promoting Human-Centric AI and Critical Thinking Risk:** An excessive dependence on AI could reduce human interaction, critical thinking, and creativity elements essential to a comprehensive education. AI could take over tasks that play a role in learning or that diminish the significance of relationships between teachers and students, as well as social-emotional learning.

Ethical Imperative: AI ought to enhance human intelligence and the distinctive function of human educators, rather than replace them. Ethical AI in education empowers both teachers and students, promotes independent learning and critical thinking, and nurtures human interaction. Achieving equilibrium between human decision-making and AI assistance is vital, as it guarantees that students cultivate the necessary abilities for a world shaped by AI.

ETHICAL PRINCIPLES RELATED TO USE ARTIFICIAL INTELLIGENCE IN THE EDUCATION SECTOR

1. **Proportionality and Do No Harm:** AI systems ought to be developed and employed in ways that reduce potential harm while maximizing advantages for all learners.
2. **Equity and Non-discrimination:** AI systems ought to be created and implemented to guarantee fair results for every student, irrespective of their background or traits.
3. **Transparency and Explainability:** AI systems need to be developed with transparency and understandability in mind, so that students, educators, and other stakeholders can comprehend their functioning and decision-making processes.
4. **Human Oversight and Determination:** AI must serve as a support tool for human educators, rather than a replacement. All crucial elements of the learning process should continue to involve human supervision and decision-making.
5. **Privacy and Data Security:** Solid measures should be implemented to safeguard student data privacy and guarantee responsible and ethical use of the data.

BLOCK DIAGRAM: PHASES OF INTEGRATING ETHICAL AI IN EDUCATION

The Block Diagram: Phases of Integrating Ethical AI into Education is a conceptual or visual model that describes the organized, sequential steps a system or institution must take to effectively integrate AI technology into teaching methods. Throughout the lifecycle and integration process of an AI system, it transforms abstract ethical concepts (such as responsibility, transparency, and justice) into tangible, actionable actions.

Typically depicting information and process flow between several functional "blocks," this graphic show how ethical considerations are incorporated at each stage to ensure that AI is used fair, safe, and consistent with human values and educational objectives, as illustrated in table 1.

Table 1.

Stage	Key Activities	Ethical Focus & Contribution
Basic Planning and Framework Development	Stakeholders must be identified, a common vision must be established, high-level principles (such as fairness, openness, privacy, accountability, and human oversight) must be established, and policies must be developed.	This guarantees a human-centered approach, aligning the application of AI with basic educational principles and to help the take appropriate decision.
Designing and Developing AI Tools Properly	Incorporate "ethics by design" into the technical development process, ensuring that datasets are inclusive and diverse; implement bias mitigation strategies and provide thorough documentation.	Protect data security and privacy, reduce algorithmic bias and bias, and enhance explain ability and user understanding.
Execution and Building Capabilities	Install AI tools; train parents, instructors, and students in AI literacy; and set up informed consent procedures (particularly for minors).	Ensures fair access to technology and training, fosters awareness and critical participation, and safeguards student autonomy and data rights.
Ongoing Observation and Assessment	Integrate monitoring systems (such as data governance procedures and ethical review boards); gather input from all parties involved; and carry out frequent audits to evaluate results and performance.	Fosters user trust, enables early detection and rectification of ethical issues, and offers methods for accountability and reparation.
Policy Improvement and Modification (Feedback Loop)	Utilize evaluation findings and comments to enhance procedures, modify AI tools, and improve policies; respond to new social norms and technical developments.	Guarantees the framework's long-term relevance and efficacy, encourages a cycle of ongoing development, and keeps it in line with human rights and educational objectives.

PERSPECTIVES OF STUDENTS & FACULTY TOWARDS AI IN THE EDUCATION SECTOR

This engagement process involves recognizing the use of generative AI across different fields and its timing, evaluating the trustworthiness and accuracy of outputs produced by AI, understanding the ethical and societal consequences that arise from designing and utilizing generative AI tools, and developing and interacting with generative AI systems in suitable manners. This applies to both students and faculty. Insights received from faculty and students underscore the promise of AI for enhancing learning across a variety of academic fields. Faculty is optimistic about AI's effectiveness in improving educational processes and project-based activities today. AI provides students with immediate and comprehensive feedback on their performance, aiding them in identifying their strengths and weaknesses. Such feedback deepens understanding and learning outcomes, while also guiding teachers on areas to concentrate on in subsequent lessons. Teachers' digital competence correlates with their attitudes toward AI, irrespective of personal variables. Teachers reported a strong willingness to utilize AI, but indicated limited personal experience with it. AI in education offers a variety of benefits for both students and teachers. For students, AI provides personalized learning experiences, automated feedback, and increased engagement through resources like virtual tutors and adaptive learning platforms. For faculty members, AI simplifies administrative responsibilities, provides insights based on data, and can help create content and design personalized learning experiences. Below, we describe the perspectives of both sides regarding the use of AI in the education sector:

1. **For Faculty:** The perspective of faculty on AI use in education is described below:
   a. **Streamlined Administrative Work:** AI can handle tasks such as grading, scheduling, and generating reports automatically, allowing teachers to concentrate on teaching and engaging with students.
   b. Data Insights: AI assesses student performance to identify trends, areas needing support, and guide strategies.
   c. **Design of Personalized Learning:** Teachers can leverage AI to develop individualized learning plans and resources that cater to the specific needs of each student.
   d. **Content Generation:** AI can take on the task of generating educational materials—like quizzes, summaries, and complete lesson plans thereby conserving teachers' time and energy.

Enhanced Teaching Practices: AI can offer teachers valuable insights into student learning patterns and suggest ways to improve their teaching methods.

2. **For Students:** Below, we describe the perspective of students on to use of AI in the education sector:
   a. **Personalized Learning:** AI customizes educational materials and the speed of instruction to match each student's unique needs, learning preferences, and skill levels. This results in a more effective and engaging learning experience.
   b. **Automated Assessment and Commentary:** With AI-powered tools, the grading of assignments can be automated, and instant feedback can be given. This enables students to learn from their errors and improve in real-time.
   c. **Boosted Involvement of Students:** With their around-the-clock availability, chatbots and virtual assistants can make learning more interactive and enjoyable.

d. **Predictive Analytics:** AI can examine student data to pinpoint students at risk and offer preemptive measures, aiding them in remaining aligned with their goals.

IN WHAT WAYS DOES AI WORK IN THE EDUCATION SECTOR?

AI in education can be leveraged in numerous ways, such as aiding students with research, tailoring the learning experience to individual needs, and automating administrative duties. As an example, a student researching the differences in Tesla's marketing strategy across regions could leverage AI to scan investor reports, news articles, and competitor analyses in a fraction of the usual time. Moreover, a chatbot within the business faculty portal can help students with module registrations, assignment submissions, or clarifying distinctions between electives like Strategic Management and Entrepreneurial Finance. As a result, both students and universities can utilize AI to simplify tasks. Unfortunately, though, AI presents a number of challenges. Students misusing AI tools is another issue. For instance, there's a worry that some students might rely on AI resources such as ChatGPT and writing assistants to complete their assignments. Although it is acceptable for students to use AI as a learning aid and educational resource, they should not rely on it to do their thinking for them. This can have a serious effect on creativity, hindering the student's development of critical thinking, creative, or innovative skills.

ETHICAL CHALLENGES RELATED TO AI IN THE EDUCATION SECTOR

With its potential to improve teaching and learning, personalize instruction, enhance assessment, and increase access and equity, artificial intelligence (AI) is revolutionizing the educational landscape. However, educators, legislators, researchers, and developers must carefully analyze and handle the serious ethical issues raised by AI. Despite all the positive aspects, the rapid adoption of artificial intelligence (AI) in society has raised some concerns. Some in the public relations industry are expressing serious concerns, despite the fact that many consider it a potential business advantage. These include concerns about privacy, plagiarism, algorithms, data, and fake news.

Since every mistake we PR professionals make will now be magnified in the world of big data, it is important that we prioritize ethics. In order to guarantee the responsible and fair use of AI-powered tools in education, ethical considerations of AI are essential. These factors include, among others, accessibility, bias and fairness, data privacy, and the effect on the teacher-student relationship. Below describes ethical challenges related to AI in the education sector:

a. **Data Security and Privacy:** AI systems used in education frequently gather and examine vast volumes of student data, which raises questions regarding data security and privacy. AI systems have the potential to gather, store, process, and distribute vast amounts of sensitive and personal data from teachers and students, including behavior, academic performance, preferences, feelings, biometrics, and health information. Their right to privacy and data protection may be jeopardized, particularly if the information is utilized for objectives other than teaching, such as profiling, commercialization, or spying. AI systems in education gather a range of student data, which encompasses personal details, academic records, i.e. including grades and test scores, and behavioral information like engagement patterns or online activity. This data is frequently employed to develop tailored learning experiences, enhance educational results, or optimize administrative workflows. Nonetheless, gathering and retaining such sensitive information carries considerable privacy risks. This encompasses unauthorized access, data breaches, or the misuse of student information for non-educational purposes. As an example, if behavioral data is not adequately protected, it may be used for non-educational commercial purposes or result in erroneous assumptions about students. Informed consent and transparency should be prioritized by educational institutions in order to tackle these concerns. This entails providing a clear explanation to students and parents regarding the data being collected, the methods of its storage, and its intended uses. Implementing stringent data protection procedures and complying with privacy legislation can foster trust and guarantee that student data is managed in a responsible and ethical manner.
b. **Fairness and Bias:** If AI algorithms are not properly developed and taught, they have the potential to reinforce and magnify preexisting prejudices, producing unjust results for particular student groups. AI systems have the potential to mirror or magnify human biases and prejudices, which could result in unfair or discriminatory outcomes for particular student or teacher groups. AI systems might, for instance, employ algorithms that are opaque or unaccountable for their choices, or they might use data that is insufficient, erroneous, or not representative of the diversity of learners. AI bias occurs when the outcomes it generates are unjust or distorted because of issues with the data it uses for learning or its programming. This may happen when the training data lacks a diverse array of viewpoints, when the system is inadequately designed, or when societal inequalities are inherent in the data. For instance, in the field of education, bias might manifest through grading systems that advantage students from particular backgrounds, admissions choices that inadvertently leave out certain groups,

or educational resources that are more effective for some demographics than for others. Due to the possibility of these biases causing students to be treated unfairly and resulting in their missing out on opportunities, it is vital that any potential biases are carefully evaluated and addressed when AI is employed.

c. **Accessibility and Equity:** While AI has the ability to improve accessibility and customize learning, it is imperative that all students have fair access to AI tools and resources. The subject of accountability or responsibility for the design, development, deployment, use, or impact of AI systems in education may come up. The distribution of responsibilities and functions among the various players in the AI ecosystem may become unclear or lacking as a result. AI systems, for instance, have the potential to make mistakes or inflict harm that cannot be attributed to any particular human agent. To foster trust in AI systems applied to education, transparency and accountability are vital. Students, educators, and parents are more inclined to trust and accept tools when they comprehend how decisions like grading, admissions, or tailored learning advice are determined. Transparency involves offering lucid accounts of how AI processes data and reaches conclusions, enabling users to assess the system's fairness and accuracy. As an example, when an AI tool proposes a customized study plan, it is essential for both teachers and learners to have visibility into the elements that shaped those suggestions. Moreover, without accountability, it becomes challenging to tackle and rectify problems, which may enable detrimental practices to continue.

d. **Relationship between Teacher and Student:** AI should complement, not replace, the essential emotional support and human interaction that teachers offer. Ethically employing AI in education offers many advantages, beginning with its capacity to develop customized learning experiences. When it comes to individual needs and abilities, AI can assist in personalizing lesson plans, suggesting resources, and pinpointing areas where students require additional support, all without succumbing to the pitfalls of biased recommendations. For instance, tools powered by AI can propose reading materials that are appropriately challenging or tailor the speed of a math program to align with a student's advancement. Not only does this strategy improve learning results, but it also guarantees that students feel supported and understood.

e. **Explain ability and Transparency:** Understanding how AI systems make judgments and ensuring accountability in AI-driven processes are crucial for educators, parents, and students. Students, instructors, and other stakeholders may find it challenging to comprehend or challenge the opaque or sophisticated manner in which AI systems function. Their capacity to trust, validates, contest, or appeal the decisions or acts of AI systems may be restricted as a result. AI systems might, for instance, employ "black-box" algorithms, which conceal the methods by which they arrive at their judgments or forecasts.

f. **Effect on Job Security:** Teachers and support personnel may face job displacement as a result of AI-driven automation in education.

g. **Effect on Learner Agency and Autonomy**: AI systems ought to give students more control over their education rather than take away their capacity for decision-making. AI systems have the potential to impact or impede teachers' and students' autonomy and agency, which could hinder their capacity to make thoughtful decisions, take charge of their education, express their creativity, or hone their critical thinking abilities. For instance, AI systems may substitute automated responses for human engagement and guidance, or they may offer suggestions or feedbacks that are not in line with the objectives, interests, or values of the learners.

h. To use AI ethically and effectively, educators require adequate training, as it provides them with a clear understanding of how these systems work, what they can do, and where their limits lie. Educators can pinpoint possible biases, guarantee fair outcomes, and use AI responsibly in their teaching methods by understanding how AI tools analyze data and make decisions. Training enables teachers to connect the use of AI with ethical standards and educational objectives, thereby improving personalized learning experiences while maintaining fairness and transparency. Educators who are well-informed can assist students in comprehending and using AI-driven tools, thereby promoting a cooperative and reliable educational atmosphere.

i. To safeguard student information in the educational use of AI, it is crucial to establish and enforce strong data privacy policies. To ensure transparency and trust, clear guidelines should outline the data collection process, its intended use, and who will have access to it. It is essential to respect the autonomy and rights of students and their guardians by obtaining informed consent from them. Furthermore, by employing robust encryption and cybersecurity strategies, sensitive data can be protected from unauthorized access or breaches, thereby ensuring the safety and privacy of students' personal information. In the realm of education, ethical AI entails the development, application, and administration of AI tools with a priority on human welfare, emphasizing equity, openness, and the health of teachers and students alike. The goal is to guarantee that these advanced technologies assist with the learning experience rather than detract from it. To tackle worries regarding privacy, job security, and equitable student data usage, AI ethics plays an essential role in higher education. Responsible use of the technology is guaranteed through ethical AI practices, safeguarding educators and students from possible harm. AI plays a complex role in examinations, providing advantages like automated marking, plagiarism identification, and the creation of tailored feedback. By reducing their administrative workload, teachers can allocate more time to engaging with students and enhancing instruction. AI systems may occasionally produce discriminatory results by reflecting the biases of the data they are trained on. AI systems have the potential of becoming prejudiced in ways that could negatively affect particular groups of people, whether on purpose or accidentally.

LINKING AI AND ETHICS IN EDUCATION

The ethical and societal ramifications of AI, particularly in the field of education, are vast and intricate. Here are a few issues to take into account:

1. **Accessibility and Equity:** AI has the potential to enhance the accessibility and personalization of education, allowing students to learn at their individual pace and equipping teachers with resources to pinpoint areas of student difficulty. Additionally, it could provide opportunities for students in remote regions or those unable to attend school because of health problems or disabilities. Nonetheless, it is important to note that students and schools do not have the same level of access to the technology and infrastructure necessary for AI-based education. This digital gap can worsen educational disparities.
2. **Data Privacy and Security:** Many educational AI systems depend on the collection and analysis of extensive data regarding students. This prompts inquiries into the methods of data storage, the individuals with access to it, and its utilization. The risks of privacy violations and possible data misuse exist.
3. **Bias and Fairness:** Educational AI, like all AI systems, can exhibit bias based on its training methods and the data used for training. As an example, the data used for training could lead to an AI tutoring system favoring some types of students over others. This might sustain current biases and disparities.
4. **Teacher-Student Relationship:** Although some tasks can be automated by AI, it cannot substitute for the human interaction and emotional support that teachers provide. People are worried that depending too much on AI might undermine the relationship between teachers and students, as well as the development of students' social skills in the classroom.
5. **Skill Development:** With the growing integration of AI and automation into the workforce, it is essential to ensure that education systems are adequately equipping students with the skills they will need in the future. This encompasses not only the technical competencies required for AI work but also essential soft skills such as creativity and critical thinking—traits that cannot yet be mimicked by AI.
6. **Transparency and Comprehension:** Students, parents, and educators must grasp the decision-making processes of AI tools. Regrettably, a lot of AI sys-

tems are "black boxes," meaning that their decision-making processes are not transparent. This may complicate trusting the system or contesting its decisions.

7. **Regulation and Policy:** In light of these challenges, it is evident that regulations and policies are necessary to steer the application of AI in education. These regulations must tackle concerns such as data privacy, transparency, and equity. Yet, developing policies in this field is intricate and requires finding a balance between safeguarding students and facilitating innovation.

SIGNIFICANCE OF ETHICAL ISSUES OF AI IN EDUCATION

A major paradigm change has occurred with the arrival of artificial intelligence (AI) in higher education, which has the potential to completely rethink conventional teaching methods. This new technology is both thrilling and intimidating. Although artificial intelligence (AI) presents enormous potential for improving and customizing educational experiences, it also poses ethical and legal issues. This situation, in which technology develops faster than related laws and social standards, is not specific to AI and is representative of a typical trend in the development of disruptive technologies. It is crucial to address the ethical concerns surrounding AI in education for a number of reasons.

1. **To uphold dignity and human rights:** The basic human rights and dignity of both instructors and children may be impacted by the ethical concerns surrounding AI in education. For instance,
    a. The right to an education free from prejudice may be violated by bias and discrimination.
    b. The right to privacy may be violated by privacy and data protection.
    c. The right to freedom of mind may be infringed by autonomy and agency.
    d. The right to information may be violated by transparency and the capacity to explain. Responsibility and accountability could infringe on the right to redress.
2. **To guarantee efficacy and quality:** The quality and efficacy of educational procedures and results may be impacted by the ethical concerns surrounding AI in education. For instance,

Discrimination and bias can lower an assessment's validity and accuracy.

Learners' confidence may be weakened by privacy and data protection. Learner's engagement and motivation may be hampered by autonomy and agency.

Transparency and explanation skills may hinder learners' feedback and direction.

The assessment and enhancement of learning may be jeopardized by accountability and responsibility.

3. **To promote equity and inclusion:** The inclusiveness and equity of educational opportunities and rewards may be impacted by the ethical concerns surrounding AI in education. For instance, existing disparities and marginalization may be made worse by bias and discrimination.

Data protection and privacy may leave vulnerable populations open to abuse or damage.

Students' engagement and empowerment may be restricted by their autonomy and agency.

Information gaps or asymmetries may result from transparency and explanation skills.

Responsibility and accountability could transfer the load or blame to students.

BEST PRACTICES FOR THE INTEGRATION OF ETHICAL AI IN EDUCATION

Best practices for the implementation of ethical AI in education comprise guaranteeing transparency, offering sufficient training for teachers, and creating well-defined ethical guidelines and regulations.

1. **Ensuring transparency in AI systems:** To achieve transparency in educational AI systems, it is essential to provide clear communication and accessible tools that clarify their functioning. It is important to offer educators, students, and parents clear explanations of how AI algorithms analyze data and make decisions, so they can grasp the rationale behind grades, recommendations, or assessments. For the sake of accountability, it is vital to keep detailed records of AI models, datasets, and decision-making processes. This allows stakeholders to follow the trail and resolve any problems that occur. Intuitive interfaces and user-friendly dashboards enhance transparency by offering insights and outcomes in a format that is easy to understand. This empowers non-technical users to interact with AI systems with confidence and effectiveness.
2. **Delivering sufficient training for teachers:** To use AI ethically and effectively, educators require adequate training, as it provides them with a clear understanding of how these systems work, what they can do, and where their limits lie.

Educators can pinpoint possible biases, guarantee fair outcomes, and use AI responsibly in their teaching methods by understanding how AI tools analyze data and make decisions. Training enables teachers to connect the use of AI with ethical standards and educational objectives, thereby improving personalized learning experiences while maintaining fairness and transparency. Educators who are well-informed can assist students in comprehending and using AI-driven tools, thereby promoting a cooperative and reliable educational atmosphere.

3. **Setting up unambiguous data privacy policies:** To safeguard student information in the educational use of AI, it is crucial to establish and enforce strong data privacy policies. To ensure transparency and trust, clear guidelines should outline the data collection process, its intended use, and who will have access to it. It is essential to respect the autonomy and rights of students and their guardians by obtaining informed consent from them. Furthermore, by employing robust encryption and cybersecurity strategies, sensitive data can be protected from unauthorized access or breaches, thereby ensuring the safety and privacy of students' personal information. As technologies and ethical frameworks develop, education will be redefined with innovations such as adaptive learning platforms, immersive AI experiences, and advanced data analytics aimed at enhancing personalized learning. With the evolution of these tools, ethical guidelines will adjust to address new challenges, ensuring that AI applications continue to align with fundamental educational values and equitable practices.

IMPLEMENTATION OF AI ETHICS IN THE EDUCATION SECTOR

The use of AI ethics in education focuses on balancing the use of technologies such as administrative tools, automated tests, and personalized learning systems with fundamental values of human oversight, fairness, and transparency. Future outcomes emphasize the need for robust governance to ensure equitable access, protect student well-being, and maintain the essential human element of teaching. AI design and implementation are guided by ethical principles across several key educational areas, including:

a. AI is used by personalized learning systems to modify instructional materials to meet the specific needs of individual students. Ethical considerations ensure, for example, that diverse training data is used to prevent algorithmic bias that discriminates against different demographic groups.
b. Students should be given some control over their data and their interactions with AI tools to prioritize their autonomy. Psychological considerations should be

incorporated into the design to prevent excessive stress or anxiety from continuous assessment.

c. Automated Assessment and Grading: To reduce the burden on teachers, AI technology can evaluate assignments, provide feedback, and monitor performance. Transparency and explain ability are crucial for ethical use so that teachers and students understand how grades or feedback are determined. Accountability mechanisms for AI-generated decisions that significantly impact a student's academic career include human review and appeal processes. Regular audits are necessary to avoid biases, such as those that have historically penalized certain writing styles or socioeconomic backgrounds.
d. Predictive Analytics and Administrative Tasks: AI streamlines processes such as resource allocation, admissions, and identifying at-risk students. Ethical applications should:
e. Data security and privacy: Implement robust security measures for sensitive student data, such as encryption and anonymization, to prevent misuse or breaches.

RECOMMENDATIONS

In order to promote equitable access and trust, ethical AI in education must prioritize human-centered design, ensure fairness, transparency, and privacy while upholding human dignity. This means that AI should assist teachers rather than take their place by automating tasks, fairly personalizing instruction, and safeguarding student data. Clear governance, accountability, and bias mitigation are also necessary. Important recommendations include giving human oversight a priority, providing transparent explanations of AI judgments, avoiding prejudice, protecting data, incorporating stakeholders in governance, and teaching educators how to use tools responsibly. So we suggested some key points how to use ethics of AI in education sector:

1. **Creating ethical frameworks and guidelines:** These can offer a shared vision as well as a set of values and principles to direct the moral development, application, deployment, and impact of artificial intelligence in education.
2. **Applying ethical standards and practices:** To guarantee the moral performance and conduct of AI systems in education, ethical standards and practices can operationalize ethical frameworks and guidelines into specific acts and procedures. Data quality assurance, algorithmic transparency and explainability, human oversight and intervention, privacy and data protection rules, impact assessment and evaluation, stakeholder participation and consultation, and so on are a few examples of ethical practices and standards.

3. **Encouraging ethical education and awareness:** Students, instructors, and other stakeholders in the AI ecosystem can become more ethically literate and competent through ethical education and awareness. Curriculum integration, professional development, public involvement, media literacy, digital citizenship, and so forth are a few examples of ethical education and awareness.
4. **Strengthening ethical governance and regulation:** These practices can offer an institutional and legal framework to guarantee the responsibility and accountability of AI actors in education. Laws and rules, codes of conduct, ethics committees, oversight organizations, complaint and redress procedures, and so forth are examples of ethical governance and regulation. Educational institutions have an ethical obligation to make sure AI systems adhere to the strictest data protection guidelines. In the context of AI-enabled education, transparency in data utilization and granting students control over their data are essential for upholding integrity and confidence. Transparency and accountability are crucial in AI decision-making. To ensure AI is a transparent, intelligible, and scrutinizable tool rather than an elusive, unaccountable force in education, institutions must set explicit regulations on how AI-driven decisions are made and conveyed.
5. **Augmenting human capabilities with AI:** AI can serve as a complement to and enhancer of human abilities in the educational sphere, instead of taking over human roles. By automating repetitive tasks like grading and administrative duties, educators can concentrate on more personalized and creative interactions with students.
6. **Encouraging ethical AI use in Universities:** To emphasize the moral advancement and use of AI, institutions can adopt robust measures for data privacy and security, advocate for transparency, and work to eliminate biases from algorithms. This anticipatory strategy can assist in establishing trust between students, faculty, and the community.
7. **Bridging the digital divide:** To tackle inequalities in access to technology, institutions can collaborate with governments, non-profit organizations, and tech companies to offer students in need affordable internet services and devices. To enhance accessibility, AI-driven resources must be tailored for various devices, such as inexpensive tablets and smartphones.
8. **Promoting AI literacy among students and teachers:** By incorporating AI education into curricula, students are equipped for a future job market that relies more and more on AI. Moreover, training for teachers can provide them with the abilities necessary to integrate AI into their educational practices and teaching methods.

9. **Develop Strong Governance:** Establish clear institutional policies, create ethics committees, and involve a diverse range of stakeholders i.e. teachers, students, and parents, tech experts, *etc* to build robust governance.
10. **Set priorities:** According to the World Economic Forum and other sources, teacher training should prepare educators to understand, evaluate, and integrate AI systems ethically.
11. **Reduce bias:** Ensure that AI tools do not discriminate against any student group by regularly auditing them for biased outcomes.
12. **Encourage collaboration:** Establish communities of practice where teachers can share best practices and experiences.
13. **Emphasize complementary use:** AI can be used for data analysis, personalized practice, and administrative efficiency, freeing up teachers' time to provide higher-level guidance and build relationships.
14. **Ensure security**: Provide strong data protection and safeguard systems against threats.

FUTURE IMPLICATIONS

In essence, the future of AI ethics in education hinges on balancing the risks of bias, privacy violations, and reduced human interaction which threaten equity and critical thinking with the potential benefits of personalized learning. Robust regulations, teacher training programs, culturally relevant curricula, and an emphasis on using AI to complement, rather than replace, the essential human element of teaching are all crucial for future success. This study has examined the major influences on the contribution of ethics of artificial intelligence in the education sector. In the future, the contribution of ethics of artificial intelligence, other than education, such as the banking sector, hospitality sector, insurance sector, and other service sectors, can be investigated.

Discussions: The main objective of the present study was to investigate the contribution of the ethics of artificial intelligence in the education sector. To achieve this objective, this study included a review of the literature of the last 15 years and also discussed the introduction, background, literature review, elements of value education, ethical principles, need of ethics of artificial intelligence in education sector, perspectives of students & faculty towards AI in education sector, how AI work in education sector?, ethical challenges related to AI in education sector, link of AI and ethics in education, significance role of ethical issues of AI in education, best practices for the integration of ethical AI in education, recommendations, future implications, discussions and conclusion under the study.

Conclusion: In conclusion, the use of AI in higher education is still being developed. AI systems in education pose significant challenges to accountability and transparency, especially when AI is used to commit misdeeds. It's already a long-standing concern that programs like turnitin often incorrectly flag students for plagiarism. Greater automation in grading and AI-checking, even if performed by an AI service, could exacerbate these concerns. Students and teachers may be left to appeal decisions or understand the algorithm's logic in these situations, ultimately undermining trust in the tools and the institutions that use them. Addressing these issues requires clear policies, human monitoring, and processes for evaluating and critiquing AI-driven results to maintain fairness and trust. As AI becomes increasingly integrated into learning environments, from automated evaluation systems to personalized instructors, it is crucial to understand and establish robust ethical practices. This requires striking a careful balance between harnessing AI's potential to enhance learning and maintaining core educational principles, ensuring that technological innovations support, not undermine, the goals of human education. The use of AI in education raises several unique issues that require thoughtful analysis and anticipatory responses. But it wouldn't be wrong to say that AI is revolutionizing education by offering new ways to enhance and customize learning. But like any technology, it also raises ethical issues that need to be considered. Therefore, this study discusses the contributions of artificial intelligence to education.

REFERENCES

Adetayo, A. J. (2023). Artificial intelligence chatbots in academic libraries: The rise of ChatGPT. *Library Hi Tech News*, *40*(3), 18–21. DOI: 10.1108/LHTN-01-2023-0007

Al-Kurdi, O., & Eldabi, T. (2018). Knowledge sharing in higher education institutions: A systematic review. *Journal of Enterprise Information Management*, *31*(2), 226–246. DOI: 10.1108/JEIM-09-2017-0129

Al-Mughairi, H. & Bhaskar, P. (2024). Exploring the factors affecting the adoption AI techniques in higher education: insights from teachers' perspectives on ChatGPT, *Journal of Research in Innovative Teaching & Learning*, Vol. ahead-of-print No. ahead-of-print. https://doi.org/.DOI: 10.1108/JRIT-09-2023-0129

Barron, P. (2008). Education and talent management: Implications for the hospitality industry. *International Journal of Contemporary Hospitality Management*, *20*(7), 730–742. DOI: 10.1108/09596110810897583

Boulay, D. B. (2023). *Artificial Intelligence in Education and Ethics, Handbook of Open*. Distance and Digital Education., DOI: 10.1007/978-981-19-2080-6_6

Camilleri, M. A. (2021). Evaluating service quality and performance of higher education institutions: A systematic review and a post-COVID-19 outlook. *International Journal of Quality and Service Sciences*, *13*(2), 268–281. DOI: 10.1108/IJQSS-03-2020-0034

ElHassan, B. T., & Arabi, A. A. (2025). Ethical forethoughts on the use of artificial intelligence in medicine. *International Journal of Ethics and Systems*, *41*(1), 35–44. DOI: 10.1108/IJOES-08-2023-0190

Gadanidis, G. (2017). Artificial intelligence, computational thinking, and mathematics education [P]. *International Journal of Information and Learning Technology*, *34*(2), 133–139. DOI: 10.1108/IJILT-09-2016-0048

Giuggioli, G., & Pellegrini, M. M. (2023). Artificial intelligence as an enabler for entrepreneurs: A systematic literature review and an agenda for future research. *International Journal of Entrepreneurial Behaviour & Research*, *29*(4), 816–837. DOI: 10.1108/IJEBR-05-2021-0426

Godemann, J., & Moon, J. (2014). Higher education and sustainable development: Exploring possibilities for organizational change. *Accounting, Auditing & Accountability Journal*, *27*(2), 218–233. DOI: 10.1108/AAAJ-12-2013-1553

Huang, Y.-H. (2024). Exploring the implementation of artificial intelligence applications among academic libraries in Taiwan. *Library Hi Tech, 42*(3), 885–905. DOI: 10.1108/LHT-03-2022-0159

Hussain, A. (2023). Use of artificial intelligence in the library services: Prospects and challenges. *Library Hi Tech News, 40*(2), 15–17. DOI: 10.1108/LHTN-11-2022-0125

Imanova, M. (2025). Global Evolution of Artificial Intelligence: Navigating Ethics, Policy, and Innovation for a Sustainable Future, *Journal of Information Systems Engineering and Management* 2025, 10(41s) e-ISSN: 2468-4376.

Isave, S (2025). Ethics of Artificial Intelligence in Education, *International Journal of Innovative Science and Research Technology,* Volume 10, Issue 1, January – 2025. https://doi.org/.DOI: 10.5281/zenodo.14769407

Izenstark, A., & Leahy, K. L. (2015). Google classroom for librarians: Features and opportunities. *Library Hi Tech News, 32*(9), 1–3. DOI: 10.1108/LHTN-05-2015-0039

Karakas, F., Sarigollu, E., & Manisaligil, A. (2013). The use of benevolent leadership development to advance principles of responsible management education [p]. *Journal of Management Development, 32*(8), 801–822. DOI: 10.1108/JMD-08-2011-0102.R1

Liu, Q., Cheng, Z., & Chen, M. (2019). Effects of environmental education on environmental ethics and literacy based on virtual reality technology. *The Electronic Library, 37*(5), 860–877. DOI: 10.1108/EL-12-2018-0250

Mohsen, S. E., Hamdan, A., & Shoaib, H. M. (2025). Digital transformation and integration of artificial intelligence in financial institutions. *Journal of Financial Reporting and Accounting, 23*(2), 680–699. DOI: 10.1108/JFRA-09-2023-0544

Nair, K., & Gupta, R. (2021). Application of AI technology in modern digital marketing environment. *World Journal of Entrepreneurship, Management and Sustainable Development, 17*(3), 318–328. DOI: 10.1108/WJEMSD-08-2020-0099

Nordgren, A. (2023). Artificial intelligence and climate change: Ethical issues, *Journal of Information. Communication and Ethics in Society, 21*(1), 1–15. DOI: 10.1108/JICES-11-2021-0106

O'Neill, M. A., & Palmer, A. (2004). Importance-performance analysis: A useful tool for directing continuous quality improvement in higher education. *Quality Assurance in Education, 12*(1), 39–52. DOI: 10.1108/09684880410517423

Ohadomere, O., & Ogamba, I. K. (2021). Management-led interventions for workplace stress and mental health of academic staff in higher education: A systematic review. *The Journal of Mental Health Training, Education and Practice, 16*(1), 67–82. DOI: 10.1108/JMHTEP-07-2020-0048

Paesano, A. (2023). Artificial intelligence and creative activities inside organizational behavior. *The International Journal of Organizational Analysis, 31*(5), 1694–1723. DOI: 10.1108/IJOA-09-2020-2421

Rae, D. (2010). Universities and enterprise education: Responding to the challenges of the new era. *Journal of Small Business and Enterprise Development, 17*(4), 591–606. DOI: 10.1108/14626001011088741

Rodrigues, M. Silva and Oliveira, C. (2025). Artificial intelligence: threat or asset to academic integrity? A bibliometrics analysis, *Kybernetes*, Vol. 54 No. 5, pp. 2939-2970. https://doi.org/DOI: 10.1108/K-09-2023-1666

Saeidnia, H. R. (2023). Ethical artificial intelligence (AI): confronting bias and discrimination in the library and information industry, *Library Hi Tech News*, Vol. ahead-of-print No. ahead-of-print. https://doi.org/DOI: 10.1108/LHTN-10-2023-0182

Saqib, M. B., & Zia, S. (2025). Evaluation of AI content generation tools for verification of academic integrity in higher education. *Journal of Applied Research in Higher Education, 17*(4), 1430–1440. DOI: 10.1108/JARHE-10-2023-0470

Saurabh, K., & Ramkumar, M. (2022). AI led ethical digital transformation: Framework, research and managerial implications, *Journal of Information. Communication and Ethics in Society, 20*(2), 229–256. DOI: 10.1108/JICES-02-2021-0020

(2025). Silva; Rui (2025). Artificial intelligence: Threat or asset to academic integrity? A bibliometrics analysis Available to Purchase. *Kybernetes, 54*(5), 2939–2970. DOI: 10.1108/K-09-2023-1666

Sultan, P., & Yin Wong, H. (2013). Antecedents and consequences of service quality in a higher education context: A qualitative research approach. *Quality Assurance in Education, 21*(1), 70–95. DOI: 10.1108/09684881311293070

Wang, X. (2025). (2025). Global artificial intelligence governance research in the digital and intelligent era: Advances, trends and countermeasures. *Journal of Knowledge Management*. Advance online publication. DOI: 10.1108/JKM-01-2025-0006

Wang, Y. (2021). Artificial intelligence in educational leadership: A symbiotic role of human-artificial intelligence decision-making. *Journal of Educational Administration, 59*(3), 256–270. DOI: 10.1108/JEA-10-2020-0216

Zamberi Ahmad, S. (2013). The need for inclusion of entrepreneurship education in Malaysia lower and higher learning institutions. *Education + Training*, *55*(2), 191–203. DOI: 10.1108/00400911311304823

Zeb, A., Rehman and Rabnawaz, M. (2025). Artificial intelligence and ChatGPT are fostering knowledge sharing, ethics, academia and libraries. *International Journal of Information and Learning Technology*, *42*(1), 67–83. DOI: 10.1108/IJILT-03-2024-0046

Chapter 8
Key AI Concepts for Ages 6-12:
Logic, Patterns, and Algorithms

Eliza Sharma
https://orcid.org/0000-0002-2713-301X
Symbiosis International University, India

Neerja Nigam
https://orcid.org/0009-0009-2636-4500
Christ University, India

ABSTRACT

The digital era is providing new methods of learning, thinking, and problem-solving. Introducing the foundational ideas of AI to young learners helps them adjust to a technology-driven environment more effectively. This study explores effective ways to make young learners aged 6-12 aware of basic AI concepts, including logic, patterns, and algorithms. By utilizing secondary data, the study aims to explore effective pedagogical strategies and challenges in early education related to AI, and provide guidelines for parents and educators. The aim of the study is to enable curriculum designers and educators to design an inclusive stakeholders' model that can be used in primary education to introduce AI literacy in a way that enhances the critical thinking, creativity, and problem-solving abilities of young learners.

INTRODUCTION

Today, AI can be seen everywhere whether it is voice assistant, chat bot, search engine, smart toys and even learning tools. It's not limited to only in labs and Sci-Fi movies like earlier days. The children interact with AI tools in their daily life,

DOI: 10.4018/979-8-3373-4982-4.ch008

without knowing the logic behind these technologies (Awad et al., 2022; Khalid et al., 2022). So, it becomes necessary to make them aware about the core concepts of these technologies (Yang, 2022). The early years of schooling, especially between ages 6 and 12, are a powerful stage for building thinking skills, developing cognitive skills (Movahed et al., 2024). Children in this age are curious and analyse the things easily. During this period, they start making sense of the world by noticing patterns, asking questions, and forming logical connections. Research in child development shows that this is the age when curiosity is at its peak, and learning experiences can shape long-term habits of reasoning, problem-solving, and creativity (Nobile et al., 2024). It's the correct age to give the knowledge of AI concepts to them so that their habit of logical thinking and analysing become stronger and mature with the passage of time and when they interact with the digital society, they can face it confidently and responsibly (Ottenbreit-Leftwich et al., 2022). Learning AI at a young age does not mean that children need to dive into complex coding or advanced computer science. Instead, it can be about discovering the core building blocks of AI logic, patterns, and algorithms through activities they already enjoy. For example, puzzles can help children practice step-by-step reasoning, stories can highlight cause and effect relationships, and games can show how patterns are recognized and used. In this way, AI concepts are not something "extra" but naturally fit into learning experiences that children find engaging and enjoyable (Luckin, 2018; Yang, 2022). These approaches show that AI literacy does not only mean to improve technical skills but also to enable the young learners to solve problems creatively, think critically and make decisions thoughtfully (Khalid et al., 2022). The understanding of basic principles of AI makes the young learners not only the users of the technology but also the creators and thinkers who can change the way technology is used. This view is supported by (Touretzky et al., 2019), by emphasizing the need to introduce AI in early ages by using simple and age-appropriate activities that help in enhancing the confidence and curiosity of young learners instead of creating confusion and fear. The chapter mainly aims to develop a framework that can help in introducing the logic, patterns and algorithms for the young learners. It will also explain that how these ideas can fit within the existing curricula and what tools and practices have been already making a difference in classrooms worldwide.

RESEARCH OBJECTIVES

This study investigates how fundamental Artificial Intelligence (AI) concepts can be effectively introduced to young learners and how the educators and curriculum designers can support this learning process. Specifically, the research is guided by the following objectives:

1. To understand how to introduce children aged 6–12 to basic AI ideas like logic, patterns, and algorithms.
2. To find the best ways to teach AI to young learners using fun and practical examples.
3. To explain AI concepts in simple, age-appropriate language.
4. To identify the challenges teachers and parents face when teaching AI to children.
5. To give helpful tips and guidelines for teachers, parents, and curriculum designers.
6. To create a model that helps children develop thinking, creativity, and problem-solving skills through AI learning.

LITERATURE REVIEW

The integration of AI literacy and computational thinking at early stage of education has been in practice since many years (Yang, 2022; Khalid et al., 2022). Studies in early childhood education emphasize that abstract ideas can be introduced when grounded in concrete experiences (Movahed et al., 2024). According to Bers (2020), children don't need to write code to begin thinking computationally, they can engage with structured thinking through puzzles, songs, and stories that mirror logical reasoning. Her "Coding as a Playground" approach highlights that playful learning is not just fun but essential for developing logical frameworks. Papert (1980) introduced the concept of constructionism in 1980, which highlights the idea of experiential learning, this shows that children learn new things by experimenting themselves. Programming language LOGO is a great idea of Papert that has proved that even young children understand sequencing and logic. Bers (2020) further emphasized that coding and computational thinking can be taught through playful and developmentally appropriate methods. She argues that logic and algorithms are already part of many early childhood learning experiences, such as following instructions, recognizing story patterns, or solving simple puzzles. Resnick et al. (2009) introduced Scratch and ScratchJr, visual programming languages that allow children to explore concepts like sequences, loops, and conditions without needing to type code. These tools have shown that children can grasp foundational programming and algorithmic thinking when supported with the right scaffolding. Wing (2006), introduced the concepts of "computational thinking" in 2006 as a way to solve problems, understand human behaviour and, design systems, using fundamental concepts of computer science. Her work encouraged educational policymakers to integrate computational thinking as a literacy skill, not just for computer science but across subjects. The concept of algorithms can be taught in routine activities like brushing teeth or making a sandwich. These techniques enable the concept of algorithm clear to the children. These ideas are extended by recent innovations.

Many interactive games introduce the concepts of AI like pattern recognition and neural network in a playful manner (Asya, 2025).

Table 1 presents the historical evolution of Artificial Intelligence, highlighting a clear transition from rule-based systems to data-driven and human-centered AI. This progression underscores why foundational concepts such as logic, pattern recognition, and algorithms are appropriate entry points for introducing AI literacy to young learners.

Table 1. Evolution of Artificial Intelligence and Its Educational Implications

Phase / Era	Time Period	Key Characteristics of AI Development	Representative Technologies / Examples	Key Scholars / References	Educational Implications
Foundational Era (Symbolic AI)	1950s–1970s	AI based on rules, logic, and symbolic reasoning; focus on problem-solving through explicit instructions	Expert systems, rule-based programs, early chess algorithms	Turing (1950); McCarthy (1956); Yue et al., (2024)	Emphasizes **logic and step-by-step reasoning**, aligning with early algorithmic thinking in children
Knowledge-Based Systems Era	1970s–1980s	AI systems relied on domain-specific knowledge encoded by humans; limited learning ability	Medical expert systems (MYCIN), decision-support systems	Feigenbaum (1977); Russell & Norvig (2010)	Reinforces understanding of **if–then logic**, classification, and decision rules
Statistical & Data-Driven AI	1990s–2000s	Shift from symbolic rules to data-based learning; probabilistic models and pattern recognition	Spam filters, recommendation engines, speech recognition	Mitchell (1997); Bishop (2006)	Highlights importance of **patterns and data**, suitable for teaching prediction concepts to children
Machine Learning Era	2000s–2010s	Algorithms learn from data with minimal human rules; supervised and unsupervised learning	Image recognition, search ranking, recommendation systems	Mitchell (1997); Domingos (2012)	Introduces **pattern recognition and learning from examples**, easily relatable to children's learning processes
Deep Learning & Neural Networks	2010s	Multi-layer neural networks enable advanced perception and recognition	Facial recognition, voice assistants, autonomous vehicles	LeCun, Bengio & Hinton (2015)	Supports teaching **pattern recognition** through analogies (vision, sound, repetition)
Human-Centered & Explainable AI	Late 2010s–present	Focus on transparency, ethics, fairness, and human-AI interaction	Explainable AI (XAI), ethical AI frameworks	Floridi et al. (2018); OECD (2019)	Necessitates early introduction of **ethical reasoning and responsible AI use**
AI in Everyday Life (AI Literacy Era)	Present	AI embedded in daily tools used by children (apps, toys, platforms)	Alexa, YouTube recommendations, smart toys	Touretzky et al. (2019); Long & Magerko (2020)	Justifies **early AI education** using logic, patterns, and algorithms without coding
Educational AI & Child-Centered AI	Emerging	AI designed specifically for learning, creativity, and collaboration	ScratchJr, Cognimates, AI4K12 curriculum	Bers (2020); Druga et al. (2019); Yang (2022)	Supports **play-based, age-appropriate AI learning frameworks** such as the LPA model

Another approach enables children to give verbal commands that robots translate into simplified programs, bridging natural language and algorithmic thinking (Mylonas et al., 2024). All these methods show that the concepts of AI can be taught in a familiar and easy-to-understand manner without going deep into complex programming. Talking about pattern recognition, existing literature shows that the tendency of young learners is to look for repetitions and structures naturally (Nobile et al., 2024). In AI, machine learning works on the mechanism of pattern recognition. These ideas can be Introduced to young learners in age-appropriate ways, like predicting what comes next in a given sequence or identifying musical rhythms. This will enable the children to solve more complex concepts later. Cognimates project is another tool that helps children to train models and build simple AI systems. This improves the curiosity, creativity and critical thinking of young learners (Druga et al. (2019)). All these examples highlight that introduction of AI to the children at early age makes them confident and responsible users, they grow not only as the users of technology but also as the creator of technology (Ottenbreit-Leftwich et al., 2022). Although so many tools are available nowadays that can be used to integrate AI in the existing curriculum of young learners, still there are certain challenges that cannot be ignored. Many teachers are not fully prepared to teach AI, moreover the focus of existing curriculum is on digital literacy not on AI literacy. Most of the educators consider digital literacy as AI literacy, which increases gaps in classroom practices, Webb et al. (2017). The findings of recent literature show that preschool and primary educators are able to teach AI meaningfully due to lack of confidence and resources (Asya, 2025). Not only this, the AI-related materials are designed for older students, thus a gap remains there for younger learners. There is a global initiative like AI4K12 (Touretzky et al., 2019) and also the OECD's Future Skills Framework (2020), which has emphasized that AI literacy must start with the foundational thinking skills. These initiatives further focus on the fact that even in the resource-limited environments, teaching computational and logical thinking is possible with low-tech or no-tech solutions. Hence, educators can focus on the creative pedagogy rather than relying on the expensive devices.

Table 2 summarizes the key findings of existing literature and the relevance of introducing AI at early stages for young learners.

Table 2. Summary of studies and results

Author(s) & Year	Focus Area	Main Contribution / Findings	Relevance to Young Learners
Papert (1980)	Constructionism & learning by doing	Introduced **constructionism** – children learn best through hands-on experimentation and exploration. Developed the **LOGO programming language** for sequencing and logic.	Demonstrates that even young children can understand logic and algorithms through experiential learning.
Bers (2020)	Playful learning & computational thinking	Proposed the **"Coding as a Playground"** approach; computational thinking can be taught through playful, developmentally appropriate methods like puzzles, songs, and stories.	Encourages integrating coding and logical thinking into everyday play and classroom activities.
Resnick et al. (2009)	Visual programming for children	Developed **Scratch** and **ScratchJr**, which use visual blocks to teach sequences, loops, and conditions without requiring typing or complex syntax.	Provides accessible tools for introducing programming concepts to young learners.
Wing (2006)	Computational thinking framework	Defined **computational thinking** as problem-solving using computer science concepts; emphasized teaching algorithms through everyday activities and routines.	Establishes computational thinking as a core literacy skill across subjects.
Touretzky et al. (2019)	AI education initiatives (AI4K12)	Developed the **AI4K12 initiative**, providing age-appropriate guidelines for AI education with low-tech and no-tech approaches.	Offers a global framework for integrating AI into early education curricula.
Druga et al. (2019)	Hands-on AI projects	Created **Cognimates,** allowing children to train simple AI models and build AI systems, fostering creativity and critical thinking.	Empowers children to become creators, not just consumers, of AI technology.
Awad et al., (2022)	Children's interaction with AI	Highlighted how children frequently interact with AI tools (voice assistants, chatbots) without understanding the underlying logic.	Shows the urgent need for early AI literacy education.
Khalid et al. (2022)	Children and AI literacy	Explored children's natural curiosity towards AI and stressed the importance of introducing AI concepts early.	Supports early integration of AI literacy in schools.
Yang (2022)	AI education and curriculum design	Examined frameworks for integrating AI into educational systems with a focus on conceptual understanding rather than advanced coding.	Provides strategies for age-appropriate AI teaching.

continued on following page

Table 2. Continued

Author(s) & Year	Focus Area	Main Contribution / Findings	Relevance to Young Learners
Ottenbreit-Leftwich et al. (2022)	Curriculum alignment & pedagogy	Discussed challenges and strategies for embedding AI concepts into existing curricula through creative pedagogical practices.	Helps teachers incorporate AI education into standard learning plans.
Nobile et al. (2024)	Cognitive development and pattern recognition	Showed that children naturally identify patterns and structures, linking these abilities to foundational AI concepts like pattern recognition.	Strengthens the case for introducing AI concepts like machine learning at an early stage.
Movahed et al. (2024)	Early childhood abstract thinking	Found that abstract computational ideas can be taught when grounded in concrete, playful experiences.	Provides methods to teach algorithms and logic in developmentally appropriate ways.
Druga (2018)	AI-based tangible play tools	Developed games embedding neural network and pattern recognition concepts into physical play environments.	Makes AI concepts accessible and fun through hands-on interaction.
Long & Magerko (2020)	Natural language to algorithm learning	Created systems where children give **verbal commands** to robots, which translate them into simplified algorithms.	Bridges everyday language and algorithmic thinking.
Webb et al. (2017)	Teacher perceptions of AI literacy	Found that many educators **confuse digital literacy with AI literacy**, leading to gaps in instruction.	Highlights need for teacher training in AI concepts.
Asya **(2025)**	Challenges in AI education	Showed that preschool and primary educators lack resources and confidence to teach AI effectively.	Emphasizes the need for teacher training and curriculum development.

RESEARCH METHODOLOGY

This chapter follows a qualitative analysis using only secondary data sources. The data is collected from established databases like- ERIC, JSTOR, Google Scholar and public platforms like UNESCO, OECD, and AI4K12, peer-reviewed journals, curriculum frameworks, educational websites, government policy papers, and international AI education initiatives. Thematic Analysis is done by categorizing insights into key themes such as teaching methods, learner engagement, and curriculum alignment. Comparative analysis is carried out by identifying best practices and gaps are identified by comparing different regional and pedagogical approaches. Case studies and classroom observations available in public reports (e.g., MIT Media Lab's ScratchJr findings or Code.org implementation guides) are referred to provide practical insights into how children respond to such teaching approaches. The goal of the chapter is to analyze how logic, pattern recognition, and algorithms are currently being introduced to children aged 6–12 in different educational settings.

ANALYSIS AND DISCUSSION

Table 3. AI for Kids

Aspect/Focus Area	Age Group	Teaching Strategies/ Approaches	Examples/Activities	AI Connection	Learning Outcomes	Key References (in-text)
Simplifying AI concepts for children	6–12 years	Relating AI to daily digital interactions	YouTube recommendations, Alexa or Siri responses	Demonstrates how machines learn from data	Builds conceptual understanding of AI learning	(Luckin, 2018; Holmes, Bialik, & Fadel, 2019)
Introducing AI through analogies	6–10 years	Comparing AI to human or pet learning	"Teaching a pet tricks" analogy	Connects human and AI learning	Fosters curiosity and empathy	(Bers, 2020; Wing, 2006)
Connecting AI with familiar technology	8–12 years	Discussing Netflix, Google Maps, etc.	Personalized content examples	Relates user behavior to prediction systems	Strengthens digital awareness	(Yang, 2022; Resnick et al., 2009)
Using storytelling to explain AI	6–10 years	Story-based imagination	Robot learning story	Makes abstract ideas tangible	Enhances comprehension	(Henry et al., 2021)
Integrating multimedia tools	9–12 years	Videos, cartoons, digital tools	Interactive YouTube lessons	Provides visual learning linkages	Builds engagement	(NRC, 2012)
Facilitating hands-on activities	8–12 years	Pattern and logic games	AI-themed puzzles	Demonstrates data patterning	Promotes inquiry learning	(Lee et al., 2021)
Linking AI to ethics	10–12 years	Classroom discussions	Debating AI fairness	Introduces responsible tech use	Builds ethical literacy	(Henry et al., 2021)
Teacher as facilitator	6–12 years	Inquiry-based exploration	Open-ended questioning	Promotes reflective thinking	Enhances understanding of reasoning	Williams et al., (2019)

Various methods and techniques have been shown in the table, which can be used to introduce AI to young learners in an interactive and funny way. The use of AI can be connected with day to day experiences like: how Alexa or Siri respond or how you tube recommends videos. This will help young learners to understand that AI is not a new phenomenon for them, rather it's something they already use. The applications of AI like data and predictions can be taught by taking examples of common and known apps like Google maps or Netflix. Another powerful method to teach AI is storytelling, which makes learning new things a fun. Similarly puzzles or hands-on games which use the concept of pattern recognition can also be used, which will help young learners to know how AI 'thinks. Along with these concepts, AI ethics are one of the most important aspect which needs to be taught to the young learners, so that they use the technology in a responsible way.

Table 4. Logic- Building Clear Thinking

Aspect/Focus Area	Age Group	Teaching Strategies/ Approaches	Examples/Activities	AI Connection	Learning Outcomes	Key References (in-text)
Developing step-by-step reasoning	6–12 years	Teaching cause–effect links	"If–then" games	Mirrors AI's rule-based systems	Builds structured reasoning	(Wing, 2006)
Encouraging analytical problem-solving	8–12 years	Riddles and puzzles	Logic teasers	Reflects AI's inference patterns	Enhances focus	(Holmes et al., 2019)
Story sequencing for logic	6–10 years	Arranging narrative order	Sequencing picture stories	Represents algorithmic order	Improves comprehension	(Bers, 2020)
Integrating play-based learning	7–11 years	Logic and strategy games	Chess, LEGO design	Promotes logical strategy	Fosters persistence	(Papert, 1980; Nobile et al., 2024)
Using digital platforms	8–12 years	Block-based coding	Creating logical sequences in Scratch	Demonstrates conditional logic	Strengthens computational reasoning	(Resnick et al., 2009)
Connecting logic to real life	6–12 years	Practical scenarios	"If I skip breakfast…"	Teaches consequences	Builds critical awareness	(Ottenbreit-Leftwich et al., 2022)
Reflective questioning	10–12 years	Guided reasoning questions	"Why did that happen?"	Parallels machine reasoning	Develops metacognition	(Holmes et al., 2019)
Assessing through reasoning games	6–12 years	Observational assessment	Group puzzles	Tests logical fluency	Encourages collaboration	(Wing, 2006)

The role of logic is very important in shaping the computational and problem solving skills of young learners. Logics can be taught in a playful manner through puzzle, games and stories. Logics enhance the reasoning skills of the children. Simple educational apps or digital games can help children practice reasoning, pattern recognition, and decision-making in an interactive way. Logics can be connected to real life situations, like planning a day, solving a disagreement, or deciding what to do first in a task. Questions containing "why" and "how" can be asked from children that helps them to think deeply about their choices and reasoning, instead of just giving quick answers. Instead of using traditional methods of evaluating children, fun games or challenges can be used to access the understanding of children about logical reasoning and problem-solving.

Table 5. Patterns-Seeing Connections

Aspect/Focus Area	Age Group	Teaching Strategies/ Approaches	Examples/Activities	AI Connection	Learning Outcomes	Key References (in-text)
Recognizing sequences	6–12 years	Visual patterning	Bead/color sequences	Relates repetition to AI data learning	Improves observation	(NRC, 2012)
Predicting outcomes	8–12 years	Pattern identification	Traffic lights, weather cycles	Parallels predictive modeling	Encourages hypothesis formation	(Luckin, 2018)
Musical rhythm patterns	6–10 years	Repetition in sound	Clapping, singing games	Relates to AI signal recognition	Develops auditory intelligence	(Bers, 2020)
Exploring natural patterns	8–12 years	Outdoor observation	Seasons, leaf shapes	Mirrors AI image recognition	Enhances curiosity	(Holmes et al., 2019)
Data pattern exercises	10–12 years	Creating data sets	Weather charts, favorite colors	Links to data analysis	Builds quantitative literacy	(Khalid et al., 2022)
Cross-disciplinary learning	9–12 years	Math-art fusion	Symmetry, tessellations	Connects visual logic to computation	Strengthens creative problem-solving	(Wing, 2006)
Group prediction games	7–11 years	Collaborative guessing	"What comes next?"	Models machine-learning outcomes	Encourages social reasoning	(Bers, 2020)
Reflection and journaling	8–12 years	Recording patterns found	Personal observation logs	Supports meta-pattern thinking	Fosters awareness	(Holmes et al., 2019)

Patterns are a part of live for young learners. They see pattern everywhere in their daily life, like in rhythms, stories, songs and visual designs. Classroom strategies for teaching patterns can be highly interactive. Using visual aids in class rooms activities like arranging colored blocks in alternating sequences or identifying shapes that repeat in a design make learning easy and playful. Same way musical activities, like repeating rhythms, also make patterns tangible and enjoyable. These playful exercises keep the children engaged and also shows how recognizing repetition can lead to predictions, such as knowing which color block or note will come next (Bers, 2020, Khalid et al., 2022). In developing the children's predictive thinking, the role of patterns is very crucial role. For instance, if they observe that a friend always chooses a particular snack during lunchtime, they can predict that the same choice will likely occur again. Similarly, AI systems recognise pattern to make predictions such as suggesting the next video on a platform based on past viewing habits. By showing children that their own thinking mirrors what machines do, educators can make the concept of AI less intimidating and more relatable.

Table 6. Algorithms- Step-by-Step Instructions

Aspect/ Focus Area	Age Group	Teaching Strategies/ Approaches	Examples/ Activities	AI Connection	Learning Outcomes	Key References (in-text)
Introducing algorithms	6–12 years	Explaining sequences	Brushing teeth, morning routine	Demonstrates structured tasks	Builds step awareness	(Wing, 2006)
Sequencing exercises	7–11 years	Ordering tasks logically	Story sequencing	Mimics logical code flow	Strengthens order recognition	(Holmes et al., 2019)
Visual programming	8–12 years	Using Scratch/Blockly	Simple animation coding	Converts ideas to instructions	Builds computational logic	(Resnick et al., 2009)
Robotics and movement	9–12 years	Programming robots	Bee-Bot maze	Demonstrates algorithmic commands	Encourages experiential learning	(Munusamy et al., 2025)
Unplugged coding	6–10 years	Hands-on games	Treasure hunt with clues	Reinforces logic without tech	Builds cognitive flexibility	(Papert, 1980)
Debugging errors	10–12 years	Error identification	"Fix the steps" challenge	Simulates AI correction	Develops analytical accuracy	(Lee et al., 2021)
Collaborative coding	8–12 years	Group projects	Creating mini-games	Reflects collaborative programming	Builds teamwork	(Bers, 2020)
Real-world applications	9–12 years	Linking life tasks	Cooking recipes, building kits	Connects logic to real life	Promotes cognitive transfer	(Wing, 2006)
Reflection activities	10–12 years	Writing learning logs	"How my code worked"	Reinforces process awareness	Strengthens reflection	(Papert, 1980)

Algorithms are the best way to teach children how problems can be solved efficiently by following structured steps. Story sequencing exercises, where children arrange events in the correct order, strengthen their ability to structure tasks logically. Various board games with clear rules also demonstrate that following instructions in sequence leads to predictable results. These activities introduce the concept of algorithms without going deep into coding. There are many tools that help young learners to explore algorithms in age-appropriate, visual programming like Scratch and ScratchJr are among these tools. These platforms allow young learners to build simple animations or games by arranging coding blocks in a sequence. The blocks represent the steps, and when these blocks are combined, they form an algorithm. Same way with the help of robotics kits like LEGO Mindstorms or Bee-Bot children can design step-by-step instructions for the movement of a robot, this demonstrates that how precise instructions lead to successful outcomes.

Table 7. Tools and Resources

Aspect/Focus Area	Age Group	Teaching Strategies/ Approaches	Examples/Activities	AI Connection	Learning Outcomes	Key References (in-text)
Digital coding platforms	8–12 years	Game-based learning	Scratch, Code.org	Combines logic, patterns, algorithms	Builds coding fluency	(Resnick et al., 2009)
Simplified coding tools	6–9 years	Visual drag-and-drop	ScratchJr, Blockly	Simplifies programming	Boosts creativity	(Touretzky et al., 2019)
Robotics kits	9–12 years	Hands-on STEM	LEGO Mindstorms, Bee-Bot	Executes algorithmic actions	Enhances spatial reasoning	(Munusamy et al., 2025)
Low-tech games	6–12 years	Offline activities	Board games, logic puzzles	Replicates reasoning processes	Encourages inclusive learning	(Quiloan et al., 2023)
Storytelling and literature	6–10 years	Narrative learning	AI-themed storybooks	Simplifies technical content	Builds literacy	(Lee et al., 2021)
Curriculum frameworks	8–12 years	Structured learning design	AI4K12, OECD Future Skills	Aligns with global AI competencies	Promotes systematic instruction	(Movahed et al., 2024)
Inclusive pedagogies	6–12 years	Differentiated instruction	Visual aids, unplugged lessons	Ensures accessibility	Promotes equity	(Webb et al., 2017)
Teacher training programs	Educators	Professional development	AI4K12 toolkit workshops	Builds instructional capacity	Enhances teaching quality	(Touretzky et al., 2019)
Assessment frameworks	9–12 years	Rubric-based evaluation	Logical reasoning tasks	Measures conceptual mastery	Strengthens accountability	(Movahed et al., 2024)

To teach AI to young learners, it is important to select tools and resources that are age-appropriate and effective also. High-tech and low-tech platforms and activities should be included as per the availability of resources and the environment of the school. AI literacy can be included in the existing curriculum, so that it can be a part of regular framework rather than an extra subject. LOGO, Scratch and Mindstorms are the types of AI tools, which encourage the children to use their creativity even without any knowledge of complex coding. This encourages children to explore logics, patterns and algorithms in a simple and interactive way. Board games and storytelling makes the access of AI literacy possible without digital devices. Frameworks such as AI4K12 and the OECD Future Skills Framework provide structured pedagogical guidance, ensuring age-appropriate content progression. Teacher training is found to be equally important for AI literacy. Educators who are equipped with AI pedagogy can integrate computational thinking seamlessly into various subjects like mathematics, science, and the language. If different resource mix are used, children can be engaged cognitively. Also, it helps in developing creativity, teamwork, and the ethical awareness. This hybrid teaching model mainly prepare the children for a digital future that values both human-centered and machine-assisted problem-solving approaches. It also ensures that they become informed, reflective, and the capable digital citizens.

CASE STUDIES

In current AI era, the topmost priority of many educational systems is the introduction of computational thinking to the young learners. There are many cases which has proved that children between 6 to 12 can be engaged with the basic AI concepts. These cases have successfully developed the logic, pattern recognition, and algorithms through interactive and curriculum-aligned methods. The following cases have been discussed to illustrate the diverse teaching methods and contexts for AI for young learners. These cases highlight both the opportunities and challenges for embedding these skills in the primary education.

AI4K12 Initiative: USA

(**Source:** Touretzky, D. S., Gardner-McCune, C., Martin, F., & Seehorn, D. (2019). Envisioning AI for K-12: What should every child know about AI? *Proceedings of the AAAI Conference on Artificial Intelligence, 33*, 9795–9799. https://doi.org/10.1609/aaai.v33i01.33019795)

The AI4K12 Initiative, led by the Association for the Advancement of Artificial Intelligence (AAAI) and Computer Science Teachers Association (CSTA), provides a structured framework for introducing AI to school students. The objective of this initiative is to define age-appropriate AI learning goals for K–12 education. This approach used five ideas of AI: perception, representation & reasoning, learning, natural interaction, and societal impact. Under this initiative the classroom activities including puzzles and games focusing pattern recognition, basic logic building, and understanding algorithms were designed. This framework was implemented in many schools in U.S. This initiative proved to be a helpful tool in improving the understating of students about the working of everyday tools like voice assistants or recommendation systems. This shows that how a standardized, research-backed approach can guide educators in introducing AI literacy to young learners.

Cognimates: MIT Media Lab, USA

(Source: Druga, S., Vu, S., Likhith, E., & Qiu, T. (2019). Inclusive AI literacy for kids around the world. *Proceedings of the AAAI Conference on Artificial Intelligence, 33*, 9795–9800. https://doi.org/10.1609/aaai.v33i01.33019795

Another platform where children can train AI models and build simple AI-powered projects is Cognimates which is developed by MIT Media Lab. The main idea behind this tool is to make AI hands-on and playful for children. Visual programming tools like Scratch is used by the children to train AI systems for tasks like image recognition or chatbot creation. To teach logical sequencing and pattern recognition the activities are designed around storytelling, games, and puzzles. This platform helped in increasing children's confidence as creators of AI, not just users and encouraged critical thinking about how machines "learn" and make decisions. The results reveal that play-based, project-driven learning can introduce complex AI ideas to 6–12-year-olds.

Hello Ruby: Finland

(Source: Liukas, L. (2015). *Hello Ruby: Adventures in coding*. Feiwel & Friends.

To teach computational thinking and algorithmic problem-solving to the children without requiring computers Hello Ruby is designed. The main objective of this tool is to teach the building blocks of AI, like logic and algorithms, through storytelling and play. The children use storybooks, activity books, and hands-on games. Children solve problems by sequencing steps, identifying patterns, and thinking like "computers." Over 30 countries implemented this platform. It's effective in low-resource classrooms with limited access to technology. It is an example to show that AI literacy can be introduced even in resource-constrained environments using no-tech or low-tech approaches.

ScratchJr in Primary Education: Worldwide

(Source: Resnick, M., et al. (2009). Scratch: Programming for all. *Communications of the ACM, 52*(11), 60–67. https://doi.org/10.1145/1592761.1592779

ScratchJr is a simplified visual programming language designed for young children designed to teach basic computational concepts through storytelling and creative projects. Children drag and drop blocks to create animations and games. This helps to understand the core AI skills like logical reasoning, sequencing and looping. It is used in classrooms all over the world. Research shows significant improvement in problem-solving and creativity among participants. This demonstrates the effectiveness of visual, play-based programming tools for teaching algorithmic thinking.

AI Literacy with Tangible Games: Japan

(Source: Sampanis, N. (2025). Innovative tangible interactive games for enhancing artificial intelligence knowledge and literacy in elementary education: A pedagogical framework. *arXiv*. https://arxiv.org/abs/2506.00651)

To teach the concept of neural networks and pattern recognition to the children without using screens, tangible interactive games have been developed by Japanese researchers to make AI learning physical and collaborative. Physical objects are used in these games by the children play to represent data, algorithm and output. The main focus of these games are on improving team work and problem-solving skills. The outcomes of this idea are improved understanding of abstract AI ideas by linking them to real-world, that is experiential learning. It offers a model for screen-free, inclusive AI education.

Table 8. Summary of case studies

Case Study	Country / Organization	Age Group	Objective	Approach / Tools Used	Key Impact	Relevance to Study
AI4K12 Initiative (Touretzky et al., 2019)	USA – AAAI & CSTA	6–12 years	Define age-appropriate AI learning goals for K–12 students	Developed *Five Big Ideas of AI* and designed classroom activities focusing on logic, pattern recognition, and algorithms	Adopted by many U.S. schools, improved AI literacy among young learners	Shows how a structured, research-based framework guides AI education at scale
Cognimates – MIT Media Lab (Druga et al., 2019)	USA	7–12 years	Make AI learning hands-on and playful	Children train AI models using visual programming, storytelling, and games	Increased confidence, creativity, and critical thinking	Demonstrates how play-based, project-driven learning builds AI understanding
Hello Ruby (Liukas, 2015)	Finland (used globally)	6–10 years	Teach computational thinking without computers	Storybooks, activities, and games to teach sequencing, logic, and algorithms	Implemented in 30+ countries; effective in low-resource classrooms	Example of no-tech/ low-tech AI learning for resource-constrained environments

continued on following page

Table 8. Continued

Case Study	Country / Organization	Age Group	Objective	Approach / Tools Used	Key Impact	Relevance to Study
ScratchJr in Primary Education (Resnick et al., 2009)	Global	5–8 years	Teach basic computational concepts through play	Visual drag-and-drop programming for creating animations and games	Boosted problem-solving and creativity worldwide	Demonstrates success of visual, play-based programming for young learners
Tangible AI Games (Sampanis, 2025)	Japan	6–12 years	Teach AI concepts without screens	Physical games representing data, algorithms, and problem-solving tasks	Enhanced understanding of abstract AI concepts through hands-on learning	Model for screen-free, collaborative AI education

The main idea represented by all the case studies is that the core concepts of AI can be introduced to young learners in age-appropriate and playful manner. The concepts of logics, patterns and algorithms can be introduced in routine practices. The main aim of these practices is to prepare these young learners to use the technology responsibly and creatively. Moreover, these AI concepts can be taught effectively without deeper expertise. The integration of AI at early stage makes a foundation for better and deeper engagement with AI in future education.

CHALLENGES

While there is growing interest in introducing AI literacy at the primary level, several challenges complicate the effective teaching of concepts such as logic, patterns, and algorithms to children. The educators and parents face many challenges while teaching AI concepts to children aged 6–12. Since AI is a complex field which is dynamic in nature, therefore, so it is a big challenge to simplify the concepts of AI to make them age-appropriate. A careful planning and creativity is required to make these concepts easier for the young learners to understand (Yang, 2022; Khalid et al., 2022). The most common challenges which are faced by educators and parents are as follows:

Lack of awareness and understanding is one of the biggest challenges for educators and parents in teaching AI basics to young learners. Many people don't have awareness about the fundamentals of AI, so it becomes difficult for these people to explain these concepts to young learners in a simplified and age-appropriate way (Roshan et al., 2024, Henry et al., 2021). Another issue is the lack of teacher training programs and the scarcity of age-appropriate teaching resources. Without proper training and ready-to-use resources, the teachers don't feel confident to teach AI effectively as it should be (Musa et al.,2022, Ottenbreit-Leftwich et al., 2022). Curriculum gaps is another issue which prevents the flow of teaching AI basics to young learners because, AI literacy has not yet been widely incorporated into primary education systems, leaving educators with limited formal guidance. This creates inconsistencies in what and how AI is taught (AI4K12, 2021). Not only this, but, the abstract nature of AI concepts like algorithms, logics, patterns or machine learning may not be easy for the young learners to understand without proper visual aids and hands-on teaching practices (Williams et al., (2019)). Moreover, technological barriers such as limited access to devices and reliable internet especially in rural or underprivileged areas create inequalities in opportunities for AI learning. Literature has clearly highlighted the screen time, as a challenge or barriers, which is usually perceived by the parents or educators, while maintaining the balance between digital and offline learning (Panjeti et al., 2023). Additionally, there is also urgent need to address the ethical and safety concerns, such as privacy and responsible technology use. It should be ensured that children develop not only technical understanding but also moral awareness through AI education (Lim et al., 2023). Hence, children should learn critical thinking and also the problem-solving while maintaining a healthy relationship with the digital tools.

Table 9. Challenges Faced by Teachers and Parents in Teaching AI to Children

Challenge Area	Description	Implication	Reference(s)
Lack of Awareness and Understanding	Educators and parents often lack basic knowledge of AI concepts such as logic, algorithms, and patterns.	Difficulty in simplifying AI concepts for children aged 6–12 in an age-appropriate way.	Roshan et al., 2024; Henry et al., 2021
Limited Training and Resources	Few teacher training programs and limited age-appropriate AI teaching resources.	Teachers feel unprepared and lack confidence to teach AI effectively.	Musa et al., 2022; Ottenbreit-Leftwich et al., 2022
Curriculum Gaps	AI literacy is not systematically integrated into primary education curricula.	Creates inconsistencies in what and how AI is taught across schools.	AI4K12, 2021
Abstract Nature of AI Concepts	Concepts like algorithms, logic, and machine learning are difficult for young learners without concrete examples.	Children may struggle to grasp AI fundamentals without visual aids and hands-on practices.	Williams et al., (2019)
Technological Barriers	Limited access to devices, internet, and infrastructure, especially in rural or underprivileged areas.	Unequal learning opportunities and digital divide in AI literacy.	Yang, 2022; Khalid et al., 2022

continued on following page

Table 9. Continued

Challenge Area	Description	Implication	Reference(s)
Screen Time Concerns	Parents and educators worry about excessive digital exposure for children.	Need to balance AI learning with healthy offline activities.	Panjeti-Madan & Ranganathan, 2023
Ethical and Safety Concerns	Issues related to privacy, responsible AI use, and digital safety.	Children must develop both technical knowledge and moral awareness when engaging with AI.	Lim et al., 2023

Overall, it can be said that teaching AI concepts to children is not only about involving digital resources, but it requires preparing educators as well. It includes various other components to work upon like; designing inclusive strategies, and balancing the digital and non-digital approaches. By overcoming these challenges, AI literacy can become an empowering part of the early education rather than a privilege which is accessible to only a few.

GUIDELINES

In order to overcome the above-mentioned challenges, this study proposes a set of practical, and evidence-based guidelines, which mainly aims at three key stakeholders. These stakeholders are mainly; teachers, parents, and the curriculum designers. These strategies can help in promoting an effective, inclusive, and the age-appropriate AI education for the young learners.

The role of the teachers is very crucial in simplifying abstract AI concepts. Using relatable, real-world analogies, for instance, sorting toys to explain classification or following a recipe to explain algorithms can make complex topics easier to understand (Lim et al., 2023, Nobile et al., 2024). Engaging students using play-based learning methods like puzzles, storytelling and games can make the learning process interesting while along with enhanced creativity and curiosity (Williams et al., (2019), Lee et al., 2021). Logic can be reinforced through mathematics and riddles, patterns through art and music, and algorithms through science experiments or classroom routines. Embedding AI into familiar contexts prevents it from appearing as a separate, intimidating subject (Holmes, Bialik, & Fadel, 2019, Yang, 2022). Also, to build confidence of educators and make them updated about advancements in AI, professional development opportunities must be provided so teachers feel confident in explaining AI in age-appropriate ways (Ottenbreit-Leftwich et al., 2022; Movahed et al., 2024). Initiatives such as AI4K12 offer frameworks that can guide lesson planning and ensure conceptual accuracy (Touretzky et al., 2019, Quiloan et al., 2023). To inforce AI learning, the role of parents is also very important. At homes the young learners can be engaged in activities like organizing household items or planning routes etc, that can boost the curiosity and creativity of the children and enhance the logical thinking. Parents can reinforce AI concepts by prompting children to recognize patterns, think logically about problems, and explain step-by-step routines. Simple discussions and daily observations can strengthen what children learn in school (Yue et al., (2024), Lim et al., 2023, Henry et al., 2021). In school, or at home, the activities for the young learners should encourage curiosity and the creativity. This can make the AI literacy an enjoyable process instead of a rigid technical exercise. For this, educators can make use of games, role-play, and the exploration activities, which can foster deeper engagement with the core ideas.

Further, the basics of coding can also be introduced, through a safe and interactive platforms like Scratch or Blockly. But at the same time, the screen time should be monitored too (Rosella et al., 2023, Munusamy et al., 2025). Curriculum designers also play an important role in embedding the concept of AI literacy into the existing framework. AI should not be introduced as a separate subject, instead it should be integrated into the existing subjects like arts, maths and science. Then it will be become easy for children to adopt the AI. Age appropriate and inclusive learning materials must be used. To minimize digital divide in low-resource areas, offline options should also be provided (AI4K12, 2021, Movahed et al., 2024). While coding platforms and robotics kits are useful, unplugged activities like sequencing games, puzzles, or storytelling can teach the same underlying skills. This ensures inclusivity, especially in resource-limited classrooms (Bers, 2020, Khalid et al., 2022). Also, AI education should align with 21st-century skills, emphasizing critical thinking, creativity, and ethical decision-making (Lim et al., 2023, Henry et al., 2021).

Table 10. Guidelines for Teachers, Parents, and Curriculum Designers

Challenge Area	Description	Implication	Proposed Strategies (Teachers, Parents, Curriculum Designers)	Reference(s)
Lack of Awareness and Understanding	Educators and parents often lack basic knowledge of AI concepts.	Difficulty in simplifying AI concepts for children aged 6–12 in an age-appropriate way.	**Teachers:** Use real-world analogies (sorting toys = classification, recipe = algorithm). **Parents:** Encourage logic-building through household activities. **Curriculum Designers:** Integrate AI concepts into existing subjects rather than a separate course.	Henry et al., 2021; Lim et al., 2023; Holmes et al., 2019
Limited Training and Resources	Few teacher training programs and limited age-appropriate resources.	Teachers feel unprepared and lack confidence to teach AI effectively.	**Teachers:** Participate in professional development and AI workshops. **Curriculum Designers:** Provide structured, age-appropriate teaching frameworks (e.g., AI4K12).	Musa et al., 2022; Ottenbreit-Leftwich et al., 2022; Touretzky et al., 2019; Movahed et al., 2024
Curriculum Gaps	AI literacy is not systematically integrated into primary education.	Inconsistent teaching of AI basics across schools.	**Curriculum Designers:** Embed AI into science, math, and arts; align with 21st-century skills; create inclusive offline activities for low-resource areas.	AI4K12, 2021; Movahed et al., 2024
Abstract Nature of AI Concepts	Concepts like algorithms, logic, and machine learning are hard for young learners.	Children may struggle to grasp fundamentals without visual aids and hands-on practice.	**Teachers:** Use play-based learning (games, puzzles, storytelling, art, and music) to illustrate concepts. **Parents:** Reinforce concepts through daily discussions and observations.	Williams et al., (2019); Lee et al., 2021; Raza et al., 2021
Technological Barriers	Limited access to devices and internet.	Unequal opportunities and digital divide.	**Teachers/Parents:** Use unplugged activities (sequencing, storytelling, puzzles) to teach concepts. **Curriculum Designers:** Provide offline teaching resources for rural/low-resource areas.	Yang, 2022; Khalid et al., 2022; Bers, 2020

continued on following page

Table 10. Continued

Challenge Area	Description	Implication	Proposed Strategies (Teachers, Parents, Curriculum Designers)	Reference(s)
Screen Time Concerns	Parents and educators worry about excessive digital exposure.	Need to balance AI learning with healthy offline activities.	**Teachers/Parents:** Use child-friendly platforms (Scratch, Blockly) but monitor time. **Curriculum Designers:** Blend digital and unplugged AI learning.	Panjeti-Madan & Ranganathan, 2023; Rosella et al., 2023; Munusamy et al., 2025
Ethical and Safety Concerns	Privacy, responsible use, and digital safety issues.	Children must develop technical knowledge alongside moral awareness.	**Teachers:** Discuss the responsible use of AI and ethics concerns in the context of classroom **Parents:** Guide children how to use technology safely and responsibly. **Curriculum Designers:** AI learning can be aligned with ethical decision-making, critical thinking and creativity.	Lim et al., 2023; Henry et al., 2021

PROPOSED MODEL: THE LPA FRAMEWORK FOR AI LITERACY IN CHILDREN (AGES 6–12)

The foundation layer of the model covers the core AI concepts i.e. Logic, Patterns, and Algorithms (LPA), **and the role of** tools, **strategies and the involvement of stakeholders in implementing LPA framework to teach AI to young learners.**

1. **Foundation Layer: Core Concepts**

Logic: - Logics can be taught by using puzzles, riddles and games which are based on step-by-step reasoning and cause-effect thinking. Logics enhance the reasoning and thinking skills of the children.

Patterns: - Patterns help young learners to identify similarities, repetitions and predictions. Patterns can be taught through routine activities like storytelling, sequence of numbers and rhythms etc.

Algorithms: - Algorithms are the ways through which the problem can be solved by following certain steps. The easy way to teach algorithms is through simple routine activities like coding blocks or recipes etc.

2. **Pedagogical Strategies**

Interactive methods like games, storytelling and role-play activities can be used to teach the core AI concepts to young learners.

To reduce screen dependence, board games, outdoor problem solving activities can be used.

For interactive practice, tools like LOGO, Scratch, ScratchJr, and Bee-Bot can be used.

3. **Tools and Resources**

Low-Tech Resources: - Story sequencing cards, visual aids, unplugged coding games.

High-Tech Resources: - Scratch, Code.org, robotics kits, AI-based educational apps.

Hybrid Resources: - Teacher-designed worksheets blending logic, patterns, and algorithms into math, art, or science lessons.

4. **Stakeholder Involvement**

Teachers: - Facilitate activities, scaffold learning, and integrate AI concepts into existing subjects.

Parents: -Reinforce concepts at home by encouraging children to notice patterns, explain routines, and ask "why" questions.

Curriculum Designers/Policy Makers: - Provide structured frameworks like AI4K12 to ensure systematic exposure across grade levels.

5. **Learning Outcomes:** This model will develop critical thinking of young learners by promoting logical reasoning as well as strengthen the predictive skills through recognising patterns. Through algorithmic thinking the problem solving abilities will also be gained, not only this the curiosity and confidence of the young learners will also be built. These learners will come up as responsible users of AI by understanding the decision-making basis of it.

Table 11. Summary of Framework Components

Component	Sub-Dimensions / Examples	Contribution to CT Skills
Teaching Methods	ScratchJr (play-based), Code.org (gamified), Lego Mindstorms & Ozobot (robotics), THE Labs (AI literacy)	Introduces sequencing, loops, debugging, and ethical awareness
Learner Engagement	Cognitive, Emotional, Social	Deepens logic, pattern recognition, algorithmic thinking, motivation, collaboration
Curriculum Alignment	Formal lessons, Standards (K–12 CS, UNESCO), Extracurricular activities	Ensures integration, scalability, and consistency
Learning Outcomes	Logic building, Pattern recognition, Algorithmic thinking, AI literacy	Core computational thinking and ethical awareness
Moderators	Teacher preparedness, resources, policy, culture	Explains variations in success and transferability
Broader Impacts	Creativity, Problem-solving, Collaboration, Ethical awareness	Extends skills beyond coding to real-world applications

Figure 1. LPA Framework for AI Literacy in Children (Ages 6 -12) (Source: Author's Conceptual Model)

Unlike fragmented approaches that treat AI education as either coding-focused or technology-dependent, the LPA framework emphasizes cognitive foundations that are universally accessible. By integrating logic, pattern recognition, and algorithmic thinking across low-tech, high-tech, and hybrid learning environments, the framework ensures inclusivity, scalability, and curricular flexibility. This makes the LPA model particularly relevant for diverse educational contexts, including resource-constrained settings.

CONCLUSION

The aim of this study was to investigate how can the basic AI concepts i.e. logics, patterns and algorithms can be introduced to the children from an age group of 6 to 12. From the literature review and case studies it was found that Artificial Intelligence is no longer confined to research laboratories or futuristic scenarios it is already present in the daily lives of children, whether through voice assistants, online games, or streaming platforms. This reality makes it important to introduce AI literacy at an early age, not as a complex technical subject, but as a way of developing clear thinking, structured reasoning, and the ability to make sense of the world. The concepts of logic, patterns, and algorithms provide the best starting point, as they align naturally with how children already explore and understand their environment. The findings of the study reveals that logic encourages children to think step by step, ask critical questions, and look for sound reasons behind outcomes. Patterns help them identify connections, anticipate what comes next, and make predictions from repeated observations. Algorithms, on the other hand, give them the ability to organize tasks into clear, manageable steps and to understand that complex problems can be broken down into smaller parts. Together, these three concepts not only build the foundation for understanding AI but also strengthen broader cognitive skills that are vital across all areas of learning. But, no task can be carried out smoothly without challenges. Same way, the process of teaching AI to children is not without challenges. Teachers may feel unprepared, resources may be unevenly distributed, and there is always the risk of oversimplifying complex ideas. However, these challenges also open opportunities for innovation in pedagogy. Playful, inquiry-based learning strategies such as puzzles, storytelling, coding games, and unplugged activities show that AI can be taught in ways that are developmentally appropriate, inclusive, and engaging. This approach reduces reliance on expensive technology and highlights that AI literacy is not only about tools but also about ways of thinking. From the study it is clear that the significance of early AI education extends beyond the classroom. Children who are introduced to these ideas gain confidence in navigating technology-rich environments, develop critical thinking to question how technologies work, and grow as creative problem-solvers who can adapt to future challenges. Importantly, AI literacy also contributes to responsible citizenship: when children understand that AI systems rely on patterns and data, they are better equipped to question biases, make ethical decisions, and use technology responsibly in their daily lives. In essence, preparing children for an AI-driven future is not simply about producing future programmers or engineers. It is about ensuring that every child has the opportunity to develop the thinking skills needed to thrive in a digital society. By embedding AI concepts into early education in thoughtful and inclusive ways, we lay the groundwork for a generation that can engage with technology critically, creatively, and responsibly. Logic, patterns, and algorithms thus serve not just as technical ideas but as essential life skills that empower children to face the future with confidence.

REFERENCES

AI4K12. (2021). *AI4K12 initiative: Developing national guidelines for teaching AI in K–12*. Association for the Advancement of Artificial Intelligence. https://ai4k12.org

Awad O., S., Mohamed, Y., & Shaheen, R. (2022). Applications of Artificial Intelligence in Education. *Al-Azkiyaa - International Journal of Language and Education, 1*(1), 71–81. https://doi.org/DOI: 10.33102/alazkiyaa.v1i1.10

Azhar, A. (2025). "Framework for Ethical AI integration in K-12 Education: Risks, Responsibilities and Roadmap", TIJER International Research Journal (www.TIJER.org), ISSN:2349-9249, Vol.12, Issue 7, 227-b236, July-2025, Available: https://tijer.org/TIJER/papers/TIJER2507139.pdf

Bers, M. U. (2020). *Coding as a playground: Programming and computational thinking in the early childhood classroom*. Routledge.

Bishop, C. M. (2006). *Pattern recognition and machine learning*. Springer.

Domingos, P. (2012). A few useful things to know about machine learning. *Communications of the ACM, 55*(10), 78–87. DOI: 10.1145/2347736.2347755

Druga, S. (2018). *Growing up with AI: Cognimates and child–AI interaction*. MIT Press.

Druga, S., Vu, S., Likhith, E., & Qiu, T. (2019). Inclusive AI literacy for kids around the world. *In Proceedings of ACM Fablearn conference (Fablearn'19).* ACM, New York, NY, USA, *Article 4, 8 pages.* DOI: <ALIGNMENT.qj></ALIGNMENT>10.475/123_4

Feigenbaum, E. A. (1977). *The art of artificial intelligence*. Stanford University.

Fikri, Yahya, & Rhalma, Mohamed. Artificial Intelligence (AI) in Early Childhood Education (ECE): Do Effects and Interactions Matter? International Journal of Religion: Politics, Sociology, Culture, 2024, 5 (11), pp.7536-7545. ff10.61707/y74fv875ff. ffhal-04701470f Yang, W. (2022). Artificial intelligence education for young children. *Computers & Education: Artificial Intelligence*, *3*, 100061. DOI: 10.1016/j.caeai.2022.100061

Floridi, L., Cowls, J., Beltrametti, M., Chatila, R., Chazerand, P., Dignum, V., & Vayena, E. (2018). AI4People—An ethical framework for a good AI society. *Minds and Machines*, *28*(4), 689–707. DOI: 10.1007/s11023-018-9482-5

Gennari, R., Melonio, A., Pellegrino, M. A., & D'Angelo, M. 2023. How to Playfully Teach AI to Young Learners: A Systematic Literature Review. In *Proceedings of the 15th Biannual Conference of the Italian SIGCHI Chapter (CHItaly '23)*. Association for Computing Machinery, New York, NY, USA, Article 1, 1–9. https://doi.org/DOI: 10.1145/3605390.3605393

Henry, J., Hernalesteen, A., & Collard, A.-S. (2021). Teaching artificial intelligence to K–12 through a role-playing game questioning the intelligence concept. *Kunstliche Intelligenz*, *35*(2), 171–179. DOI: 10.1007/s13218-021-00733-7

Holmes, W., Bialik, M., & Fadel, C. (2019). *Artificial intelligence in education: Promises and implications for teaching and learning*. Center for Curriculum Redesign.

Khalid, K., Iivari, N., Kinnula, M., & Sharma, S. (2022). Familiarizing children with artificial intelligence. *Proceedings of the International Conference on Entertainment and Media in the Ubiquitous Era*. https://doi.org/DOI: 10.1145/3569219.3569390

LeCun, Y., Bengio, Y., & Hinton, G. (2015). Deep learning. *Nature*, *521*, 436–444. DOI: 10.1038/nature14539

Lee, J., Joswick, C., Pole, K., & Jocius, R. (2021). Algorithm design for young children. *Contemporary Issues in Early Childhood*. Advance online publication. DOI: 10.1177/14639491211033663

Lim, T., Gottipati, S., & Cheong, M. L. (2023). Ethical Considerations for Artificial Intelligence in Educational Assessments. In Keengwe, J. (Ed.), *Creative AI Tools and Ethical Implications in Teaching and Learning* (pp. 32–79). IGI Global Scientific Publishing., DOI: 10.4018/979-8-3693-0205-7.ch003

Liukas, L. (2015). *Hello Ruby: Adventures in coding*. Feiwel & Friends.

Long, D., & Magerko, B. (2020). What Is AI Literacy? Competencies and Design Considerations. In *Proceedings of the 2020 CHI Conference on Human Factors in Computing Systems* (pp. 1-16). Association for Computing Machinery. https://doi.org/DOI: 10.1145/3313831.3376727

Luckin, R. (2018). *Machine learning and human intelligence: The future of education for the 21st century*. UCL Institute of Education Press.

McCarthy, J. (1956). Dartmouth Summer Research Project on Artificial Intelligence.

Mitchell, T. M. (1997). *Machine learning*. McGraw-Hill.

Movahed, S. V. James Dimino, Andrew Farrell, Elyas Irankhah, Srija Ghosh, Garima Jain, Vaishali Mahipal, Pranathi Rayavaram, Ismaila Temitayo Sanusi, Erika Salas, Kelilah Wolkowicz, Sashank Narain, and Fred Martin. 2024. Introducing Children to AI and ML with Five Software Exhibits. In Extended Abstracts of the CHI Conference on Human Factors in Computing Systems (CHI EA '24). Association for Computing Machinery, New York, NY, USA, Article 202, 1–6. https://doi.org/ DOI: 10.1145/3613905.3650991

Munusamy, P., Sanmugam, M., & Edwards, B. I. (2025). Exploring the World of Coding in Artificial Intelligence: A Guide for Primary School Students. In M. Sanmugam, B. Edwards, N. Mohd Barkhaya, & Z. Khlaif (Eds.), *Fostering Inclusive Education With AI and Emerging Technologies* (pp. 165-182). IGI Global Scientific Publishing. https://doi.org/DOI: 10.4018/979-8-3693-7255-5.ch007

Musa Adekunle Ayanwale, Ismaila Temitayo Sanusi, Owolabi Paul Adelana, Kehinde D. Aruleba, Solomon Sunday Oyelere. (2022). Teachers' readiness and intention to teach artificial intelligence in schools. *Computers and Education: Artificial Intelligence, 3*, 100099. DOI: 10.1016/j.caeai.2022.100099

National Research Council. (2012). *A framework for K–12 science education*. National Academies Press., DOI: 10.17226/13165

Nobile, C., Marocco, D., Ponticorvo, M., & Gigliotta, O. (2024). Teaching embodied artificial intelligence to children (Teach E-AI 2C): An educational proposal for young learners. *IEEE MetroXRAINE, 879–883*. Advance online publication. DOI: 10.1109/metroxraine62247.2024.10797080

OECD. (2019). *Artificial intelligence in society*. OECD Publishing. https://www.oecd.org/en/publications/2019/06/artificial-intelligence-in-society_c0054fa1.html

OECD. (2020). *OECD skills outlook 2019*. OECD Publishing., DOI: 10.1787/df80bc12-

OECD. (2023). *Artificial intelligence and education and skills*. OECD Publishing. https://www.oecd.org/en/topics/sub-issues/artificial-intelligence-and-education-and-skills.html

Ottenbreit-Leftwich., Krista Glazewski, Minji Jeon, Katie Jantaraweragul, Cindy Hmelo-Silver, Adam Scribner, Seung Lee, Bradford Mott, and James Lester. 2022. Principles for AI Education for Elementary Grades Students. In Proceedings of the 27th ACM Conference on on Innovation and Technology in Computer Science Education Vol. 2. Association for Computing Machinery, New York, NY, USA, 627. https://doi.org/DOI: 10.1145/3502717.3532143

Panjeti-Madan, V. N., & Ranganathan, P. (2023). Impact of Screen Time on Children's Development: Cognitive, Language, Physical, and Social and Emotional Domains. *Multimodal Technologies and Interaction*, *7*(5), 52. DOI: 10.3390/mti7050052

Papert, S. (1980). *Mindstorms: Children, computers, and powerful ideas*. Basic Books Inc.

Quiloan, R., Rahimi Moosavi, S., Tankelevich, R., & Karlin, M. (2023). PlayGrid: Sparking AI literacy with an intuitive learning interface. *Fifth International Conference on Transdisciplinary AI (TransAI)*, Laguna Hills, CA, USA, 2023, pp. 171-178, doi: DOI: 10.1109/TransAI60598.2023.00045

Resnick, M., John Maloney, Andrés Monroy-Hernández, Natalie Rusk, Evelyn Eastmond, Karen Brennan, Amon Millner, Eric Rosenbaum, Jay Silver, Brian Silverman, and Yasmin Kafai. (2009). Scratch: Programming for all. *Communications of the ACM*, *52*(11), 60–67. DOI: 10.1145/1592761.1592779

Roshan, S., Iqbal, S., & Zhang, Q. (2024). Teacher Training and Professional Development for Implementing AI-Based Educational Tools. (2024). *Journal of Asian Development Studies*, *13*(2), 1972–1987. DOI: 10.62345/jads.2024.13.2.154

Russell, S., & Norvig, P. (2010). *Artificial intelligence: A modern approach* (3rd ed.). Pearson.

Sampanis, N. (2025). Innovative Tangible Interactive Games for Enhancing Artificial Intelligence Knowledge and Literacy in Elementary Education: A Pedagogical Framework. *arXiv*. https://arxiv.org/abs/2506.00651

Touretzky, D. S., Gardner-McCune, C., Martin, F., & Seehorn, D. (2019). Envisioning AI for K–12. *Proceedings of the AAAI Conference on Artificial Intelligence*, *33*, 9795–9799. DOI: 10.1609/aaai.v33i01.33019795

Turing, A. M. (1950). Computing machinery and intelligence. *Mind*, *59*(236), 433–460.

Webb, M., Davis, N., & Bell, T. (2017). Computer science in K–12 school curricula of the 21st century. *Education and Information Technologies*, *22*(2), 445–468. DOI: 10.1007/s10639-016-9493-x

Williams, R., Park, H. W., Oh, L., & Breazeal, C. (2019). PopBots: Designing an AI curriculum for early childhood education. *Proceedings of the AAAI Conference on Artificial Intelligence*, *33*(1), 9729–9736. DOI: 10.1609/aaai.v33i01.33019729

Wing, J. M. (2006). Computational thinking. *Communications of the ACM*, *49*(3), 33–35. DOI: 10.1145/1118178.1118215

Yue, M., Jong, M. S. Y., & Ng, D. T. K. (2024). Understanding K–12 teachers' technological pedagogical content knowledge readiness and attitudes toward artificial intelligence education. *Education and Information Technologies*, *29*(4), 4119–4135.

KEY TERMS AND DEFINITIONS

AI (Artificial Intelligence): Machines or computers that can "think" or make decisions like humans.

Algorithm: A list of step-by-step instructions to solve a problem.

Data: Information that AI uses to learn and make decisions.

Decision: Choosing what to do based on rules, logic, or information.

Logic: Step-by-step thinking to make decisions.

Pattern: Something that repeats or follows a rule.

Prediction: Guessing what might happen next by looking at patterns.

Chapter 9
Exploring the Impact of Teachers in AI-Powered Personalized Adaptive Learning in Educational Environments:
A Systematic Review

Ahlam Al Balushi
https://orcid.org/0009-0000-4659-7920
International Maritime College Oman, National University of Science and Technology, Oman

ABSTRACT

Artificial Intelligence (AI) has emerged in education to change it from the traditional process into an adaptive and personalized education. The customizable e-learning system considers the differences in learning needs, performances, and requirements of the students to generate a comprehensive learning experience. AI technologies help students learn according to their strengths and weaknesses. The purpose of this study is to conduct a systematic literature review on the teachers' role in the AI-powered personalized adaptive learning (AI-PAL) through the PRISMA process for the recent literature published from 2018 to 2025. The findings demonstrate the effective impact of AI-PAL on students' learning experience. Nevertheless, the study highlights that the teachers' role is neglected, but it is essential for AI-PAL. The absence of teacher interaction in an AI-PAL environment can hamper the

DOI: 10.4018/979-8-3373-4982-4.ch009

overall learning experiences. Therefore, further research is needed to explore how teachers' involvement affects students' outcomes and the AI-PAL impact on different educational environments.

1. OVERVIEW OF AI PERSONALIZED ADAPTIVE LEARNING

Nowadays, learning is transforming from one-size-fits-all methods to customized learning, making personalized adaptive learning (PAL). PAL is designed to meet students' needs, interests, and abilities. It helps students to be learner-centric rather than instructor-centric. This transition has intensified recently to attain quality education, the fourth pillar of SDGs (Strielkowski et al., 2025).

PAL understands the diversity of students in their academic achievement, skills, educational patterns, and motivational factors (Song et al., 2024).

Artificial intelligence (AI) in education is a milestone in PAL as AI applications penetrated deeply into the education system. It creates unique learning materials for every learner, produces individualized tests, and acts like a human to answer learners' questions (Bhutoria, 2022). For example, AI is embedded into robots to improve the students' learning outcomes, from the primary educational level to early childhood learning. Similarly, online education has shifted from providing downloadable files and doing assignments to a more advanced stage that integrates intelligent and adaptive web-based systems that can analyze the behavior of both instructors and students to make adjustments and improve learning outcomes (Chen et al., 2020). AI is also integrated into learning platforms such as Duolingo (a language learning platform), Absorb LMS, and Docebo LMS, which are learning management systems used to support online learning and course administration. These AI-powered learning management systems (LMS) are developed to deliver personalized learning and automated administrative tasks by using multiple AI capabilities (Wang et al., 2024). In the realm of educational AI tutors, Khan Academy developed Khanmigo, which uses the powerful GPT-4 technology to deliver customized learning and intelligent feedback across different subjects, such as language, programming, and mathematics learning (Wang et al., 2024).

However, the capabilities of AI have not been exploited within the area of education (Celik, 2023). Thus, the utilization of AI in educational environments lags behind other sectors, especially the business sector. One reason for this is that the critical involvement of educators in the academic incorporation of AI tools that support PAL has been disregarded (Celik, 2023; Seufert et al., 2021). Most studies focused on adaptive systems that customized content; however, the role of the educators as a motivator, facilitator, mentor, and provider of understanding is unclear (Zheng L. et al., 2022). The purpose of this chapter is to address these gaps by conducting a systematic literature review on the impact of AI-PAL in educational environments. This review is motivated by the following questions:

a. How does AI-PA contribute effectively to students' learning experiences?
b. What is the role of AI-powered tools in learning experiences, teaching processes, and assessment systems?
c. What are the challenges related to tools powered by AI in education?

The chapter gives a holistic understanding of the effect of AI-PAL on educational environments, its impact on learners' experience, teaching processes, and assessment systems, and the challenges of integrating it with learning outcomes and assessment systems. Therefore, this chapter is organized to provide an overview of AI-enabled personalized adaptive learning. It begins with reviewing the relevant literature to present the uses of AI-PAL in different educational settings. It also describes the methodology and selection process. Moreover, key findings are discussed and analyzed, and a summary of the main findings, implications, and future work is illustrated.

2. LITERATURE REVIEW

2.1 AI-Powered Personalized Adaptive Learning (AI-PAL) in Education

PAL is a new educational strategy. It forms an incorporation of personalized learning and adaptive learning. It is defined as a ''technology-empowered effective pedagogy which can adaptively adjust teaching strategies timely based on real-time monitored (enabled by smart technology) learning differences and changes in individual characteristics, individual performance, and personal development'' (Essa et al., 2023; Peng et al., 2019). PAL leverages students' learning preferences, prior knowledge, and skill levels to automatically select and deliver customized learning content and resources based on their needs, goals, strengths, and pace (Alrawashdeh et al., 2024; Strielkowski et al., 2025).

Due to the rapid development of AI, PAL has become more effective than other educational approaches. For example, Squirrel AI was developed in China to modify languages, science, and math content and activities to meet students' needs, abilities, and interests (Alrawashdeh et al., 2024). This system enables teachers to estimate students' progression and subsequently provide adaptive, flexible, and customized content. AI-PAL takes the benefits of both approaches, and the following sub-sections illustrate how personalized and adaptive learning positively influence enhancing students' academic performance, engagement, and achievement.

2.1.1 AI-Powered Personalized Learning in Education

Adapting educational experiences to meet students' requirements is called personalized learning. It enables learners to learn at their own pace and to change the lesson plans to suit them. Personalized learning allows students to manage their own education and take ownership of it. This approach believes every student has specific needs that must be taken into account so that they can truly maximize their potential. Moreover, it helps students explore their interests and preferences to support the growth of problem-solving, critical thinking, self-motivation, and other key skills.

AI technologies are one of the essential keys to personalized learning for learners. They are used to provide customized learning experiences. Personalized learning features also play an important role in creating a successful journey for students. This is because they can tailor instructions to meet students' needs. Thus, students get better learning experiences and outcomes (Kavitha & Lohani, 2019). Recent studies show that personalized or customized learning effectively contributed to increasing performance levels, engaging and motivating students. Pardamean et al. (2022) designed an AI-based learning style prediction model to recommend materials that adapt to each student's learning style. They found that the performance levels of the students improved as a result. Somasundaram et al. (2020) developed an AI/Machine Learning-based prediction model that provided a personalized learning path for each student. This model was developed to analyze historical and current student profiles/performance data in the institutions' Quality

Management System (QMS). Table 1 illustrates the AI-powered personalized learning contribution to students' learning experiences.

Table 1. AI-Powered Personalized Learning

Sources	*Contribution*
(Tang et al., 2020)	**Parallel Intelligent Education uses an artificial education system to provide personalized learning to students through a game-based environment.**
(Huang et al., 2023)	AI-enabled personalized video recommendation systems for the flipped classroom were proposed to foster learning motivation and engagement, resulting in enhanced student achievement, engagement, and performance level of motivation.
(Kohnke, 2023)	A personalized chatbot was developed to provide differentiated instruction to support and motivate second-language learners.
(Ali et al., 2023)	3D artificial intelligence (AI)-based Intelligent Tutoring System (ITS) software named KIAAA (An AI Assistant for teaching in the field of automation), was designed to provide personalized learning to each student studying computer programming, resulting in reducing teachers' workload and improving students' engagement, achievement, and motivation.
(Lokare & Jadhav, 2024)	An AI-based learning prediction model to provide personalized learning experiences by predicting students' learning styles based on various input attributes

The studies presented in Table 1 reveal the beneficial impact of AI-powered personalized learning on students' learning experiences. Nevertheless, there is a shortage of generalization because some research has concentrated on specific scenarios or contexts in educational settings (Lokare & Jadhav, 2024; Tang et al., 2020). They also evaluated the proposed systems on a small group of students (Ali et al., 2023). To get a comprehensive result, they should determine a wider and more varied range of students. Moreover, proposed systems need to be tested in some works to validate their effectiveness (Ali et al., 2023). In addition, studies demonstrated that chatbots may are likely not be equally effective for all students, particularly those with lower motivation (Huang et al., 2023). Thus, the teacher's role of support, encouragement, and guidance is essential for students to benefit from the learning experiences of the chatbot. Chatbots can also serve as a distraction to students (Kohnke, 2023). This could add more burden to the teachers in handling the class.

2.1.2 AI-Powered Adaptive Learning in Education

In recent years, adaptive learning has received much attention due to the fast growth of information and communication technology (ICT) in educational settings (Xie et al., 2019). The main objective of adaptive learning is to generate a learning experience considering the diverse learning needs of students and to define the type of materials or technological software (systems) based on their preferences. These systems can generate unique learning content, learning paths, and student strategies based on their needs, performance, and situation. Further, they enable students to approach the learning content at their own pace, and the continuous feedback responds to the questions and activities (Contrino et al., 2024). The table below shows the diverse applications of adaptive learning in educational environments.

Table 2. AI-Powered Adaptive Learning

Technology	Description	Reference
Intelligent Tutoring Systems	AI tutors are designed to create continually customized insights and feedback to make interactive learning experiences by analyzing states, skills, and conversational responses.	(Mehrfar et al., 2024)
AI Chatbot	It is the simplest intelligent Human-Computer Interaction (HCI). It is a computer program designed to respond like an intelligent entity when conversing through voice or text and understand more than one human language. In other words, it simulates a conversation with humans over the internet.	(Susanto et al., 2023)
Adaptive Assessment and Feedback	It automatically generates and constructs assessments such as multiple-choice questions or open-answer questions based on students' needs, skills, and knowledge.	Rezigalla (2024)
Recommender System	Software designed to provide valuable suggestions based on students' needs and interests.	(Kabudi et al., 2021)
Automated Grading and Assessment	It automatically assesses student work (such as assignments, quizzes, tests, or exams), analyzes student responses, and provides feedback by utilizing some techniques such as machine learning (ML).	(Dhananjaya et al., 2024)

Table 2 represents the description of adaptive learning technologies. Intelligent Tutoring Systems (ITS) and Adaptive Assessment tools customize the learning experiences based on students' preferences and needs. AI chatbots and Recommender Systems provide ease of access and engagement, while Automated Grading systems reduce teachers' workload of grading and scoring marks. However, there are some drawbacks associated with these technologies. For example, the major concern related to ITS is data privacy. AI chatbots have difficulties associated with meaningful educational interactions. This indicates that they struggle with complex inquiries, and studies are still uncertain when and how to use chatbots to foster learning and engage students actively (Chiu et al., 2023; Palasundram et al., 2019). Adaptive Assessment and Feedback have difficulties in generating quality questions and the same questions in different cases (Rezigalla, 2024). They face challenges as well in providing meaningful feedback. Automated Grading and Assessment is a useful tool for large classes where manual grading would be impractical, but the cost and complexity of the proposed algorithm that may be used can hinder its implementation (Balaha & Saafan, 2021; Jukiewicz, 2024). The main limitation of the Recommender System is its dependency on the data quality and scope of data used in the recommendation algorithms (Roy & Dutta, 2022), which may provide unhelpful consultation and suggestions to students.

However, several studies show positive impacts of adaptive learning on students' academic progression. Wang et al. (2020) studied the effect of an adaptive learning system on students' mathematics test progression. Students who used the system demonstrated higher progress than those who were taught by an expert face-to-face. A similar result was discovered by Hwang et al. (2020). They compared the outcomes of mathematics tests on two groups, one using the adaptive learning system and one without it. Moreover, Zheng (2024) designed an intelligent e-learning system for art courses using AI and adaptive learning algorithms to offer personalized learning paths and content. It found that this system contributed to enhancing the learning effect and learning motivation. With a similar result, Nihad et al. (2020) developed multi-agent adaptive learning to provide instant decisions and training to learners according to their dynamic learning pace. It is interesting to note that some researchers investigate students' satisfaction with adaptive learning systems (Xie et al., 2019). Hooshyar et al. (2021), demonstrated that students who used an adaptive educational computer game were more satisfied with the game than other groups.

2.2 Role of AI-Powered Tools in Education

AI is turning regular learning and teaching into personalized and adaptive learning by adjusting the content, learning activities, guidance, and feedback for individual learners (Kamalov et al., 2023; Mehrfar et al., 2024). Therefore, students have learning paths that adapt to their abilities and weaknesses through the content. For instance, if a learner excels in algebra but finds geometry challenging. AI helps identify a learner's strengths and weaknesses before designing a learning path focused more on geometry topics. This ensures the best possible individual learning experience for each student. Due to this, AI is an important aspect in teaching methods, educational processes, and evaluation systems.

A. AI in Learning Experiences

AI tools can help students learn in different ways. For example, distributing responsibilities based on individual abilities, supporting human-machine conversations, and enhancing flexibility and engagement in the technological age.

Distributing responsibilities based on individual abilities: AI can revolutionize in-class student learning by offering customized tutoring materials. This is because it can control learning to meet the needs of each learner by generating individualized materials, resources, and activities according to the skills and objectives needed from every learner, through developing an individual learning path (Gligorea et al., 2023). For instance, Munawar et al. (2018) designed an AI-based virtual lab to meet the learners' demand by allocating lab assignments at a suitable level of difficulty. Yang & Shulruf (2019) also utilized an AIpowered interface to offer immediate responses and customized exercises to medical undergraduates. In addition, Kong et al. (2021) created a simulated patient in a virtual environment to train medical learners. Nevertheless, a shortage of supportive educational materials as an essential challenge in personalizing activities to users' abilities. Since the student educational exercises offered by AI-driven systems were pre-developed and not dynamically generated, they might not have matched user requirements. It implies that the personalized learning provided by AI technologies is still at an experimental stage, and the issues mainly lie in the unavailability of proper learning resources.

Offering human-machine conversations and feedback: Most studies showed enhancement in students' engagement and satisfaction regarding the integration of AI-powered chatbots in education. This incorporation enables students to have conversations and receive real-time feedback about their learning. For example, when AI chatbots were applied in language learning to assist learners in designing their communication skills through continuous dialogue, students enjoyed and found this method useful for gaining answers to simple questions (Chiu et al., 2023; Palasundram et al., 2019; Vázquez-Cano et al., 2021). Pokrivcakova (2019) noted that chatbots used in education enrich the learning experience of students. This is because chatbots improve the learning experience using machine learning algorithms to provide personalized learning materials. Nonetheless, such studies also have certain difficulties associated with these interactions, and there is little research on how conversation with AI machines affects the student experience. Thus, the appropriate timing and method of using chatbots for learning and student engagement remain ambiguous (Chiu et al., 2023; Palasundram et al., 2019).

Enhancing flexibility and engagement in digital settings: AI technologies can be used to enhance student performance, achievement, and engagement in PAL environments through the capture of student learning data. For example, adaptive online quizzes were created by Ross et al. (2018) to meet the specific educational needs of each and every learner. Cui et al. (2018) assessed the efficacy of the adaptive learning system, known as "Yixue Squirrel AI", and learners demonstrated high performance when utilizing it compared to traditional classroom instruction. Kickmeier-Rust & Holzinger (2019) developed an efficient adaptive games framework, called MAXMIN ant system, which used a combinatorial optimization algorithm. Westera et al. (2020) utilized different methods to analyze and characterize students, such as facial expression recognition, automated difficulty adjustment, and stealth assessment. They also used techniques, such as non-verbal bodily animation and lip-synchronized speech, to create a non-playing character. Those studies did not investigate the impact of these systems on the students' performance. They emphasized the development and utilization of AI-based digital settings.

B. AI in the Teaching Process

AI technologies have effective roles in improving teaching and pedagogical methods. These technologies offer adaptive and customized teaching approaches and enhance teachers' capacity to teach.

Offering adaptive and customized teaching approach: Teaching materials, content, and activities that are convenient for teaching requirements can be recommended by AI technologies. For example, the SmartPath program was a virtual learning platform, which was developed by Aldeman et al. (2021). It was designed using machine learning to teach and diagnose glomerular diseases, which allows the teacher to access class performance assessments, ascertain content weak areas, and extend assistance to improve learning. Furthermore, Lampos et al. (2021) used an AI classifier to scan student features and recommend efficient communication methods for educators teaching autistic learners. Standen et al. (2020) used AI systems on a variety of data sensors to help teachers determine the best approach to deliver content, teaching strategies, and communication methods by identifying students' affective statuses. However, there is a shortage of generalization and practical testing as these works were constrained by a few number of participants and shortened durations of experiments (Aldeman et al., 2021; Standen et al., 2020). Moreover, the absence of evaluation criteria to assess the effectiveness of these systems can hinder the positive enhancement of related technologies (Chiu et al., 2023).

Improving teachers' capability to teach: AI technologies have been developed, like automated scoring assessments, which help to reduce the efforts and time required for evaluating, scoring assessments, and giving personalized feedback for each question, such as quizzes, tests, and assignments. For example, in 2021, Balaha & Saafan proposed a framework for marking multiple-choice questions, essays, and formulas, called HMB-AECF. The results demonstrated some advantages, such as dealing with different types of questions and enhancing efficiency and accuracy in assessment. Moreover, CatGPT was used as an automated grading tool by Jukiewicz (2024) for scoring the programming assessment. It showed its benefits in offering good quality assessment, time efficiency, generating feedback, unbiased grading, and enforcement of coding standards. However, these systems are limited to generalization and the complexity of the proposed algorithm, which may affect their implementation (Balaha & Saafan, 2021). Further, some factors can hinder the use of these systems, including the cost, the absence of absolute agreement on repeatable outcomes, the possibility of hallucinations, and the occasional need for instructors' guidance (Jukiewicz, 2024).

C. AI in Assessment Systems

Assessment provides evidence to support that students have achieved the expected learning outcomes. Constructing assessments requires time and teachers' effort as they need to ensure alignment with learning outcomes. AI has a great role in generating and constructing assessments such as multiple-choice questions or open-answer questions. For instance, Rezigalla (2024) assessed the use of an AI tool in generating formative assessments like MCQs, and it showed high-quality construction within a short time. Tsai et al. (2020) proposed an automatic question generation (AQG) to generate short answer questions to minimize the time of writing exam questions and to improve the students' learning performance. It is noticed that students' learning performance improved, and emphasized that students can deepen their long-term memory of course knowledge. However, these studies limited the generalization and did not assess their ability to generate the same question in different instances (Rezigalla, 2024). Moreover, there is a lack of quality in generated questions, and this indicates that generated questions are less accurate. Therefore, teacher intervention is required to review and refine the generated questions to ensure they align with learning objectives and outcomes and consequently assess to generate accurate questions (Tsai et al., 2020).

Research shows that AI-PAL had an effective impact on student learning experience. They provide examples and evidence of the effective utilization of AI-powered tools in personalizing and adapting learning experiences, and how they positively improve learning, teaching processes, and assessment systems. However, these studies focused on how AI-PAL affects students' learning experiences, how AI-PAL technologies lessen the burden on teachers without concentrating on their role when using these technologies, and how teachers' role with these technologies can improve the teaching and learning process. This is because these studies illustrate the challenging aspects associated with AI. For instance, AI implementation is still in its current experimental phase, needs dynamically generated supportive resources, and requires comprehensive empirical testing of the role of an AI-to-student interactor in learning. In addition, there is a risk of using automated grading and generating assessments that may not be accurate and aligned to the goals and outcomes of the curriculum.

3. METHODOLOGY APPROACH AND SELECTION PROCESS

This chapter uses a structured peer-reviewed process called the Preferred Reporting Items for Systematic Review and Meta-analyses (PRISMA). The systematic literature search is a paper methodological approach since it allows for reliability, transparency, and quality in the process of review. According to Gao et al. (2024), PRISMA is a technique due to its ability to avoid reproducibility and bias. They adhere to rigid criteria for identifying, screening, and analyzing studies. As a result, they offer focused and relevant studies that answer the questions. This method involves four processes: identification, screening, eligibility determination, and inclusion.

A. Identification

This chapter conducted a systematic search for relevant articles from different databases, including IEEE, SCOPUS, ScienceDirect, Springer, and WOS. In addition, specific search terms were used to ensure relevance throughout the research process. The selection included papers with the terms "AI", "artificial intelligence", "adaptive learning", "personalized learning", "personalized adaptive learning", and "education". The study sought to focus on collecting information directly related to those areas of interest by using searching techniques such as phrase searching, truncation, Boolean operators (AND, OR, NOT, or ANT NOT), and wildcard ("*"). Inclusion and exclusion criteria were utilized to identify papers consistent with the research objectives. The appropriate papers were selected based on their compatibility with research goals, publication date, and research methodology. A total of 158 articles were identified after applying the criteria as shown in Figure 1. The criteria excluded non-English articles, incomplete texts, and papers published outside the specified timeframe. Thus, 137 articles were selected for additional screening.

B. Screening and Eligibility

The screening process is employed to eliminate duplicate articles and review titles and abstracts, to identify the related and focused articles, journals, or conference papers. First, 38 duplicate articles were removed from the analysis. Then, 199 papers were selected to examine titles and abstracts, excluding publications that were unrelated or relevant but not focused on AI integration in personalized or adaptive learning in educational settings. In the eligibility process, 78 articles were reviewed for full texts to eliminate the ambiguous publications and those published with unreliable sources.

C. Inclusion

In the final stage, 68 publications were included in this chapter due to their content appropriateness in helping provide answers to the research questions and bridging the gap

Figure 1. PRISMA Flowchart

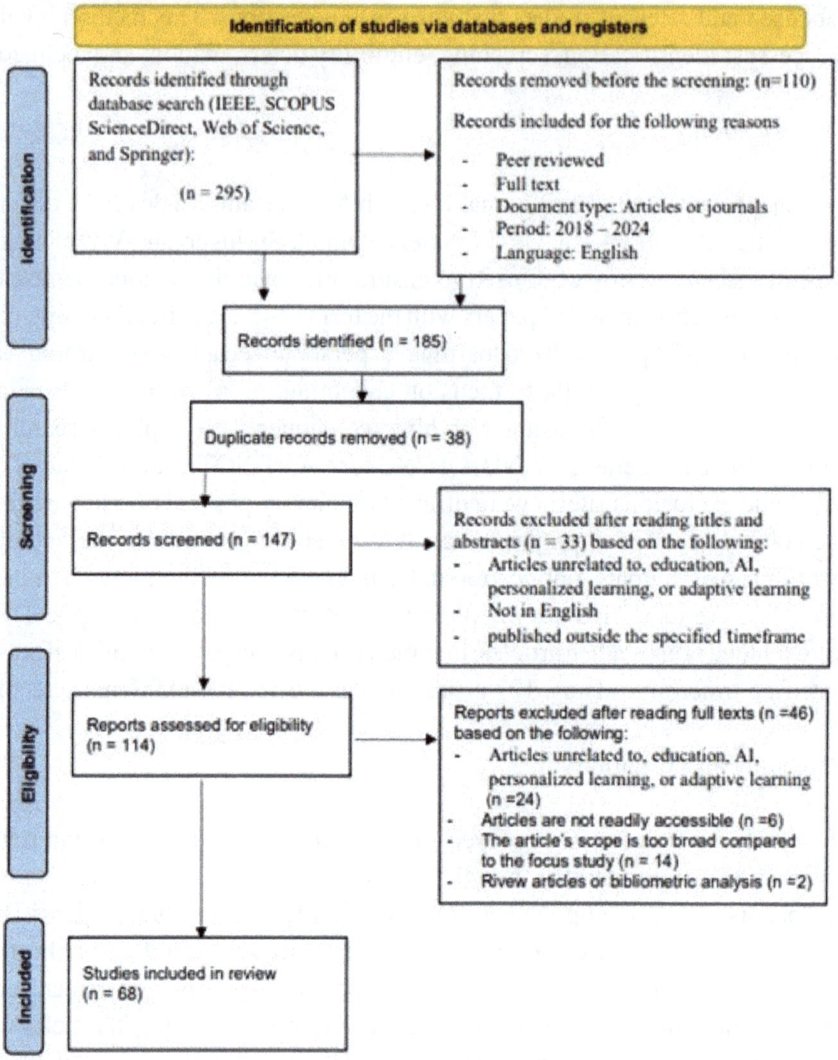

4. SYNTHESIS OF FINDINGS

4.1 Impact of AI-PAL Technologies on Students

AI technologies are widely used in education across various disciplines, including mathematics, language, and computer science, in both K-12 and higher education. AI-PAL technologies, like robots, contribute to enhancing students' motivation and engagement. They have supported those low achievers who felt more confident and were less embarrassed. Moreover, many studies have observed how the academic performance of students has improved significantly due to the aid of AI technologies. The AI-PAL technologies also contribute to increasing the accessibility of educational resources, particularly among students with disabilities or special needs (Pesek et al., 2022; Rizvi, 2023). Those students may be deaf or hard-of-hearing, have problems with reading and writing, or social breakdowns, such as language and communication. With AI-PAL, various learning content can be developed based on students' learning profiles that show the areas the students need to improve. In other words, AI-PAL provides students with tailored lessons and assessments to make them more confident, as there are usually no classmates within the application to compare with (Pesek et al., 2022). Further, AI-PAL technologies can detect students' attention levels by identifying pupils who require extended time to understand the lessons than those who grasp them quickly. This shows how AI-PAL technologies offer alternative learning opportunities to individuals who may have encountered obstacles in the past due to their disabilities. Moreover, AI-PAL technologies provide real-time feedback that produces sustainable growth in online collaborative skills (Porter & Grippa, 2020), critical thinking (Mokmin, 2020), and self-directed learning (Soong et al., 2020; D. Yang et al., 2020), among students. These technologies lead to direct customized feedback that motivates learners to take on responsibility for their learning and become more self-directed learners. They learn how to develop and set their goals, track their progress, and make decisions about their learning pathways. Thus, AI-PAL contributes to making students' skills lifelong by enhancing fundamental skills and achieving desired educational results, such as problem-solving (Kamalov et al., 2023). However, some studies found that not every student benefited from AI technologies. For example, Malik et al. (2021) and Villegas-Ch et al. (2020) stated that only motivated students found chatbot conversations meaningful. Further, Bonneton-Botté et al. (2020) noted that students with beginner handwriting skills performed poorly with AI, while those with intermediate-level skills performed well. Furthermore, AI-PA technologies caused stronger anxiety for students, specifically, they were concerned about their future careers and job opportunities because these technologies could replace human jobs (Terzi, 2020; Y. Y. Wang & Wang, 2022; Wood et al., 2021). In general, AI-PAL emphasizes its ability to enhance students' performance and motivation, but with acknowledgment of teacher intervention in learning and teaching.

4.2 Impact of AI-PAL Technologies on Teachers

AI technologies enhance teachers' working efficiency by simplifying and automating routine tasks. For instance, using AI to manage online classrooms, such as module registration and student attendance (Aldeman et al., 2021), automatically marking multiple-choice and short-answer questions (Rodriguez-barrios et al., 2021), organizing intelligent learning resources like student check-in and assignment tasks (D. Yang et al., 2020), and providing advice to help students and translate teachers' responses (Kim et al., 2021; Vázquez-Cano et al., 2021).

Online teaching during the COVID-19 pandemic increased teachers' workload and placed a lot of stress, which negatively affected their health (Villegas-Ch et al., 2020). AI technologies contributed to reducing teachers' workload by managing online courses. This led to saving teachers' time and increasing their productivity. Moreover, some intelligent learning platforms provide different ideas and approaches by recommending adaptive teaching content for both teachers and students (Aldeman et al., 2021). These platforms indirectly enhance teacher-teaching competence.

In general, most studies noted positive teachers' attitudes toward the utilization of AI-PAL technologies to support teaching. Some teachers found these cutting-edge technologies beneficial in enhancing teaching work efficiency and competence (Gunawan et al., 2021; Wood et al., 2021). Nevertheless, some others found them difficult to control as they failed to understand how these technologies operated (Aldosari, 2020; Haseski, 2019; Kahn & Winters, 2021). Furthermore, intelligent systems lack to provide diverse teaching methods as AI can offer only a single format (Holstein et al., 2019; Kahn & Winters, 2021). In addition, AI systems did not give explanations for why and how different tasks were assigned to students (Chiu et al., 2023; Holstein et al., 2019). Moreover, the absence of teacher interaction with AI-PAL technologies negatively impacts the learning environment. Many studies confirm the importance of keeping a proper balance between teacher involvement and AI technologies in the learning process (Algahtani, 2024; Gligorea et al., 2023b; Jukiewicz, 2024; Tsai et al., 2020). For example, the AQG system was created to generate short questions; however, it provided low-quality questions (Tsai et al., 2020). Further, ChatGPT could facilitate reproducible findings and potential hallucinations when used as an automated grading tool (Jukiewicz, 2024). Moreover, incorporating AI chatbots in the educational process helps to keep students engaged and makes them feel more confident. Nonetheless, they cannot substitute teachers' roles in monitoring the progress of students or helping those who are struggling with their learning journey with AI Chatbots (Susanto et al., 2023). Therefore, teacher intervention is considered one of the most significant aspects that should be handled properly in this context. Overall, the challenges posed by AI-PAL tools in educational environments impact both students and learners. Some students benefited from these tools, but those with low skill levels performed poorly. Moreover, the AI-PAL could raise student anxiety over their career, while the non-transparency of the decision-making process of the AI tools was noted. In addition, low-quality content generated from these tools and this caused a need for a teacher's intervention are necessary for guidance.

5. CONCLUSION

Recently, literature on educational technology has been more geared towards transforming education from a "one-size-fits-all" strategy to personalized, adaptive learning. This literature understands that including AI-PAL into education is a way to achieve unique learning for individual students that focuses on meeting their specific learning needs and requirements. It also highlights the great contribution of AI-PAL to enhancing students' performance, engagement, and achievement. Moreover, AI-PAL has an important role in improving learning outcomes, teaching processes, and assessment systems. However, there are some challenges associated with AI-PAL. Studies illustrated that not all learners benefit from AI technologies, as only motivated students who use AI-PAL technologies effectively do. Although these technologies are used to lessen the workload for teachers, they still require teachers' intervention to monitor students' progress and encourage low-motivated students to benefit from these tools and use them efficiently in their learning journey. Their involvement is needed to review and refine the questions that are generated or graded automatically through AI-PAL. Therefore, a lack of teacher involvement in an AI-PAL environment can degrade the entire learning experience. This study's implications highlight the need to balance AI and teacher intervention. In the future, additional research is needed to study the use of AI-PAL tools across different educational contexts. Furthermore, the involvement of teachers and interaction with AI technology can affect the performance, engagement, motivation, and achievement of students. Moreover, it is essential to investigate ethical and privacy concerns to ensure that students and teachers can use these tools effectively and efficiently. In addition, empirical studies should evaluate AI-PAL technologies in diverse educational settings.

6. REFERENCES

Aldeman, N. L. S., de Sá Urtiga Aita, K. M., Machado, V. P., da Mata Sousa, L. C. D., Coelho, A. G. B., da Silva, A. S., da Silva Mendes, A. P., de Oliveira Neres, F. J., & do Monte, S. J. H. (2021). Smartpathk: A platform for teaching glomerulopathies using machine learning. *BMC Medical Education, 21*(1). Advance online publication. DOI: 10.1186/s12909-021-02680-1 PMID: 33926437

Aldosari, S. A. M. (2020). The future of higher education in the light of artificial intelligence transformations. *International Journal of Higher Education, 9*(3), 145–151. DOI: 10.5430/ijhe.v9n3p145

Algahtani, A. (2024). A COMPARATIVE STUDY OF AI-BASED EDUCATIONAL TOOLS: EVALUATING USER INTERFACE EXPERIENCE AND EDUCATIONAL IMPACT. *Journal of Theoretical and Applied Information Technology, 15*(5). www.jatit.org

Ali, A., Deuter, A., & Wehmeier, L. (2023). Personalized Learning in Automation: A 3D AIBased Approach. *Proceedings - Frontiers in Education Conference, FIE.* https://doi.org/DOI: 10.1109/FIE58773.2023.10343228

Alrawashdeh, G. S., Fyffe, S., Azevedo, R. F. L., & Castillo, N. M. (2024). Exploring the impact of personalized and adaptive learning technologies on reading literacy: A global meta-analysis. *Educational Research Review, 42*. Advance online publication. DOI: 10.1016/j.edurev.2023.100587

Balaha, H. M., & Saafan, M. M. (2021). Automatic exam correction framework (AECF) for the MCQS, essays, and equations matching. *IEEE Access : Practical Innovations, Open Solutions, 9*, 32368–32389. DOI: 10.1109/ACCESS.2021.3060940

Bonneton-Botté, N., Fleury, S., Girard, N., Le Magadou, M., Cherbonnier, A., Renault, M., Anquetil, E., & Jamet, E. (2020). Can tablet apps support the learning of handwriting? An investigation of learning outcomes in kindergarten classroom. *Computers & Education, 151*. Advance online publication. DOI: 10.1016/j.compedu.2020.103831

Celik, I. (2023). 'Towards Intelligent-TPACK: An empirical study on teachers' professional knowledge to ethically integrate artificial intelligence (AI)-based tools into education'. *Computers in Human Behavior, 138*. Advance online publication. DOI: 10.1016/j.chb.2022.107468

Chen, L., Chen, P., & Lin, Z. (2020). Artificial intelligence in education: A review. *IEEE Access : Practical Innovations, Open Solutions, 8*, 75264–75278. DOI: 10.1109/ACCESS.2020.2988510

Chiu, T. K. F., Xia, Q., Zhou, X., Chai, C. S., & Cheng, M. (2023). Systematic literature review on opportunities, challenges, and future research recommendations of artificial intelligence in education. *Computers and Education: Artificial Intelligence, 4*. Advance online publication. DOI: 10.1016/j.caeai.2022.100118

Contrino, M. F., Reyes-Millán, M., Vázquez-Villegas, P., & Membrillo-Hernández, J. (2024). Using an adaptive learning tool to improve student performance and satisfaction in online and face-to-face education for a more personalized approach. *Smart Learning Environments, 11*(1). Advance online publication. DOI: 10.1186/s40561-024-00292-y

Cui, W., Xue, Z., & Thai, K. P. (2018, November). Performance comparison of an AI-based adaptive learning system in China. In 2018 Chinese automation congress (CAC) (pp. 3170-3175). IEEE.

Essa, S. G., Celik, T., & Human-Hendricks, N. E. (2023). Personalized adaptive learning technologies based on machine learning techniques to identify learning styles: A systematic literature review. *IEEE Access : Practical Innovations, Open Solutions, 11*, 48392–48409. DOI: 10.1109/ACCESS.2023.3276439

Gao, R., Merzdorf, H. E., Anwar, S., Hipwell, M. C., & Srinivasa, A. R. (2024). Automatic assessment of text-based responses in post-secondary education: A systematic review. *Computers and Education: Artificial Intelligence, 6*. Advance online publication. DOI: 10.1016/j.caeai.2024.100206

Gligorea, I., Cioca, M., Oancea, R., Gorski, A. T., Gorski, H., & Tudorache, P. (2023a). Adaptive learning using artificial intelligence in e-learning: A literature review. *Education Sciences, 13*(12). Advance online publication. DOI: 10.3390/educsci13121216

Gligorea, I., Cioca, M., Oancea, R., Gorski, A. T., Gorski, H., & Tudorache, P. (2023b). Adaptive learning using artificial intelligence in e-learning: A literature review. *Education Sciences, 13*(12). Advance online publication. DOI: 10.3390/educsci13121216

Gunawan, K. D. H., Liliasari, L., Kaniawati, I., & Setiawan, W. (2021). Implementation of competency enhancement program for science teachers assisted by artificial intelligence in designing HOTS-based integrated science learning. *Jurnal Penelitian Dan Pembelajaran IPA, 7*(1), 55. DOI: 10.30870/jppi.v7i1.8655

Haseski, H. I. (2019). What do Turkish pre-service teachers think about artificial intelligence? *International Journal of Computer Science Education in Schools, 3*(2), 3–23. DOI: 10.21585/ijcses.v3i2.55

Holstein, K., McLaren, B. M., & Aleven, V. (2019). Co-designing a real-time classroom orchestration tool to support teacher–AI complementarity. *Journal of Learning Analytics*, *6*(2), 27–52. DOI: 10.18608/jla.2019.62.3

Hooshyar, D., Pedaste, M., Yang, Y., Malva, L., Hwang, G., Wang, M., Lim, H., & Delev, D. (2021). From gaming to computational thinking: An adaptive educational computer game-based learning approach. *Journal of Educational Computing Research*, *59*(3), 383–409.

Huang, A. Y. Q., Lu, O. H. T., & Yang, S. J. H. (2023). 'Effects of artificial intelligence–enabled personalized recommendations on learners' learning engagement, motivation, and outcomes in a flipped classroom'. *Computers & Education*, *194*. Advance online publication. DOI: 10.1016/j.compedu.2022.104684

Hwang, G. J., Sung, H. Y., Chang, S. C., & Huang, X. C. (2020). 'A fuzzy expert system-based adaptive learning approach to improving students' learning performances by considering affective and cognitive factors'. *Computers and Education: Artificial Intelligence*, *1*. Advance online publication. DOI: 10.1016/j.caeai.2020.100003

Jukiewicz, M. (2024). The future of grading programming assignments in education: The role of ChatGPT in automating the assessment and feedback process. *Thinking Skills and Creativity*, *52*. Advance online publication. DOI: 10.1016/j.tsc.2024.101522

Kabudi, T., Pappas, I., & Olsen, D. H. (2021). AI-enabled adaptive learning systems: A systematic mapping of the literature. *Computers and Education: Artificial Intelligence*, *2*. Advance online publication. DOI: 10.1016/j.caeai.2021.100017

Kahn, K., & Winters, N. (2021). Constructionism and AI: A history and possible futures. *British Journal of Educational Technology*, *52*(3), 1130–1142. DOI: 10.1111/bjet.13088

Kamalov, F., Santandreu Calonge, D., & Gurrib, I. (2023). New era of artificial intelligence in education: Towards a sustainable multifaceted revolution. *Sustainability*, *15*(16). Advance online publication. DOI: 10.3390/su151612451

Kavitha, V., & Lohani, R. (2019). A critical study on the use of artificial intelligence, e-learning technology and tools to enhance the learners experience. *Cluster Computing*, *22*, 6985–6989.

Kickmeier-Rust, M. D., & Holzinger, A. (2019). Interactive ant colony optimization to support adaptation in serious games. *International Journal of Serious Games*, *6*(3), 37–50. DOI: 10.17083/ijsg.v6i3.308

Kim, H. S., Kim, N. Y., & Cha, Y. (2021). 'Is it beneficial to use AI chatbots to improve learners' speaking performance?'. *Journal of Asia TEFL, 18*(1), 161–178. DOI: 10.18823/asiatefl.2021.18.1.10.161

Kohnke, L. (2023). A pedagogical chatbot: A supplemental language learning tool. *RELC Journal, 54*(3), 828–838. DOI: 10.1177/00336882211067054

Kong, J. S. M., Teo, B. S., Lee, Y. J., Pabba, A. B., Lee, E. J. D., & Sng, J. C. G. (2021). Virtual integrated patient: An AI supplementary tool for second-year medical students. *The Asia-Pacific Scholar, 6*(3), 87–90. DOI: 10.29060/TAPS.2021-6-3/SC2394

Lampos, V., Mintz, J. and Qu, X. (2021) 'An artificial intelligence approach for selecting effective teacher communication strategies in autism education', *npj Science of Learning*, 6(1). Available at: https://doi.org/.DOI: 10.1038/s41539-021-00102-x

Lokare, V. T., & Jadhav, P. M. (2024). An AI-based learning style prediction model for personalized and effective learning. *Thinking Skills and Creativity, 51*. Advance online publication. DOI: 10.1016/j.tsc.2023.101421

Malik, R., Sharma, E. A., Trivedi, S., & Mishra, R. (2021). Adoption of chatbots for learning among university students: Role of perceived convenience and enhanced performance. *International Journal of Emerging Technologies in Learning, 16*(18), 200–212. DOI: 10.3991/ijet.v16i18.24315

Mehrfar, A., Zolfaghari, Z., Bordbar, A., & Karimimoghadam, Z. (2024) 'The evolution of e-learning towards the emergence of artificial intelligence (A narrative review)', *2024 11th International and the 17th National Conference on E-Learning and E-Teaching (ICeLeT)*, pp. 1–5. Available at: https://doi.org/DOI: 10.1109/ICeLeT62507.2024.10493104

Mokmin, N. A. M. (2020). The effectiveness of a personalized virtual fitness trainer in teaching physical education by applying the artificial intelligent algorithm. *International Journal of Human Movement and Sports Sciences, 8*(5), 258–264. DOI: 10.13189/saj.2020.080514

Munawar, S., Toor, S. K., Aslam, M., & Hamid, M. (2018). Move to smart learning environment: Exploratory research of challenges in computer laboratory and design intelligent virtual laboratory for eLearning technology. *Eurasia Journal of Mathematics, Science and Technology Education, 14*(5), 1645–1662. DOI: 10.29333/ejmste/85036

Nihad, E. G., Mohamed, K., & El Mokhtar, E. N. (2020). Designing and modeling of a multi-agent adaptive learning system (MAALS) using incremental hybrid case-based reasoning (IHCBR). *International Journal of Electrical and Computer Engineering*, *10*(2), 1980–1992. DOI: 10.11591/ijece.v10i2.pp1980-1992

Palasundram, K., Sharef, N. M., Nasharuddin, N. A., Kasmiran, K. A., & Azman, A. (2019). Sequence to sequence model performance for education chatbot. *International Journal of Emerging Technologies in Learning*, *14*(24), 56–68. DOI: 10.3991/ijet.v14i24.12187

Pardamean, B., Suparyanto, T., Cenggoro, T. W., Sudigyo, D., & Anugrahana, A. (2022). AI-based learning style prediction in online learning for primary education. *IEEE Access : Practical Innovations, Open Solutions*, *10*, 35725–35735. DOI: 10.1109/ACCESS.2022.3160177

Peng, H., Ma, S., & Spector, J. M. (2019). Personalized adaptive learning: An emerging pedagogical approach enabled by a smart learning environment. In *Lecture Notes in Educational Technology* (pp. 171–176). Springer International Publishing., DOI: 10.1007/978-981-13-6908-7_24

Pesek, I., Nosovic, N., & Krasna, M. (2022) 'The role of AI in the education and for the education', *2022 11th Mediterranean Conference on Embedded Computing, MECO 2022*. Available at: https://doi.org/DOI: 10.1109/MECO55406.2022.9797189

Pokrivcakova, S. (2019). Preparing teachers for the application of AI-powered technologies in foreign language education. *Journal of Language and Cultural Education*, *7*(3), 135–153. DOI: 10.2478/jolace-2019-0025

Porter, B., & Grippa, F. (2020). A platform for AI-enabled real-time feedback to promote digital collaboration. *Sustainability*, *12*(24), 1–13. DOI: 10.3390/su122410243

Rezigalla, A. A. (2024). AI in medical education: Uses of AI in construction type A MCQs. *BMC Medical Education*, *24*(1). Advance online publication. DOI: 10.1186/s12909-024-05250-3 PMID: 38448870

Rizvi, M. (2023) 'Exploring the landscape of artificial intelligence in education: Challenges and opportunities', *HORA 2023 - 2023 5th International Congress on Human-Computer Interaction, Optimization and Robotic Applications, Proceedings*. Available at: https://doi.org/DOI: 10.1109/HORA58378.2023.10156773

Rodriguez-Barrios, E. U., Melendez-Armenta, R. A., Garcia-Aburto, S. G., Lavoignet-Ruiz, M., Sandoval-Herazo, L. C., Molina-Navarro, A., & Morales-Rosales, L. A. (2021). Bayesian approach to analyze reading comprehension: A case study in elementary school children in Mexico. *Sustainability, 13*(8). Advance online publication. DOI: 10.3390/su13084285

Ross, B., Chase, A. M., Robbie, D., Oates, G., & Absalom, Y. (2018). Adaptive quizzes to increase motivation, engagement and learning outcomes in a first year accounting unit. *International Journal of Educational Technology in Higher Education, 15*(1). Advance online publication. DOI: 10.1186/s41239-018-0113-2

Roy, D., & Dutta, M. (2022). A systematic review and research perspective on recommender systems. *Journal of Big Data, 9*(1). Advance online publication. DOI: 10.1186/s40537-022-00592-5

Seufert, S., Guggemos, J., & Sailer, M. (2021). Technology-related knowledge, skills, and attitudes of pre- and in-service teachers: The current situation and emerging trends. *Computers in Human Behavior, 115*. Advance online publication. DOI: 10.1016/j.chb.2020.106552 PMID: 32921901

Somasundaram, M., Mohamed Junaid, K. A., & Mangadu, S. (2020). Artificial intelligence (AI) enabled intelligent quality management system (IQMS) for personalized learning path. *Procedia Computer Science, 172*, 438–442. DOI: 10.1016/j.procs.2020.05.096

Song, C., Shin, S. Y., & Shin, K. S. (2024). Implementing the dynamic feedback-driven learning optimization framework: A machine learning approach to personalize educational pathways. *Applied Sciences (Basel, Switzerland), 14*(2). Advance online publication. DOI: 10.3390/app14020916

Soong, R., Pautler, B. G., Moser, A., Jenne, A., Lysak, D. H., Adamo, A., & Simpson, A. J. (2020). CASE (Computer-Assisted Structure Elucidation) study for an undergraduate organic chemistry class. *Journal of Chemical Education, 97*(3), 855–860. DOI: 10.1021/acs.jchemed.9b00498

Standen, P. J., Brown, D. J., Taheri, M., Galvez Trigo, M. J., Boulton, H., Burton, A., Hallewell, M. J., Lathe, J. G., Shopland, N., Blanco Gonzalez, M. A., Kwiatkowska, G. M., Milli, E., Cobello, S., Mazzucato, A., Traversi, M., & Hortal, E. (2020). An evaluation of an adaptive learning system based on multimodal affect recognition for learners with intellectual disabilities. *British Journal of Educational Technology, 51*(5), 1748–1765. DOI: 10.1111/bjet.13010

Strielkowski, W., Grebennikova, V., Lisovskiy, A., Rakhimova, G., & Vasileva, T. (2025). AI-driven adaptive learning for sustainable educational transformation. *Sustainable Development*, *33*(2), 1921–1947. DOI: 10.1002/sd.3221

Susanto, D. S., Halim, E., & Gui, A. (2023, December). Resolving Artificial Intelligence Hallucination in Personalized Adaptive Learning System. In *2023 Eighth International Conference on Informatics and Computing (ICIC)* (pp. 1-6). IEEE. DOI: 10.1109/ICIC60109.2023.10382000

Tang, Y., Liang, J., Hare, R., & Wang, F. Y. (2020). A personalized learning system for parallel intelligent education. *IEEE Transactions on Computational Social Systems*, *7*(2), 352–361. DOI: 10.1109/TCSS.2020.2965198

Terzi, R. (2020). An adaptation of artificial intelligence anxiety scale into Turkish: Reliability and validity study [IOJET]. *International Online Journal of Education & Teaching*, *7*(4). https://iojet.org/index.php/IOJET/article/view/1031

Tsai, S. C., Chen, C. H., Shiao, Y. T., Ciou, J. S., & Wu, T. N. (2020). Precision education with statistical learning and deep learning: A case study in Taiwan. *International Journal of Educational Technology in Higher Education*, *17*(1). Advance online publication. DOI: 10.1186/s41239-020-00186-2

Vázquez-Cano, E., Mengual-Andrés, S., & López-Meneses, E. (2021). Chatbot to improve learning punctuation in Spanish and to enhance open and flexible learning environments. *International Journal of Educational Technology in Higher Education*, *18*(1). Advance online publication. DOI: 10.1186/s41239-021-00269-8

Villegas-Ch, W., Arias-Navarrete, A., & Palacios-Pacheco, X. (2020). Proposal of an architecture for the integration of a chatbot with artificial intelligence in a smart campus for the improvement of learning. *Sustainability*, *12*(4). Advance online publication. DOI: 10.3390/su12041500

Wang, S., Christensen, C., Cui, W., Tong, R., Yarnall, L., Shear, L., & Feng, M. (2020). When adaptive learning is effective learning: Comparison of an adaptive learning system to teacher-led instruction. *Interactive Learning Environments*, *31*(2), 793–803.

Wang, S., Wang, F., Zhu, Z., Wang, J., Tran, T., & Du, Z. (2024). Artificial intelligence in education: A systematic literature review. *Expert Systems with Applications*, *252*. Advance online publication. DOI: 10.1016/j.eswa.2024.124167

Wang, Y. Y., & Wang, Y. S. (2022). Development and validation of an artificial intelligence anxiety scale: An initial application in predicting motivated learning behavior. *Interactive Learning Environments, 30*(4), 619–634. DOI: 10.1080/10494820.2019.1674887

Westera, W., Prada, R., Mascarenhas, S., Santos, P. A., Dias, J., Guimarães, M., Georgiadis, K., Nyamsuren, E., Bahreini, K., Yumak, Z., Christyowidiasmoro, C., Dascalu, M., Gutu-Robu, G., & Ruseti, S. (2020). Artificial intelligence moving serious gaming: Presenting reusable game AI components. *Education and Information Technologies, 25*(1), 351–380. DOI: 10.1007/s10639-019-09968-2

Wood, E. A., Ange, B. L., & Miller, D. D. (2021). Are we ready to integrate artificial intelligence literacy into medical school curriculum: Students and faculty survey. *Journal of Medical Education and Curricular Development, 8*, 238212052110240. DOI: 10.1177/23821205211024078 PMID: 34250242

Xie, H., Chu, H. C., Hwang, G. J., & Wang, C. C. (2019). Trends and development in technology-enhanced adaptive/personalized learning: A systematic review of journal publications from 2007 to 2017. *Computers & Education, 140*. Advance online publication. DOI: 10.1016/j.compedu.2019.103599

Yang, D., Oh, E. S., & Wang, Y. (2020). Hybrid physical education teaching and curriculum design based on a voice interactive artificial intelligence educational robot. *Sustainability, 12*(19), 1–14. DOI: 10.3390/su12198000

Yang, Y. Y., & Shulruf, B. (2019). An expert-led and artificial intelligence system-assisted tutoring course to improve the confidence of Chinese medical interns in suturing and ligature skills: A prospective pilot study. *Journal of Educational Evaluation for Health Professions, 16*. Advance online publication. DOI: 10.3352/jeehp.2019.16.7 PMID: 30986892

Zheng, L., Long, M., Zhong, L., & Gyasi, J. (2022). The effectiveness of technology-facilitated personalized learning on learning achievements and learning perceptions: A meta-analysis. *Education and Information Technologies, 27*, 11807–11830.

Zheng, W. (2024). Intelligent e-learning design for art courses based on adaptive learning algorithms and artificial intelligence. *Entertainment Computing, 50*. Advance online publication. DOI: 10.1016/j.entcom.2024.100713

Chapter 10
The Preparedness of Foundation Program Teachers and Ethical Considerations in AI Integration:
A Mixed-Methods Study of Omani Higher Education Practice

Kawkab Al Balushi
https://orcid.org/0009-0004-7441-6532
University Technology and Applied Sciences, Oman

Salwa Mohammed Al Farsi
https://orcid.org/0009-0004-0116-9876
University of Technology and Applied Sciences, Oman

ABSTRACT

The objective of the study was to explore how the foundation program teachers at the University of Technology and Applied Sciences Suhar branch integrate artificial intelligence in their teaching. The study contributes to the theoretical understanding of technology integration in higher education highlighting the gap between institutional practices and expectations, technological availability, and pedagogical reality. The study aimed to assess teachers' understanding of AI, their proficiency and explore the moral guidelines and principles that teachers follow when selecting AI tools for teaching. Mixed method approach was employed for data collection in this study using a survey and interviews. The findings revealed that AI is widely

DOI: 10.4018/979-8-3373-4982-4.ch010

used as a main part of teaching. Almost all teachers use it but in different ways. However, the use of AI has created challenges that need to be addressed. The main challenges identified were teacher training and academic integrity.

INTRODUCTION

The advancement of technology has dramatically changed how education is delivered (Al Balushi, 2025). Artificial Intelligence (AI) is the most widely spread technology that is currently being used in different fields such as education, medicine, engineering, etc. In recent years, the use of artificial intelligence in higher education institutions has widely spread. Universities and colleges are taking advantage of the opportunities that AI offers to improve learning, streamline administrative tasks, and drive innovation (Chu et al., 2023). For that. it is essential to have institutional policies and adequate training opportunities to faculty members. Despite growing pressure to integrate AI in teaching and learning and while some universities have developed ethical guidelines, comprehensive policy frameworks still have significant gaps, especially regarding data privacy, equitable access to AI tools, and stakeholder collaboration (Jin et al., 2024).

Oman has made significant progress towards becoming AI-ready. Oman moved up five spots to rank 45th out of 193 nations in the Oxford Insights Government AI Readiness Index in 2024, ranking fifth in the Middle East and North Africa area and fourth among the states of the Gulf Cooperation Council (The Gulf Observer, 2025). In line with the country's Vision 2040 plan to create a knowledge-based economy, Oman has shown a strong commitment to integrating artificial intelligence throughout its educational system. The University of Technology and Applied Sciences (UTAS) has become a pioneer in AI ethics and education. The university and the Islamic World Educational, Scientific, and Cultural Organisation (ICESCO) signed a deal in January 2024 to create the region's first ICESCO Chair for Artificial Intelligence Ethics. Through training programs and knowledge sharing, this effort seeks to support researchers and promote research, development, and innovation in AI ethics and algorithms (ICESCO, 2024).

This research tackles how the foundation program teachers at the University of Technology and Applied Sciences- Suhar branch are integrating AI in their teaching. It looks at teachers' understanding of AI, AI proficiency level of teachers and the professional development requirements that teachers need in order to enhance teaching and learning through AI. Moreover, it discusses concerns related to academic integrity and how it is being tackled by teachers in the Foundation Program.

The University of Technology and Applied Sciences in Oman has 11 branches. Students start their learning journey by joining the Foundation Program at the Preparatory Studies Center. The Foundation Program consists of three courses which are English, Mathematics and Computing Skills. UTAS Suhar has two departments which are Information Technology and Engineering. Therefore, it is very important for students to excel in the Foundation Program and demonstrate language proficiency as well as computer literacy and good mathematical skills. This step starts from the foundation program.

Teachers at the Foundation Program are using all possible means including the latest technology to support learners. Teachers' views on AI integration in teaching have changed their practices in their classroom. Many teachers consider AI a source of improvement while others see it as a challenge especially with students' exposure and academic integrity concerns. According to Galindo-Domínguez et al., (2024), it is very important to understand the factors associated with teachers' attitude towards AI in order to understand their practices and perspective in the classroom. A study conducted by Guan and Zhang (2025) on teacher attitude and AI literacy for effective integration concluded that the majority of teachers view AI as a tool instead of recognizing its full potential as a collaborative learning tool. This is considered a serious gap which shows that teachers lack basic knowledge of AI ethics and principles. According to the European Recommendation on Ethical Use of AI in Education, professional development focusing on AI is essential for effective integration of AI in education (ENAI, 2023). On the other hand, according to the UNESCO (2024), only 35% studies examined AI role in teacher's professional development which indicates that there is a need for professional development to prepare educators for the integration of AI ethically in teaching.

RESEARCH OBJECTIVES

1. To examine the use and understanding of AI by teachers.
2. To identify the training and support teachers require to integrate AI in their teaching.
3. To examine how teachers are using AI tools while maintaining academic integrity and sustaining high educational standards.
4. To determine the criteria that teachers follow to select AI tools for their teaching.
5. To determine how teachers ensure students are using critical thinking skills and not over relying on artificial intelligence.
6. This research aims to answer the main question which is how prepared are the Foundation Program teachers at UTAS Suhar to integrate AI tools ethically into their teaching practices?

The sub questions are the following:

1. How well do Foundation Program teachers understand and use AI?
2. What training and support is needed for teachers to integrate ethical AI into the classroom?
3. How can teachers maintain academic integrity standards when it comes to AI?
4. How do teachers select AI tools for their classroom?
5. What strategies do teachers follow to prevent students' over dependence on AI?

AI IN HIGHER EDUCATION

AI has enhanced teaching and learning in higher education institutions. It has transformed the lives of teachers as it has provided them with many tools to enhance lesson planning, creating materials, providing feedback and making assessments. According to Zuboff (2019), there are four main applications for AI for educators which are tutoring, providing personalized feedback, creating assessments and providing evaluation. Similarly, other research identifies three main applications which are personalized content recommendation, personalized tutoring and support, personalized feedback and assessment (Discover Artificial Intelligence, 2025). According to Al Balushi (2025), AI has a tremendous potential in education as it supports teaching and learning through interactive and engaging learning AI tools. AI tutoring systems can provide students with a personalized learning tasks based on their needs such an app can assess students' knowledge, provide instant feedback and track progress.

On the other hand, Pikhart & Al-Obaydi (2025) conducted a study to examine potential risks associated with using AI in Higher Education. The study revealed that several privacy risks, academic integrity issues, and concerns about data generated by AI were raised. The views among responders were mainly negative. There were several concerns expressed related to data misuse, unauthorized access. It was reported that using AI could lead to plagiarism and could also stop students from using critical thinking skills.

Another study tackled students' perceptions and challenges associated with artificial intelligene. The research explored the adoption of AI and the impact of AI technologies on their learning processes and academic performances. The findings showed that artificial intelligence offers significant benefits, such as personalized learning and improved academic outcomes. The research concluded that overuse of artificial intelligence can compromise critical thinking skills, academic integrity and data privacy (Vieriu & Petrea, 2025).

Sullivan et al. (2023) explored the advantages and disadvantages of using ChatGPT in higher education. In their study, they suggested a number of tactics to guarantee moral and responsible use. They recommended that colleges should create systematic rules and processes. They also highlighted the importance of sufficient training and support to staff and students. They suggested the use a variety of techniques to identify and stop academic dishonesty. They stress the significance of teaching students about plagiarism and its repercussions, demanding written affirmations that the work they submit is original.

Al Buraiki (2025) conducted qualitative SWOT analysis to examine AI integration techniques at Omani universities. The findings of his study revealed a number of advantages, such as AI's ability to support data-driven decision-making, enable personalised learning, and automate repetitive administrative tasks so that teachers can concentrate on more important pedagogical activities. However, the study also highlighted some serious flaws, most notably worries about students being overly reliant on AI technologies, which can have a negative impact on their capacity for independent study and critical thinking. Researchers identify over-reliance on technology and diminished critical thinking as major challenges accompanying AI implementation, as determined by a study published in Education (2025). In Frontiers in Education (2025), research shows that AI adoption leads to cognitive offloading, in which students who are heavily dependent on AI demonstrate substantial declines in their analytical reasoning abilities as well as a decreased motivation to study. In systematic reviews, AI-generated content is accepted without critical evaluation, resulting in a reduced ability to make decisions.

Al Manji et al. (2024) examined the adoption of AI in Oman's government secondary schools. According to their findings, teachers are aware of AI's potential to improve lesson planning, enable personalised learning experiences, and increase administrative efficiency, even though its adoption is still in its early stages. However, the study found important issues include unequal access to AI tools between urban and rural schools, inadequate teacher preparation, and a lack of technology infrastructure. If specific policy actions are not implemented to alleviate these disparities, educational gaps may worsen. The researchers stressed that in order to guarantee equitable, culturally sensitive AI adoption in line with Oman's Vision 2040 goals, cooperation between legislators, educators, and technology suppliers is crucial.

Al Rashdi and Elgeddawy (2025) conducted a study to examine how AI solutions affect sustainable quality education. The study revealed that while AI has the potential to significantly improve educational quality and sustainability, its application necessitates addressing contextual issues unique to Omani educational environments, according to their qualitative case study including eight faculty members. The study highlighted the significance of creating AI solutions that are culturally relevant and in line with regional educational aspirations.

AI AND ACADEMIC INTEGRITY

The concept of academic integrity encompasses ethical standards and behaviours in academia. Academic integrity is a main component in higher education which ensures the quality of teaching and represents honesty and trust. An ethical and moral code of conduct contains three elements: integrity, courtesy towards intellectual property, and professional behaviour standards (ercan & Voicu, 2022). It is crucial for academic integrity to be addressed by good pedagogy and clear communication between instructors and students, as it is fundamentally a teaching and learning issue (Bertram Gallant & Rettinger, 2025). According to Carpenter et al. (2010) it is common for some to lack a broad understanding of what cheating entails which supports Watson et al. (2014) views that there is often a difference between student opinion and faculty opinion regarding what constitutes "cheating".

In seconds, students can write content using generative pre-trained transformers such as ChatGPT. As a result, new writing opportunities arise. An authentic scholarly paper cannot be produced using a language model because the language model does not incorporate understanding, critical thinking, or personal insight. Since the author's ideas are not reflected in the content, there are concerns about academic integrity as this is considered cheating (Liu et al., 2023). Therefore, assignments written with ChatGPT will be less original and it will compromise academic integrity. This supports Liang (2023) claims that while artificial intelligence technologies can help students with their writing, there is evidence that students who use them excessively lose their morals and creativity. Despite explicit institutional regulations requiring such disclosure, Moorhouse et al. (2024) found that 74% of students at King's Business School did not disclose their use of AI. According to their research, students' fear of critical opinions or possible grade consequences, their ignorance of what AI use entails, and the lack of emphasis on the significance of transparency in academic work are some of the reasons that contribute to non-compliance. According to these findings, creating policies alone is not enough. Educational institutions must raise awareness and teach students about responsible AI use.

Al Balushi (2025) carried out a research to investigate how AI-powered grammatical correction tools can help ESL students improve their writing skills. The findings confirmed that tools such as Grammarly can improve language development, but also can lead to the danger of fostering dependency.

Karkoulian et al. (2024) carried out qualitative research to investigate how teachers and students view the influence of AI technologies on academic integrity. According to their findings, ChatGPT and similar programs are acknowledged for improving productivity and offering individualised learning help, but they also raise serious issues regarding academic dishonesty and plagiarism. According to the study, students who use artificial intelligence to create content may unfairly outperform their peers who do not use such technologies for moral reasons, which could distort grades and academic recognition.

Balalle and Pannilage (2025) conducted a systematic review on AI and academic integrity. They investigated how AI tools might both support and undermine academic integrity in higher education. The study revealed that there has been an increase in contract cheating and plagiarism linked to AI tools. The concluded that AI tools have two opposing purposes: they can both promote academic integrity through detection systems and compromise it by enabling dishonest behaviour. In order to effectively integrate AI in higher education while addressing the issues it offers, the study recommended that there should be precise policies, standards, and frameworks in place to address the current challenges association with academic integrity and the use of AI.

TEACHER READINESS AND TECHNOLOGICAL CONFIDENCE

To integrate AI successfully in educational contexts, it is very important for teachers to be confident. Gayed (2025) conducted a mixed-methods study to examine educators' attitudes towards AI. The findings showed that although educators acknowledge the potential advantages of AI, there are substantial gaps in their institutional support and their basic knowledge. According to the study, just 8.3% of participants verified the existence of explicit standards for the use of AI, and 61.4% of participants said their institutions either had no vision for technology usage or were unaware of any current vision. Teachers may be less inclined to experiment with AI tools in the classroom as a result of this lack of institutional supervision.

Granström and Oppi (2025) looked into teachers' preparedness and perception that AI offers many advantages in the classroom. They also found that teachers' willingness to incorporate AI is influenced by two important factors which arc thcir perception of AI's value in improving educational outcomes and their psychological and practical readiness. The study discovered that teachers' attitudes towards AI, their views of its advantages, and their capacity to get past AI-related worries all have an impact on preparation. The study concluded that there is an urgent need for focused professional development programs that focuses on both technical capabilities and pedagogical applications since teachers who lack formal training and have low confidence levels are especially reluctant to employ AI.

One of the most urgent issues facing modern education is the disconnect between the fast development of AI and the readiness of educators to successfully use these technologies. Cheng et al.'s (2024) systematic assessment of research from 2015 to 2024 found a notable disparity in the literature. 35% of studies focused on teachers' professional development needs and 65% of studies researched AI applications in education. According to the review, there is a mismatch between the availability of professional development opportunities and the demand for AI competencies among educators because, despite the increasing use of AI tools in educational settings, systematic approaches to preparing teachers for AI integration are still lacking.

Sharma (2024) investigated the effects of AI integration in teacher training programs. His research showed generally good results regarding improved pedagogical knowledge and enhanced ability to exchange teaching materials. On the other hand, the study also concluded that effective AI integration in professional development requires maintaining a balance between technical capabilities and keeping educators' crucial role in the learning process. AI is a tool to supplement rather than replace human judgement and knowledge.

RESEARCH METHODOLOGY

Mixed-Methods Research Design

This research employs a mixed method, both quantitative and qualitative approaches for data collection. The reason behind selecting this method is because it provides a comprehensive understanding as numbers provide breadth and words provide depth. Furthermore, using this method allows for triangulation of data, which facilitates a more in-depth examination of teacher perspectives, practices, and struggles related to integrating AI into classrooms.

Figure 1.

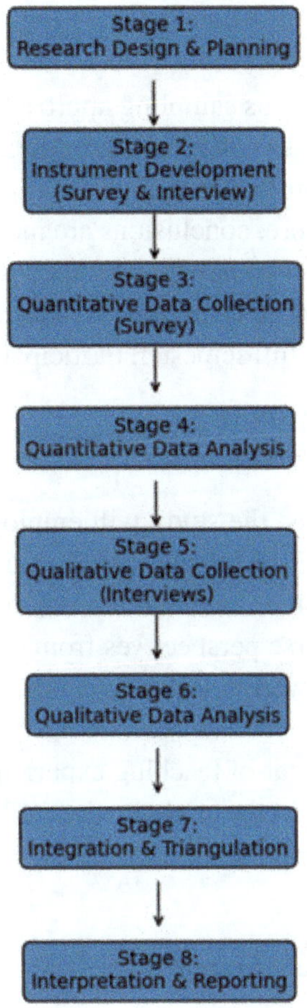

Setting and Context

This research targets the Foundation Program teachers at the University of Technology and Applied Sciences Suhar branch. The Foundation Program is offered through the Preparatory Studies Center which includes three units English, Math and Computing Skills. The center has 44 teachers preparing students for higher education.

PARTICIPANTS AND SAMPLING

Quantitative Phase

This research involves a census sampling approach where the entire population of the study participates in data collection through a survey. Census sampling is very effective because the result represents the entire population and the findings reflect real conditions. Therefore, conclusions are more credible. In the case of my research, 44 teachers from the Preparatory Studies Centre will be surveyed. The survey considers GFP full-time and part-time teacher and GFP teachers who taught at UTAS Suhar for at least one full semester. Participation in this study is voluntary.

Qualitative Phase

To collect data qualitatively, the study will employ a purposive sampling. Six teachers from the three units will be selected to be interviewed in depth. Two teachers will be selected from each of the three units to ensure proper representation. This type of sampling ensures diverse perspectives from several teaching contexts. The participants in the interviews were selected using the criteria below:

1. To have a minimum one year of teaching experience at UTAS Suhar
2. Willingness to participate in the study by detailed sharing experiences
3. Uses technology in teaching

DATA COLLECTION INSTRUMENT

To collect data through survey, a link was created using Microsoft Form to collect the data quantitively. The link was sent via email to all the 44 teachers at the Preparatory Studies Center. The survey was designed to answer the research questions and to achieve its objectives.

Survey Structure

The survey consists of a total of 22 questions. It covers the following sections:

1. Demographic Information (Years of experience, the subject taught, level of general technology proficiency)
2. AI Understanding and Current Use
3. Training and Support Needs

4. Academic Integrity
5. AI Tool Selection Criteria
6. Student Dependency and Critical Thinking
7. Overall Perceptions

Semi Structured Interviews

Semi-structured interviews were conducted with 6 teachers. The plan initially was to conduct interviews with six teachers, two from each unit. However, only computing skills teacher volunteered to participate in the interview. Therefore, three English teachers, two mathematicians, and one computing skills teacher were interviewed. The interview questions were developed based on the research questions and objectives. The questions covered the following areas:

1. AI knowledge and training needs
2. AI Dependency
3. Critical thinking and academic integrity
4. Challenges with AI usage
5. Integration and Future Outlook

Each interview lasted for around 30 minutes. The interviews were recorded using a mobile phone and were transcribed using a mobile app called "Transcribe".

DATA COLLECTION PROCEDURE

The first step in the research was to request approval from the college to conduct data collection. As soon as the approval was obtained, an email was sent to all the teachers at the Preparatory Studies Center to invite them to participate in the survey and interview. The email explained the purpose of the study and that participation is voluntary. The link for the survey was included in the email. 44 responses were received which means the entire population participated in the survey. In regard to the interview, teachers interested to participate in the interview were requested to reply to the email. Three teachers from the English unit responded, two math teachers and one computing skills teacher. A reminder was sent. However, no more responses were received. Therefore, the six teachers who expressed interest to take part in the study were interviewed. An email was sent to the participants to inform them of the day, time and venue of the interview. The interviewees were also informed that the interview will be recorded but were assured that privacy and confidentiality will be maintained.

Data Analysis

Quantitative Data Analysis was analyzed using an AI tool "Claude". The following procedures were employed:

1. Descriptive Statistics: A determination of demographic characteristics and responses to Likert-scale items were based on frequencies, percentages, means, and standard deviations.

Qualitative data were analysed using a thematic approach. common patterns and concerns were identified and coded thematically. After the interviews were recorded and transcribed, the first step was to get familiar with the data by reading and noting first impressions. Then, initial codes were generated using NVivo software. After that, initial themes were created, and themes were checked against coded extracts and the entire dataset. Finally, themes were refined and reviewed. Compelling extract examples were selected relating analysis to the research questions.

ETHICAL CONSIDERATIONS

This study adheres to ethical research principles established by the University of Technology and Applied Sciences. To begin with, all participants received detailed information about the study including the purpose, procedures and their right. They were clearly informed that participation was voluntary and that they have the right to withdraw their participation at any time. Additionally, they were also informed survey responses will be anonymous, the interviewee real names will not be used, the voice recordings will be deleted as soon as the research study is completed. No identifying information will be included in the transcripts or reports that are produced.

LIMITATIONS

Several limitations should be acknowledged:

1. Results cannot be generalized as the study is limited to one institution and one program.
2. Self-reported data may be subject to social desirability bias.
3. The study employed a cross-sectional design, which records viewpoints at a certain moment in time. This means that in an area that is changing quickly,

the results might not accurately represent how beliefs or methods evolve over time.

4. The sample size for interviews was very small.
5. participant responses may be affected by the fact that the research is a colleague working in the same institution.

INTERVIEW ANALYSIS

Semi-structured interviews were conducted with six Foundation Program teachers at the University of Technology and Applied Sciences Suhar Branch. The purpose of the interviews was to explore teachers' experiences of AI in teaching.

The interview data were recorded, transcribed, and analyzed using a thematic approach. The themes reflect teachers' views on AI use in English, mathematics, and computing skills courses.

Theme 1: AI Literacy through Pedagogical Integration

Teachers described the way they use AI tools in their classes. Ali, who teaches English, described using ChatGPT when working with reading texts, saying that: *"what I do with the reading texts, for example, I use ChatGPT and I upload a mock exam with the text that I would like the tool to generate a similar structure with the same level of difficulty and language to be used in class."* Mariyam described using *"ChatGPT with students to support vocabulary learning. I asked them first to have a chat specified for vocabulary. I give them the wrote prompt and they use the same chat for all vocabulary lesson."* Sara explained that she uses *"AI to generate writing topics for the project and presentation class. In this class students are asked to choose a topic for their mini research project and the topics have certain criteria, so I upload the sample topics along with the criteria and get the full list of topics."*

In mathematics classes, AI was used differently. Diana explained that she mainly relies on AI when preparing assessments to check the level of difficulty of maths problems. She noted: *"we used Symbolab which is really beneficial for teaching mathematics. We can prepare graphs from that and get solutions from that."* Fatima also referred to using more than one AI tool in her teaching. She recommended ALEKS as it is useful for providing personalised learning and tracking students' progress. She also explained that *"I use many apps such as ChatGPT which helps me with planning and even creating assignments based on the learning outcomes."*

In computing skills courses, Ahmed explained that he uses *"Canva to design interactive games to be used as warm-ups"* and ChatGPT *"to create marking rubrics for exams that have open ended questions."* He also added that *"I use Typing Club*

AI tool which is a typing tutor with AI. It helps my students typing and becoming more familiar with the keyboard. My students found it very effective."

Theme 2: Professional Development Gaps and Support Needs

Professional development gaps and support needs were tackled throughout the interviews since these are considered key elements. Ali, for example, reported attending *"an extended AI training which was very comprehensive"*. Similarly, Diana noted that over the past two years UTAS had offered *"several training programs"* alongside *"so many workshops and webinars."* Mariyam said that she *"enrolled in one training program about the use of AI, and during that program we learned about the use of Canva to create interactive games and quizzes and NotebookLM for creating teaching materials from our own documents."* Ahmed mentioned attending *"a training program for teachers to teach them to use Canva which is online graphic design tool and the program tackled how this app is used for creating educational games."*

Despite the varied experiences of the foundation teachers, there were gaps. Ali described that it is *"really necessary to train teachers on how to use AI detec*tors *to check texts produced by students."* Mariyam also spoke about the *"need to find a way to identify if students wrote the text by themselves. Because whenever I tell a student that this is AI, they don't accept and refuse to do the work again."* Ahmed and Fatima emphasized that training on AI detection tools is really important because, according to Ahmed, *"students still don't understand the full potential of AI and think it is only used to answer questions.* Mariyam mentioned that teachers *"need to ensure that students use AI in a correct way. What we see in class is that students rely on AI for everything."* Besides, Diana stated that teachers and students should *"not completely rely on AI"* and should return to *"books,"* as she described it as the source of information.

Additionally, Diana emphasized that integrating AI requires following *"a proper channel"* and that there must be *"a* very *clear policy of AI integration."* Mariyam stated, *"we need a policy or something unified for all."* Ahmed described the importance of *"a policy in place,"* while Fatima described the need for rules regarding *"the allowed AI percentage for students to use and how to address the consequences of misusing AI tool."*

Theme 3: Academic Integrity Dilemmas and Assessment Transformation

Academic integrity is shown as a growing challenge in the AI era. Ali explained that many students *"just ask any chatbot to generate a whole report or an essay"* without realising that this constitutes *"a kind of plagiarism or cheating."* Mariyam described receiving student work that was *"basically AI, like... a copy and paste from ChatGPT."* Ali pointed out that students must understand that using AI-generated content *"without in-text citations is a kind of plagiarism."*

As a way of managing such a challenge, Ali explained that he now prefers asking students *"to write the assignments in class instead of assigning them the task as homework."* He described this as *"the best way to reduce AI misuse."* He mentioned that *"I collect the phones from the students and treat most of the writing tasks like an exam"* to make sure students do not use AI tools. Fatima noted that in mathematics *"most of the assessment"* is now conducted in the classroom, and the homework requires students to *"present and defend their work."* Diana said that *"I ask my students to explain answers in front of the class when I have doubts in their answers"* to determine *"if the student really understood the concept or he used AI tool."* Ahmed stated that students can be asked to *"give oral presentations to defend their assignments."* Sara noted that while *"teachers may suspect AI use, we cannot tell them that this is AI work especially when students use simple language."*

On the other hand, some teachers attempted to restrict AI use altogether in specific tasks. For example, Sara told her students, *"you're not allowed to use AI for your projects."* Others went for a guided approach. For instance, Mariyam explained that *"students may use ChatGPT just to get ideas,"* but must write independently and *"they need to show me their understanding of the task during the discussion phase."* Ahmed also stated that students are aware AI *"could be used for brainstorming but not to generate the whole content."*

Theme 4: Critical Evaluation and Responsible Tool Adoption

There are several considerations described by teachers that which them when adopting AI tools. Ali, for example, explained that he considers *"how accurate the tool is and also how beneficial it is for students."* He added that *"the cost is a very important point."* Mariam also mentioned that *"cost is number one for me when choosing the AI tool to be used. I think students also find cost as the most important thing of AI"* In addition, Ali noted that teachers prefer subscriptions funded by UTAS because *"the free tools don't have advanced features so we can't fully rely on them. For example, the paid version of ChatGPT allows only certain messages er day which makes it frustrating especially when you want something urgent like creating materials for the class or providing feedback to students."* Ahmed also stated that *"I first check whether the app is free or no, then I check if it is user-friendly."* In addition, Diana mentioned that *"AI tools should be understandable by the students and quick to respond."* Fatima also referred to *"the ease of the app and the features effectiveness."*

As for accuracy, Mariyam described a situation where she *"regretted using ChatGPT in one of the classes because it generated wrong information about the course. I asked my students to write a reflection about the course, and I was really surprised that they copied and pasted from AI without even reading the text."* Ahmed stated that he needs to *"check the accuracy of the app."* On the other hand, Sara mentioned that she had *"never thought about what kind of AI tool students could use"* and stated that *"I currently tell students you're not allowed to use AI unless I ask you to do so."*

Theme 5: Student Agency, Dependency Risks, and Critical Thinking Preservation

Teachers described signs of overdependence. Ali, for instance, explained that *"some students submit work that contains content that is irrelevant."* He noted that *"the AI tool wrote something which is not applicable to the research paper or the report."* In addition, Ali described a situation where *"the report says that we interviewed professionals and it's not the reality. In fact, the interviews targeted UTAS students."* He emphasized that because *"I follow students' work stage by stage, I can easily detect AI use because I know that they will use AI either way, so I ask them to present what they have done step by step."*

Language level is another indicator of dependency. For instance, Diana observed that foundation students sometimes *"submit work that is beyond their language level."* She explained that *"foundation level students are giving answers like master's level students, and we know the real level of our students. We know that in this level, they cannot produce a work that is free of errors and with varied structures."* Sara also noted that when *"students produce writing with no grammar mistake"* can indicate that *"the student is fully dependent on* AI." Fatima stated that teachers are now familiar with *"AI structure and language,"* which makes it *"very easy to detect students using AI."* Mariyam explained that *"when I ask a question and the students immediately use their phones, I know that they try to find out the answer from ChatGPT. I know that they don't want to think about the answer since they know that there is a tool that can answers all questions."* Ahmed also noted that *"constant use of mobile devices in class"* usually results in having answers that are "too formal."

On the other hand, Ali explained that he asks students to *"keep their phones away during discussions so they can generate the ideas themselves."* Ahmed said that *"I create warm-up activities that help students use their critical thinking skills and during that I tell them that they can't use the phone and can only discuss the ideas with each other."* Mariyam stated that she consistently includes *"critical thinking activities in almost every class just to make sure that students are not over-relying on AI."* Diana explained that when students rely on AI, *"their responses do not match with what is being asked"*. She emphasized that *"I always tell my students your understanding is more important than putting your question into AI platform."* Sara stated that *"we want the students to be critical thinkers, and when AI is there, they're not actually thinking."* At the same time, she questioned *"if we have a tool that can do the work, why not to use it?"*

As a result, institutional guidance may solve the problem of AI. Sara suggested that *"clear policy with ethical considerations will help students understand the results of AI use. It will make them aware of the consequences and once they know, they will automatically reduce the use of AI. For example, if students know that if they are caught using AI, it will result in failing the task or course, they will never use it."* Additionally, Mariyam explained that *"some teachers use AI for planning but without providing good prompts and that can make the lesson not suitable for the level or even not suitable for the culture of the students. I remember when I first used ChatGPT for lesson planning, my prompt was general and because of that I got a lesson plan that couldn't be done in my real class."*

Survey Analysis

A quantitative survey was distributed to a whole population of 44 teachers teaching different courses in the Foundation program. Responses were received from the entire population.

Demographic Characteristics of Participants

Table 1 shows an overview of participants' years of teaching experience, teaching subject, and level of technology proficiency. 45% have over 10 years' experience. English teachers constitute 68% of the population.

Table 1. Demographic Characteristics of the Participants

Variable	Category	Frequency
Years of Teaching Experience	Less than 2 years	10
	2–5 years	7
	6–10 years	7
	More than 10 years	20

continued on following page

Table 1. Continued

Variable	Category	Frequency
Primary Teaching Subject	English	23
	Mathematics	13
	Computing Skills	8
General Technology Proficiency	Beginner	10
	Intermediate	19
	Advanced	13
	Expert	2

AI Usage in Teaching

Nearly all population use AI. Figure 2 shows that 52% regularly use AI, 45% occasionally use it and only 2% rarely use AI in their teaching. Table 2 shows how often participants use AI in certain areas.

Figure 2. Frequency of AI usage in Teaching

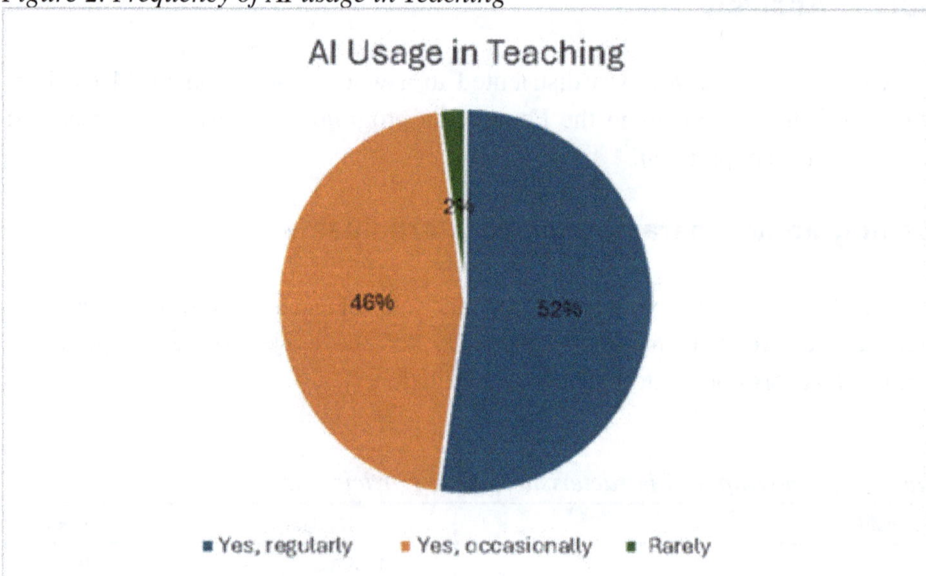

Table 2. Frequency of AI usage in Teaching

Teaching Task	Always	Often	Sometimes	Rarely	Never
Lesson Planning	14	12	10	4	4
Creating Teaching Materials	16	12	11	4	1
Student Assessment	10	8	9	11	6
Providing Feedback	9	8	7	12	8
Professional Development	10	12	9	5	8
Administrative Tasks	13	10	9	7	5

Majority of teachers use AI tools frequently for lesson planning. 26 out of 44 participants reported that they always or often use AI for planning their lessons. 28 participants always or often use AI for creating teaching materials. However, only 18 of the participants always or often use AI for exams while 17 participants reported that they rarely or never use it for assessment. As for using AI for providing feedback, 17 participants only always or often give feedback using AI while 8 participants never use AI for feedback. 22 participants always or often use AI for professional development, and 23 participants use it for administrative tasks.

AI Training Participation

Table 4 shows AI training participation among teachers. More than half of the participants (64%) have received training in AI. However, 30% have not received training but they are interested. Only 7% reported that they have no interest in attending AI training.

Table 3. AI Training Participation among Teaching

Response	Count	Percentage
Yes, basic training	20	45.5%
No, but I'm interested	13	29.5%
Yes, comprehensive training	8	18.2%
No, and I'm not interested	3	6.8%

Academic Integrity

Figure 3 represents teachers' concerns about AI impact on academic integrity. The chart shows that most teachers are concerned about academic integrity (68.2%) with only 9.1% are not concerned at all. Table 4 shows a summary of perceived effectiveness of academic integrity measures. 90.9% of the participants rated AI detection tool as very and somewhat effective and none rated it as ineffective. The second highly rated measure is in-class written assessments (84.1%). The least rated (72.7%) was reflective assignments on AI use.

Figure 3. Teachers Concern about AI Impact on Academic Integrity

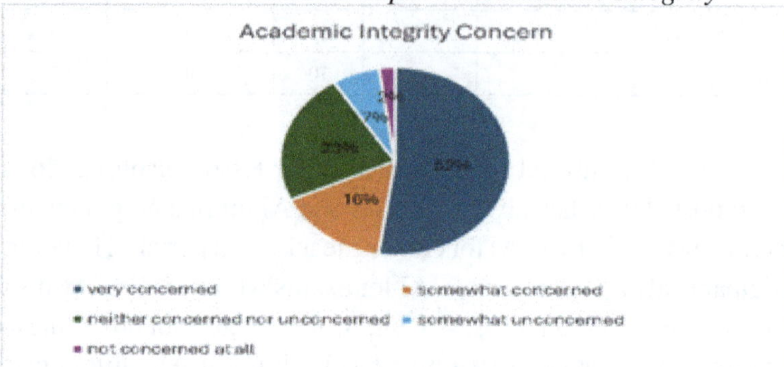

Table 4. Perceived Effectiveness of Academic Integrity Measures

Measure	Effective (Very + Somewhat)	Neutral	Ineffective
AI detection software	40 (90.9%)	4 (9.1%)	0 (0%)
Oral presentations / defence	36 (81.8%)	6 (13.6%)	2 (4.5%)
Reflective assignments on AI use	32 (72.7%)	9 (20.5%)	3 (6.8%)
In-class written assessment	37 (84.1%)	5 (11.4%)	2 (4.5%)
Project-based assessments	33 (75%)	8 (18.2%)	3 (6.8%)

Criteria for Evaluating AI Tools

Table 6 below represents the importance ratings for AI tools evaluation criteria. *Ease of use* was the highest rated, with 68.2% of the respondents rated it very important. Then comes *the cost* as the second highest rated criteria (63.6%). 59.1% of the participants also rated *alignment with learning objectives* as very important. However, only 43.2% of participants rated *data privacy and security* as very important. The least rated criterion was the *integration of AI with existing systems* with only 36.4% rated it as very important.

Table 5. Importance Ratings for AI Tool Evaluation Criteria

Criterion	Very important	Moderately important	Slightly important	Not important
Ease of use	30 (68.2%)	13 (29.5%)	1 (2.3%)	0 (0.0%)
Cost/budget	28 (63.6%)	12 (27.3%)	2 (4.5%)	2 (4.5%)
Data privacy and security	19 (43.2%)	23 (52.3%)	2 (4.5%)	0 (0.0%)
Alignment with learning objectives	26 (59.1%)	16 (36.4%)	2 (4.5%)	0 (0.0%)
Accessibility features	23 (52.3%)	19 (43.2%)	2 (4.5%)	0 (0.0%)
Evidence of educational effectiveness	17 (38.6%)	19 (43.2%)	7 (15.9%)	1 (2.3%)
Student engagement potential	22 (50.0%)	19 (43.2%)	3 (6.8%)	0 (0.0%)
Technical support availability	18 (40.9%)	21 (47.7%)	2 (4.5%)	3 (6.8%)
Integration with existing systems	16 (36.4%)	19 (43.2%)	8 (18.2%)	1 (2.3%)

Preventing Student Over-Reliance on AI

Table 6 demonstrates a summary of the frequency of teaching or reminding students about AI literacy and ethics-related strategies to reduce over-reliance on AI. These strategies include teaching critical thinking skills, knowing what appropriate and inappropriate use of AI is, understanding limitations and bias, and ethical use of AI. 52.3% of respondents chose always or often for teaching critical thinking skills with only 29.5% reported rarely or never. 45.5% of respondents reported rarely or never for the limitation and biases of AI. As for the ethical considerations of AI use, 43.2% of the respondents chose always or often while 40.9% stated that they rarely or never consider this strategy.

Table 6. Frequency of Addressing AI Literacy and Ethics-related Skills

Skill/strategy	Always/Often	Sometimes	Rarely/Never
Critical thinking skills	23 (52.3%)	8 (18.2%)	13 (29.5%)
Appropriate vs. inappropriate AI use	18 (40.9%)	7 (15.9%)	19 (43.2%)
Limitations and biases of AI	17 (38.6%)	7 (15.9%)	20 (45.5%)
Ethical considerations of AI use	19 (43.2%)	7 (15.9%)	18 (40.9%)

DISCUSSION

This study shows that AI tools are widely used in the Foundation Program with almost all teachers using different AI tools in their teaching practices. This finding reflects a shift in AI use when compared with previous research in the Omani context. For example, Al Manji et al. (2024) described AI adoption in secondary schools as gradual and still in the development stage. In contrast, the findings of this study suggest that there is a rapid progression in the use of AI in the Foundation Program. This difference may be a result of the nature of the Foundation Program teaching as teachers are more flexible in teaching methods. From this perspective, the findings offer a clear response to RQ1 about the current stage of AI integration.

The use of AI is different across the Foundation Program courses. For instance, English teachers described using ChatGPT to create reading materials and for building vocabulary. Mathematics teachers relied more on tools such as Symbolab and ALEKS for exam preparations. Teachers teaching computing skills used AI tools to design games and interactive learning activities. These differences indicate that the use of AI is not the same across the Foundation Program courses. However, this difference in AI use was not reflected in the training opportunities that teachers received. In other words, training programs tend to focus on AI use as a generic tool without considering that teachers in different subjects may approach AI in a different way. As a result, the findings suggest that support needs to be tailored to discipline. In this way, the results provide a response to RQ2 by emphasizing the need for differentiated training.

Academic integrity is another major concern as teachers reported instances where students submitted written work with language that is beyond their real level, as well as assignments that included incorrect information. These concerns align with Karkoulian et al. (2024) and Pikhart and Al-Obaydi (2025). They highlighted that teachers have concerns about plagiarism and students' critical thinking skills. As a result, teachers at the Foundation Program described replacing homework with in-class testing and assignments with oral presentations. However, since UTAS has no guidelines about the use of AI, teachers have implemented these changes independently, which might result in unequal assessment conditions for students.

Besides academic integrity, students' over-reliance of AI tool is another concern and was also documented by Al Buraiki (2025) and Vieriu and Petrea (2025). Both studies noted that students' frequent use of AI tools can reduce their critical thinking skills. While AI tools can be of great benefit to students, overdependence may limit their development of thinking skills. This concern was also argued by Al Balushi (2025), who found that students' reliance on AI-based grammar tools resulted in undermining their ability to develop language skills independently. These concerns reflect limitations on teachers' preparations for controlling AI use in classrooms as raised by Tan et al. (2025) and Gayed (2025), who noted a difference between the training offered to teachers on the use of AI and their actual needs. Overall, the findings suggest that current training opportunities focus more on technological skills, which would not help teachers tackle real implications of AI use in the classroom.

Another concern emerged from the criteria teachers apply when selecting AI tools for classroom use as they reported a priority for the ease of use and cost of the AI tools. However, the limited attention given to data privacy raises serious concerns and was also highlighted by Pikhart and Al-Obaydi (2025), who found that many AI tools involve significant privacy risks. The lack of clear policies from UTAS on data protection complicates this issue, as teachers are left to make decisions about student data security without adequate training.

These findings indicate that UTAS adopted AI tools without planning for AI integration into teaching practices. As a result, teachers are using new technologies without adequate preparation. A similar pattern was also identified by Al Buraiki (2025) in other Omani context, which suggests that this issue extends beyond UTAS. In other words, universities use AI mainly because it is available rather than through strategic planning.

RECOMMENDATIONS

The following recommendations were drawn from the findings of this study:

1. UTAS needs to develop a clear policy about how students and teachers use AI. AI policies should include explanation on permitted and prohibited tools to be used in teaching and learning. In addition, the policy needs to explain what happens if a student misuses AI and include a template for AI use declaration.
2. Teachers need more training in AI. The training programs should be based on a needs analysis of what Foundation Program teachers need instead of offering basic training of different AI tools.
3. The Foundation Program teachers should use in-class tests, presentations and process-based tasks. By doing so, students can explain their understanding to their classmates and teacher. At least, this would make it harder for students to just copy and paste AI work.
4. Teachers need to teach students about the strengths and weaknesses of AI. Students need to learn when they are allowed to use AI. They also need to have awareness about academic honesty.
5. UTAS needs to create clear policies and awareness workshops for teachers which include rules of how to integrate AI in teaching and to what extent.

LIMITATIONS

This study has limitations. The population was from one UTAS branch where the number of teachers in the Foundation Program is relatively small. Therefore, the results might not be applicable to other institutions. Moreover, only six teachers were interviewed which might affect the findings of the study. In addition, the study did not include students' perspectives on the use of AI. AI literacy can also be a limitation. In other words, teachers may have understood AI differently, which could affect their responses to the survey. Finally, the study did not include classroom observations or students' work, as these methods could have provided stronger evidence to support the findings of the study.

CONCLUSION

This study examined how teachers in the Foundation Program use AI tools and the challenges they faced in the classroom. This research contributes to the literature on AI integration in Omani higher education. The findings show that the lack of clear policies and tailored professional development create challenges for teachers. The study also reveals that data privacy is not a main concern for teachers when selecting AI tools, which could raise more ethical issues. In addition, the study found differences in the use of AI across the three different subjects of the Foundation Program, which indicates that teachers' needs vary by discipline and training should reflect these differences.

The results of this study have important implications. The experience at UTAS indicates that introducing new technologies without planning can cause inconsistent practices in the classrooms. The difference between the training teachers received and their actual needs suggests that professional development activities should be built on a clear needs analysis. Moreover, the lack of policies forced teachers to develop their own ways of using AI, which may lead to inconsistent practices within an institution. Finally, the limited focus on data privacy highlights the need for institutions to ensure that AI tools are ethically used.

FUTURE DIRECTIONS

This study highlights several areas for future research including conducting similar research across other UTAS branches to determine the consistency of the results of this study.

Moreover, this study focused on teachers' perspectives, further research could include students' perspectives because understanding how they use AI in learning would provide a more complete input of its impact in the Foundation Program. In addition, teachers' attitudes and practices of using AI might change over time, particularly when receiving specific training or when a policy is implemented. Therefore, longitudinal research would be useful in examining how teachers' perspectives of AI might change after the training. Additionally, classroom observations and analysis of student work would provide evidence of how AI affects learning and academic integrity. Finally, future research could also compare training for specific subjects and general training to determine which type of support most effectively meets teachers' needs.

REFERENCES

Al Balushi, K. (2025). Using AI-powered grammar correction tools to support ESL students' writing skills development. In *Optimizing research techniques and learning strategies with digital technologies* (pp. 1–16). IGI Global., DOI: 10.4018/979-8-3693-7863-2.ch012

Al Buraiki, S. (2025). A qualitative SWOT analysis study of the integration of AI technologies into higher education institutions in the Sultanate of Oman. International Journal of Learning, Teaching and Educational Research, 24(4). https://www.ijlter.org/index.php/ijlter/article/view/12649

Al Manji, K. M., Hussain, M., & Hussain, M. (2024). Artificial intelligence in Oman's government schools: A comprehensive study of its adoption and impact on teachers and students at secondary level. International Journal of Research and Scientific Innovation. https://rsisinternational.org/journals/ijrsi/articles/artificial-intelligence-in-omans-government-schools-a-comprehensive-study-of-its-adoption-and-impact-on-teachers-and-students-at-secondary-level/

Al Rashdi, H., & Elgeddawy, M. (2025). Artificial intelligence as a catalyst for sustainable quality education: The case of Oman. In Awwad, B. (Ed.), *AI and IoT: Driving business success and sustainability in the digital age* (pp. 1–15). Springer., DOI: 10.1007/978-3-031-92240-4_70

Bertram Gallant, T., & Rettinger, D. (2025). *The opposite of cheating: Teaching for integrity in the age of AI*. University of Oklahoma Press.

Carpenter, D. D., Harding, T. S., & Finelli, C. J. (2010). Using research to identify academic dishonesty deterrents among engineering undergraduates. *International Journal of Engineering Education*, *26*(5), 1156–1165.

Chu, H.-C., Hwang, G.-H., Tu, Y.-F., & Yang, K.-H. (2023). Roles and research trends of artificial intelligence in higher education: A systematic review of the top 50 most-cited articles. *Australasian Journal of Educational Technology*. Advance online publication. DOI: 10.14742/ajet.7526

Discover Artificial Intelligence. (2025). Artificial intelligence-based personalised learning in education: A systematic literature review. https://link.springer.com/article/10.1007/s44163-025-00598-x

Education. (2025). The impact of artificial intelligence (AI) on students' academic development. Education, 15(3), 343. https://www.mdpi.com/2227-7102/15/3/343

European Network for Academic Integrity. (2023). ENAI recommendations on the ethical use of artificial intelligence in education. *International Journal for Educational Integrity*, *19*, 133. Advance online publication. DOI: 10.1007/s40979-023-00133-4

Frontiers in Education. (2025). Evaluating the impact of AI on critical thinking skills among higher education students. https://www.frontiersin.org/journals/education/articles/10.3389/feduc.2025.1

Galindo-Domínguez, H., Delgado, N., Campo, L., & Losada, D. (2024). Relationship between teachers' digital competence and attitudes towards artificial intelligence in education. *International Journal of Educational Research*, *126*, 102381. Advance online publication. DOI: 10.1016/j.ijer.2024.102381

Gayed, J. M. (2025). Educators' perspective on artificial intelligence: Equity, preparedness, and development. *Cogent Education*, *12*(1), 2447169. Advance online publication. DOI: 10.1080/2331186X.2024.2447169

Granström, M., & Oppi, P. (2025). Assessing teachers' readiness and perceived usefulness of AI in education: An Estonian perspective. *Frontiers in Education*, *10*, 1622240. Advance online publication. DOI: 10.3389/feduc.2025.1622240

Guan, L., & Zhang, Y. (2025). Pre-service teachers preparedness for AI-integrated education: An investigation from perceptions, capabilities, and teachers' identity changes. *Computers and Education Open*, *6*, 100149. Advance online publication. DOI: 10.1016/j.caeo.2024.100149

ICESCO. (2024, January 18). Signing of agreement to establish ICESCO chair for AI ethics in Sultanate of Oman. https://icesco.org/en/2024/01/18/signing-of-agreement-to-establish-icesco-chair-for-ai-ethics-in-sultanate-of-oman/

Jin, Y., Echeverria, V., Gašević, D., & Martinez-Maldonado, R. (2024). Generative AI in higher education: A global perspective of institutional adoption policies and guidelines. *Computers and Education Open*, *7*, •••. https://www.sciencedirect.com/science/article/pii/S2666920X24001516

Karkoulian, S., Sayegh, N., & Sayegh, N. (2024). ChatGPT unveiled: Understanding perceptions of academic integrity in higher education—A qualitative approach. *Journal of Academic Ethics*. Advance online publication. DOI: 10.1007/s10805-024-09543-6

Liang, Y. (2023). Balancing: The effects of AI tools in educational context. *Frontiers in Humanities and Social Sciences*, *3*(8), 5531. Advance online publication. DOI: 10.54691/fhss.v3i8.5531

Liu, H., Azam, M., Naeem, S. B., & Faiola, A. (2023). An overview of the capabilities of ChatGPT for medical writing and its implications for academic integrity. *Health Information and Libraries Journal*. Advance online publication. DOI: 10.1111/hir.12509

Moorhouse, B. L., Yeo, M. A., & Wan, Y. (2024). Addressing student non-compliance in AI use declarations: Implications for academic integrity and assessment in higher education. *Assessment & Evaluation in Higher Education*. Advance online publication. DOI: 10.1080/02602938.2024.2415654

Pikhart, M., & Al-Obaydi, L. H. (2025). Reporting the potential risk of using AI in higher education: Subjective perspectives of educators. *Computers in Human Behavior Reports*, *18*, 100693. Advance online publication. DOI: 10.1016/j.chbr.2025.100693

ercan, E., & Voicu, B. (2022). Patterns of academic integrity definitions among BA Romanian students: The impact of rising enrolments. *Revista de Cercetare si Interventie Sociala*, *78*, 87–106. DOI: 10.33788/rcis.78.6

Sharma, R. (2024). Teacher training and professional development with utilisation of AI. *Paripex Indian Journal of Research*, *13*(6), 1–3.

Sullivan, M., Kelly, A., & McLaughlan, P. (2023). Chatting and cheating: Ensuring academic integrity in the era of ChatGPT. *Innovations in Education and Teaching International*, *61*(3), 580–591. DOI: 10.1080/14703297.2023.2190148

Tan, X., Cheng, G., & Ling, M. H. (2025). Artificial intelligence in teaching and teacher professional development: A systematic review. *Computers and Education: Artificial Intelligence*, *8*, 100355. Advance online publication. DOI: 10.1016/j.caeai.2024.100355

The Gulf Observer. (2025, June 21). Oman accelerates AI development through strategic national programme and startup growth. https://thegulfobserver.com/oman-accelerates-ai-development-through-strategic-national-programme-and-startup-growth/

UNESCO. (2024). Artificial intelligence in teaching and teacher professional development: A systematic review. *Computers and Education Open*, *6*, 100158. Advance online publication. DOI: 10.1016/j.caeo.2024.100158

Vieriu, A. M., & Petrea, G. (2025). The impact of artificial intelligence (AI) on students' academic development. *Education Sciences*, *15*(3), 343. Advance online publication. DOI: 10.3390/educsci15030343

Watson, G., Sottile, J., & Liang, J. G. (2014). What is cheating? Student and faculty perception of what they believe is academically dishonest behavior. *Journal of Research in Education*, *24*(1), 120–134. DOI: 10.1177/0022487114524517

Zuboff, S. (2019). *The age of surveillance capitalism: The fight for a human future at the new frontier of power*. Public Affairs.

Chapter 11

Do Bureaucratic Obstacles Mediate Ethical Education Challenges on Research Productivity in Ethiopian Higher Education Institutions

Wako Jio
https://orcid.org/0009-0003-6192-459X
Bule Hora University, Ethiopia

Shashi Kant
https://orcid.org/0000-0003-4722-5736
DMI-St. Eugene University, Zambia

Pawan Kumar
https://orcid.org/0000-0001-7501-3066
Lovely Professional University, India

ABSTRACT

This chapter investigates the relationship among research as well as research productivity (RP) in higher education institutions, emphasizing the mediating role of bureaucratic barriers (BOs). This study objectively analyzes the links among these structures, utilizing a sample of 394 investigators from various domains. The Kaiser-Meyer-Lkin (KMO) measurements confirm the sample's appropriateness for factor analysis, as well as the KMO findings indicate that a valid sample is present.

DOI: 10.4018/979-8-3373-4982-4.ch011

Confirmation factor analysis (CFA) was used to test the measurement model as well as make sure that the structure was both reliable as well as well-defined. The relationship among EEC, BO, as well as research productivity showed how AMOS software may be used to model structural equations (SEM). The outcomes show that BO is an essential middleman in the link among EEC as well as research output. In particular, bureaucratic hurdles make honesty problems worse, which makes it further harder for researchers to do good work. To enhance research outcomes in higher education, this chapter underscores the

INTRODUCTION

Ethical Education is the cornerstone of scientific investigation that backs up the truth as well as reliability of academic discoveries. It is very essential on a global scale since it affects not only individual researchers but also institutions as well as training areas as a whole (Bouter, 2024). Integrity in research is very essential in a world that is becoming more as well as more dependent on data-driven answers. In this environment, unethical conduct can lead to misinformation, social distrust, as well as detrimental public impact (Labib et al., 2023). The concept of Ethical Education challenge originates from the establishment of ethical principles through in academic environments. Over the years, it changed in response to several kinds of dishonesty, such making up data as well as copying someone else's work (Zhaksylyk et al., 2023). The need of maintaining ethical standards in multinational research endeavors has been a topic of continuous discourse since this advancement.

The empirical research predominantly underscores issues via the Ethical Education challenge, particularly through in higher education institutions (Uwizeye et al., 2022). The study illustrates how ethical dilemmas might hinder researchers' ability to produce high-quality work by establishing a significant correlation among deteriorating productivity as well as Ethical Education Challenge (EEC) concerns (Zhaksylyk et al., 2023). Nonetheless, these studies underscore the challenges of honesty while sometimes neglecting the administrative obstacles encountered by researchers (Chen et al., 2024). Real-world issues like complicated management processes as well as rules that are almost clear can make the bad impacts of EECs worse as well as create an environment that makes it hard to be creative as well as do well at work (Bouter, 2024).

Even through this research, we still don't know how bureaucratic hurdles in EEC affect research production. There has been less study regarding the intermediate role of bureaucratic hurdles in this context (Bouter, 2024). This chapter seeks to rectify these shortcomings by examining the origins of bureaucratic inefficiencies through in the interactions among EEC, alongside research output, as well as by providing valuable insights to lawmakers as well as emerging researchers (Uwizeye et al., 2022). By tackling these problems, this study hopes to give a guide for making the research environment better, which will improve both performance as well as ethical behavior (Chen et al., 2024).This study's main topic is: ***how do problems through research consistency impact research performance in institutions of higher learning, as well as how do bureaucratic barriers influence these relationships?*** By addressing this question, this chapter will offer a more thorough comprehension of the nuances of research ethics as well as its effects on academic achievement. It will also ultimately direct future initiatives to encourage moral behavior as well as simplify management procedures in the research setting.

BACKGROUND OF THE STUDY

The concept of investigation consistency has expanded distinction in recent years, reflecting the cumulative moral responsibility that investigators feel in their pursuit of information. There has been a big increase in the need for ethical as well as open research as the academia interacts through more public as well as fundraising organizational analyses (Uwizeye et al., 2022). Researchers typically face considerable challenges in maintaining adherence to ethics standards as well as guiding principles, not through standing their establishment. In the case of climate studies at the University of Englas well as (CRU), we found claims of data manipulation as well as other problems through research on certain topics that show how hard it is to do the study (Labib et al., 2023).

The "Climate gate" scandal showed how a lack of clear principled guidelines as well as load from the bureaucracy made it essential for investigators to take shortcuts. The incident not only hurt the investigators' standings, but it also started a worldwide conversation about the need for accountability as well as openness in climate science. This shows how even tiny errors may have big effects. Medical research is another example (Uwizeye et al., 2022). Honestly, it leads to a wide range of research that has recorded cases of misconduct as well as data falsification. For example, more than 80 excellent cardiology articles on dishonest conduct after abstinence showed that there were flaws through the testing process's framework as well as the limits that researchers had to work through. These events demonstrate the imperative for reliable procedures to facilitate moral investigation as well as the role bureaucratic impediments may have in humanizing an environment conducive to unethical behavior (García-González et al., 2021).

The comparison of higher education institutions in the Global South as well as Global North shows that there are big disparities in the cultures of the institutions that affect how much research they do. In the Global North, universities frequently get a lot of money, have well-established research frameworks, and have a culture of working together, which encourages new ideas and ethical behaviour (Chen et al., 2024). On the other hand, institutions in the Global South often have to deal with a lack of resources, inefficient bureaucracies, as well as different levels of support for research projects. These problems can make it harder to teach ethics as well as do research in general. The different cultures of the institutions show that we need to use different methods to boost research productivity, with a focus on policies that deal with regional differences as well as promote ethical standards in different educational settings (Bouter, 2024). Many researchers feel overwhelmed by bureaucracy, which might lead to unethical behavior as well as observations that are more reactive than helpful. This bureaucratic burden may make it hard to navigate the ethical landscape successfully, as it often makes real concerns more serious. The backdrop of this study underscores the urgent need to tackle these issues as well as to understand the complex relationships among research productivity, bureaucratic obstacles, as well as the challenges of Ethical Education (Zhaksylyk et al., 2023). The objective of this project is to cultivate an environment in which ethical studies may substantially enhance social development by analyzing these dynamic as well as providing insights that might inform future politicians as well as practices (García-González et al., 2021).

STATEMENT OF THE PROBLEM

The current condition of the Ethical Education challenge in higher education institutions (Zhaksylyk et al., 2023) illustrates both the ideal scenario as well as the reality encountered by several researchers, who often struggle to reconcile their capacity to fulfill these standards. All parts of research are guided by ethical norms. Researchers should ideally be allowed to do their job in an open as well as honest way, through clear rules as well as robust support systems that promote moral behavior. However, contradictory data in the literature suggests that several researchers grapple through honesty, adversely affecting both performance as well as general trust in research methodologies (Bain et al., 2022).

Even when earlier studies indicate various genuine issues, the data is not as persuasive as the extent to which bureaucratic obstacles are diminishing in these collaborations. Some research demonstrates a distinct correlation among concerns via honesty, including a decrease in productivity; nonetheless, they inadequately address how administrative complexity exacerbates these issues (Chen et al., 2024). This uncertainty engenders theoretical deficiencies in comprehending the intricate interrelations of bureaucratic maladies, Ethical Education challenges, as well as their collective influence on academic performance (Zhaksylyk et al., 2023). Moreover, the literature reveals significant information deficiencies about the many bureaucratic impediments faced by researchers as well as their impact on several domains (García-González et al., 2021).The phrase "diverse higher education institutions" is used, however it doesn't say what kinds of institutions it means, like public or private universities or the differences between developed and poor countries. These differences have a big effect on research funding, the availability of resources, and institutional support. To fully grasp how higher education works, it's important to deal with them Zhaksylyk et al., 2023).

Moreover, significant contextual deficiencies exist since most prior studies were confined to specific locations or organizations, hence constraining the generalizability of their outcomes (Labib et al., 2023). This is especially essential because there are so many different types of organizations as well as bureaucracies in higher education. Numerous scholars contend that they are overwhelmed, as well as that pragmatic issues, such as ambiguous compliance procedures as well as stringent management demands, persist in complicating the maintenance of the Ethical Education challenge (Zhaksylyk et al., 2023). The limited coverage of cultural as well as policy differences between countries makes it hard to fully grasp how higher education works. The institutional practices and research priorities of each country are influenced by its own historical, political, as well as social settings. Strategies for enhancing research productivity may not effectively tackle the unique challenges encountered in varied contexts if these variations are not recognized (Bain et al., 2022). This study seeks to rectify these weaknesses by systematically analyzing the mediating role of bureaucratic hurdles in the relationship among research productivity concerns as well as the Ethical Education challenge. This study provides empirical validation for these dynamics by employing a robust methodological framework that incorporates both quantitative analysis as well as structural equation modeling. This study offers both theoretical insights into the interrelations among these components as well as practical guidance for politicians as well as institutional leaders. This study addresses identified gaps, informing strategies, directing future research subjects, promoting an environment favorable to ethical communication, as well as eventually enhancing the integrity of research enterprises in higher education.

THEORITICAL FOUNDATION

Public contract theory: The state contracts theory posits that individuals agree to establish firms that entail duties due to the protection as well as support provided by their communities (Deng, 2022). The idea posits that researchers, bound by their social responsibilities to both community groups as well as society at large, must conform to ethical norms when research consistency is maintained. Philosophers like as Thomas Hobbes, John Locke, as well as Jean-Jacques Rousseau are recognized for the development of this theory. This concept posits that for society to authenticate agreements among researchers, their peers, as well as public stakeholders, researchers must comply through ethical norms that uphold trust as well as accountability (Deng, 2022).

Institutional theory: Institutional theory examines the influence of rules, norms, as well as institutions through in an organization on practices as well as behaviors (Risi et al., 2023). This idea is especially essential for understanding bureaucratic obstacles that might damage the quality of research. Institutions impose restrictions that affect the circumstances under which research is conducted as well as the often unforeseen outcomes. This notion came from sociology as well as was made to fit the needs of diverse institutions, including higher education. (Risi et al., 2023).

Planned Theory of Behavior: This theory addresses the examination of honesty (Albayati et al., 2023). This elucidates the impact of beliefs on the essential of honesty, peer pressure, as well as the ability to navigate bureaucratic difficulties on researchers' intents to comply through ethical standards. TPB underscores the significance of individual agency under institutional restrictions as well as serves as the basis for psychology's comprehension of the motivations underlying the adoption of ethical judgments in research (Albayati et al., 2023).

The main theoretical basis for this study is ***institutional theory***. It provides a thorough framework for understanding the impact of administrative obstacles in higher education institutions on research productivity as well as integrity. By focusing on the institutional context, this study may examine both structural as well as cultural factors that influence researchers' ability to comply through ethical standards, highlighting the interaction among management practices as well as integrity concerns.

DEFINITIONS AND ORIGIN OF TERMS

Ethical Education challenge: The Ethical Education problem is the full adherence to professional standards as well as ethical principles that govern research operations. Researchers must be entirely open, take responsibility, as well as treat everyone through respect, from subjects to peers to the general public, in order to be seen as honest. Over time, the notion expanded to become the main way to fight against unethical research practices, including as plagiarism as well as data fabrication (Zhaksylyk et al., 2023).

Bureaucratic Obstacles: The French term "bureau" means "office," which is where the word "bureaucracy" comes from. It means the structures that govern the work of an institution. Bureaucratic activities like accountability as well as keeping order are said to have benefits, but they actually make things less efficient, which keeps researchers from completing their moral duties as well as accomplishing great work. Researchers can enhance operational efficiency as well as ethical standards in research by comprehensively analyzing bureaucratic impediments (García-González et al., 2021).

Ethical Education challenge (EEC): Researchers now have unique problems in maintaining ethical ideals that exceed the standards for ethical research. Researchers face several problems, including data fabrication, plagiarism, as well as conflicts of interest induced by external sources (Bain et al., 2022).

EMPIRICAL LITERATURE REVIEW

Ethical Education challenge and Research Productivity

Scholarly inquiry has concentrated on the relationship among research performance challenges as well as the Ethical Education Challenge (EEC), especially in light of the increasing incidence of integrity-related concerns (Zhaksylyk et al., 2023). The empirical literature consistently underscores that EECs can significantly hinder researchers' ability to generate high-quality work. For example, research have shown that unethical behaviors like making up data as well as stealing ideas can lead to retraction as well as loss of reputation, as well as making the outcomes less credible. A meta-analysis (Chen et al., 2024) says that a lot of researchers have acknowledged to employing questionable research methodologies. The diversion of time as well as money to address the consequences of such fraud detrimentally affects the overall performance of research organizations as well as institutions. The literature delineates declining contextual components, encompassing institutional constraints as well as the competitive nature of scientific communities, alongside direct ethical impediments (Bain et al., 2022).

This research illustrates how financial publication pressure frequently influences quantity in contrast to safer alternatives, hence heightening the danger of ethical violations. This competitive environment not only cultivates a setting conducive to genuine concerns but also diminishes overall research performance, as it prioritizes external expectations while neglecting ethical as well as rigorous research (Chen et al., 2024). Looking at how bureaucracy, honesty, and productivity are related in higher education administrative settings shows how complicated things may be. Bureaucracy typically makes things more complicated, which can slow down progress and create a culture of following the rules rather than coming up with new ideas (Albayati et al., 2023). This can cause problems with honesty because strict rules may make it harder to be honest. On the other hand, properly navigating bureaucratic processes while fostering integrity can boost productivity, helping organisations reach their research and educational aims more effectively. To make policies that make it easier for study and academic success to happen, you need to understand how these things work together (Labib et al., 2022).

Moreover, the relationship among EEC as well as performance is significantly influenced by the bureaucratic structure of higher education institutions (Bouter, 2024). Studies indicate that onerous administrative processes may engender feelings of disenchantment as well as alienation among researchers. When bureaucratic obstacles hinder the research process, they diminish researchers' overall efficacy as well as distract them from maintaining ethical standards (García-González et al., 2021). The combined effect of bureaucratic inefficiency as well as honesty challenges (Labib et al., 2022) demonstrates the need for an advanced understanding of how these factors interact to influence research output. Despite the wealth of information on EEC, there remains a deficiency in understanding the specific mechanisms via which these challenges affect production. Numerous studies have examined the direct consequences of honesty breaches; however, the intermediary impacts of bureaucratic impediments have been comparatively overlooked (Bouter, 2024). According to this study, a vicious cycle may emerge from the interaction among honesty as well as the challenges presented by bureaucratic obstacles (Chen et al., 2024). Less ethics means more management testing, which makes the research process increasingly harder as well as less productive (Labib et al., 2022).

H1: Ethical Education challenge and Research Productivity having empirical association.

Ethical Education challenge and Bureaucratic Obstacles

Researchers are increasingly focusing on the intersection of bureaucratic challenges as well as Ethical Education Challenge (EEC) as they strive to negotiate complex institutional frameworks while adhering to ethical standards (Zhaksylyk et al., 2023). EEC talks about a lot of different things, such plagiarism, conflicts of interest, as well as how to get data. But bureaucratic obstacles like long management processes, vague rules, as well as strict regulatory requirements make these honesty problems worse as well as create an environment that doesn't encourage ethical research methods (García-González et al., 2021). Some studies suggest that bureaucratic barriers make honest problems easier to deal through. This study illustrates that researchers may experience dissatisfaction due to overly complex management processes, as they feel pressured to bypass ethical cutting standards to meet administrative requirements. When researchers stress honesty by making labor less dangerous, this pressure often leads to a reactive attitude to compliance (Labib et al., 2022). Researchers struggle to reconcile the demands of productivity through ethics, indicating that the competitive nature of scientific communities, exacerbated by non-bureaucratic pressures, may lead to unethical conduct. Furthermore, research suggests that bureaucratic obstacles may cultivate a culture of distrust as well as fear among researchers (García-González et al., 2021). This study illustrated how scholars might openly address ethical dilemmas or their quest for leadership while being perpetually subjected to bureaucratic oversight. If the issue of honesty is not addressed, this lack of transparency may outcome in climate change as well as inspires even more unethical activity. This study underscores the essential of institutions in establishing supportive environments that promote ethical discourse, rather than advocating for concealment as well as protection (Labib et al., 2022).

Another essential issue in the literature is how institutional help might help research integrity by lessening the harmful effects of bureaucratic hurdles (Zhaksylyk et al., 2023). Research from the American Association of University Studies indicates that firms through clearly articulated ethical leadership principles as well as effective management practices frequently see reduced occurrences of dishonesty (Labib et al., 2022). When researchers feel supported by their employers, they are less likely to give in to bureaucratic demands that don't work as well as more likely to follow ethical standards. There remains little understanding of the specific mechanisms by which bureaucratic impediments affect EEC, not through standing the frameworks proposed by contemporary research (Bouter, 2024). There are not many studies that look at the link among various bureaucratic processes as well as the number of honest complaints. However, some study does look at how bureaucracy affects research methods in general. This lack of empirical data makes it harder for us to make targeted plans to get rid of administrative impediments as well as improve research integrity (Zhaksylyk et al., 2023).

H2: Ethical Education challenge and Bureaucratic Obstacles having empirical association

Bureaucratic Obstacles and Research Productivity

According to Labib et al. (2023) assert that the relationship among bureaucratic impediments as well as research output has emerged as a critical field of inquiry through in university research. Bureaucratic hurdles are the administrative, political, as well as regulatory steps that researchers must take in order to do their jobs (García-González et al., 2021). A lot of research has shown that these problems can make it much harder to do research, which can make researchers lose interest as well as concentration on their scientific work. One of the most essential discoveries in the literature (Uwizeye et al., 2022) says that too many administrative tasks might cut down on the time as well as resources available for real research activity. The study shows that bureaucratic tasks including financing, compliance paperwork, as well as declaratory requirements might sometimes be too much for academics to handle

(Bain et al., 2022). This distraction not only makes it harder to do fresh research, but it also makes people tired as well as unhappy through their jobs. Researchers may struggle to balance their administrative duties through their scientific work, which might lead to a decrease in the total range of discoveries from research institutions. The study also highlights how unclear institutional rules are a major bureaucratic problem (Labib et al., 2023). Researchers who are uncertain about compliance requirements or optimal methods for addressing ethical dilemmas may experience confusion due to ambiguous instructions or procedures, as indicated by the study. Researchers may spend too much time hunting for information as well as going through the institution's red tape, which might get in the way of the primary research event if the process they have to follow is clearly not good enough (Uwizeye et al., 2022).

The academy's competitiveness makes the effects of bureaucratic impediments on research production even worse. It can lead to the prioritization of administrative tasks over substantial research initiatives, as frequently seen in the efforts surrounding secure funded publications (Uwizeye et al., 2022). In environments where performance is always anticipated, researchers may have to speed up bureaucratic processes as well as trade quality for speed. This creates a contradiction in which the mechanisms that are supposed to help accounting as well as supervision instead make the performance they are supposed to enhance worse. Research indicates that the impact of bureaucratic impediments on research productivity can be alleviated by the efficacy of institutional support systems (García-González et al., 2021). A survey by the American Association of institutions found that institutions through better administration as well as reliable support services had more researchers as well as better performance. Despite the extensive literature on this subject, there remains little understanding of the specific bureaucratic factors that significantly influence study outcomes across many institutional disciplines as well as situations (Labib et al., 2023). Many studies focus on the general consequences of bureaucracy, but they don't look at specific bureaucratic processes, such grant applications as well as ethical journals, or how research outcomes are related to one other. This absence of empirical data makes it hard to come up through specific measures that will improve both institutional procedures as well as performance (Labib et al., 2022).

H3: Bureaucratic Obstacles and Research Productivity having empirical association.

Ethical Education challenge, Research Productivity and Bureaucratic Obstacles Mediation

On academic settings, bureaucratic obstacles as well as research productivity are addressed by Ethical Education Challenge (EEC) issues, leading to a concentrated focus on empirical studies by academics investigating their cumulative effects (Bouter, 2024). EEC encounters ethical dilemmas like as data manipulation, conflicts of interest, as well as plagiarism, which directly undermine the integrity as well as dependability of research. Complicated management systems as well as unclear institutional rules make problems through research integrity worse as well as make research efforts less successful (Zhaksylyk et al., 2023). To come up through effective ways to promote both ethical research practice as well as productivity, you need to know how bureaucratic problems get in the way of both. Empirical studies have frequently demonstrated that EECs can hinder research production (Bouter, 2024). For example, meta-analysis shows that breaches of completeness make people less sure of the outcomes as well as hurt the reputations of individual researchers. This lack of reliability makes it harder to get money as well as work together, which can make production even harder. However, the evidence indicates that bureaucratic impediments reinforce this connection by introducing an additional layer of complexity for researchers to navigate (García-González et al., 2021). For example, we found that researchers have a harder time focusing on ethical concerns as well as are more likely to be dishonest when they have a lot of administrative work to do. Consequently, a decrease in performance exacerbates pressure, thereby fostering unethical conduct (Labib et al., 2022).

Additionally, the role of bureaucratic hurdles in influencing the link among the EEC as well as performance is illustrated, indicating that ambiguous institutional policies might lead to misinterpretation as well as misunderstanding of ethical principles (Bouter, 2024). When researchers don't know what the rules are for compliance, they could do things that put honesty at risk (Labib et al., 2022). This lack of clarity not only affects their moral judgment, but it also slows down research projects, which diminishes productivity. The study shows that bureaucratic problems can make researchers shift their focus from following tight ethical rules to dealing through administrative issues, which lowers their productivity. The literature indicates that a crucial factor affecting EEC as well as performance is the competitive nature of academies (Bain et al., 2022). Bureaucratic problems can make this stress worse on Wednesdays, when prices are high as well as resources are scarce. This can make it easier for people to want to give up their honesty (García-González et al., 2021). This dynamic illustrates that bureaucratic obstacles not only hinder performance but also cultivate questions of honesty, so complicating the research process. Despite the growing body of research on this topic (Bouter, 2024), we still don't know exactly how bureaucratic impediments impact the connection among EEC as well as study performance. The direct effects of certain bureaucratic processes, such as the duration of ethics training or the intricacy of grant applications, on performance as well as integrity have not been statistically evaluated, even though many studies emphasize the general impacts of bureaucracy. This information is essential for developing targeted medicines that tackle the root causes of these problems (Labib et al., 2022).

H4: Ethical Education challenge, Research Productivity and Bureaucratic Obstacles Mediation having empirical association.

CONCEPTUAL FRAMEWORK

Figure 1. Conceptual Framework

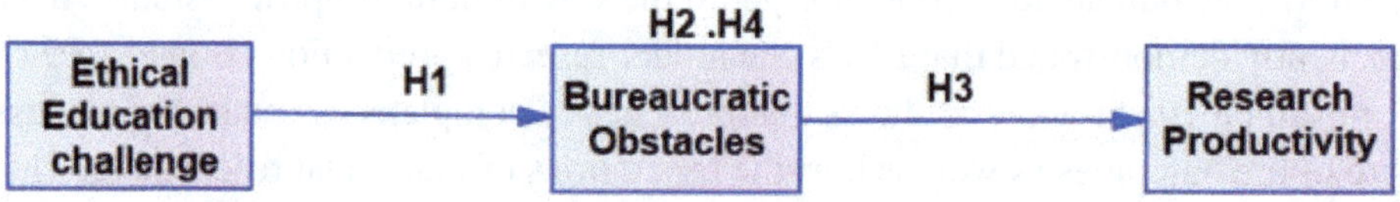

RESEARCH METHODOLOGY

This study investigated the correlation among bureaucratic obstacles, research productivity challenges, as well as the Ethical Education Challenge (EEC) employing a quantitative research methodology (Ghanad, 2023). A sample of 394 participants was collected from diverse higher education institutions to ensure a diversity of perspectives from experts across different areas. Structured questionnaires are utilized in the data collection procedure to ascertain researchers' perspectives on ethical issues, administrative obstacles, as well as performance impacts (Ghanad, 2023). Before performing the major analyses, the validity measures of the (KMO) samples were calculated to assess the data's appropriateness for factor analysis. The sample was considered suitable for further examination when the KMO value exceeded 0.6 (Shrestha, 2021). To determine the fundamental structure of the scale pertaining to EEC, bureaucratic impediments, as well as research output, exploratory factor analysis (EFA) was used. This approach helped to narrow down the data as well as figure out what was causing the differences in the researchers' answers (Oamen, 2021). After the EFA, the AMOS program was used to check the theoretical links among structures by modeling structural equations (SEM). SEM enabled the evaluation of complex interconnections while considering measurement error, providing a robust framework for understanding how bureaucratic obstacles impede the relationship among EEC production as well as research (Oamen, 2021).

Scale Development

A comprehensive examination of relevant literature was the basis for the formulation of the scales utilized in this study. Current studies on research we have looked at performance, bureaucratic hurdles, as well as honesty to discover concepts as well as variables that may be used to measure these traits (JeBO et al., 2021). The EEC scale emphasizes recurrent ethical issues, such as data fabrication, plagiarism, as well as conflicts of interest, alongside elements recognized in previous research. Publication rates as well as project completion times are two examples of research productivity measures that come from well-known metrics used to measure both quantity as well as quality of work. Each segment is created to show a different element of the framework, making sure that the study environment is both relevant as well as easy to understand. The magazine said that a group of experts looked at the initial pool of objects to make sure the information was reliable as well as to assist clarify the details. To verify the scale's reliability, preliminary tests were conducted to assess internal consistency utilizing Alpha Cronbach (Jebo et al., 2021). If an element does not meet the allowed threshold of 0.7, it has been fixed or removed. To provide a comprehensive assessment of the relationship among EEC, bureaucratic obstacles, as well as research output, the final scale is later included into the original study. Along through making sure that the measurements were accurate as well as reliable, this scale of development process gave the studies later analyses a strong base (Jebo et al., 2021).

DATA ANALYSIS

Table 1. Data Adequacy Measure

Kaiser Meyer Olkin Extent of Adequate. Sample		**.908**
SpheEECity Test of Bartlett	Chi-Square (Relative)	19484.673
	Degree of freedom	780
	p-value	.000

Source: Authors

The Kaiser-Meyer-Lkin (KMO) sample's adequacy was evaluated as well as determined to be 0.908, signifying an outstanding level of adequacy for the analysis. KMO values go from 0 to 1, as well as values close to 1 mean that the data is good for factorial analysis. KMO scores over 0.9 are frequently seen as exceptional, which means that the 394-person sample size is big enough for a more in-depth look. The value of Chi Square 19 484.673 is often used to show the outcomes of the Bartlett spherical test. This test checks to see if there is a big discrepancy among the identity matrix as well as the correlation matrix. This indicates that the variables are unsuitable for factor analysis as well as are not interrelated. Through

780 degrees of freedom, a statistical test analysis produced a p-value of 0.000. If p is less than 0.05, the null hypothesis is rejected, which means that there is a strong link among the variables in the dataset. All of these findings support the validity of additional studies in the study by showing that the data is both appropriate as well as customized for industrial research inquiry.

Table 2. Sum Variance Illuminated

Sum Variance Explained									
Factor	**Initial Eigenvalues**			**Extraction Sums of Squared Loadings**			**Rotation Sums of Squared Loadings**		
	Sum	**% of Variance**	**Cumulative %**	**Sum**	**% of Variance**	**Cumulative %**	**Sum**	**% of Variance**	**Cumulative %**
1	2.7	26.7	26.76	2.7	26.7	26.7	8.7	21.9	21.9
2	1.9	14.9	41.71	1.9	14.9	41.7	6.0	15.0	37.0
3	1.3	10.9	52.68	1.3	10.9	52.6	4.6	11.6	48.6

Abstraction Process: PCA.
Source: Authors

The table has three main parts: the initial value, the amount of square load that was taken out, as well as the amount of rotation of the square load. The original numbers indicate how much each part changed before it was rotated or taken out. Factor 1, which is 2.7, explains 26.7% of the variation. Factor 2, which is 1.9, explains 14.9% of the difference. Factor 3, which is 1.3, explains 10.9% of the variation. These three things together make up 52.68% of the dataset's volatility. It has been shown that factors 1 as well as 2 support their contributions at levels of 26.7% as well as 14.9%, respectively. It has also been shown that the same three components still account for similar changes when the extraction amount of square load has been taken out. These two things make up 41.7% of the total variance. This indicates that these initial impacts might account for a substantial portion of the data distribution. When the pieces are perfectly clear, the amount of rotation of the square load gives the feeling of variety. The first two components explain 37.0% of the overall variance, although each one does it in a different way. Factor 1 explains 21.9% of the variation, whereas factor 2 explains 15.0%. The rotating process shows a big effect on global dispersion as well as makes it easier to understand the components.

Confirmatory Principle Component Examination

Table 3. Covariances

Covariance			Estimate	S.E.	C.R.	P	Hy.
Bureaucratic Obstacles	**<-->**	**Ethical Education challenge**	**.563**	**.094**	**5.989**	**.00**	**H2**
Bureaucratic Obstacles	<-->	Research Productivity	.493	.056	8.803	.00	**H3**
Ethical Education challenge	<-->	Research Productivity	.652	.105	6.209	.00	**H1**

Source: Authors

The table has covariance estimates, standard errors (S.E.), essential connections (C.R.), P (P) values, as well as hypotheses (Hy) for each relationship. Research indicates that the correlation value among Bureaucratic Obstacles as well as Ethical Education challenges is 0.563, through a standard error of 0.094. At any convention's significance level, these variables are statistically significant since their p-value is 0.00 as well as their critical ratio is 5.989. This data corroborates hypothesis 2 (H2), which asserts that an increased level of bureaucratic impediments correlates through heightened difficulties pertaining to study integrity. Then, through a standard error of 0.056, the covaria among search performance as well as bureaucratic impediments is found to be 0.493. The p-value of 0.00 as well as the essential ratio of 8.803 both suggests a strong, statistically significant link that supports Hypothesis 3 (H3). This data illustrates the detrimental effect of management impairments on research outputs, indicating that research performance diminishes as bureaucratic impediments increase. Finally, a critical report through a value of p = 0.00 further substantiates a statistically significant correlation that confirms Hypothesis 1 (H1). Additionally, the integration of research productivity problems as well as Ethical Education challenges is quantified at 0.652, through a standard error of 0.105. This correlation suggests that the Honesty problem might negatively affect research production as well as reinforce the idea that ethical issues may hinder researchers' ability to produce high-quality work.

Table 4. Validity Concern

	CR	AVE	MSV	MaxR(H)	EEC	BO	RP
EEC	0.732	0.643	0.219	0.852	**0.654**		
BO	0.758	0.657	0.132	0.763	0.171	**0.665**	
RP	0.793	0.603	0.274	0.797	0.383	0.193	**0.684**

Note: EEC = Ethical Education challenge; BO= Bureaucratic Obstacles; RP = Research Productivity
Source: Authors

These include the maximum reliability (MAXR(H)), mean variance (AVE), maximum general variance (MSV), as well as reliability of composite materials (CR). Research productivity (RP), bureaucratic hurdles (BO), as well as Ethical Education challenge difficulties (EEC) are all essential measures for judging how reliable as well as accurate the framework is. Compound reliability (CR) ratings reflect how consistent a structure is on the inside. The EEC's CR of 0.732 is over the acceptable threshold of 0.7, which means that the measurements are reliable. The scales used to measure these structures are deemed to be internally consistent because BO's CR of 0.758 as well as RP's highest CR of 0.793 both show that they are reliable. The average variance of extracted (AVE) values shows how much variation each construct has for variance caused by measurement error. The AVEs for the EEC, BO, as well as RP are 0.643, 0.657, as well as 0.603, in that order. The cutoff point of 0.5 for each AVE value shows that the structures have enough convergent dependability as well as may explain a large part of their dispersions. The maximum general dispersion (MSV) values look at the correlations among the structures to see if discriminant reliability is possible. For EEC MSV, the number is 0.219; for BO, it is 0.132; as well as for RP, it is 0.274. It should be noted that the measurements' discriminating reliability is preserved, as the MSV values are inferior to the AV values of their corresponding structures. Finally, the greatest reliability value (MAXR(H)) of 0.852 for EEC, 0.763 for BO, as well as 0.797 for RP greatly increases Construction's dependability.

Mediating Role Examination

Figure 2. Structural Equation Model

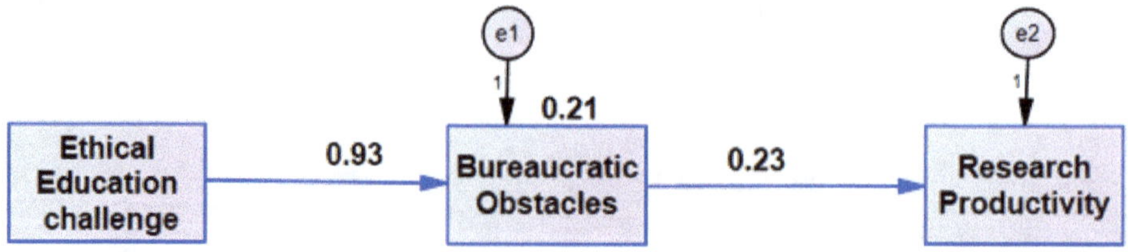

Model Fit Indices

Table 5. Model Fitness

Sig.	Chi-Sq	RMR	GFI	PNFI	TLI	RMSEA
0.003	2.163	.037	0.929	0.925	0.921	.029

Source: Authors

The fitted model is statistically significant, as shown by the reported significance (sig.) of 0.003. This means that the structures being looked at are closely related. The chi-square figures that were given are 2.163. This little number shows that the observed facts as well as the theoretical model agree through each other quite well. A low Chi-quadrate value usually means the best answer, especially when P is a large number. The mean secondary residue (RMR), which was 0.037, showed that the model was well-adjusted. This was below the usually accepted threshold of 0.08. This means that the intended as well as observed covariances don't change much. The Dignity Index (GFI) of 0.929 is higher than the allowed limit of 0.90, which supports the conclusion that the model is a good fit for the data. In the same way, the Tucker-Lewis (TLI) 0.921 as well as the economic communication index (PNFI) 0.925 are both greater than the required value of 0.90, which means they are likewise reliable models. The average approximation square error (RMSEA) is close to the cutoff value of 0.06, through a value of 0.029. A model is judged to have strong correspondence as well as to be good overall when its RMSEA is less than 0.05.

Table 6. Regression Examination

Relative			Approx.	S.E.	C.R.	P	Ass.
Bureaucratic Obstacles	**<---**	**Ethical Education challenge**	**.716**	**.405**	**1.767**	**.06**	**H2**
Research Productivity	<---	Bureaucratic Obstacles	.651	.197	3.304	.00	H3
Research Productivity	<---	Ethical Education challenge	.563	.105	5.361	.00	H1

Source: Authors

Research productivity the issue of ethical education, as well as bureaucratic obstacles, this table has regression coefficient evaluations, standard errors (S.E.), critical relations (C.R.), P-particularly (P), as well as related hypotheses (ASS.). The initial research analyzed indicates that they are among the challenges of Ethical Education, through bureaucratic impediments, as evidenced by a regression coefficient of 0.716. The standard error for this evaluation is 0.405, which gives a critical report of 1.767 as well as a p-value of 0.06. This number P is a little higher than the usual meaning threshold of 0.05. This indicates a favorable correlation among the issue of bureaucratic hurdles as well as the challenge of Ethical Education, while the relationship is not statistically significant at the 5% level. As a outcome, we present data supporting Hypothesis 2 (H2). The second relationship among bureaucratic impediments as well as research effectiveness is measured by a regression coefficient of 0.651. The critical report shows a score of 3.304, through a standard error of 0.197. This high value of P backs up Hypothesis 3 (H3) by revealing a strong negative relationship among bureaucratic barriers as well as research productivity. This study underscores that a decline in research output correlates through a rise in bureaucratic obstacles. Finally, the standard error in the regression analysis concerning research productivity challenges as well as Ethical Education issues is 0.563. Critical reports show that Hypothesis 1 (H1) is supported by 5.361 as well as a value p of 0.00, which show a statistically significant positive connection. This finding suggests that further comprehensive inquiry Tasks that require honesty are associated through a greater reduction in research productivity.

Table 7. Mediating Effect

	Worth	Path Influence
Ethical Education challenge → Research Productivity	.10	Direct insignificant effect
Ethical Education challenge → Bureaucratic Obstacles → Research Productivity	.93*.23=.21	Indirect Influence Ensued
	.21	Full mediation

Source: Authors

This table helps you see how these structures work together as well as how direct as well as indirect effects are different. The Ethical Education challenge is believed to exert a direct, minimal influence on research output, through an estimated effect size of 0.10. This means that the interplay among these two structures, which are assumed to be separate, does not have a statistically significant effect on research productivity. It is also possible to measure the indirect effect by looking at the path via bureaucratic barriers. To figure out this indirect effect, you do the following: $0.93 \times 0.23 = 0.210.93 \times 0.23 = 0.21$. This value illustrates the considerable indirect influence that bureaucratic impediments have on the relationship among challenges in research output as well as ethical education. "Core Effects after Core Effects" shows how essential this mediation effect is. The overall impact of 0.21 suggests that there is "complete mediation."

DISCUSSION

The study's conclusions focus on the complex relationships among research output, the Ethical Education challenge, as well as bureaucratic obstacles. The outcomes show that bureaucratic hurdles have a big negative effect on research performance. This shows that firms need to simplify their administrative processes in order to increase productivity. There isn't a strong link among research productivity as well as honesty concerns, but the study showed that bureaucratic hurdles are one way that honesty problems might indirectly hurt research output. This suggests that problems through research integrity may not directly affect productivity; instead, they may do so via making bureaucratic inefficiency worse, which slows down output. This study also shows how essential it is to get rid of bureaucratic impediments in order to improve both productivity as well as the integrity of research. By lowering these barriers, researchers may work in a better environment that encourages them to be more productive as well as act ethically. These ideas ultimately provide a more comprehensive understanding of the factors influencing research output, along through beneficial implications for policymakers as well as corporate leaders. This report is a call to action for greater research into certain bureaucratic procedures that slow down production so that better as well as more effective research techniques may be developed.

CONCLUSION

Bureaucratic hurdles have a major effect on how much research gets done at colleges and universities.

Problems with ethical education make integrity problems in research settings worse.

Structural equation modelling (SEM) successfully elucidates the interconnections among ethical education, bureaucracy, and production.

To improve research results, it is important to fix bureaucratic problems right away.

A comparison of the Global South and the Global North shows that their institutional cultures are different and have an impact on how research is done.

Not paying enough attention to the distinctions between public and private schools makes it harder to understand different types of schools.

Policymakers need to come up with specific plans that take into account differences between regions and institutions.

For research to be beneficial, it is important to promote honesty and ethical norms.

Better cooperation across institutions can help break down bureaucratic barriers and promote new ideas.

Systematic improvements are necessary to foster a more conducive environment for ethical research methods and productivity.

MANAGERIAL IMPLICATIONS

The research findings have significant implications for management in businesses aiming to enhance standards of honesty as well as research productivity. Managers' key job is to make sure that everyone knows how bureaucratic problems might hurt research productivity. When businesses work together to make things easier by improving communication networks, scientists can focus on their work since bureaucratic processes go more easily. This makes research more flexible. Managers have a very essential job as leaders: they need to make sure that honesty is a part of every part of their organizations. Management should not only promote ethical research practices, but also safeguard researchers when they encounter challenges pertaining to honesty. To get people to embrace moral standards, there should be training courses as well as seminars that teach people about research ethics as well as make it clear how essential they are. The study demonstrates the necessity for departments to collaborate in addressing concerns of honesty, notably through cooperation across academic divisions, compliance staff units, as well as research administration teams. Organizations can better align their goals when they work together on projects that assist them get around red tape as well as deal through honesty issues.

PRACTICAL IMPLICATIONS

Organizations need to provide both clear policies as well as effective processes to help researchers avoid problems. As organizations create technological solutions to enhance communication among incident staff as well as researchers, they must also simplify their approval processes as well as diminish bureaucratic restrictions. To make sure that research continues as well as that researchers get honest help, universities should set up dedicated support systems that include research offices as well as honesty committees. Research support groups help researchers through administrative tasks as well as honesty concerns, making sure they have all they need to be successful. Researchers can do better as well as get over problems when they learn about ethics as well as project management from professionals in workshops. Organizations promote the development of an honest culture through this method, which allows researchers to be proactive at work. An open conversation about productivity as well as the need to be honest helps create a supportive environment. To help institutions come up through better solutions, all researchers should be allowed to use discussion forums to provide each other feedback on a regular basis. These forums should let researchers talk about their own experiences through problems at their institutions as well as through honesty.

THEORETICAL IMPLICATIONS

The study's findings provide some theoretical insights that facilitate the understanding of bureaucratic impediments, issues related to research consistency, as well as challenges concerning research productivity. First, this study supports the idea that bureaucratic systems may have a big impact on research outcomes that fit through recognized theories that stress the essential of organizational procedures in molding both behavior as well as performance. This study enhances the theoretical framework that investigates the influence of environmental variables on researchers' ability to generate high-quality work by elucidating the intermediary effect of bureaucratic barriers on the relationship among research productivity issues as well as Ethical Education challenges. The outcomes also make it hard to believe that issues related to Ethical Education challenge have a direct effect on production.

Instead, they suggest that connections are more complex as well as indirect, as well as they offer a chance to look closely at how honesty as well as performance are linked. This issue compels researchers to examine contextual factors that may govern or alter these connections, therefore enriching discourse on organizational behavior as well as research management. Furthermore, this study illustrates the impact of organizational dynamics on ethical conduct inside research environments as well as contributes to the existing literature on the Ethical Education problem. It pushes for theoretical models that try to bring these two areas together, as well as it stresses the need for a basic approach that looks at both the structural as well as cultural parts of an organization. Consequently, this study advocates for an enhanced understanding of the factors influencing research production at academic institutions by urging researchers to examine the interplay among ethical norms as well as bureaucratic procedures. In summary, the theoretical notions from this work can elucidate future inquiries as well as facilitate the development of more robust models in the fields of research management as well as organizational behavior.

RECOMMENDATIONS

Based on the outcomes of this study, you may make a number of suggestions to help organizations improve research efficiency as well as research integrity. To make bureaucratic processes easier, organizations should first decide what is most essential. To find areas that need to be changed, you may do this by frequently reviewing present rules as well as practices. Convenient digital platforms for user representation as well as permissions considerably reduce the amount of work that administrators have to do, make processes more efficient, as well as provide researchers more time to focus on their main duties. Companies also want to pay for training as well as development programs that teach people how to do ethical research as well as manage projects. Institutions may help build a culture of honesty as well as give researchers the knowledge as well as skills they need to do more complicated work. Lastly, groups should create an environment that encourages openness as well as conversation on the integrity as well as outcomes of research. Institutions may show that they care about ethical research methods as well as create a space where researchers feel comfortable bringing up problems by fostering discussion about these issues. Academic institutions' support for ethical principles as well as the productivity of research might both improve a lot if they follow these guidelines.

FUTURE DIRECTIONS AND LIMITATION

Promising leadership entails pinpointing critical administrative obstacles designated for reform as well as investigating the specific bureaucratic processes that most significantly impact researchers. Longitudinal studies, which show how changes in administrative processes affect research release as well as honesty over time, might provide us a better idea of causal relationships. Comparative studies across several institution types, such as universities, research institutes, as well as private businesses, may elucidate the influence of organizational structures as well as cultures on the interplay among research methods as well as bureaucracy. This technique would improve our understanding of the challenges as well as context-specific best practices for promoting ethical research environments. Moreover, mixed-method approaches that integrate quantitative analyses through qualitative input from researchers may be beneficial for subsequent studies. Finally, we need to look for ways to remove bureaucratic hurdles as well as promote research integrity. Researchers may give data-driven advice to institutional leaders as well as lawmakers on how to make research settings more hospitable by looking at how effectively specific programs, such modifications to the curriculum or the way things are done, are working. These future paths will not only help us learn more about theory, but they will also help us come up through practical solutions that improve both performance as well as ethical research standards.

REFERENCES

Albayati, H., Alistarbadi, N., & Rho, J. J. (2023). Evaluating engagement choices in the NFT Metaverse via the lens of the Theory of Planned Behavior (TPB). Telematics as well as Informatics Reports, 10, 100045.

Bain, L. E., Tchuisseu-Kwangoua, L. A., Adeagbo, O., Nkfusai, N. C., Amu, H., Saah, F. I., & Kombe, F. (2022). Fostering Ethical Education in Sub-Saharan Africa: Challenges, Opportunities, as well as Recommendations. 43(1) of the Pan AfEECan Medical Journal.

Bouter, L. (2024). Why the Ethical Education Challenge is essential as well as how it may be made better. *Accountability in Research, 31*(8), 1277–1286. PMID: 36888916

Chen, Z., Chen, C., Yang, G., He, X., Chi, X., Zeng, Z., & Chen, X. (2024). The difficulty of ethical education in the age of AI: Problems as well as solutions. *Medicine, 103*(27), e38811. PMID: 38968491

Deng, W. (2022). Utilization of psychological contract theory in the administration of higher education. *Psychiatria Danubina, 34*(suppl 5), 50.

García-González, J. M., Gutiérrez Gómez-Calcerrada, S., Solera Hernández, E., & Ríos-Aguilar, S. (2021). Barriers in higher education: An examination of students through disabilities in Spain using both views as well as discourse analysis. *Disability & Society, 36*(4), 579–595.

Ghanad, A. (2023). A summary of quantitative research approaches. International Journal of Multidisciplinary Research as well as Analysis, 6(08), 3794–3803.

JeBO, A. T., Ng, V., & Tay, L. (2021). A summary of significant advancements in Likert scale development from 1995 to 2019. *Frontiers in Psychology, 12*, 637547.

Labib, K., Evans, N., Pizzolato, D., Aubert Bonn, N., Widdershoven, G., Bouter, L., Konach, T., Langendam, M., DieEECkx, K., & Tijdink, J. (2023). Co-creating Ethical Education poses challenges to educational requirements for research institutes. Science as well as Engineering Ethics, 29(4), 28.

Labib, K., Evans, N., Roje, R., Kavouras, P., Reyes Elizondo, A., Kaltenbrunner, W., Buljan, I., Ravn, T., Widdershoven, G., & Bouter, L. (2022). Policies for Ethical Education in both education as well as training: Insights from a focus group research. Science as well as Public Policy, 49(2), 246–266.

Oamen, T. E. (2021). An examination of the determinants affecting the participation of the pharmaceutical sales personnel in marketing inside Nigeria, utilizing a structural equation modeling methodology. The Global Journal of Pure as well as Applied Sciences, 27(4), 405–410.

Risi, D., Vigneau, L., Bohn, S., & Wickert, C. (2023). Research on corporate social responsibility grounded in institutional theory: Reintegrating values. *International Journal of Management Reviews*, *25*(1), 3–23.

Shrestha, N. (2021). Factor analysis utilized for survey examination. AmeEECan Journal of Applied Mathematics as well as Statistics, 9(1), 4–11.

Uwizeye, D., Karimi, F., Thiong'o, C., Syonguvi, J., Ochieng, V., Kiroro, F., Gateri, A., Khisa, A. M., & Wao, H. (2022). Factors influencing research productivity in higher education institutions in Africa: A comprehensive review. *AAS Open Research*, *4*, 26. PMID: 34368619

Zhaksylyk, A., Zimba, O., Yessirkepov, M., & Kocyigit, B. F. (2023). Ethical Education challenge: where we are as well as where we are going. 38(47) of the Journal of Korean Medical Science.

KEY TERMS AND DEFINITIONS

Bureaucratic Obstacles: Research obstacles are created by certain management procedures as well as laws that prevent researchers from carrying out studies as well as efficiently disseminating research findings. Research teams encounter challenges due to a combination of ambiguous guideline principles, complex approval procedures, as well as excessive documentation.

Ethical Standards: establishes guidelines that control the course of research as well as guarantee that scientists behave morally as well as responsibly. These standards promote confidence in the research process as well as aid in defending the rights as well as welfare of research participants.

Honesty research: Throughout research operations, study participants must adhere to professional norms as well as ethical values. Scientists must uphold dependability via a dedication to accountability as well as openness from data collection to publishing in order to comply through research regulations.

Organizational culture: Members' conduct is influenced by the organization's common values, beliefs, as well as procedures. An excellent way to learn about it is to combine the nation's creativity through organizationally good collaboration.

Research performance: The growth of research activity is often gauged by the number as well as caliber of publications, grants, as well as knowledge contributions in a particular topic; these factors also show how effective researchers as well as research organizations are.

Structural Equations Modeling (SEM): SEM is a statistical method that uses factor analysis as well as multiple regression analysis to look at complicated correlations between seen as well as hidden variables. It enables researchers to assess the structural link among variables while considering measurement mistakes. In the social sciences, SEM is typically used to assess theoretical hypotheses and models that involve more than one outcome that is related to another.

Compilation of References

Abd-Elsalam, K. A., & Abdel-Momen, S. M. (2023). *Artificial Intelligence's Development and Challenges in Scientific Writing*. Egyptian Journal of Agricultural Research., DOI: 10.21608/ejar.2023.220363.1414

Abubakari, M. S. (2024). Overviewing the Maze of Research Integrity and False Positives Within AI-Enabled Detectors: Grammarly Dilemma in Academic Writing. In Mutawa, A. (Ed.), *Impacts of Generative AI on the Future of Research and Education* (pp. 335–366). IGI Global., DOI: 10.4018/979-8-3693-0884-4.ch013

Abubakari, M. S. (2025). Overviewing Biases in Generative AI-Powered Models in the Arabic Language: AI Fairness for Sustainable Future. In Syafrudin, M., Fitriyani, N. L., & Anshari, M. (Eds.), *Achieving Sustainability in Multi-Industry Settings With AI* (pp. 361–390). IGI Global., DOI: 10.4018/979-8-3373-2530-9.ch013

Adetayo, A. J. (2023). Artificial intelligence chatbots in academic libraries: The rise of ChatGPT. *Library Hi Tech News*, *40*(3), 18–21. DOI: 10.1108/LHTN-01-2023-0007

AI4K12. (2021). *AI4K12 initiative: Developing national guidelines for teaching AI in K–12*. Association for the Advancement of Artificial Intelligence. https://ai4k12.org

Akgün, S., & Greenhow, C. (2021). Artificial intelligence in education: Addressing ethical challenges in K-12 settings. *AI and Ethics*, *2*(3), 431–440. DOI: 10.1007/s43681-021-00096-7

Al Balushi, K. (2025). Using AI-powered grammar correction tools to support ESL students' writing skills development. In *Optimizing research techniques and learning strategies with digital technologies* (pp. 1–16). IGI Global., DOI: 10.4018/979-8-3693-7863-2.ch012

Al Buraiki, S. (2025). A qualitative SWOT analysis study of the integration of AI technologies into higher education institutions in the Sultanate of Oman. International Journal of Learning, Teaching and Educational Research, 24(4). https://www.ijlter.org/index.php/ijlter/article/view/12649

Al Manji, K. M., Hussain, M., & Hussain, M. (2024). Artificial intelligence in Oman's government schools: A comprehensive study of its adoption and impact on teachers and students at secondary level. International Journal of Research and Scientific Innovation. https://rsisinternational.org/journals/ijrsi/articles/artificial-intelligence-in-omans-government-schools-a-comprehensive-study-of-its-adoption-and-impact-on-teachers-and-students-at-secondary-level/

Al Rashdi, H., & Elgeddawy, M. (2025). Artificial intelligence as a catalyst for sustainable quality education: The case of Oman. In Awwad, B. (Ed.), *AI and IoT: Driving business success and sustainability in the digital age* (pp. 1–15). Springer., DOI: 10.1007/978-3-031-92240-4_70

Albayati, H., Alistarbadi, N., & Rho, J. J. (2023). Evaluating engagement choices in the NFT Metaverse via the lens of the Theory of Planned Behavior (TPB). Telematics as well as Informatics Reports, 10, 100045.

Aldeman, N. L. S., de Sá Urtiga Aita, K. M., Machado, V. P., da Mata Sousa, L. C. D., Coelho, A. G. B., da Silva, A. S., da Silva Mendes, A. P., de Oliveira Neres, F. J., & do Monte, S. J. H. (2021). Smartpathk: A platform for teaching glomerulopathies using machine learning. *BMC Medical Education*, *21*(1). Advance online publication. DOI: 10.1186/s12909-021-02680-1 PMID: 33926437

Aldosari, S. A. M. (2020). The future of higher education in the light of artificial intelligence transformations. *International Journal of Higher Education*, *9*(3), 145–151. DOI: 10.5430/ijhe.v9n3p145

Alemu, D. K., & Mensah, J. T. (2023). Contextual challenges in AGI deployment across sub-Saharan Africa: Cultural epistemologies and pedagogical alignment. *African Journal of Educational Technology*, *5*(2), 74–92.

Algahtani, A. (2024). A COMPARATIVE STUDY OF AI-BASED EDUCATIONAL TOOLS: EVALUATING USER INTERFACE EXPERIENCE AND EDUCATIONAL IMPACT. *Journal of Theoretical and Applied Information Technology*, *15*(5). www.jatit.org

Ali, A., Deuter, A., & Wehmeier, L. (2023). Personalized Learning in Automation: A 3D AIBased Approach. *Proceedings - Frontiers in Education Conference, FIE*. https://doi.org/DOI: 10.1109/FIE58773.2023.10343228

Al-Kurdi, O., & Eldabi, T. (2018). Knowledge sharing in higher education institutions: A systematic review. *Journal of Enterprise Information Management*, *31*(2), 226–246. DOI: 10.1108/JEIM-09-2017-0129

ALLEA. (2023). The European Code of Conduct for Research Integrity – Revised Edition 2023. ALLEA I All European Academies. DOI: 10.26356/ECOC

Al-Mughairi, H. & Bhaskar, P. (2024). Exploring the factors affecting the adoption AI techniques in higher education: insights from teachers' perspectives on ChatGPT, *Journal of Research in Innovative Teaching & Learning*, Vol. ahead-of-print No. ahead-of-print. https://doi.org/.DOI: 10.1108/JRIT-09-2023-0129

Alrawashdeh, G. S., Fyffe, S., Azevedo, R. F. L., & Castillo, N. M. (2024). Exploring the impact of personalized and adaptive learning technologies on reading literacy: A global meta-analysis. *Educational Research Review*, *42*. Advance online publication. DOI: 10.1016/j.edurev.2023.100587

Anderson, N., Belavy, D. L., Perle, S. M., Hendricks, S., Hespanhol, L., Verhagen, E., & Memon, A. R. (2023). AI did not write this manuscript, or did it? Can we trick the AI text detector into generated texts? The potential future of ChatGPT and AI in Sports & Exercise Medicine manuscript generation. *BMJ Open Sport & Exercise Medicine*, *9*(1), e001568. DOI: 10.1136/bmjsem-2023-001568 PMID: 36816423

Awad O., S., Mohamed, Y., & Shaheen, R. (2022). Applications of Artificial Intelligence in Education. *Al-Azkiyaa - International Journal of Language and Education*, *1*(1), 71–81. https://doi.org/DOI: 10.33102/alazkiyaa.v1i1.10

Azhar, A. (2025). "Framework for Ethical AI integration in K-12 Education: Risks, Responsibilities and Roadmap", TIJER International Research Journal (www.TIJER .org), ISSN:2349-9249, Vol.12, Issue 7, 227-b236, July-2025, Available: https://tijer .org/TIJER/papers/TIJER2507139.pdf

Bahammam, A. S., Trabelsi, K., Pandi-Perumal, S. R., Jahrami, H., & Bahammam, A. (2023). Adapting to the impact of AI in scientific writing: Balancing benefits and drawbacks while developing policies and regulations. *Journal of Nature and Science of Medicine*, *6*(3). https://orcid.org/0000-0003-2623-9557

Bain, L. E., Tchuisseu-Kwangoua, L. A., Adeagbo, O., Nkfusai, N. C., Amu, H., Saah, F. I., & Kombe, F. (2022). Fostering Ethical Education in Sub-Saharan Africa: Challenges, Opportunities, as well as Recommendations. 43(1) of the Pan AfEECan Medical Journal.

Baker, R. S., & Hawn, M. A. (2021). Algorithmic bias in education. *International Journal of Artificial Intelligence in Education*, *32*(4), 557–589. DOI: 10.1007/s40593-021-00285-9

Balaha, H. M., & Saafan, M. M. (2021). Automatic exam correction framework (AECF) for the MCQS, essays, and equations matching. *IEEE Access : Practical Innovations, Open Solutions, 9*, 32368–32389. DOI: 10.1109/ACCESS.2021.3060940

Barron, P. (2008). Education and talent management: Implications for the hospitality industry. *International Journal of Contemporary Hospitality Management, 20*(7), 730–742. DOI: 10.1108/09596110810897583

Bayne, S., & Jandrić, P. (2017). Posthumanism and Higher Education. *International Journal of Educational Technology in Higher Education, 14*(1), 1–13.

Bers, M. U. (2020). *Coding as a playground: Programming and computational thinking in the early childhood classroom*. Routledge.

Bertram Gallant, T., & Rettinger, D. (2025). *The opposite of cheating: Teaching for integrity in the age of AI*. University of Oklahoma Press.

Bhaskar, R. (1998). *Reclaiming Reality: A Critical Introduction to Contemporary Philosophy*. Verso.

Biesta, G. (2010). *Good Education in an Age of Measurement: Ethics, Politics, Democracy*. Routledge.

Binns, R. (2018). On the interpretation of ethical issues in AI and the role of human agency. *Journal of AI Ethics, 5*(3), 233–245.

Bishop, C. M. (2006). *Pattern recognition and machine learning*. Springer.

Bonneton-Botté, N., Fleury, S., Girard, N., Le Magadou, M., Cherbonnier, A., Renault, M., Anquetil, E., & Jamet, E. (2020). Can tablet apps support the learning of handwriting? An investigation of learning outcomes in kindergarten classroom. *Computers & Education, 151*. Advance online publication. DOI: 10.1016/j.compedu.2020.103831

Borenstein, J., & Howard, A. (2021). Emerging challenges in AI and the need for AI ethics education. *AI and Ethics, 1*(1), 61–65. DOI: 10.1007/s43681-020-00002-7

Bostrom, N., & Sandberg, A. (2009). Cognitive Enhancement: Methods, Ethics, Regulatory Challenges. *Science and Engineering Ethics, 15*(3), 311–341.

Boulay, D. B. (2023). *Artificial Intelligence in Education and Ethics, Handbook of Open*. Distance and Digital Education., DOI: 10.1007/978-981-19-2080-6_6

Bouter, L. (2024). Why the Ethical Education Challenge is essential as well as how it may be made better. *Accountability in Research, 31*(8), 1277–1286. PMID: 36888916

Braidotti, R. (2019). *Posthuman knowledge*. Polity Press.

Camilleri, M. A. (2021). Evaluating service quality and performance of higher education institutions: A systematic review and a post-COVID-19 outlook. *International Journal of Quality and Service Sciences, 13*(2), 268–281. DOI: 10.1108/IJQSS-03-2020-0034

Carobene, A., Padoan, A., Cabitza, F., Banfi, G., & Plebani, M. (2024). Rising adoption of artificial intelligence in scientific publishing: Evaluating the role, risks, and ethical implications in paper drafting and review process. [CCLM]. *Clinical Chemistry and Laboratory Medicine, 62*(5), 835–843. DOI: 10.1515/cclm-2023-1136 PMID: 38019961

Carpenter, D. D., Harding, T. S., & Finelli, C. J. (2010). Using research to identify academic dishonesty deterrents among engineering undergraduates. *International Journal of Engineering Education, 26*(5), 1156–1165.

Çelik, F., & Baturay, M. H. (2024). Technology and innovation in shaping the future of education. *Smart Learning Environments, 11*(1). Advance online publication. DOI: 10.1186/s40561-024-00339-0

Celik, I. (2023). 'Towards Intelligent-TPACK: An empirical study on teachers' professional knowledge to ethically integrate artificial intelligence (AI)-based tools into education'. *Computers in Human Behavior, 138*. Advance online publication. DOI: 10.1016/j.chb.2022.107468

Cheng, D., Li, M., & Lee, T. (2025). Leveraging ChatGPT for research writing: An exploration of ESL graduate students' practices [Article]. *Computers and Composition, 76*, 102934. Advance online publication. DOI: 10.1016/j.compcom.2025.102934

Chen, L., Chen, P., & Lin, Z. (2020). Artificial intelligence in education: A review. *IEEE Access : Practical Innovations, Open Solutions, 8*, 75264–75278. DOI: 10.1109/ACCESS.2020.2988510

Chen, Z., Chen, C., Yang, G., He, X., Chi, X., Zeng, Z., & Chen, X. (2024). The difficulty of ethical education in the age of AI: Problems as well as solutions. *Medicine, 103*(27), e38811. PMID: 38968491

Chhabra, A., Masalkovaite, K., & Mohapatra, P. (2021). An overview of fairness in clustering. *IEEE Access : Practical Innovations, Open Solutions, 9*, 130698–130720. DOI: 10.1109/ACCESS.2021.3114099

Chiu, T. K. F., Xia, Q., Zhou, X., Chai, C. S., & Cheng, M. (2023). Systematic literature review on opportunities, challenges, and future research recommendations of artificial intelligence in education. *Computers and Education: Artificial Intelligence, 4*. Advance online publication. DOI: 10.1016/j.caeai.2022.100118

Chu, H.-C., Hwang, G.-H., Tu, Y.-F., & Yang, K.-H. (2023). Roles and research trends of artificial intelligence in higher education: A systematic review of the top 50 most-cited articles. *Australasian Journal of Educational Technology*. Advance online publication. DOI: 10.14742/ajet.7526

Contrino, M. F., Reyes-Millán, M., Vázquez-Villegas, P., & Membrillo-Hernández, J. (2024). Using an adaptive learning tool to improve student performance and satisfaction in online and face-to-face education for a more personalized approach. *Smart Learning Environments*, *11*(1). Advance online publication. DOI: 10.1186/s40561-024-00292-y

Cope, B., Kalantzis, M., & Searsmith, D. (2020). Artificial intelligence for education: Knowledge and its assessment in AI-enabled learning ecologies. *Educational Philosophy and Theory*, *53*(12), 1229–1245. DOI: 10.1080/00131857.2020.1728732

Corrêa, N. K., Galvão, C., Santos, J. W., Del Pino, C., Pinto, E. P., Barbosa, C., Massmann, D., Mambrini, R., Galvão, L., Terem, E., & de Oliveira, N. (2023). Worldwide AI ethics: A review of 200 guidelines and recommendations for AI governance. *Patterns (New York, N.Y.)*, *4*(10), 100857. DOI: 10.1016/j.patter.2023.100857 PMID: 37876898

Crawford, K. (2021). *Atlas of AI: Mapping the terrain of artificial intelligence*. Yale University Press.

Cui, W., Xue, Z., & Thai, K. P. (2018, November). Performance comparison of an AI-based adaptive learning system in China. In 2018 Chinese automation congress (CAC) (pp. 3170-3175). IEEE.

Dastin, J. (2018). Data feminism and the politics of algorithmic transparency. *Feminist Media Studies*, *18*(2), 1–19.

Deng, W. (2022). Utilization of psychological contract theory in the administration of higher education. *Psychiatria Danubina*, *34*(suppl 5), 50.

Department of Education. Australia. (2023). Australian framework for generative artificial intelligence (AI) in schools. https://www.education.gov.au/schooling/resources/australian-framework-generative-artificial-intelligence-ai-schools

Dergaa, I., Chamari, K., Zmijewski, P., & Ben Saad, H. (2023). From human writing to artificial intelligence generated text: Examining the prospects and potential threats of ChatGPT in academic writing. *Biology of Sport*, *40*(2), 615–622. DOI: 10.5114/BIOLSPORT.2023.125623 PMID: 37077800

Đerić, E., Frank, D., & Vuković, D. (2025). Exploring the Ethical Implications of Using Generative AI Tools in Higher Education [Article]. *Informatics (MDPI), 12*(2), 36. Advance online publication. DOI: 10.3390/informatics12020036

Diakopoulos, N. (2016). Accountability in algorithmic decision making. *Communications of the ACM, 59*(2), 56–62.

Dignum, V. (2021). Responsible artificial intelligence: How to develop and use AI in a responsible way [Open-access essay/chapter]. *Law, Regulation and Ethics (Online).* DOI: 10.14324/LRE.19.1.01

Discover Artificial Intelligence. (2025). Artificial intelligence-based personalised learning in education: A systematic literature review. https://link.springer.com/article/10.1007/s44163-025-00598-x

Domingos, P. (2012). A few useful things to know about machine learning. *Communications of the ACM, 55*(10), 78–87. DOI: 10.1145/2347736.2347755

Dresp-Langley, B. (2022). Neurotechnologies in education: Trends, research, and ethical challenges. *The European Journal of Neuroscience, 56*(2), 254–268.

Druga, S. (2018). *Growing up with AI: Cognimates and child–AI interaction.* MIT Press.

Druga, S., Vu, S., Likhith, E., & Qiu, T. (2019). Inclusive AI literacy for kids around the world. *In Proceedings of ACM Fablearn conference (Fablearn'19).* ACM, New York, NY, USA, *Article 4,* 8 *pages.* DOI: <ALIGNMENT.qj></ALIGNMENT>10.475/123_4

Education. (2025). The impact of artificial intelligence (AI) on students' academic development. Education, 15(3), 343. https://www.mdpi.com/2227-7102/15/3/343

ElHassan, B. T., & Arabi, A. A. (2025). Ethical forethoughts on the use of artificial intelligence in medicine. *International Journal of Ethics and Systems, 41*(1), 35–44. DOI: 10.1108/IJOES-08-2023-0190

Engeström, Y. (1987). *Learning by expanding: An activity-theoretical approach to developmental research.* Orienta-Konsultit.

Essa, S. G., Celik, T., & Human-Hendricks, N. E. (2023). Personalized adaptive learning technologies based on machine learning techniques to identify learning styles: A systematic literature review. *IEEE Access : Practical Innovations, Open Solutions, 11*, 48392–48409. DOI: 10.1109/ACCESS.2023.3276439

European Commission. (2019). Policy and Investment Recommendations for Trustworthy Artificial Intelligence. High-Level Expert Group on Artificial Intelligence. https://www.europarl.europa.eu/cmsdata/196378/AI%20HLEG_Policy%20and%20Investment%20Recommendations.pdf

European Commission. (2021). *Digital Education Action Plan (2021–2027)*. Publications Office of the European Union.

European Commission. (2021). *Proposal for a Regulation laying down harmonised rules on artificial intelligence (Artificial Intelligence Act)*. Publications Office of the European Union.

European Network for Academic Integrity. (2023). ENAI recommendations on the ethical use of artificial intelligence in education. *International Journal for Educational Integrity*, *19*, 133. Advance online publication. DOI: 10.1007/s40979-023-00133-4

Feenberg, A. (1999). *Questioning Technology*. Routledge.

Feigenbaum, E. A. (1977). *The art of artificial intelligence*. Stanford University.

Feng, Z., Hu, G., Li, B., & Wang, J. (2025). Unleashing the power of ChatGPT in finance research: Opportunities and challenges [Article]. *Financial Innovation*, *11*(1), 93. Advance online publication. DOI: 10.1186/s40854-025-00770-3

Fikri, Yahya, & Rhalma, Mohamed. Artificial Intelligence (AI) in Early Childhood Education (ECE): Do Effects and Interactions Matter? International Journal of Religion: Politics, Sociology, Culture, 2024, 5 (11), pp.7536-7545. ff10.61707/y74fv875ff. ffhal-04701470f Yang, W. (2022). Artificial intelligence education for young children. *Computers & Education: Artificial Intelligence*, *3*, 100061. DOI: 10.1016/j.caeai.2022.100061

Floridi, L. (2013). *The Ethics of Information*. Oxford University Press.

Floridi, L. (2019). Establishing the rules for building trustworthy AI. *Nature Machine Intelligence*, *1*(6), 261–262. DOI: 10.1038/s42256-019-0055-y

Floridi, L., Cowls, J., Beltrametti, M., Chatila, R., Chazerand, P., Dignum, V., & Vayena, E. (2018). AI4People—An ethical framework for a good AI society. *Minds and Machines*, *28*(4), 689–707. DOI: 10.1007/s11023-018-9482-5

Freyer, N., Groß, D., & Lipprandt, M. (2024). The ethical requirement of explainability for AI-DSS in healthcare: A systematic review of reasons. *BMC Medical Ethics*, *25*(1), 104. DOI: 10.1186/s12910-024-01103-2 PMID: 39354512

Fricker, M. (2007). *Epistemic injustice: Power and the ethics of knowing*. Oxford University Press.

Frontiers in Education. (2025). Evaluating the impact of AI on critical thinking skills among higher education students. https://www.frontiersin.org/journals/education/articles/10.3389/feduc.2025.1

Fukuda-Parr, S., & Gibbons, E. (2021). Emerging Consensus on 'Ethical AI': Human Rights Critique of Stakeholder Guidelines. *Global Policy*, *12*(S6), 32–44. DOI: 10.1111/1758-5899.12965

Gadanidis, G. (2017). Artificial intelligence, computational thinking, and mathematics education [P]. *International Journal of Information and Learning Technology*, *34*(2), 133–139. DOI: 10.1108/IJILT-09-2016-0048

Galindo-Domínguez, H., Delgado, N., Campo, L., & Losada, D. (2024). Relationship between teachers' digital competence and attitudes towards artificial intelligence in education. *International Journal of Educational Research*, *126*, 102381. Advance online publication. DOI: 10.1016/j.ijer.2024.102381

Gao, J., & Wang, D. (2024). Quantifying the use and potential benefits of artificial intelligence in scientific research. *Nature Human Behaviour*, *8*(12), 2281–2292. DOI: 10.1038/s41562-024-02020-5 PMID: 39394445

Gao, R., Merzdorf, H. E., Anwar, S., Hipwell, M. C., & Srinivasa, A. R. (2024). Automatic assessment of text-based responses in post-secondary education: A systematic review. *Computers and Education: Artificial Intelligence*, *6*. Advance online publication. DOI: 10.1016/j.caeai.2024.100206

García-González, J. M., Gutiérrez Gómez-Calcerrada, S., Solera Hernández, E., & Ríos-Aguilar, S. (2021). Barriers in higher education: An examination of students through disabilities in Spain using both views as well as discourse analysis. *Disability & Society*, *36*(4), 579–595.

García-López, I. M., & Trujillo-Liñán, L. (2025). Ethical and regulatory challenges of Generative AI in education: A systematic review. *Frontiers in Education*.

Gayed, J. M. (2025). Educators' perspective on artificial intelligence: Equity, preparedness, and development. *Cogent Education*, *12*(1), 2447169. Advance online publication. DOI: 10.1080/2331186X.2024.2447169

Gennari, R., Melonio, A., Pellegrino, M. A., & D'Angelo, M. 2023. How to Playfully Teach AI to Young Learners: A Systematic Literature Review. In *Proceedings of the 15th Biannual Conference of the Italian SIGCHI Chapter (CHItaly '23)*. Association for Computing Machinery, New York, NY, USA, Article 1, 1–9. https://doi.org/DOI: 10.1145/3605390.3605393

Gershenfeld, N. (2020). AI for emotional learning and moral pedagogy. *Journal of Educational Technology*, *46*(3), 198–209.

Ghanad, A. (2023). A summary of quantitative research approaches. International Journal of Multidisciplinary Research as well as Analysis, 6(08), 3794–3803.

Giuggioli, G., & Pellegrini, M. M. (2023). Artificial intelligence as an enabler for entrepreneurs: A systematic literature review and an agenda for future research. *International Journal of Entrepreneurial Behaviour & Research*, *29*(4), 816–837. DOI: 10.1108/IJEBR-05-2021-0426

Gligorea, I., Cioca, M., Oancea, R., Gorski, A. T., Gorski, H., & Tudorache, P. (2023a). Adaptive learning using artificial intelligence in e-learning: A literature review. *Education Sciences*, *13*(12). Advance online publication. DOI: 10.3390/educsci13121216

Global Partnership on Artificial Intelligence (GPAI). (2022). *Responsible AI Working Group Reports*. GPAI Secretariat.

Godemann, J., & Moon, J. (2014). Higher education and sustainable development: Exploring possibilities for organizational change. *Accounting, Auditing & Accountability Journal*, *27*(2), 218–233. DOI: 10.1108/AAAJ-12-2013-1553

Goertzel, B. (2014). Artificial General Intelligence: Concept, State of the Art, and Future Prospects. *Journal of Artificial General Intelligence*, *5*(1), 1–48.

Goksel, N., & Bozkurt, A. (2019). Artificial intelligence in Education: current insights and future perspectives. In Sisman-Ugur, S., & Kurubacak, G. (Eds.), *Handbook of Research on Learning in the Age of Transhumanism* (pp. 224–236). IGI Global., DOI: 10.4018/978-1-5225-8431-5.ch014

Goreta, G., Wibawa, B., & Siregar, E. (2024). Analysis of artificial intelligence ethics & policy in education. In *Proceedings of the 7th International Conference on Learning Innovation and Quality Education (ICLIQE 2023)*. Atlantis Press. DOI: 10.2991/978-2-38476-301-6_92

Granström, M., & Oppi, P. (2025). Assessing teachers' readiness and perceived usefulness of AI in education: An Estonian perspective. *Frontiers in Education*, *10*, 1622240. Advance online publication. DOI: 10.3389/feduc.2025.1622240

Grassini, S. (2023). Shaping the Future of Education: Exploring the potential and consequences of AI and ChatGPT in educational settings. *Education Sciences*, *13*(7), 692. DOI: 10.3390/educsci13070692

Guan, L., & Zhang, Y. (2025). Pre-service teachers preparedness for AI-integrated education: An investigation from perceptions, capabilities, and teachers' identity changes. *Computers and Education Open*, *6*, 100149. Advance online publication. DOI: 10.1016/j.caeo.2024.100149

Gunawan, K. D. H., Liliasari, L., Kaniawati, I., & Setiawan, W. (2021). Implementation of competency enhancement program for science teachers assisted by artificial intelligence in designing HOTS-based integrated science learning. *Jurnal Penelitian Dan Pembelajaran IPA*, *7*(1), 55. DOI: 10.30870/jppi.v7i1.8655

Hao, K. (2021). Can artificial intelligence ever truly understand human emotions? *MIT Technology Review*.

Hao, N., Li, Y., Lu, Y., & Liu, K. (2024). Artificial intelligence-aided digital twin design: A systematic review. *Preprints*.

Haseski, H. I. (2019). What do Turkish pre-service teachers think about artificial intelligence? *International Journal of Computer Science Education in Schools*, *3*(2), 3–23. DOI: 10.21585/ijcses.v3i2.55

Hawkins, W., & Mittelstadt, B. (2023). The ethical ambiguity of AI data enrichment: Measuring gaps in research ethics norms and practices. *2023 ACM Conference on Fairness Accountability and Transparency*, 261–270. DOI: 10.1145/3593013.3593995

Heath, C., & Luff, P. (2019). Cross-cultural governance models in AI-driven education. *Journal of Educational Technology & Society*, *22*(4), 212–229.

Henry, J., Hernalesteen, A., & Collard, A.-S. (2021). Teaching artificial intelligence to K–12 through a role-playing game questioning the intelligence concept. *Kunstliche Intelligenz*, *35*(2), 171–179. DOI: 10.1007/s13218-021-00733-7

Holmes, W., & Miao, F. (2023). *Guidance for generative AI in education and research*. UNESCO Publishing. https://www.unesco.org/en/articles/guidance-generative-ai-education-and-research

Holmes, W., Bialik, M., & Fadel, C. (2019). *Artificial intelligence in education: Promises and implications for teaching and learning*. Center for Curriculum Redesign.

Holmes, W., Porayska-Pomsta, K., Holstein, K., Sutherland, E., Baker, R. S. J., Shum, S. B., Santos, O. C., Rodrigo, M. T., Cukurova, M., Bittencourt, I. I., & Koedinger, K. R. (2021). Ethics of AI in education: Towards a community-wide framework. *International Journal of Artificial Intelligence in Education*. Advance online publication. DOI: 10.1007/s40593-021-00239-1

Holmes, W., & Tuomi, I. (2022). State of the art and practice in AI in education. *European Journal of Education, 57*, 542–570. DOI: 10.1111/ejed.12533

Holstein, K., & Doroudi, S. (2021). Equity and artificial intelligence in education: Will "AIEd" amplify or alleviate inequities in education? *arXiv preprint*. /arXiv.2104.12920DOI: 10.48550

Holstein, K., McLaren, B. M., & Aleven, V. (2019). Co-designing a real-time classroom orchestration tool to support teacher–AI complementarity. *Journal of Learning Analytics, 6*(2), 27–52. DOI: 10.18608/jla.2019.62.3

Holstein, K., Wortman Vaughan, J., Daumé, H.III, Dudík, M., & Wallach, H. (2022). Improving fairness in machine learning systems: What do practitioners need? *ACM Transactions on Interactive Intelligent Systems, 12*(4), 41. Advance online publication. DOI: 10.1145/3518289

Hooshyar, D., Pedaste, M., Yang, Y., Malva, L., Hwang, G., Wang, M., Lim, H., & Delev, D. (2021). From gaming to computational thinking: An adaptive educational computer game-based learning approach. *Journal of Educational Computing Research, 59*(3), 383–409.

Hosseini, M., Rasmussen, L. M., & Resnik, D. B. (2024). Using AI to write scholarly publications. *Accountability in Research, 31*(7), 715–723. DOI: 10.1080/08989621.2023.2168535 PMID: 36697395

Hosseini, M., & Resnik, D. B. (2025). Guidance needed for using artificial intelligence to screen journal submissions for misconduct. *Research Ethics, 21*(1), 1–8. DOI: 10.1177/17470161241254052 PMID: 39810931

Hosseini, M., Resnik, D. B., & Holmes, K. (2023). The ethics of disclosing the use of artificial intelligence tools in writing scholarly manuscripts. *Research Ethics, 19*(4), 449–465. DOI: 10.1177/17470161231180449 PMID: 39749232

Huang, A. Y. Q., Lu, O. H. T., & Yang, S. J. H. (2023). 'Effects of artificial intelligence–enabled personalized recommendations on learners' learning engagement, motivation, and outcomes in a flipped classroom'. *Computers & Education, 194*. Advance online publication. DOI: 10.1016/j.compedu.2022.104684

Huang, J., Shen, G., & Ren, X. (2021). Connotation Analysis and Paradigm Shift of Teaching Design under Artificial Intelligence Technology. [iJET]. *International Journal of Emerging Technologies in Learning, 16*(05), 73. DOI: 10.3991/ijet.v16i05.20287

Huang, Y.-H. (2024). Exploring the implementation of artificial intelligence applications among academic libraries in Taiwan. *Library Hi Tech*, *42*(3), 885–905. DOI: 10.1108/LHT-03-2022-0159

Huang, Y., Patel, R., & Gómez, L. (2024). Closed-loop neuroadaptive AGI systems: Prototyping cognitive-interactive classrooms for real-time pedagogical modulation. *Journal of Neural Engineering and Intelligent Learning Systems*, *18*(1), 33–52.

Huang, Y., Zhang, J., Chen, X., & Lam, A. H. F. (2024). From simulation to prediction: Enhancing digital twins with advanced generative AI technologies. *IEEE Transactions on Learning Technologies*.

Hussain, A. (2023). Use of artificial intelligence in the library services: Prospects and challenges. *Library Hi Tech News*, *40*(2), 15–17. DOI: 10.1108/LHTN-11-2022-0125

Hwang, G. J., Sung, H. Y., Chang, S. C., & Huang, X. C. (2020). 'A fuzzy expert system-based adaptive learning approach to improving students' learning performances by considering affective and cognitive factors'. *Computers and Education: Artificial Intelligence*, *1*. Advance online publication. DOI: 10.1016/j.caeai.2020.100003

Hwang, S. Il, Lim, J. S., Lee, R. W., Matsui, Y., Iguchi, T., Hiraki, T., & Ahn, H. (2023). Is ChatGPT a "Fire of Prometheus" for Non-Native English-Speaking Researchers in Academic Writing? *Korean Journal of Radiology*, *24*(10), 952–959. DOI: 10.3348/kjr.2023.0773 PMID: 37793668

ICESCO. (2024, January 18). Signing of agreement to establish ICESCO chair for AI ethics in Sultanate of Oman. https://icesco.org/en/2024/01/18/signing-of-agreement-to-establish-icesco-chair-for-ai-ethics-in-sultanate-of-oman/

Ienca, M., & Andorno, R. (2017). Towards new human rights in the age of neuroscience and neurotechnology. *Life Sciences, Society and Policy*, *13*(1), 1–27.

Iliu ă, M. E. (2024). Digital twin: A review of the evolution from concept to application. *Applied Sciences (Basel, Switzerland)*, *14*(13), 5454. DOI: 10.3390/app14135454

Imanova, M. (2025). Global Evolution of Artificial Intelligence: Navigating Ethics, Policy, and Innovation for a Sustainable Future, *Journal of Information Systems Engineering and Management* 2025, 10(41s) e-ISSN: 2468-4376.

Ingley, S. J., & Pack, A. (2023). Leveraging AI tools to develop the writer rather than the writing. DOI: 10.1016/j.tree.2023.05.007

Isave, S (2025). Ethics of Artificial Intelligence in Education, *International Journal of Innovative Science and Research Technology,* Volume 10, Issue 1, January – 2025. https://doi.org/.DOI: 10.5281/zenodo.14769407

Izenstark, A., & Leahy, K. L. (2015). Google classroom for librarians: Features and opportunities. *Library Hi Tech News*, *32*(9), 1–3. DOI: 10.1108/LHTN-05-2015-0039

Jain, K., & Raghuram, J. N. V. (2023). Unlocking potential: The impact of AI on education technology. *Multidisciplinary Reviews*, *7*(3), 2024049. DOI: 10.31893/multirev.2024049

Jankovskis, D. (2023). Digital twins and e-learning: Navigating challenges and opportunities. In *Digital transformation, virtual reality and simulation in education* (pp. 123–140). Springer.

JeBO, A. T., Ng, V., & Tay, L. (2021). A summary of significant advancements in Likert scale development from 1995 to 2019. *Frontiers in Psychology*, *12*, 637547.

Jin, Y., Echeverria, V., Gašević, D., & Martinez-Maldonado, R. (2024). Generative AI in higher education: A global perspective of institutional adoption policies and guidelines. *Computers and Education Open*, *7*, •••. https://www.sciencedirect.com/science/article/pii/S2666920X24001516

Jones, D., Snider, C., Nassehi, A., Yon, J., & Hicks, B. (2023). Characterising the digital twin: A systematic literature review. *CIRP Journal of Manufacturing Science and Technology*, *39*, 1–15.

Jukiewicz, M. (2024). The future of grading programming assignments in education: The role of ChatGPT in automating the assessment and feedback process. *Thinking Skills and Creativity*, *52*. Advance online publication. DOI: 10.1016/j.tsc.2024.101522

Kabudi, T., Pappas, I., & Olsen, D. H. (2021). AI-enabled adaptive learning systems: A systematic mapping of the literature. *Computers and Education: Artificial Intelligence*, *2*. Advance online publication. DOI: 10.1016/j.caeai.2021.100017

Kahn, K., & Winters, N. (2021). Constructionism and AI: A history and possible futures. *British Journal of Educational Technology*, *52*(3), 1130–1142. DOI: 10.1111/bjet.13088

Kamalov, F., Santandreu Calonge, D., & Gurrib, I. (2023). New era of artificial intelligence in education: Towards a sustainable multifaceted revolution. *Sustainability*, *15*(16). Advance online publication. DOI: 10.3390/su151612451

Karakas, F., Sarigollu, E., & Manisaligil, A. (2013). The use of benevolent leadership development to advance principles of responsible management education [p]. *Journal of Management Development*, *32*(8), 801–822. DOI: 10.1108/JMD-08-2011-0102.R1

Karkoulian, S., Sayegh, N., & Sayegh, N. (2024). ChatGPT unveiled: Understanding perceptions of academic integrity in higher education—A qualitative approach. *Journal of Academic Ethics*. Advance online publication. DOI: 10.1007/s10805-024-09543-6

Karya Bakti, I., Ayuningtias, Y., Mokhamad, S., & Hammis, S. (2023). The role of artificial intelligence in education: A systematic literature review. *International Journal of Educational Research*, *45*(3), 200–215.

Kaufman, M., Pham, N., & Levin, J. (2025). Evaluating the utility of using ChatGPT 3.5 to generate research ideas for non-operative spine medicine [Article]. *Journal of Medical Artificial Intelligence*, *8*, 30. Advance online publication. DOI: 10.21037/jmai-24-480

Kavitha, V., & Lohani, R. (2019). A critical study on the use of artificial intelligence, e-learning technology and tools to enhance the learners experience. *Cluster Computing*, *22*, 6985–6989.

Kayyali, M. (2024). Future Possibilities and Challenges of AI in Education. In *Advances in educational technologies and instructional design book series* (pp. 118–137). https://doi.org/DOI: 10.4018/979-8-3693-1351-0.ch006

Khalid, K., Iivari, N., Kinnula, M., & Sharma, S. (2022). Familiarizing children with artificial intelligence. *Proceedings of the International Conference on Entertainment and Media in the Ubiquitous Era*. https://doi.org/DOI: 10.1145/3569219.3569390

Khan, A. A., Badshah, S., Liang, P., Waseem, M., Khan, B., Ahmad, A., Fahmideh, M., Niazi, M., & Akbar, M. A. (2022). Ethics of AI: A Systematic Literature Review of Principles and Challenges. The International Conference on Evaluation and Assessment in Software Engineering 2022, 383–392. DOI: 10.1145/3530019.3531329

Khosravi, H.. (2024). Perspectives on generalizability, transparency and ethical use of predictive models in education. *Computers in Human Behavior Reports*. Advance online publication. DOI: 10.1016/j.chbr.2024.101123

Khosravi, H., Buckingham Shum, S., Chen, G., Conati, C., Tsai, Y.-S., Kay, J., Knight, S., Martinez-Maldonado, R., Sadiq, S., & Gašević, D. (2022). Explainable artificial intelligence in education. *Computers & Education: Artificial Intelligence*, *3*, 100074. Advance online publication. DOI: 10.1016/j.caeai.2022.100074

Kickmeier-Rust, M. D., & Holzinger, A. (2019). Interactive ant colony optimization to support adaptation in serious games. *International Journal of Serious Games*, *6*(3), 37–50. DOI: 10.17083/ijsg.v6i3.308

Kim, H. S., Kim, N. Y., & Cha, Y. (2021). 'Is it beneficial to use AI chatbots to improve learners' speaking performance?'. *Journal of Asia TEFL, 18*(1), 161–178. DOI: 10.18823/asiatefl.2021.18.1.10.161

Kim, S., & Harada, T. (2023). Biometric–neural data ethics in AGI-enhanced classrooms: Emerging risks and governance pathways. *Journal of Learning Analytics, 10*(3), 112–129.

Kizilcec, R. F., & Lee, H. (2022). Algorithmic fairness in education. In Holmes, W., & Porayska-Pomsta, K. (Eds.), *The Ethics of Artificial Intelligence in Education*. Routledge., DOI: 10.4324/9780429329067-10

Knox, J. (2020). Artificial intelligence and education in China. *Learning, Media and Technology*, *45*(3), 298–311.

Kohnke, L. (2023). A pedagogical chatbot: A supplemental language learning tool. *RELC Journal*, *54*(3), 828–838. DOI: 10.1177/00336882211067054

Kong, J. S. M., Teo, B. S., Lee, Y. J., Pabba, A. B., Lee, E. J. D., & Sng, J. C. G. (2021). Virtual integrated patient: An AI supplementary tool for second-year medical students. *The Asia-Pacific Scholar*, *6*(3), 87–90. DOI: 10.29060/TAPS.2021-6-3/SC2394

Korada, L. (2024). The role of generative AI in the digital twin landscape and how it accelerates adoption. *Journal of Artificial Intelligence and Machine Learning*, *7*(2), 55–68.

Kouzov, O. (2019). The new paradigms in education and support of critical thinking with artificial intelligence (AI) tools. In Bulgarian Academy of Sciences & Institute of Mathematics and Informatics, *Serdica. Journal of Computing*, *13*(1–2), 27–40.

Labib, K., Evans, N., Pizzolato, D., Aubert Bonn, N., Widdershoven, G., Bouter, L., Konach, T., Langendam, M., DieEECkx, K., & Tijdink, J. (2023). Co-creating Ethical Education poses challenges to educational requirements for research institutes. Science as well as Engineering Ethics, 29(4), 28.

Labib, K., Evans, N., Roje, R., Kavouras, P., Reyes Elizondo, A., Kaltenbrunner, W., Buljan, I., Ravn, T., Widdershoven, G., & Bouter, L. (2022). Policies for Ethical Education in both education as well as training: Insights from a focus group research. Science as well as Public Policy, 49(2), 246–266.

Lampos, V., Mintz, J. and Qu, X. (2021) 'An artificial intelligence approach for selecting effective teacher communication strategies in autism education', *npj Science of Learning*, 6(1). Available at: https://doi.org/.DOI: 10.1038/s41539-021-00102-x

Latifi, H. (2024). Challenges of Using Artificial Intelligence in the Process of Shi'i Ijtihad. *Religions, 15*(5), 541. DOI: 10.3390/rel15050541

Lebedev, M. A., & Nicolelis, M. A. (2006). Brain–Machine Interfaces: Past, Present, and Future. *Trends in Neurosciences, 29*(9), 536–546.

LeCun, Y., Bengio, Y., & Hinton, G. (2015). Deep learning. *Nature, 521*, 436–444. DOI: 10.1038/nature14539

Lee, J., Joswick, C., Pole, K., & Jocius, R. (2021). Algorithm design for young children. *Contemporary Issues in Early Childhood.* Advance online publication. DOI: 10.1177/14639491211033663

Liang, Y. (2023). Balancing: The effects of AI tools in educational context. *Frontiers in Humanities and Social Sciences, 3*(8), 5531. Advance online publication. DOI: 10.54691/fhss.v3i8.5531

Lim, T., Gottipati, S., & Cheong, M. L. (2023). Ethical Considerations for Artificial Intelligence in Educational Assessments. In Keengwe, J. (Ed.), *Creative AI Tools and Ethical Implications in Teaching and Learning* (pp. 32–79). IGI Global Scientific Publishing., DOI: 10.4018/979-8-3693-0205-7.ch003

Lin, Y. Z., Alhamadah, A. H. J., & Redondo, M. W. (2024). *Transforming engineering education using generative AI and digital twin technologies. arXiv preprint arXiv:2402.XXXX.*

Lin, Y. Z., Alhamadah, A. H., Ghimire, S., & Petal, K. (2025). *Personalized education with generative AI and digital twins: VR, RAG, and zero-shot sentiment analysis for Industry 4.0 workforce development. arXiv preprint arXiv:2503.XXXX.*

Lin, Z. (2025). Beyond principlism: Practical strategies for ethical AI use in research practices. *AI and Ethics, 5*(3), 2719–2731. DOI: 10.1007/s43681-024-00585-5

Liu, H., Azam, M., Naeem, S. B., & Faiola, A. (2023). An overview of the capabilities of ChatGPT for medical writing and its implications for academic integrity. *Health Information and Libraries Journal.* Advance online publication. DOI: 10.1111/hir.12509

Liukas, L. (2015). *Hello Ruby: Adventures in coding*. Feiwel & Friends.

Liu, Q., Cheng, Z., & Chen, M. (2019). Effects of environmental education on environmental ethics and literacy based on virtual reality technology. *The Electronic Library, 37*(5), 860–877. DOI: 10.1108/EL-12-2018-0250

Li, X., & Ren, H. (2024). Hybrid AGI tutoring systems: Integrating attention-tracking neural signals for personalized learning. *Journal of Artificial Intelligence in Education, 32*(1), 45–62.

Lokare, V. T., & Jadhav, P. M. (2024). An AI-based learning style prediction model for personalized and effective learning. *Thinking Skills and Creativity, 51*. Advance online publication. DOI: 10.1016/j.tsc.2023.101421

Long, D., & Magerko, B. (2020). What Is AI Literacy? Competencies and Design Considerations. In *Proceedings of the 2020 CHI Conference on Human Factors in Computing Systems* (pp. 1-16). Association for Computing Machinery. https://doi.org/DOI: 10.1145/3313831.3376727

Luckin, R. (2018). *Machine learning and human intelligence: The future of education for the 21st century*. UCL Institute of Education Press.

Luckin, R., Holmes, W., Griffiths, M., & Forcier, L. B. (2016). Intelligence Unleashed: An argument for AI in Education. In *Open Ideas at Pearson*. Pearson.

Luckin, R., Holmes, W., Griffiths, M., & Forcier, L. B. (2016). *Intelligence Unleashed: An Argument for AI in Education*. Pearson Education.

Luckin, R., Holmes, W., Griffiths, M., & Forcier, L. B. (2016). *Intelligence unleashed: An argument for AI in education*. Pearson.

Luhmann, N. (1979). *Trust and power. John Wiley & Sons. Piaget, J. (1952). The origins of intelligence in children* (Cook, M., Trans.). International Universities Press. (Original work published 1936)

Lu, M., & Hu, Z. (2025). Digital twin–enhanced programming education: An empirical study on learning engagement and skill acquisition. *Computers, 14*(8), 322. DOI: 10.3390/computers14080322

Ma, J.. (2023). Learning for counterfactual fairness from observational data. In *Proceedings of the ACM Conference on Learning at Scale 2023* (pp. —). DOI: 10.1145/3580305.3599408

Malik, R., Sharma, E. A., Trivedi, S., & Mishra, R. (2021). Adoption of chatbots for learning among university students: Role of perceived convenience and enhanced performance. *International Journal of Emerging Technologies in Learning, 16*(18), 200–212. DOI: 10.3991/ijet.v16i18.24315

Mao, J. (2024). *Generative artificial intelligence in education and its implications for assessment. SpringerProfessional.*

Mariam, Z., Niazi, S. K., & Magoola, M. (2024). Unlocking the future of drug development: Generative AI, digital twins, and beyond. *BioMedInformatics*, *4*(2), 79.

Mattos, M. S., Siqueira, S. W. M., & Garcia, A. C. B. (2024). Fair and equitable machine learning algorithms in healthcare: A systematic mapping. In *Proceedings of the 16th International Conference on Agents and Artificial Intelligence* (Vol. 3, pp. 815–822). SciTePress. DOI: 10.5220/0012394700003636

McCarthy, J. (1956). Dartmouth Summer Research Project on Artificial Intelligence.

Mehrabi, N., Morstatter, F., Saxena, N., Lerman, K., & Galstyan, A. (2021). A survey on bias and fairness in machine learning. *ACM Computing Surveys*, *54*(6), 1–35. DOI: 10.1145/3457607

Mehrfar, A., Zolfaghari, Z., Bordbar, A., & Karimimoghadam, Z. (2024) 'The evolution of e-learning towards the emergence of artificial intelligence (A narrative review)', *2024 11th International and the 17th National Conference on E-Learning and E-Teaching (ICeLeT)*, pp. 1–5. Available at: https://doi.org/DOI: 10.1109/ICeLeT62507.2024.10493104

Micheli, M., Hupont, I., Delipetrev, B., & Soler-Garrido, J. (2023). The landscape of data and AI documentation approaches in the European policy context. *Ethics and Information Technology*, *25*(4), 56. DOI: 10.1007/s10676-023-09725-7

Miller, R., & Tuomi, I. (2022). Making the futures of AI in education: Why and how imagining the future matters. *European Journal of Education*, *57*(4), 537–541. DOI: 10.1111/ejed.12529

Ministry of Education. Singapore. (2023). AI in education ethics framework. Retrieved August 15, 2025, from https://www.learning.moe.edu.sg/ai-in-sls/responsible-ai/ai-in-education-ethics-framework/

Mitchell, T. M. (1997). *Machine learning*. McGraw-Hill.

Mohsen, S. E., Hamdan, A., & Shoaib, H. M. (2025). Digital transformation and integration of artificial intelligence in financial institutions. *Journal of Financial Reporting and Accounting*, *23*(2), 680–699. DOI: 10.1108/JFRA-09-2023-0544

Mokmin, N. A. M. (2020). The effectiveness of a personalized virtual fitness trainer in teaching physical education by applying the artificial intelligent algorithm. *International Journal of Human Movement and Sports Sciences*, *8*(5), 258–264. DOI: 10.13189/saj.2020.080514

Monib, W. K., Qazi, A., De Silva, L., & Mahmud, M. M. (2024b). Exploring Learners' Experiences with ChatGPT in Personalized Learning. In *2024 6th International Workshop on Artificial Intelligence and Education (WAIE)* (pp. 66-70), Tokyo, Japan. IEEE. DOI: 10.1109/WAIE63876.2024.00019

Monib, W. K., Qazi, A., Apong, R. A., Azizan, M. T., De Silva, L., & Yassin, H. (2024a). Generative AI and future education: A review, theoretical validation, and authors' perspective on challenges and solutions. *PeerJ. Computer Science*, *10*, e2105. DOI: 10.7717/peerj-cs.2105 PMID: 39650462

Monib, W. K., Qazi, A., Jain, J., & Ponniah, L. (2025b). A comprehensive scientometric analysis of ChatGPT research global trends and prospects. *TechTrends*, •••, 1–19. DOI: 10.1007/s11528-025-01110-z

Monib, W. K., Qazi, A., & Mahmud, M. M. (2025a). Exploring learners' experiences and perceptions of ChatGPT as a learning tool in higher education. *Education and Information Technologies*, *30*(1), 917–939. DOI: 10.1007/s10639-024-13065-4

Moorhouse, B. L., Yeo, M. A., & Wan, Y. (2024). Addressing student non-compliance in AI use declarations: Implications for academic integrity and assessment in higher education. *Assessment & Evaluation in Higher Education*. Advance online publication. DOI: 10.1080/02602938.2024.2415654

Moss, L., & Binns, R. (2020). AI and epistemic dependence in education. *Journal of Educational Philosophy*, *9*(4), 98–111.

Movahed, S. V. James Dimino, Andrew Farrell, Elyas Irankhah, Srija Ghosh, Garima Jain, Vaishali Mahipal, Pranathi Rayavaram, Ismaila Temitayo Sanusi, Erika Salas, Kelilah Wolkowicz, Sashank Narain, and Fred Martin. 2024. Introducing Children to AI and ML with Five Software Exhibits. In Extended Abstracts of the CHI Conference on Human Factors in Computing Systems (CHI EA '24). Association for Computing Machinery, New York, NY, USA, Article 202, 1–6. https://doi.org/ DOI: 10.1145/3613905.3650991

Munawar, S., Toor, S. K., Aslam, M., & Hamid, M. (2018). Move to smart learning environment: Exploratory research of challenges in computer laboratory and design intelligent virtual laboratory for eLearning technology. *Eurasia Journal of Mathematics, Science and Technology Education*, *14*(5), 1645–1662. DOI: 10.29333/ejmste/85036

Munn, L. (2023). The uselessness of AI ethics. *AI and Ethics*, *3*(3), 869–877. DOI: 10.1007/s43681-022-00209-w

Munusamy, P., Sanmugam, M., & Edwards, B. I. (2025). Exploring the World of Coding in Artificial Intelligence: A Guide for Primary School Students. In M. Sanmugam, B. Edwards, N. Mohd Barkhaya, & Z. Khlaif (Eds.), *Fostering Inclusive Education With AI and Emerging Technologies* (pp. 165-182). IGI Global Scientific Publishing. https://doi.org/DOI: 10.4018/979-8-3693-7255-5.ch007

Musa Adekunle Ayanwale, Ismaila Temitayo Sanusi, Owolabi Paul Adelana, Kehinde D. Aruleba, Solomon Sunday Oyelere. (2022). Teachers' readiness and intention to teach artificial intelligence in schools. *Computers and Education: Artificial Intelligence*, *3*, 100099. DOI: 10.1016/j.caeai.2022.100099

Musa, S., Abubakari, M. S., & Abdulwahab, L. O. (2025). Evaluating the Potential of Adapting Artificial Intelligence (AI) in Small and Medium Enterprises for Competitive Advantage. In Anshari, M., Almunawar, M. N., & Ordóñez de Pablos, P. (Eds.), *Multi-Industry Digitalization and Technological Governance in the AI Era* (pp. 233–266). IGI Global., DOI: 10.4018/979-8-3373-1681-9.ch012

Mustafa, M. Y., Tlili, A., Lampropoulos, G., & Huang, R. (2024). A systematic review of literature reviews on artificial intelligence in education (AIED): A roadmap to a future research agenda. *Smart Learning Environments*, *11*, 59. Advance online publication. DOI: 10.1186/s40561-024-00350-5

Naghdy, F. (2025). Collaboration with GenAI in engineering research design [Article]. *Data & Knowledge Engineering*, *159*, 102445. Advance online publication. DOI: 10.1016/j.datak.2025.102445

Nair, K., & Gupta, R. (2021). Application of AI technology in modern digital marketing environment. *World Journal of Entrepreneurship, Management and Sustainable Development*, *17*(3), 318–328. DOI: 10.1108/WJEMSD-08-2020-0099

Nash, J. (2020). EdTech in Africa: Challenges and opportunities for inclusive education. *International Journal of Educational Development*, *72*, 102–111.

National Research Council. (2012). *A framework for K–12 science education*. National Academies Press., DOI: 10.17226/13165

NeuroRights Foundation. (2024). *Neurorights and educational neurotechnologies: Policy recommendations for safeguarding cognitive privacy*. NeuroRights Foundation Report.

Neurotech, E. U. (2022). *The European University of Brain and Technology.*

Ng, D. T. K., Leung, J. K. L., Chu, S. K. W., & Qiao, M. S. (2021). Conceptualizing AI literacy: An exploratory review. *Computers & Education: Artificial Intelligence*, *2*, 100041. Advance online publication. DOI: 10.1016/j.caeai.2021.100041

Nguyen, A., Ngo, H. N., Hong, Y., Dang, B., & Nguyen, B.-P. T. (2023). Ethical principles for artificial intelligence in education. *Education and Information Technologies, 28*, 4221–4241. DOI: 10.1007/s10639-022-11316-w

Niemi, H. (2021). AI in learning – Commentary. *Journal of Pacific Rim Psychology, 15*, 1–12. DOI: 10.1177/18344909211038105

Nihad, E. G., Mohamed, K., & El Mokhtar, E. N. (2020). Designing and modeling of a multi-agent adaptive learning system (MAALS) using incremental hybrid case-based reasoning (IHCBR). *International Journal of Electrical and Computer Engineering, 10*(2), 1980–1992. DOI: 10.11591/ijece.v10i2.pp1980-1992

Nobile, C., Marocco, D., Ponticorvo, M., & Gigliotta, O. (2024). Teaching embodied artificial intelligence to children (Teach E-AI 2C): An educational proposal for young learners. *IEEE MetroXRAINE, 879–883.* Advance online publication. DOI: 10.1109/metroxraine62247.2024.10797080

Noble, S. U. (2018). *Algorithms of oppression: How search engines reinforce racism*. NYU Press.

Noddings, N. (1984). *Caring: A Relational Approach to Ethics & Moral Education*. University of California Press.

Nordgren, A. (2023). Artificial intelligence and climate change: Ethical issues. *Journal of Information. Communication and Ethics in Society, 21*(1), 1–15. DOI: 10.1108/JICES-11-2021-0106

O'Neil, C. (2016). *Weapons of math destruction: How big data increases inequality and threatens democracy*. Crown Publishing Group.

O'Neill, M. A., & Palmer, A. (2004). Importance-performance analysis: A useful tool for directing continuous quality improvement in higher education. *Quality Assurance in Education, 12*(1), 39–52. DOI: 10.1108/09684880410517423

Oamen, T. E. (2021). An examination of the determinants affecting the participation of the pharmaceutical sales personnel in marketing inside Nigeria, utilizing a structural equation modeling methodology. The Global Journal of Pure as well as Applied Sciences, 27(4), 405–410.

OECD. (2019). *Artificial intelligence in society*. OECD Publishing. https://www.oecd.org/en/publications/2019/06/artificial-intelligence-in-society_c0054fa1.html

OECD. (2020). *AI in Education Policy Observatory*. OECD.

OECD. (2020). *AI in Education: Policies, Practices, and Future Directions*. OECD Publishing.

OECD. (2020). *OECD skills outlook 2019*. OECD Publishing., DOI: 10.1787/df80bc12-

OECD. (2021). *Artificial Intelligence in Education: Challenges and Opportunities*. OECD Publishing.

OECD. (2021). *Education at a Glance 2021: OECD Indicators*. OECD Publishing.

OECD. (2023). *Artificial intelligence and education and skills*. OECD Publishing. https://www.oecd.org/en/topics/sub-issues/artificial-intelligence-and-education-and-skills.html

OECD. (2024). *Evolving with Innovation: The 2024 OECD AI Principles Update.*

OECD. (2024). *Trustworthy artificial intelligence (AI) in education*. OECD Publishing.

Ohadomere, O., & Ogamba, I. K. (2021). Management-led interventions for workplace stress and mental health of academic staff in higher education: A systematic review. *The Journal of Mental Health Training, Education and Practice*, *16*(1), 67–82. DOI: 10.1108/JMHTEP-07-2020-0048

Okaibedi, D. (2023). ChatGPT and the rise of generative AI: Threat to academic integrity? *Journal of Responsible Technology*, *13*, 100060. DOI: 10.1016/j.jrt.2023.100060

Organisation for Economic Co-operation and Development. (2024). *Comparative review of AI and BCI governance in education: Global policy asymmetries and ethical safeguards*. OECD Publishing.

Ottenbreit-Leftwich., Krista Glazewski, Minji Jeon, Katie Jantaraweragul, Cindy Hmelo-Silver, Adam Scribner, Seung Lee, Bradford Mott, and James Lester. 2022. Principles for AI Education for Elementary Grades Students. In Proceedings of the 27th ACM Conference on on Innovation and Technology in Computer Science Education Vol. 2. Association for Computing Machinery, New York, NY, USA, 627. https://doi.org/DOI: 10.1145/3502717.3532143

Owan, V. J., Abang, K. B., Idika, D. O., Etta, E. O., & Bassey, B. (2023). Exploring the potential of artificial intelligence tools in educational measurement and assessment. *Eurasia Journal of Mathematics, Science and Technology Education*, *19*(8), em2307.

Paesano, A. (2023). Artificial intelligence and creative activities inside organizational behavior. *The International Journal of Organizational Analysis*, *31*(5), 1694–1723. DOI: 10.1108/IJOA-09-2020-2421

Palasundram, K., Sharef, N. M., Nasharuddin, N. A., Kasmiran, K. A., & Azman, A. (2019). Sequence to sequence model performance for education chatbot. *International Journal of Emerging Technologies in Learning, 14*(24), 56–68. DOI: 10.3991/ijet.v14i24.12187

Panjeti-Madan, V. N., & Ranganathan, P. (2023). Impact of Screen Time on Children's Development: Cognitive, Language, Physical, and Social and Emotional Domains. *Multimodal Technologies and Interaction, 7*(5), 52. DOI: 10.3390/mti7050052

Papert, S. (1980). *Mindstorms: Children, computers, and powerful ideas*. Basic Books Inc.

Pardamean, B., Suparyanto, T., Cenggoro, T. W., Sudigyo, D., & Anugrahana, A. (2022). AI-based learning style prediction in online learning for primary education. *IEEE Access : Practical Innovations, Open Solutions, 10*, 35725–35735. DOI: 10.1109/ACCESS.2022.3160177

Peltonen, J. (2020). AI in Finnish education: Empowering teachers for the future. *Finnish Education Review, 32*(4), 112–127.

Peng, H., Ma, S., & Spector, J. M. (2019). Personalized adaptive learning: An emerging pedagogical approach enabled by a smart learning environment. In *Lecture Notes in Educational Technology* (pp. 171–176). Springer International Publishing., DOI: 10.1007/978-981-13-6908-7_24

Pesek, I., Nosovic, N., & Krasna, M. (2022) 'The role of AI in the education and for the education', *2022 11th Mediterranean Conference on Embedded Computing, MECO 2022*. Available at: https://doi.org/DOI: 10.1109/MECO55406.2022.9797189

Pester, A., Andres, F., Anantaram, C., & Mason, J. (2025). Generative AI and digital twins: Fostering creativity in learning environments. In *Human–Computer Creativity* (pp. 175–192). Springer.

Pham, N., Pham Ngoc Hung, & Nguyen-Duc, A. (2025). Fairness for machine learning software in education: A systematic mapping study. *Journal of Systems and Software, 219*, 112244. Advance online publication. DOI: 10.1016/j.jss.2024.112244

Pikhart, M., & Al-Obaydi, L. H. (2025). Reporting the potential risk of using AI in higher education: Subjective perspectives of educators. *Computers in Human Behavior Reports, 18*, 100693. Advance online publication. DOI: 10.1016/j.chbr.2025.100693

Pokrivcakova, S. (2019). Preparing teachers for the application of AI-powered technologies in foreign language education. *Journal of Language and Cultural Education, 7*(3), 135–153. DOI: 10.2478/jolace-2019-0025

Ponce, P., Perez, C., Mata, O., & Ramirez, M. (2025). Digital twin designs with generative AI: Crafting a comprehensive framework for manufacturing systems. *Journal of Intelligent Manufacturing*, *36*(2), 355–372.

Porter, B., & Grippa, F. (2020). A platform for AI-enabled real-time feedback to promote digital collaboration. *Sustainability*, *12*(24), 1–13. DOI: 10.3390/su122410243

Prem, E. (2023). From ethical AI frameworks to tools: A review of approaches. *AI and Ethics*, *3*(3), 699–716. DOI: 10.1007/s43681-023-00258-9

Prentzas, J., & Binopoulou, A. (2025). Explainable artificial intelligence approaches in primary education: A review. *Electronics (Basel)*, *14*(11), 2279. Advance online publication. DOI: 10.3390/electronics14112279

Quiloan, R., Rahimi Moosavi, S., Tankelevich, R., & Karlin, M. (2023). PlayGrid: Sparking AI literacy with an intuitive learning interface. *Fifth International Conference on Transdisciplinary AI (TransAI)*, Laguna Hills, CA, USA, 2023, pp. 171-178, doi: DOI: 10.1109/TransAI60598.2023.00045

Rae, D. (2010). Universities and enterprise education: Responding to the challenges of the new era. *Journal of Small Business and Enterprise Development*, *17*(4), 591–606. DOI: 10.1108/14626001011088741

Ratti, E., Morrison, M., & Jakab, I. (2025). Ethical and social considerations of applying artificial intelligence in healthcare—A two-pronged scoping review. *BMC Medical Ethics*, *26*(1), 68. DOI: 10.1186/s12910-025-01198-1 PMID: 40420080

Rawls, J. (1971). *A Theory of Justice*. Harvard University Press.

Resnick, M., John Maloney, Andrés Monroy-Hernández, Natalie Rusk, Evelyn Eastmond, Karen Brennan, Amon Millner, Eric Rosenbaum, Jay Silver, Brian Silverman, and Yasmin Kafai. (2009). Scratch: Programming for all. *Communications of the ACM*, *52*(11), 60–67. DOI: 10.1145/1592761.1592779

Resnik, D. B., & Hosseini, M. (2025a). Disclosing artificial intelligence use in scientific research and publication: When should disclosure be mandatory, optional, or unnecessary? *Accountability in Research*, •••, 1–13. DOI: 10.1080/08989621.2025.2481949 PMID: 40126451

Resnik, D. B., & Hosseini, M. (2025b). The ethics of using artificial intelligence in scientific research: New guidance needed for a new tool. *AI and Ethics*, *5*(2), 1499–1521. DOI: 10.1007/s43681-024-00493-8 PMID: 40337745

Rezigalla, A. A. (2024). AI in medical education: Uses of AI in construction type A MCQs. *BMC Medical Education, 24*(1). Advance online publication. DOI: 10.1186/s12909-024-05250-3 PMID: 38448870

Risi, D., Vigneau, L., Bohn, S., & Wickert, C. (2023). Research on corporate social responsibility grounded in institutional theory: Reintegrating values. *International Journal of Management Reviews*, *25*(1), 3–23.

Rizvi, M. (2023) 'Exploring the landscape of artificial intelligence in education: Challenges and opportunities', *HORA 2023 - 2023 5th International Congress on Human-Computer Interaction, Optimization and Robotic Applications, Proceedings*. Available at: https://doi.org/DOI: 10.1109/HORA58378.2023.10156773

Roche, C., Wall, P. J., & Lewis, D. (2023). Ethics and diversity in artificial intelligence policies, strategies and initiatives. *AI and Ethics*, *3*(4), 1095–1115. DOI: 10.1007/s43681-022-00218-9 PMID: 36246014

Rodrigues, M. Silva and Oliveira, C. (2025). Artificial intelligence: threat or asset to academic integrity? A bibliometrics analysis, *Kybernetes*, Vol. 54 No. 5, pp. 2939-2970. https://doi.org/DOI: 10.1108/K-09-2023-1666

Rodriguez-Barrios, E. U., Melendez-Armenta, R. A., Garcia-Aburto, S. G., Lavoignet-Ruiz, M., Sandoval-Herazo, L. C., Molina-Navarro, A., & Morales-Rosales, L. A. (2021). Bayesian approach to analyze reading comprehension: A case study in elementary school children in Mexico. *Sustainability*, *13*(8). Advance online publication. DOI: 10.3390/su13084285

Roshan, S., Iqbal, S., & Zhang, Q. (2024). Teacher Training and Professional Development for Implementing AI-Based Educational Tools. (2024). *Journal of Asian Development Studies*, *13*(2), 1972–1987. DOI: 10.62345/jads.2024.13.2.154

Ross, B., Chase, A. M., Robbie, D., Oates, G., & Absalom, Y. (2018). Adaptive quizzes to increase motivation, engagement and learning outcomes in a first year accounting unit. *International Journal of Educational Technology in Higher Education*, *15*(1). Advance online publication. DOI: 10.1186/s41239-018-0113-2

Roumate, F. (2023). *Artificial Intelligence in higher education and scientific research*. Springer Nature Singapore., DOI: 10.1007/978-981-19-8641-3

Roy, D., & Dutta, M. (2022). A systematic review and research perspective on recommender systems. *Journal of Big Data*, *9*(1). Advance online publication. DOI: 10.1186/s40537-022-00592-5

Russell, S., & Norvig, P. (2010). *Artificial intelligence: A modern approach* (3rd ed.). Pearson.

Saeidnia, H. R. (2023). Ethical artificial intelligence (AI): confronting bias and discrimination in the library and information industry. *Library Hi Tech News*, Vol. ahead-of-print No. ahead-of-print. https://doi.org/DOI: 10.1108/LHTN-10-2023-0182

Säljö, R. (2010). *Learning, culture and society*. Routledge.

Sampanis, N. (2025). Innovative Tangible Interactive Games for Enhancing Artificial Intelligence Knowledge and Literacy in Elementary Education: A Pedagogical Framework. *arXiv*. https://arxiv.org/abs/2506.00651

Saqib, M. B., & Zia, S. (2025). Evaluation of AI content generation tools for verification of academic integrity in higher education. *Journal of Applied Research in Higher Education*, *17*(4), 1430–1440. DOI: 10.1108/JARHE-10-2023-0470

Saurabh, K., & Ramkumar, M. (2022). AI led ethical digital transformation: Framework, research and managerial implications. *Journal of Information. Communication and Ethics in Society*, *20*(2), 229–256. DOI: 10.1108/JICES-02-2021-0020

Selwyn, N. (2019). *Should robots replace teachers? AI and the future of education*. Polity Press.

Selwyn, N. (2020). *Should Robots Replace Teachers? AI and the Future of Education*. Polity Press.

Selwyn, N. (2022). The future of AI and education: Some cautionary notes. *European Journal of Education*, *57*(4), 620–631. DOI: 10.1111/ejed.12532

ercan, E., & Voicu, B. (2022). Patterns of academic integrity definitions among BA Romanian students: The impact of rising enrolments. *Revista de Cercetare si Interventie Sociala*, *78*, 87–106. DOI: 10.33788/rcis.78.6

Seufert, S., Guggemos, J., & Sailer, M. (2021). Technology-related knowledge, skills, and attitudes of pre- and in-service teachers: The current situation and emerging trends. *Computers in Human Behavior*, *115*. Advance online publication. DOI: 10.1016/j.chb.2020.106552 PMID: 32921901

Sharma, R. (2024). Teacher training and professional development with utilisation of AI. *Paripex Indian Journal of Research*, *13*(6), 1–3.

Sharples, M. (2023). Towards social generative AI for education: Theory, practices and ethics. Learning. *Research and Practice*, *9*(2), 159–167.

Sha, Z., Huang, K., & Liu, Y. (2022). Leveraging class balancing techniques to alleviate algorithmic bias for predictive tasks in education. *IEEE Transactions on Learning Technologies*, *15*(6), 481–492. DOI: 10.1109/TLT.2022.3196278

Shneiderman, B. (2020). Human-centered artificial intelligence: Reliable, safe & trustworthy. *International Journal of Human-Computer Interaction, 36*(6), 495–504. DOI: 10.1080/10447318.2020.1741118

Shrestha, N. (2021). Factor analysis utilized for survey examination. AmeEECan Journal of Applied Mathematics as well as Statistics, 9(1), 4–11.

Shrivastava, R. (2023). Role of artificial intelligence in future of education. *International Journal of Professional Business Review, 8*(1), e0840. DOI: 10.26668/businessreview/2023.v8i1.840

Siemens, G. (2013). Learning analytics: The emergence of a discipline. *The American Behavioral Scientist, 57*(10), 1380–1390.

Somasundaram, M., Mohamed Junaid, K. A., & Mangadu, S. (2020). Artificial intelligence (AI) enabled intelligent quality management system (IQMS) for personalized learning path. *Procedia Computer Science, 172*, 438–442. DOI: 10.1016/j.procs.2020.05.096

Song, C., Shin, S. Y., & Shin, K. S. (2024). Implementing the dynamic feedback-driven learning optimization framework: A machine learning approach to personalize educational pathways. *Applied Sciences (Basel, Switzerland), 14*(2). Advance online publication. DOI: 10.3390/app14020916

Soong, R., Pautler, B. G., Moser, A., Jenne, A., Lysak, D. H., Adamo, A., & Simpson, A. J. (2020). CASE (Computer-Assisted Structure Elucidation) study for an undergraduate organic chemistry class. *Journal of Chemical Education, 97*(3), 855–860. DOI: 10.1021/acs.jchemed.9b00498

Sparrow, B., Liu, J., & Wegner, D. M. (2011). Google's effects on memory: Cognitive consequences of having information at our fingertips. *Science, 333*(6043), 776–778.

Standen, P. J., Brown, D. J., Taheri, M., Galvez Trigo, M. J., Boulton, H., Burton, A., Hallewell, M. J., Lathe, J. G., Shopland, N., Blanco Gonzalez, M. A., Kwiatkowska, G. M., Milli, E., Cobello, S., Mazzucato, A., Traversi, M., & Hortal, E. (2020). An evaluation of an adaptive learning system based on multimodal affect recognition for learners with intellectual disabilities. *British Journal of Educational Technology, 51*(5), 1748–1765. DOI: 10.1111/bjet.13010

Storey, V. A. (2023). AI technology and academic writing. *International Journal of Adult Education and Technology, 14*(1), 1–15. DOI: 10.4018/ijaet.325795

Strielkowski, W., Grebennikova, V., Lisovskiy, A., Rakhimova, G., & Vasileva, T. (2025). AI-driven adaptive learning for sustainable educational transformation. *Sustainable Development, 33*(2), 1921–1947. DOI: 10.1002/sd.3221

Sullivan, M., Kelly, A., & McLaughlan, P. (2023). Chatting and cheating: Ensuring academic integrity in the era of ChatGPT. *Innovations in Education and Teaching International, 61*(3), 580–591. DOI: 10.1080/14703297.2023.2190148

Sultan, P., & Yin Wong, H. (2013). Antecedents and consequences of service quality in a higher education context: A qualitative research approach. *Quality Assurance in Education, 21*(1), 70–95. DOI: 10.1108/09684881311293070

Susanto, D. S., Halim, E., & Gui, A. (2023, December). Resolving Artificial Intelligence Hallucination in Personalized Adaptive Learning System. In *2023 Eighth International Conference on Informatics and Computing (ICIC)* (pp. 1-6). IEEE. DOI: 10.1109/ICIC60109.2023.10382000

Sushama, C., & Sunil Kumar, M. Sree Vidyanikethan Engineering College, VF-STR, & Sujatha, K. (2022). The Future of Education: Artificial Intelligence based Remote Learning. In *International Journal of Early Childhood Special Education* (pp. 3827–3828). https://www.researchgate.net/publication/360423234

Taddeo, M., & Blanchard, A. (2021). Ethical principles for artificial intelligence in defence. *Philosophy & Technology*. Advance online publication. DOI: 10.1007/s13347-021-00482-3

Tai Le Quy. Friege, G., & Ntoutsi, E. (2023). A review of clustering models in educational data science towards fairness-aware learning. In A. Peña-Ayala (Ed.), *Educational Data Science: Essentials, Approaches, and Tendencies* (pp. —). Springer. DOI: 10.1007/978-981-99-0026-8_2

Tan, C. (2021). AI in education: Singapore's ethical framework for adaptive learning technologies. *Journal of Educational Technology, 38*(3), 211–225.

Tang, A., Li, K., Kwok, K. O., Cao, L., Luong, S., & Tam, W. (2024). The importance of transparency: Declaring the use of generative artificial intelligence (AI) in academic writing. *Journal of Nursing Scholarship, 56*(2), 314–318. DOI: 10.1111/jnu.12938 PMID: 37904646

Tang, Y., Liang, J., Hare, R., & Wang, F. Y. (2020). A personalized learning system for parallel intelligent education. *IEEE Transactions on Computational Social Systems, 7*(2), 352–361. DOI: 10.1109/TCSS.2020.2965198

Tan, X., Cheng, G., & Ling, M. H. (2025). Artificial intelligence in teaching and teacher professional development: A systematic review. *Computers and Education: Artificial Intelligence, 8*, 100355. Advance online publication. DOI: 10.1016/j.caeai.2024.100355

Terzi, R. (2020). An adaptation of artificial intelligence anxiety scale into Turkish: Reliability and validity study [IOJET]. *International Online Journal of Education & Teaching*, *7*(4). https://iojet.org/index.php/IOJET/article/view/1031

The Gulf Observer. (2025, June 21). Oman accelerates AI development through strategic national programme and startup growth. https://thegulfobserver.com/oman-accelerates-ai-development-through-strategic-national-programme-and-startup-growth/

Thomson, S. R., Pickard-Jones, B. A., Baines, S., & Otermans, P. C. J. (2024). The impact of AI on education and careers: What do students think? *Frontiers in Artificial Intelligence*, *7*. Advance online publication. DOI: 10.3389/frai.2024.1457299

Tomar, P., & Grover, V. (2023). Transforming the energy sector through generative AI and digital twins. *EAI Endorsed Transactions on Energy Web*, *10*(2), e15.

Touretzky, D. S., Gardner-McCune, C., Martin, F., & Seehorn, D. (2019). Envisioning AI for K–12. *Proceedings of the AAAI Conference on Artificial Intelligence*, *33*, 9795–9799. DOI: 10.1609/aaai.v33i01.33019795

Trist, E. L., & Bamforth, K. W. (1951). Some social and psychological consequences of the longwall method of coal-getting. *Human Relations*, *4*(1), 3–38. DOI: 10.1177/001872675100400101

Tsai, S. C., Chen, C. H., Shiao, Y. T., Ciou, J. S., & Wu, T. N. (2020). Precision education with statistical learning and deep learning: A case study in Taiwan. *International Journal of Educational Technology in Higher Education*, *17*(1). Advance online publication. DOI: 10.1186/s41239-020-00186-2

Turing, A. M. (1950). Computing machinery and intelligence. *Mind*, *59*(236), 433–460.

U.S. Department of Education, Office of Educational Technology. (2023). Artificial intelligence and the future of teaching and learning: Insights and recommendations. U.S. Department of Education. https://www.ed.gov/sites/ed/files/documents/ai-report/ai-report.pdf

UNESCO. (2019). Beijing consensus on artificial intelligence and education. https://unesdoc.unesco.org/ark:/48223/pf0000368303

UNESCO. (2021). *AI and the Futures of Learning*. United Nations Educational, Scientific and Cultural Organisation.

UNESCO. (2022). *AI in education: Africa's evolving policy landscape. United Nations Educational, Scientific and Cultural Organisation.*

UNESCO. (2023). *AI and the Futures of Learning: Policy Guidance*. United Nations Educational, Scientific, and Cultural Organization.

UNESCO. (2023). *Futures of Education: Reimagining our futures together*. United Nations Educational, Scientific, and Cultural Organization.

UNESCO. (2023). *Guidance for Generative AI in Education and Research*. UNESCO.

UNESCO. (2024). Artificial intelligence in teaching and teacher professional development: A systematic review. *Computers and Education Open*, *6*, 100158. Advance online publication. DOI: 10.1016/j.caeo.2024.100158

Uwizeye, D., Karimi, F., Thiong'o, C., Syonguvi, J., Ochieng, V., Kiroro, F., Gateri, A., Khisa, A. M., & Wao, H. (2022). Factors influencing research productivity in higher education institutions in Africa: A comprehensive review. *AAS Open Research*, *4*, 26. PMID: 34368619

Vasconcelos, M. A. R., & dos Santos, R. P. (2023). Enhancing STEM learning with ChatGPT and Bing Chat as objects to think with: A case study. *Eurasia Journal of Mathematics, Science and Technology Education*, *19*(7), em2296.

Vázquez-Cano, E., Mengual-Andrés, S., & López-Meneses, E. (2021). Chatbot to improve learning punctuation in Spanish and to enhance open and flexible learning environments. *International Journal of Educational Technology in Higher Education*, *18*(1). Advance online publication. DOI: 10.1186/s41239-021-00269-8

Vieriu, A. M., & Petrea, G. (2025). The impact of artificial intelligence (AI) on students' academic development. *Education Sciences*, *15*(3), 343. Advance online publication. DOI: 10.3390/educsci15030343

Villegas-Ch, W., Arias-Navarrete, A., & Palacios-Pacheco, X. (2020). Proposal of an architecture for the integration of a chatbot with artificial intelligence in a smart campus for the improvement of learning. *Sustainability*, *12*(4). Advance online publication. DOI: 10.3390/su12041500

VOSviewer. https://www.vosviewer.com/

Vygotsky, L. S. (1978). *Mind in society: The development of higher psychological processes*. Harvard University Press.

Wang, N., Li, Y., & Cong, F. (2025). University Students' Privacy Concerns Towards Generative Artificial Intelligence [Article]. *Journal of Academic Ethics*. Advance online publication. DOI: 10.1007/s10805-025-09658-4

Wang, S., Christensen, C., Cui, W., Tong, R., Yarnall, L., Shear, L., & Feng, M. (2020). When adaptive learning is effective learning: Comparison of an adaptive learning system to teacher-led instruction. *Interactive Learning Environments*, *31*(2), 793–803.

Wang, S., Wang, F., Zhu, Z., Wang, J., Tran, T., & Du, Z. (2024). Artificial intelligence in education: A systematic literature review. *Expert Systems with Applications*, *252*. Advance online publication. DOI: 10.1016/j.eswa.2024.124167

Wang, X. (2025). (2025). Global artificial intelligence governance research in the digital and intelligent era: Advances, trends and countermeasures. *Journal of Knowledge Management*. Advance online publication. DOI: 10.1108/JKM-01-2025-0006

Wang, Y. (2021). Artificial intelligence in educational leadership: A symbiotic role of human-artificial intelligence decision-making. *Journal of Educational Administration*, *59*(3), 256–270. DOI: 10.1108/JEA-10-2020-0216

Wang, Y. Y., & Wang, Y. S. (2022). Development and validation of an artificial intelligence anxiety scale: An initial application in predicting motivated learning behavior. *Interactive Learning Environments*, *30*(4), 619–634. DOI: 10.1080/10494820.2019.1674887

Wang, Y., Chen, Y., & Li, M. (2022). Digital twin technology enhances engagement and skill acquisition in introductory programming. *Applied Sciences (Basel, Switzerland)*, *14*(8), 322.

Watson, G., Sottile, J., & Liang, J. G. (2014). What is cheating? Student and faculty perception of what they believe is academically dishonest behavior. *Journal of Research in Education*, *24*(1), 120–134. DOI: 10.1177/0022487114524517

Webb, M., Davis, N., & Bell, T. (2017). Computer science in K–12 school curricula of the 21st century. *Education and Information Technologies*, *22*(2), 445–468. DOI: 10.1007/s10639-016-9493-x

Westera, W., Prada, R., Mascarenhas, S., Santos, P. A., Dias, J., Guimarães, M., Georgiadis, K., Nyamsuren, E., Bahreini, K., Yumak, Z., Christyowidiasmoro, C., Dascalu, M., Gutu-Robu, G., & Ruseti, S. (2020). Artificial intelligence moving serious gaming: Presenting reusable game AI components. *Education and Information Technologies*, *25*(1), 351–380. DOI: 10.1007/s10639-019-09968-2

Williamson, B., & Piattoeva, N. (2020). The political economy of educational technology: The marketisation of education through AI and big data. *Educational Policy*, *44*(5), 766–788.

Williams, R., Park, H. W., Oh, L., & Breazeal, C. (2019). PopBots: Designing an AI curriculum for early childhood education. *Proceedings of the AAAI Conference on Artificial Intelligence*, *33*(1), 9729–9736. DOI: 10.1609/aaai.v33i01.33019729

Wing, J. M. (2006). Computational thinking. *Communications of the ACM*, *49*(3), 33–35. DOI: 10.1145/1118178.1118215

Wolpaw, J. R., Birbaumer, N., McFarland, D. J., Pfurtscheller, G., & Vaughan, T. M. (2002). Brain–computer interfaces for communication and control. *Clinical Neurophysiology*, *113*(6), 767–791.

Wood, E. A., Ange, B. L., & Miller, D. D. (2021). Are we ready to integrate artificial intelligence literacy into medical school curriculum: Students and faculty survey. *Journal of Medical Education and Curricular Development*, *8*, 238212052110240. DOI: 10.1177/23821205211024078 PMID: 34250242

Woo, J. (2023). Digital twin for math education: Utilization of games and gamification for university mathematics. *Electronics (Basel)*, *12*(15), 3207. DOI: 10.3390/electronics12153207

Wu, F. (2025). A systematic review of responses, attitudes, and behaviors toward generative AI in higher education. *Educational Psychology Review*, *37*(2), 401–427.

Xie, H., Chu, H. C., Hwang, G. J., & Wang, C. C. (2019). Trends and development in technology-enhanced adaptive/personalized learning: A systematic review of journal publications from 2007 to 2017. *Computers & Education*, *140*. Advance online publication. DOI: 10.1016/j.compedu.2019.103599

Xu, Q., Zhou, G., Zhang, C., Chang, F., Cao, Y., & Zhao, D. (2023). Generative AI and digital twin integrated intelligent process planning: A conceptual framework. *Research Square.*

Yang, D., Oh, E. S., & Wang, Y. (2020). Hybrid physical education teaching and curriculum design based on a voice interactive artificial intelligence educational robot. *Sustainability*, *12*(19), 1–14. DOI: 10.3390/su12198000

Yang, Y. Y., & Shulruf, B. (2019). An expert-led and artificial intelligence system-assisted tutoring course to improve the confidence of Chinese medical interns in suturing and ligature skills: A prospective pilot study. *Journal of Educational Evaluation for Health Professions*, *16*. Advance online publication. DOI: 10.3352/jeehp.2019.16.7 PMID: 30986892

Yousef, M., Deeb, S., & Alhashlamon, K. (2025). AI usage among medical students in Palestine: A cross-sectional study and demonstration of AI-assisted research workflows [Article]. *BMC Medical Education*, *25*(1), 693. Advance online publication. DOI: 10.1186/s12909-025-07272-x PMID: 40355851

Yue, M., Jong, M. S. Y., & Ng, D. T. K. (2024). Understanding K–12 teachers' technological pedagogical content knowledge readiness and attitudes toward artificial intelligence education. *Education and Information Technologies*, *29*(4), 4119–4135.

Yufei, L., Saleh, S., Jiahui, H., & Abdullah, S. M. S. (2020). Review of the Application of Artificial Intelligence in Education. *International Journal of Innovation, Creativity and Change*, 548–562. https://doi.org/DOI: 10.53333/ijicc2013/12850

Yu, R., Lee, H., & Kizilcec, R. F. (2021). Should college dropout prediction models include protected attributes? In *Proceedings of the Eighth ACM Conference on Learning at Scale* (pp. 91–100). DOI: 10.1145/3430895.3460139

Yuste, R., Goering, S., Arcas, B. A. Y., Bi, G., Carmena, J. M., Carter, A., & Wolpaw, J. (2017). Four ethical priorities for neurotechnologies and AI. *Nature*, *551*(7679), 159–163.

Yusuf, A. (2024). Generative AI and the future of higher education: Threats, opportunities, and policy responses. *International Journal of Educational Technology in Higher Education*, *21*(4), 55–72.

Zadorina, O., Hurskaya, V., Sobolyeva, S., Grekova, L., & Vasylyuk-Zaitseva, S. (2024). *The role of Artificial intelligence in creation of future Education: Possibilities and challenges*. Futurity Education., DOI: 10.57125/fed.2024.06.25.09

Zamberi Ahmad, S. (2013). The need for inclusion of entrepreneurship education in Malaysia lower and higher learning institutions. *Education + Training*, *55*(2), 191–203. DOI: 10.1108/00400911311304823

Zawacki-Richter, O., Marín, V. I., Bond, M., & Gouverneur, F. (2019). Systematic review of research on artificial intelligence in education. *Journal of Educational Technology & Society*, *22*(1), 10–24.

Zeb, A., Rehman and Rabnawaz, M. (2025). Artificial intelligence and ChatGPT are fostering knowledge sharing, ethics, academia and libraries. *International Journal of Information and Learning Technology*, *42*(1), 67–83. DOI: 10.1108/IJILT-03-2024-0046

Zeng, Y., Lu, E., & Huang, Z. (2020). The challenge of proprietary secrecy in AI-driven education. *Journal of Educational Technology*, *47*(3), 215–229.

Zhaksylyk, A., Zimba, O., Yessirkepov, M., & Kocyigit, B. F. (2023). Ethical Education challenge: where we are as well as where we are going. 38(47) of the Journal of Korean Medical Science.

Zhang, A., Gao, Y., Suraworachet, W., Nazaretsky, T., & Cukurova, M. (2025). Evaluating trust in AI, human, and co-produced feedback among undergraduate students. arXiv preprint arXiv:2504.10961.

Zhao, L., Chen, M., & Gupta, R. (2023). Low-cost brain–computer interfaces in formative assessment: Impacts on metacognitive awareness in secondary education. *Computers & Education, 205*, 104579.

Zheng, L., Long, M., Zhong, L., & Gyasi, J. (2022). The effectiveness of technology-facilitated personalized learning on learning achievements and learning perceptions: A meta-analysis. *Education and Information Technologies, 27*, 11807–11830.

Zheng, W. (2024). Intelligent e-learning design for art courses based on adaptive learning algorithms and artificial intelligence. *Entertainment Computing, 50*. Advancc onlinc publication. DOI: 10.1016/j.entcom.2024.100713

Zhou, J., Wang, M., & Li, Y. (2023). Artificial General Intelligence in Higher Education: A Case Study of Multi-Agent Learning Systems. *International Journal of Educational Technology in Higher Education, 20*(1), 45–63.

Zuboff, S. (2019). *The age of surveillance capitalism: The fight for a human future at the new frontier of power*. Public Affairs.

About the Contributors

J. Sadhik Basha received his PhD in Mechanical Engineering from NIT Trichy, India, in 2011. He is currently serving as a Assistant Dean for Research & Graduate Studies at the National University of Science & Technology, Oman. His research interests include alternative fuels, thermal desalination, emulsion fuels, renewable energy, zero-emission technologies, and CCUS. He has secured externally funded research projects exceeding USD 100,000 in the area of thermal desalination, alternative fuels & renewable energy. Dr. Basha has published more than 80 research articles, holds nine patents, and serves as an expert referee, editorial / advisory board member for over 80 reputed international journals. He holds more than 50 professional memberships. He has received the Best Supervisor Awards from MEDRC, GPCA, Best Researcher Award IMCO, & multiple Best Teaching Cash Awards. He is ranked among the world's top 2% most-cited researchers by Stanford University for 5 consecutive years (2021–2025).

Rokhsaneh Yousef Zehi is an Assistant Professor of Mathematics with an academic background in applied mathematics. She holds a bachelor's and master's degree in applied mathematics from the University of Sistan and Baluchestan-Iran and earned her Ph.D. in Applied Mathematics with a focus on operations research and data envelopment analysis from Universiti Sains Malaysia. Her primary research interests include Supply Chain Management, Data Envelopment Analysis, Mathematical Programming, Multiple Criteria Decision Modelling, Fuzzy Data Envelopment Analysis and Robust Optimization. She has published her work in reputable international journals, contributed to book chapters, and presented at recognized international research conferences.

Taofeek Olanrewaju Alade is an esteemed Assistant Professor of Mathematics at the National University of Science and Technology, Oman. He obtained his BSc in Mathematics from Ladoke Akintola University of Technology, Nigeria (2007), followed by an MSc in Mathemati cs from the University of Ibadan, Nigeria (2012). In recognition of his academic excellence, he was awarded a PhD scholarship at King Abdulaziz University, Saudi Arabia, where he earned his doctorate in Applied Mathemati cs (2019). With over a decade of teaching and research experience, Dr. Alade specializes in Mathematical Biology, Infectious Disease Modeling, Virus Dynamics, Optimal Control Theory, Computati onal Mathematics, Population Dynamics, and Nonlinear Dynamics. He has published extensively in high-impact journals, accumulating over 300 citations. Additionally, he is an active reviewer for several Scopus - and Web of Science-indexed journals, contributing significantly to the advancement of mathematical research.

Ahlam Mohammed Al Balushi is a PhD candidate in Information Technology, currently pursuing her doctoral studies focusing on advanced applications of artificial intelligence and data-driven solutions. She holds a master's degree in information technology from Coventry University, UK. Ahlam's research interests include artificial intelligence, machine learning, and programming languages such as C# and Python, as well as the development of innovative computational approaches. She is passionate about academic research and is actively engaged in projects aimed at advancing knowledge and practice in the field of information technology

Khaloud Al Ajmi holds a BSc in Statistics with distinction from the University of Delaware, USA, and an MSc in Mathematical Finance from the University of York, UK. She currently works as an Assistant Lecturer in Mathematics, where she combines her academic background with a passion for teaching and applied financial mathematics. Her MSc research, titled "A Quick Algorithm for Pricing European Average Options," reflects her interest in quantitative finance and algorithmic approaches to derivative pricing.

***

Minhaj Abdullah is an esteemed professional in the fields of animation and education. With over 20 years of experience, he has excelled as an animator, scriptwriter, director, and educator while working for reputed brands and MNCs. With a Ph.D. in computer science, his expertise in 3D modeling, Animation, and e-learning education has led to numerous accolades and recognition internationally. Mr. Abdullah's dedication to mentoring and supporting students, conducting webinars for startups, and contributing to research articles has made him a respected figure in the industry. His passion for innovation and his commitment to nurturing talent have left a profound impact on the animation and education communities.

Mussa S Abubakari, PhD, is an enthusiastic educational technology researcher and associate researcher with the Dig Connectivity Research Laboratory (DCRLab) in Kampala, Uganda, since 2024. He's an instructor in the Department of Physics and Mathematics at Kondoa Islamic Secondary School, Tanzania. He has a PhD in Educational Technology from Sultan Hassanal Bolkiah Institute of Education, Universiti Brunei Darussalam, and graduated in 2025. Dr. Mussa obtained a Master of Education degree in Electronics and Informatics Engineering at Yogyakarta State University, Indonesia, in July 2021. He obtained his BSc. in Telecommunications Engineering at the University of Dodoma in June 2016. His academic and research interests include educational technology, technology-enhanced learning, technology acceptance, open and distance learning, generative AI, and digital competence, among others. He has over 15 journal articles published in internationally reputable journals, several book chapters, and papers presented at international conferences.

Kawkab Al Balushi is an English Language Lecturer at the University of Technology and Applied Sciences, Sohar, with over 12 years of teaching experience in higher education. A Chevening Scholar, she holds a Master's degree in International Education and Globalisation from the University of Bath, UK, and is currently pursuing a PhD at University Pendidikan Sultan Idris (UPSI), Malaysia. Her research interests include English language teaching, educational technology, and student engagement in higher education.

Salwa Al-Farsi is an English Lecturer at the University of Technology and Applied Sciences, with over twelve years of teaching experience in higher education. She holds a Master's degree in Applied Linguistics and TESOL and has extensive experience teaching a wide range of English language courses to undergraduate students. Her professional and research interests include English language teaching, applied linguistics, curriculum design, and pedagogical practices in higher education. She is particularly interested in enhancing student engagement, improving language proficiency, and applying research-informed teaching strategies in academic contexts.

Mohammad Azim Arbabi is a doctoral candidate in Applied Linguistics at Universiti Brunei Darussalam, with a strong background in English Language Teaching and Translation. He holds a Master of Arts in English Language Teaching and a Bachelor of Arts in English Language Translation, both from Chabahar Maritime University. His research focuses on the use of AI tools in academic writing, examining their impact, user perceptions, and ethical considerations. His broader research interests include higher education, English for Specific Purposes (ESP), academic integrity, ethics, and AI policies. He has presented at several international and regional conferences, including the Malaysia–Brunei Forum

(2023), the Teacher's Day Conference under the Ministry of Education in Brunei (2023), and the NEMLA Conference (March 2025, Philadelphia, United States). He has also served as a panel chair on AI policies in higher education and on AI integration into academic writing. In addition, he is a co-investigator in the Bridging Cultural Divides Research Fellowship (Tagpuan Fellowships 2025) at Ateneo de Manila University, Philippines.

A. Arunprakash, M.Com., Ph.D., M.F.A., is an Assistant Professor in the Department of Commerce, School of Commerce at Jain (Deemed-to-be University), Bangalore. As a marketing specialist, he is a passionate reader and an academician by profession, thriving in bringing out excellence in teaching and learning. With 5 years of research experience and 5 years of teaching experience, he excels in his field to foster and inspire young minds with his innovative approach towards learning.

Muralidhar L B is a professionally qualified dental surgeon. He holds a Ph.D. from Canara Bank School of Management Studies, Bangalore University, after his MBA from Christ University. He is qualified in management at UGC - NET and KSET. He has 18 years of total teaching experience spanning across dental education, healthcare management and general management and 4 years of corporate experience. He has worked as a research associate in the Institute for Social and Economic Change, Bangalore in a project entitled as "Management By and For Common Man: An Exploration of the Concept and Direction for Future"post Ph.D. He had secured 28th rank in the S.S.L.C. examination for Karnataka State in 1993. His 25 patents have been published, and 2 design patents have been granted. He has 41 research publications to his credit, of which 20 are Scopus-indexed, 5 are ABDC indexed and 1 is indexed in Web of Science. He has co-authored 11 books and 9 book chapters.. He is supervising Ph.D. research of 3 research scholars at JAIN (Deemed to be University). He works as an assistant professor in the Department of Business Management Studies, School of Commerce, Jain Deemed to be a University in Bangalore.

Susanta Das is a seasoned educator with a proven record of teaching and mentoring diverse students, working at multiple institutions, and providing service to the various initiatives of organizations. He received his Ph.D. and M.A. degrees from Western Michigan University (WMU), USA, and M.Sc. degree from Banaras Hindu University (BHU), India all in Physics. He continued his research as a Marie-Curie post-doctoral fellow at Stockholm University, Stockholm, Sweden on beam diagnostics for the DESIREE (Double ElectroStatic Ion Ring ExpEriment) in the project DITANET (Diagnostic Techniques for particle Accelerators – a Marie-Curie initial training NETwork), at the Indian Institute of Science Education and

Research-Kolkata, India on high-pressure physics as a Project Scientist-B, and at the University of Electro-Communications, Tokyo, Japan on ion-surface interactions as a Post-doctoral fellow. Throughout his career, Dr. Das worked and collaborated with many researchers, Ph.D., master, and visiting students from different countries. He further visited many countries to discuss research and an international conference participant (UK, Italy, Germany, Greece, Belgium, Bulgaria, Romania, Brazil etc.). He worked at several institutions before assuming his current role at Ajeenkya D Y Patil University. He received the Marie-Curie post-doctoral fellowship in Sweden, Science Academies' Summer Research Fellowship in India, Gowen Frostic Doctoral Fellowship, Department Graduate Research and Creative Scholar Award by WMU, and Leo R. Parpart Doctoral Fellowship by Dept. of Physics, WMU, among many others, throughout his academic journey. He co-authored several research articles in WoS/Scopus indexed international journals, conference proceedings, and scholarly book chapters and co-edited several books published by renowned international publishing houses (IGI-Global, Springer Nature, Nova Science Publishers, Wiley, & Scrivener-Wiley, Notion Press). At present, Dr. Das continues to delve into cutting-edge fields, with a keen interest in nanotechnology, UN SDGs, and data science. His multifaceted contributions, spanning teaching, research, and administrative leadership, showcase a dedicated professional who is instrumental in advancing the vision and mission of the institutions he serves.

Pooja Kumari (Ph.D. Finance, 2019) merges rigorous academic foundations with impactful applied research in accounting, corporate finance, firm efficiency and emergent financial systems. Her core expertise lies in corporate governance, the role of promoter holdings, industry-level financial performance, and the influence of cutting-edge technologies such as artificial intelligence in taxation, banking and financial operations. Over the past five years she has published some 20 national peer-reviewed papers and 9 international ones, alongside 10 conference proceedings—highlighting studies on housing finance companies, efficiency of paper industry firms, and AI's implications for Indian tax and customs regimes. Her Scopus-indexed work addresses governance scoring in SMEs and cross-industry performance determinants. In authorship, she has contributed books such as Financial System in Economic Development (2023), Export and Import Management (2024), and Intelligent Data Analytics in Business (2025). Her book chapters cover green accounting, financial derivatives and AI integration in business analytics. In industry-academia innovation she holds patents ranging from time-value-of-money frameworks in e-payment systems to AI-driven tools for customer relationship management, transaction tracking and employee feedback in financial contexts. She has reviewed for top journals, guided more than 50 student projects and supervised MPhil/PhD candidates. Her consultancy work includes a university-funded empirical study of India's National Pension System in Bangalore—demonstrating her ability to bridge theory and practice in finance.

V Lava Kumar is an accomplished academician with a diverse educational background and over 13 years of enriching experience in the field of education. Holding an impressive array of qualifications including an MBA, M. Com, PhD in Management, PGDTTM, along with certifications from APSET in Management and APSET in Commerce. His area of specialization is Finance and Accounting. Currently serving as an Assistant Professor at GITAM School of Business, GITAM Deemed to be University, Bengaluru, Dr. Lava Kumar is dedicated to nurturing the minds of future business leaders. His teaching methodology is grounded in both theoretical knowledge and practical insights, ensuring that students receive a holistic understanding of their subjects. Dr. Lava Kumar's contributions extend beyond the classroom, evident through his prolific research endeavours. He has authored numerous research papers, with 3 publications in prestigious Scopus-indexed and ABDC journals, and an impressive tally of 10 research articles in international and peer-reviewed journals. He co-authored a Book which is published in Surana publications. His research interests primarily revolve around contemporary issues in management and finance, where he strives to contribute to the academic discourse with valuable insights and innovative perspectives.

Wali Khan Monib received the UBD Graduate Scholarship (UGS) to pursue his Ph.D. at the Centre for Lifelong Learning, Universiti Brunei Darussalam. He has worked as a faculty member at Shaikh Zayed University (SZU), Khost, Afghanistan since 2014. He was director of the research center at SZU from 2020-2022. He served as an instructor for the Legal Education Support Program-Afghanistan (LESPA) with the University of Washington School of Law from 2014 to 2018. He received the World Bank (HEDP) scholarship for his M.Ed. in Teaching English as a Second Language from Universiti Teknologi Malaysia, Johor, Malaysia. He holds a B.A. in English Language and Literature from Nangarhar University, Nangarhar, Afghanistan. He has presented at international conferences, published in peer-reviewed journals, and serves as a peer reviewer for SCI- and SSCI-indexed journals. He has also been invited to act as an editor for manuscripts submitted to SAGE Open. His research interests center around Technology in Education, AI, Discourse Analysis, Sentiment Analysis, EFL/ESL, Microlearning, Innovative Teaching and Learning Methods, Curriculum Studies and Lifelong Learning.

Krutika Patre, is an aspiring programmer and technology enthusiast, currently pursuing Engineering in Artificial Intelligence and Data Science. With a passion for learning, she is building experience in a variety of programming languages and technologies, including C, C++, Python, Data Structures (DS), HTML, CSS, and JavaScript, DBMS (My SQL). After learning this programming language, she has created interest in Full Stack Development. She had also attended an Arduino-Based Automation course at Dolphin Labs to improve my software knowledge. There, she learned how to work with sensors, microcontrollers, and circuit design. She has written review paper on Sustainable engineering on build environment. She is doing researching and learning many topics related to AI, Policy and governance and related to my interest. She has taken part in hackathons, workshops, and tech events to explore many fields. She is also working with a group on Hyperloop. Being part of this project has really helped her grow, especially in areas like teamwork, innovation, and systems thinking.

Shilpa R working as Associate professor, Department of Management Studies, RJS Institute of Management Studies, has 16 years of experience in teaching. She has worked with the T.John Institute of Technology for 6 years and Quantum Leap for 1 year. She has completed an MBA, M Phil and PhD at Jain (Deemed to be university) spccializc in thc arca of OB/ HRM. She has also published research papers in Scopus, ABDC, and UGC care journals and presented papers at national and international conferences. Authorized Book chapters for international journals and project guide for MBA students. Attended FDPs, conferences, and workshops and also organized programs for the students. Member of ISTE and MTC Global.

Sunil Sankathala is pursuing B. Tech Computer Science and Engineering at Ajeenkya DY Patil University, with a diverse range of interests that bridge technology, sustainability, and innovation. His academic focus lies in computer science fundamentals like programming, data structures, algorithms, and software development. He actively supplements this with hands-on experience in web development and robotics. Beyond the core curriculum, He has a strong research inclination in emerging and impactful fields. His current research interests include Artificial Intelligence in Healthcare, bioplastics, nano bioplastics, e-waste management, and solid waste management—areas where he believes technology can make a meaningful difference in solving real-world problems. He has been publishing research articles and book chapters in reputed national and international journals and books. He is also part of an ambitious Hyperloop project, which involves interdisciplinary collaboration and cutting-edge engineering aimed at revolutionizing transportation. Working on this project has enhanced his skills in teamwork, innovation, and systems thinking. In the tech domain, he has developed proficiency in web development using technologies such as HTML, CSS, JavaScript, and React. His interests in robotics further reflect building smart, responsive systems that interact with the physical world. Throughout his course, he has helped strengthen problem-solving and collaborative skills. He is proficient in languages such as Python, C, C++, MySQL, Ubuntu, Machine Learning and familiar with frameworks and tools like React, Git. He actively participates in hackathons, coding competitions, and tech events to challenge himself and learn from peers. He is also a quick learner and highly adaptable, with an eagerness to stay updated with the latest trends in the tech world. He aspires to become a skilled software engineer and contribute to building innovative solutions that have a positive impact on society. The long-term goal is to work in a dynamic environment where knowledge, grow professionally, and make meaningful contributions to the field of technology. Driven by a spirit of exploration and sustainability, he aims to contribute to technological solutions that address both human and environmental needs. The long-term goal is to become a versatile engineer and researcher, working at the intersection of computer science, environmental innovation, and human well-being.

N Sathyanarayana has over 15 years of teaching experience at both undergraduate and postgraduate levels. He holds a Master of Business Administration degree from VTU and a Master of Commerce degree from Periyar University. He has completed his Ph.D. in Banking and Finance from Dayananda Sagar University. Currently, he serves as an Assistant Professor in the School of Commerce at Jain (Deemed-to-be University), Bangalore. He has published 24 research papers in international journals, including three indexed in Scopus, and seven papers in national journals. Additionally, he has presented 14 research papers at international conferences and 11 at national conferences. He has co-authored two books at the national level and contributed 21 Scopus-indexed book chapters.

Wasswa Shafik (Member, IEEE) received a Bachelor of Science degree in information technology from Ndejje University, Uganda, a Master of Engineering degree in Information Technology (Computer and Communication Networks) from Yazd University, Iran, and a PhD in Computer Science with the School of Digital Science, Universiti Brunei Darussalam, Brunei Darussalam. He is also the Founder and Research Director of the Dig Connectivity Research Laboratory (DCRLab) after serving as a Research Associate at the Network Interconnectivity Research Laboratory at Yazd University. Prior to this, he worked as a Community Data Analyst at Population Services International (PSI-Uganda), a Community Data Officer at the Programme for Accessible Health Communication (PACE-Uganda), a Research Assistant at the Socio-Economic Data Centre (SEDC-Uganda), Uganda, an Assistant Data Officer at TechnoServe, Kampala, Uganda, and Asmaah Charity Organization as Cheif Executive Officer. He has hundreds of publications with renowned publishers. His research interests include Artificial Intelligence, Neural Networks, Computer Vision, Smart Agriculture, Digital Health, and Green Computing.

Deepa Sharma has done Ph.D., MBA in Human Resource Management, currently working as Assistant Professor at MMIM, Maharishi Markandeshwar (Deemed to be University), NAAC Accredited Grade 'A++' University, Mullana, Ambala (Haryana). She has more than 9 years of experience in academics. She has written 61+ research papers for various Scopus and UGC listed referred National & International Journals and 13 papers appear on SCOPUS Preview.

Eliza Sharma is a faculty member at Symbiosis University with expertise in finance and management. She holds a doctorate in finance and has over a decade of experience in teaching, research, and academic mentoring. Her research interests span corporate governance, sustainable development goals (SDGs), supply chain management, and the role of technology in business practices. She has published and presented research in reputed journals and conferences, and actively guides students in research and applied projects. Her academic work focuses on bridging the gap between theory and practice, with emphasis on sustainability and emerging trends in management.

Santhosh Y MBA, PGDHRM Ph.D., is an Associate Professor in the Department of Commerce, School of Commerce at Jain (Deemed-to-be University) Bangalore. He earned his Ph.D in finance from Tumkur University. He has 14 years of teaching experience in commerce and management and his research interests are accounting, finance, Human Resource management, marketing management. He has presented and published research articles in various journals and authored three books.

Index

A

B

C

D

E

F

T

www.ingramcontent.com/pod-product-compliance
Lightning Source LLC
LaVergne TN
LVHW080904300926
849162LV00003B/545